The Haynes
OBD-II
& Electronic Engine Management Systems
Manual

by Bob Henderson
and John H Haynes
Member of the Guild of Motoring Writers

**The Haynes Automotive Repair Manual
for understanding, troubleshooting and
repairing engine management systems**

ABCDE
FGHIJ
KLMNO

Haynes Publishing Group
Sparkford Nr Yeovil
Somerset BA22 7JJ England

Haynes Publishing Group
861 Lawrence Drive
Newbury Park
California 91320 USA

Acknowledgements

Thanks are due to the Robert Bosch Corporation for the use of certain illustrations. Technical authors who contributed to this project are John Wegmann, Jay Storer and Mike Stubblefield.

© **Haynes North America, Inc. 2006**
With permission from J.H. Haynes & Co. Ltd.

A book in the Haynes Automotive Repair Manual Series

Printed in the U.S.A.

ISBN-13: 978-1-56392-612-9

ISBN-10: 1-56392-612-1

Library of Congress Catalog Card Number 2006920350

While every attempt is made to ensure that the information in this manual is correct, no liability can be accepted by the authors or publishers for loss, damage or injury caused by any errors in, or omissions from, the information given.

06-272

Contents

Chapter 1
Introduction

Chapter 2
Manufacturer's warranties

Chapter 3
Tools

Chapter 4
Basic troubleshooting

Chapter 5
Powertrain management basics

Chapter 6
OBD-II monitors

Chapter 7
Trouble code retrieval

Chapter 8
Trouble codes

Chapter 9
Diagnostic routines

Chapter 10
Component replacement procedures

Chapter 11
OBD-II and performance programming

1 Introduction

Background of on-board diagnostics

To understand the present level of vehicle diagnostics, one must step back a few decades to see how far the technology has come. While on-board diagnostics (OBD) is not an active participant in vehicle emissions, its development is integrally tied to that of emissions control systems for cars and trucks.

When vehicle manufacturers first began to respond to a public clamor for cleaner air, and paid even more attention to Federal recommendations that evolved into emissions standards/goals to be met, the science of emissions control was in its infancy. The early part of the Seventies saw some rather hastily-added, quick-fix emissions controls added to all domestic cars. These controls often robbed engine power, hurt economy and resulted in giving what the public called "smog controls" a bad reputation. When the catalytic converter was introduced in the mid-Seventies, things got a little better because the converter cleaned the exhaust emissions so well that manufacturers could remove or modify some of the earlier devices and improve driveability.

On-board diagnostics could not take place until cars were equipped with computer controls. General Motors vehicles had an early version of OBD on some of their 1980 vehicles. As the electronic fuel injection and other functions became controlled by the vehicle computer (the PCM, or Powertrain Control Module as it is called today), implementing OBD became more practical. California has led the way in tightening emissions restrictions, and by the late Eighties had required an OBD system for all cars to be sold in that state. Auto and light truck manufacturers had to develop the hardware and software to provide the diagnostic capability.

The aim of the original OBD system was to promote

cleaner air by ensuring that emission control components kept working. Many states started including a "smog check" in their annual or biennial mandatory vehicle safety check program. But a lot can happen to emission controls in the year between tests, and these simplified emission tests only "sniffed" the tailpipe output while the car was stationary, not running on the road. Also, these tests were "pass or fail," so the motorist whose car failed was on his own to find a shop to diagnose what made the emissions too high and to then repair the car so it could be retested.

The OBD idea was to have the vehicle do its own monitoring of emission controls, all the time, and what's more, to assign numbered codes that would identify the problem area, and finally to keep these "trouble codes" stored in the vehicle's computer. A warning light on the car's dash would indicate to the driver that there was a problem with the emissions system, and when the car was brought to a shop, the technician could extract the codes and know the parts of the emissions system he should examine, test and repair.

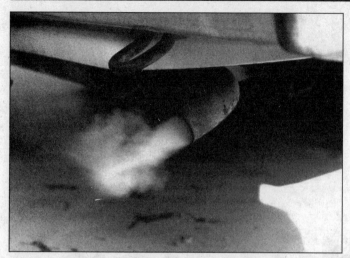
OBD-II was designed to catch emissions control problems before they progress to a stage like this

The development of OBD-II

There were some natural learning-curve difficulties with the original OBD system, now referred to as OBD-I. There was a lack of cooperation and standardization among the world's many car manufacturers. It seemed each car had a different legend on the dashboard warning light, which could read "Service Engine Soon" on one car and "Check Engine" on another. The driver didn't always know that this light indicated a problem with his car's emissions system only, and that it should be repaired right away.

The car manufacturers all had their own versions of codes, making them more difficult for technicians to read and diagnose, and since the dash light often went out after awhile, some motorists forgot about the problem, perhaps thinking that the car had "repaired itself." When Congress passed the Clean Air Act of 1990, the next level of OBD monitoring was mandated, and most of the issues from the earlier system were addressed.

The OBD-II system required all manufacturers to use a uniform set of letters/numbers for the codes, share the same definitions of each code, and have a standardized warning light in all cars. The connector in the vehicle where a scan tool can be connected is now also of uniform design among manufacturers.

Under OBD-II, not only are engine emissions controls monitored, but also all parts of the fuel system are monitored for escaping vapors, and sensors keep track of the effectiveness of the catalytic converter. Emission control components can set a code even if they haven't failed, but have lost 50% of their effectiveness. Earlier repair of these components should result in cleaner air for all of us, and total exhaust or vapor emissions have so far been reduced by as much as 100% from previous years.

The OBD-II regulations were mandated for all 1996 model cars, but some 1994 models and most 1995 models already had the system in place. There is a chance that someday there will be an even more advanced monitoring system called OBD-III, in which your car's computer can be accessed remotely by roadside sensors that transmit wireless data to state agencies, so that drivers with cars that are "out of compliance" can be notified that they need repairs.

What does the warning light mean?

Although your OBD-II vehicle may still have a light designation of "Check Engine" or "Service Engine Soon", to the government, manufacturers and technicians it is universally known now as the MIL, which stands for Malfunction Indicator Lamp. Whatever the designation, the light plays a key part in reducing vehicle-produced air pollution by alerting the driver of a need for service of emissions components. When the light glows, it is not a cause for immediate alarm, so you don't need to pull over immediately. Some diagnostic trouble codes are set and stored in the computer without triggering the MIL. Other problems that require attention will turn on the MIL, and this tells you that you should hook-up a code reader or scan tool to see what trouble code has been set, or schedule a checkup at your dealership or other repair facility. Sometimes, the MIL light will come on, and then go off a short time later or on the next trip with the vehicle, indicating a transitory "glitch" that may now be OK. If the problem goes away, that's good, but even so, the PCM will store "history" information about that intermittent problem, which can be of help to you or a service technician some time later.

One of the common triggers for the MIL is the fuel filler cap. Since the OBD-II system monitors your vehicle's fuel system very closely for escaping vapors, a fuel cap that isn't tightened securely after refueling may set a code. Check

with your owner's manual for recommendations about tightening the fuel cap to prevent this. In general, most newer cars require you to turn the cap until you hear a click.

✳ When the MIL on your instrument panel blinks instead of glows, this tells you the emissions problem is more serious. Again, this doesn't mean you have to make a panic stop, but you should get off the highway if you can and travel at lower speeds until you get to the nearest repair facility.

On some newer vehicles, there is another indicator light on the instrument panel bearing a "Maint Reqd" symbol. This has nothing to do with the OBD-II system, but is merely a helpful reminder that it's time to have your oil and filter changed. The light is linked to the PCM to turn on this light at the proper interval.

We should be thankful for the development of emission systems and on-board diagnostics, since it has resulted in cleaner air for all of us. Additionally, since some of the malfunctions that set codes in OBD-II can also hurt driveability and fuel economy, warning drivers of these problems can save motorists aggravation and money as well.

✳ Every time you start your vehicle, make it a habit to notice the MIL light. It should light for a moment during startup, and it's a good way to make sure the bulb is OK. If it doesn't light during that first turn of the Key to ON, then the bulb may be burned out or there could be a problem with the MIL communication system. Whatever the cause, you should have this checked out at a service facility, so the MIL can continue to keep our air cleaner by serving as the early warning system of problems with the emissions controls.

Notes

2 Manufacturer's warranties

Before you dive under the hood to troubleshoot or fix a problem related to emissions, there are some things you should know about the federally-mandated extended warranty, designed to protect you from the cost of repairs to any emission-related failures beyond your control.

There are actually TWO emission control warranties - the "Design and Defect Warranty" and the "Performance Warranty." We will discuss them separately. It's interesting to note that today there are actually some vehicles which do not have emissions control warranties, such as "zero emissions" vehicles like electric cars that have no emissions equipment to begin with.

Emissions Defect Warranty

Federal (most states)

Basically, the federal requirement for the Emissions Defect Warranty covers the repair of all emission control related parts (including other engine parts which are not emissions controls per se but whose failure could hamper the performance of emissions controls) which fail during the first two years or the first 24,000 miles of service on passenger cars and light trucks (defined as trucks with less than 8500 pounds GVWR rating). According to Federal law, the manufacturer must repair or replace the defective part free of charge if an original equipment part or system fails

2.1 You'll find the details of your vehicle's specific emissions components warranty coverage in the overall warranty book that comes with your new car

because of a defect in materials or workmanship and the failure would cause your vehicle to exceed Federal emissions standards.

All manufacturers have established procedures to provide owners with this coverage, and some even offer consumer protection that is longer than what is federally required. For instance, most late-model vehicles have 3-year/36,000 mile coverage of the emissions components.

The Emissions Defect Warranty applies to used vehicles, too. It doesn't matter whether you bought the vehicle new or used; if the vehicle hasn't exceeded the warranty time or mileage limitations, the warranty applies. If you own some type of vehicle other than a car, read the description of the emissions warranty in your owner's manual or warranty booklet to determine the length of the warranty on your vehicle.

What parts or repairs are covered by the warranty?

Coverage includes all parts whose primary purpose is to control emissions and all parts that have an effect on emissions.

List A

1 Air flow sensor
2 Air/fuel feedback control system and sensors
3 Air induction system
4 Altitude compensation system
5 Catalytic converter
6 Cold-start enrichment system
7 Controls for deceleration
8 Electronic ignition system
9 Exhaust pipe (manifold to catalytic converter)
10 Electronic engine control sensors and switches
11 Evaporative emission control system
12 Exhaust gas recirculation (EGR) system
13 Exhaust heat control valve
14 Exhaust manifold
15 Fuel filler cap and neck restrictor
16 Fuel injection system
17 Fuel injection supply manifold
18 Fuel tank
19 Idle air bypass valve
20 Ignition coil and/or control module
21 Intake manifold
22 Malfunction Indicator Lamp (MIL)/On-Board Diagnostic (OBD) system
23 PCV system and oil filler cap
24 Powertrain control module (PCM)
25 Secondary air injection system
26 Spark control components
27 Spark plugs and ignition wires
28 Synchronizer assembly
29 Throttle body assembly (MFI)

Also covered are a number of minor parts that are associated with the emissions components listed above, such as bulbs, hoses, gaskets, belts, wiring, fuel lines, etc.

In addition to the coverage described above for the parts listed in the Emissions Defects Warranty, certain critical emissions components are covered for a much longer period in a Performance Warranty. The standard is 8-years/80,000 miles for:

List B

1 Catalytic converter
2 Electronic emissions control unit (PCM)
3 Onboard emissions diagnostic device (diagnostic port and MIL light and circuit)

California models (also Massachusetts, New York, Maine, and Vermont)

Requirements for vehicles to meet California's strict standards are different than those of most other states, and this can lead to some consumer confusion. The warranty manual that comes with your car has two sections that describe the difference between the Federal and California standards. Make sure you're reading the correct part of your booklet.

If you're not sure whether your car is a "federal" or "California" model, check the VECI label under the hood. It should say whether the vehicle is certified for sale in California (or the other states listed above that have adopted the California standards). These states, and some others, have an I/M (inspection and maintenance) check program that is designed to check vehicle emissions and ensure that the vehicles pass a standard test. Consumers may refer to this as a "smog" test, but it would be more correct to call it a "clean air" check, since that is the result of keeping vehicle emissions systems maintained regularly.

In these states, the above "list A" of covered parts must be covered for 3-years/36,000 miles, which is what most manufacturers have voluntarily offered for all their cars and light trucks anyway, so there is little change there. However, the performance warranty also states that if your vehicle fails a state emissions test, the manufacturer must cover all repairs necessary to allow the vehicle to pass, and this covers all of the components on list A.

Another difference in these states is that the long-term Performance portion of the emissions warranty covers more components for the longer period, even **without** failing a test. The long-term portion is for 7-years/70,000 miles but covers more items. The items covered differ with the manufacturer and with the specific vehicle being discussed, but these are some of the additional items that may be covered:

Fuel tank
Intake manifold
Fuel pump module
Exhaust manifold
Fuel injectors
Distributor
Exhaust pipes
Charcoal canister

If - after reading the lists above and the manufacturer's description of your warranty coverage in your owner's manual or warranty booklet - you're still confused about whether certain parts are covered, contact your dealer service department or the manufacturer's zone or regional representative.

Can any part of a warranty repair be charged to you?

No! You can't be charged for any labor, parts or miscellaneous items necessary to complete the job when a manufacturer repairs or replaces any part under the emissions warranty. For example, if a manufacturer agrees to replace a catalytic converter under the emissions warranty, you shouldn't be charged for the catalyst itself or for any pipes, brackets, adjustments or labor needed to complete the replacement.

How do you know if you're entitled to coverage?

If you or a reliable mechanic can show that a part in one of the listed systems is defective, it's probably covered under the emissions warranty. When you believe you've identified a defective part that might be covered, you should make a warranty claim to the person identified by the manufacturer in your owner's manual or warranty booklet.

What should you do if your first attempt to obtain warranty coverage is denied?

1 Ask for the complete reason - in writing - for the denial of emissions warranty coverage;
2 Ask for the name(s) of the person(s) who determined the denial of coverage;
3 Ask for the name(s) of the person(s) you should contact to appeal the denial of coverage under the emissions warranty.

Once you've obtained this information, look in your owner's manual or warranty booklet for the name of the person designated by the manufacturer for warranty assistance and contact this person.

How does maintenance affect your warranty?

Performance of scheduled maintenance is YOUR responsibility. You're expected to either perform scheduled maintenance yourself, or have a qualified repair facility perform it for you. If a part failure can be directly attributed to poor maintenance of your vehicle or vehicle abuse (proper operation of the vehicle is usually spelled out in your owner's manual or maintenance booklet), the manufacturer might not be liable for replacing that part or repairing any damage caused by its failure. To assure maximum benefit from your emissions control systems in reducing air pollution, as well as assuring continued warranty coverage, you should have all scheduled maintenance performed, or do it yourself. It's a good idea to document all maintenance procedures and save all related receipts. However . . .

Do you have to show any maintenance receipts before you can make a warranty claim?

No! Proof of maintenance isn't required to obtain coverage under the emissions warranty. If a listed part is defective in materials or workmanship, the manufacturer must provide warranty coverage. Of course, not all parts fail because of defects in materials or workmanship. Though you're not automatically required to show maintenance receipts when you make a warranty claim, there is one circumstance in which you will be asked for proof that scheduled maintenance has been performed. If it looks as if a part failed because of a lack of scheduled maintenance, you can be required to prove that the maintenance was performed.

Can anyone besides dealers perform scheduled maintenance recommended by the manufacturer?

Absolutely! Scheduled maintenance can be performed by anyone who is qualified to do so, including you (as long as the maintenance is performed in accordance with the manufacturer's instructions). If you're going to take the vehicle to a repair facility, refer to your owner's manual or maintenance booklet and make a list of all scheduled maintenance items before you go. When you get there, don't simply ask for a "tune-up" or a "15,000 mile servicing." Instead, specify exactly what you want done. Then make sure the work specified is entered on the work order or receipt that you receive. This way, you'll have a clear record that all scheduled maintenance has been done.

If you buy a used vehicle, how do you know whether it's been maintained properly?

Realistically, you don't. But it never hurts to ask the seller to give you the receipts that prove the vehicle has been properly maintained according to the schedule. These receipts are proof that the work was done properly and on time, if the question of maintenance ever arises. And once you buy a used vehicle, you should continue to maintain it in accordance with the maintenance schedule in the owner's manual or warranty booklet (If the seller doesn't have these items anymore, buy new ones at the dealer).

What if the dealer claims your vehicle can pass the emissions test without repair?

The law doesn't require you to fail the emissions test to trigger the warranty. If any test shows that you have an emissions problem, get it fixed while your vehicle is still within the warranty period. Otherwise, you could end up failing a future test because of the same problem - and paying for the repairs yourself. If you doubt your original test results or the dealer's results, get another opinion to support your claim.

What kinds of reasons can the manufacturer use to deny a claim?

As long as your vehicle is within the age or mileage limits explained above, the manufacturer can deny coverage under the Performance Warranty only if you've failed to properly maintain and use your vehicle. Proper use and maintenance of the vehicle are your responsibilities. The manufacturer can deny your claim if there's evidence that your vehicle failed an emissions test as a result of:

a) Vehicle abuse, such as off-road driving, or overloading; or

b) Tampering with emission control parts, including removal, intentional damage or modification

c) Improper maintenance, including failure to follow maintenance schedules and instructions

d) Misfueling: The use of improper fuels.

If any of the above have taken place, and seem likely to have caused the particular problem which you seek to have repaired, then the manufacturer can deny coverage. If your claim is denied for a valid reason, you may have to pay the costs of the diagnosis. Therefore, you should always ask for an estimate of the cost of the diagnosis before work starts.

Can anyone besides a dealer perform scheduled maintenance?

Yes! Scheduled maintenance can be done by anyone with the knowledge and ability to perform the repair. For your protection, we recommend that you refer to your owner's manual to specify the necessary items to your mechanic. And get an itemized receipt or work order for your records. You can also maintain the vehicle yourself, as long as the maintenance is done in accordance with the manufacturer's instructions included with the vehicle. Make sure you keep receipts for parts and a maintenance log to verify your work.

Why maintenance is important to emissions control systems

Emission control has led to many changes in engine design. As a result, most vehicles don't require tune-ups and other maintenance as often. But some of the maintenance that is required enables your vehicle's emission controls to do their job properly. Failure to do this emissions-related maintenance can cause problems. For example, failure to change your spark plugs at the specified interval can lead to misfiring and eventual damage to your catalytic converter. Vehicles that are well-maintained and tamper-free don't just pollute less - they get better gas mileage, which saves you money. Regular maintenance also gives you better performance and catches engine problems early, before they get serious - and costly.

How do you make a warranty claim?

Bring your vehicle to a dealer or any facility authorized by the manufacturer to perform warranty repairs to the vehicle or its emissions control system. Notify them that you wish to obtain a repair under the Performance Warranty. You should have with you a copy of your emissions test report as proof of your vehicle's failure to pass the emissions test. And bring your vehicle's warranty statement for reference. The warranty statement should be in your owner's manual or in a separate booklet provided by the manufacturer with the vehicle.

How do you know if your claim has been accepted as valid?

After presenting your vehicle for a Performance Warranty claim, give the manufacturer 30 days to either repair the vehicle or notify you that the claim has been denied. If your inspection/maintenance program dictates a shorter deadline, the manufacturer must meet that shorter deadline. Because of the significance of these deadlines, you should get written verification when you present your vehicle for a Performance Warranty claim.

The manufacturer can accept your claim and repair the vehicle, or deny the claim outright, or deny it after examining the vehicle. In either case, the reason for denial must be provided in writing with the notification.

What happens if the manufacturer misses the deadline for a written claim denial?

You can agree to extend the deadline, or it may be automatically extended if the delay is beyond the control of the manufacturer. Otherwise, a missed deadline means the manufacturer forfeits the right to deny the claim. You are then entitled to have the repair performed at the facility of your choice, at the manufacturer's expense.

If your claim is accepted, do you have to pay for either the diagnosis or the repair?

You can't be charged for any costs for diagnosis of a valid warranty claim. Additionally, when a manufacturer repairs, replaces or adjusts any part under the Performance Warranty, you may not be charged for any parts, labor or miscellaneous items necessary to complete the repair. But if your vehicle needs other repairs that aren't covered by your emissions warranty, you can have that work performed by any facility you choose.

Can your regular repair facility perform warranty repairs?

If you want to have the manufacturer pay for a repair under the Performance Warranty, you MUST bring the vehicle to a facility authorized by the vehicle manufacturer to repair either the vehicle or its emission control systems. If your regular facility isn't authorized by the manufacturer, tell your mechanic to get your "go-ahead" before performing any repair that might be covered by the Performance Warranty.

What should you do if the manufacturer won't honor what you feel is a valid warranty claim?

As we said earlier, if an authorized warranty representative denies your claim, you should contact the person designated by the manufacturer for further warranty assistance. Additionally, you're free to pursue any independent legal actions you deem necessary to obtain coverage. Finally, the EPA is authorized to investigate the failure of manufacturers to comply with the terms of this warranty. If you've followed the manufacturer's procedure for making a claim and you're still not satisfied with the manufacturer's determination, contact the EPA by writing:

Manager, Certifications and Compliance Division (6405J)
Warranty Claims
U.S. Environmental Protection Agency
Ariel Rios building
1200 Pennsylvania Ave., N.W.
Washington, D.C. 20460

California drivers can contact the California Air Resources Board (CARB) at:

State of California Air Resources Board
Mobile Source Operations Division
P.O. Box 8001
El Monte, CA 91731-2990

Notes

3 Tools

Lots of interesting high-tech gadgets are available for testing the sensors, actuators, emission control devices and fuel system components involved with a computer controlled engine management system. Simple visual checks may identify some problems, but many problems arising in the OBD-II system can be very difficult to diagnose, even with the proper tools. To pinpoint the cause of a Malfunction

3.1 Trouble code readers simplify the task of extracting trouble codes

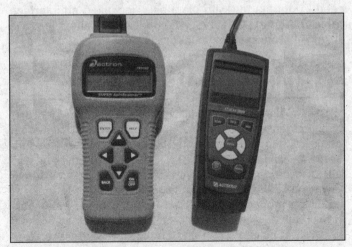

3.2 Scanners, like these from Actron and AutoXray are powerful diagnostic aids and an absolute necessity for diagnosing OBD-II system problems - programmed with comprehensive diagnostic information, they can tell you just about anything you want to know about your engine management system

Indicator Light (MIL) coming on, or most driveability issues, you'll most likely need more than your eyeballs and a flashlight. When it comes to looking into the OBD-II system, the most useful tool in your arsenal is the scanner. From there, other, more common tools and instruments may come into play.

Trouble-code readers, scan tools and software

Trouble-code readers

Trouble code readers are a cost-effective way to extract trouble codes stored in your PCM **(see illustration 3.1)**. Once you've obtained a code and know in which circuit or system the problem lies, you can often get away with finishing up the diagnosis with a multimeter. Most code readers will also allow you to erase the code with a push of a button after repairs are made. What you *can't* do with a code reader, however, is look into the OBD-II system and see what's going on in there. For that you'll need some sort of a scan tool.

Scan tools

Scan tools (or "scanners"), once prohibitively expensive, are now priced within the grasp of most Do-It-Yourselfers and are indispensable for diagnosing problems with the OBD-II system. Hand-held digital scanners **(see illustration 3.2)** are the most powerful and versatile tools for analyzing engine management systems. Shop around carefully when you're thinking about buying a scanner. Some scan tools are limited in their usage, in that they are capable of reading generic, or P0 codes only (the standardized codes shared by all auto manufacturers). This isn't necessarily bad, however, since this will help you figure out most problems related to an MIL light coming on. Others, although more expensive, can read manufacturer-specific trouble codes (P1, P2 and P3 codes). These are sometimes referred to as "enhanced" codes. Additionally, the higher-end scan tools can read codes related to other computer-run systems throughout the vehicle **(see illustration 3.3)**.

3.3 Professional-level scan tools can reveal even more of the goings-on in your vehicle's computer systems. Some can also download software upgrades from the Internet and re-program the PCM to correct potential driveability problems discovered by the vehicle manufacturer (tools like these are *very* expensive)

3.4 Diagnostic software, such as this kit from Auterra, turns your computer into the scan tool, saving the extra cost of buying a scanner but providing you with similar information

Scan tools can do more than just output trouble codes. They can give you real-time sensor data which will enable you to determine if a particular sensor is working as it should. What a scan tool *can't* do is tell you exactly what the problem related to a particular trouble code is.

PC-based software

Software (see illustration 3.4) is available that enables your computer or PDA to interface with the engine management computer, just like a scan tool. In some ways it is even more user-friendly than a scan tool, since more information can be displayed, graphically, at one time.

A PDA loaded with scan-tool software makes a really handy, economical scan tool. A laptop computer-turned-scanner may be the best bet, though, because of the size of its monitor, and it can still be used when test driving the vehicle. A desktop PC will also work, but isn't nearly as convenient because of its lack of portability.

Warning: *When using a laptop computer in the vehicle, keep it off of your lap when driving! If the vehicle is equipped with a passenger-side airbag, keep it off of the passenger's lap, too. In the event of an accident, the last thing you want is a computer being launched into your (or your passenger's) face! Also, when using any scan tool while driving the vehicle, keep your eyes on the road - not the scanner. Most scan tools are capable of recording and storing data, which can be played back after the test drive.*

Scan-tool software kits usually include everything you need to get started with diagnosis, including an interface cable that attaches to your computer and plugs into the diagnostic connector of your vehicle.

Digital multimeter

The multimeter is a small, hand-held diagnostic tool that combines an ohmmeter and voltmeter (and sometimes an ammeter) into one handy unit. A multimeter can measure the voltage and resistance in a circuit. Many emission and fuel injection devices and systems are electrically powered, so the multimeter is an essential tool.

There are two types of multimeters: Conventional units (a box with two leads) and probe types (small, hand-held units with a built-in probe and one flexible lead) (see illustrations 3.5 and 3.6). Probes - which are about the same size as a portable soldering pen - are easier to use in tight spaces because of their compact dimensions. And you don't need three hands to hold a meter and two test leads all at the same time (you can hold the meter in one hand and the single lead in the other). But probes usually have less fea-

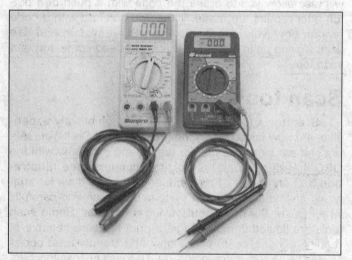

3.5 These two high-impedance digital multi-meters are accurate, versatile and inexpensive, but each unit is equipped with a different type of lead: the one on the left uses insulated alligator clips which don't have to be held in place, freeing your hands for using the meter itself; the unit on the right has a pair of probes, which are handy for testing wires and terminals inside connectors (our advice? Buy both types of leads, or make your own)

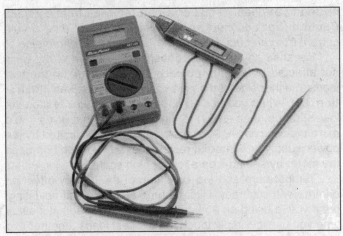

3.6 A probe-style meter like the unit on the right is small and easy to use because one of the probes is integrated into the housing, leaving your other hand free to hold the single ground lead

3.7 To make a voltage measurement, turn the mode switch or knob on your multimeter to the Volts DC position and hook up the meter in PARALLEL to the circuit being tested; if you hook it up in series, like an ammeter/ohmmeter, you won't get a reading and you could damage something (note how the positive probe is being used to make contact with a wire through the backside of the connector without unplugging the connector)

tures than conventional units.

Why a digital multimeter? Partly because digital meters are easier to read, particularly when you're trying to read tenths of a volt or ohm. But mainly you need a digital meter - instead of an "analog" (needle type) - because digital multimeters are more accurate than analog meters. More specifically, you need a high-impedance digital voltmeter. This kind won't damage sensitive electronic circuits.

Using a multimeter to read voltage is simply a matter of selecting the voltage range and hooking up the meter IN PARALLEL (see illustration 3.7) to the circuit being checked. Older analog (needle-type) meters have always allowed a certain amount of voltage to "detour" through this parallel circuit, which affects the accuracy of the measurement being taken.

This leaking voltage isn't that important when you're measuring 12-volt circuits - and you just want to know if a circuit has 12 or 13 or 14 volts present. If some of the voltage trickles through the meter itself, your judgment call about the health of the circuit is unaffected. But many engine control circuits operate at five volts or less; and some of them operate in the millivolt (thousandths of a volt) range. So voltage readings must be quite accurate - in many cases to the tenth, hundredth or even thousandth of a volt. Even if an older analog meter could measure voltage values this low (and even if you could read them!), the readings would be inaccurate because of the voltage detouring out of the circuit into the meter.

High-impedance digital meters have 10-Meg ohms (10 million ohms) resistance built into their circuitry to prevent voltage leaks through the meter. And this is the main reason we specify a digital voltmeter. When you shop around for a good meter, you may find a newer analog type meter with a high-resistance circuit design similar to that of a digital meter, but it will still be difficult to read when performing low-voltage tests, so don't buy it - get a digital model!

Some of the more sophisticated multimeters (see illustration 3.8) can perform many of the same functions as

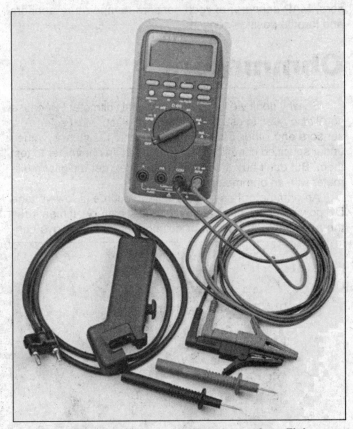

3.8 Top-of-the line multimeters like this one from Fluke can do a lot of things besides just measure volts, amps and ohms - using a wide array of adapters and cables, most of which are included in the basic kit, they can check the status of all the important information sensors, measure the duty cycle of idle air control motors, and even measure the pulse width of the fuel injectors

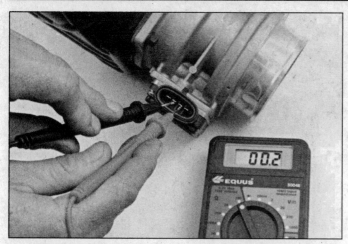

3.9 To measure resistance, select the appropriate range of resistance and touch the meter probes to the terminals you're testing; the polarity (which terminal you touch with which lead) makes no difference on an ohmmeter because it's self-powered and the circuit is turned off

scanners, such as checking camshaft and crankshaft position sensors, fuel injection on-time, IAC motors, MAF sensors, MAP sensors, oxygen sensors, temperature sensors and throttle position sensors.

Ohmmeters

So why don't we just specify a digital voltmeter? Because you'll also need to use an ohmmeter a lot too: Most solenoids, sensors and other devices have specific resistance values under specified conditions, so you'll need an ohmmeter to test them. But don't buy a separate ohmmeter; get a digital multimeter with an ohmmeter built in.

An ohmmeter has its own voltage source (a low-voltage DC power supply, provided by a dry-cell battery). It measures the resistance of a circuit or component and is always con-

3.10 Get a thermometer with a range from zero to about 220-degrees - there are automotive-specific thermometers available, but a cooking thermometer will work

nected to a "dead" circuit or a part removed from a circuit. **Caution:** *Don't connect an ohmmeter to a "live" (hot) circuit; current from an outside source will damage an ohmmeter.*

Because an ohmmeter doesn't use system voltage, it's not affected by system polarity. You can hook up the test leads to either side of the part you want to test **(see illustration 3.9)**. When you use an ohmmeter, start your test on the lowest range, then switch to a higher range that gives you a more precise reading. Voltage and current are limited by the power supply and internal resistance, so you won't damage the meter by setting it on a low or high scale.

Temperature and the condition of the battery affect an ohmmeter's accuracy. Digital ohmmeters are self-adjusting, but if you're using an analog meter, you must adjust it every time you use it: Simply touch the two test leads together and turn the zero adjustment knob until the needle indicates zero ohms, or continuity, through the meter on the lowest scale.

Thermometer

If you're going to be testing temperature sensors, get a good automotive thermometer **(see illustration 3.10)** capable of reading from zero to about 220-degrees F. If you can't find an automotive-specific unit, a good cooking thermometer will work.

Vacuum gauge

Measuring intake manifold vacuum is a good way to diagnose all kinds of things about the condition of an engine. Manifold vacuum is tested with a vacuum gauge **(see illustration 3.11)**, which measures the difference in pressure between the intake manifold and the outside atmosphere. If the manifold pressure is lower than the atmospheric pressure, a vacuum exists. Most gauges measure vacuum in inches of mercury (in-Hg). As vacuum increases (or atmospheric pressure decreases), the reading will increase. Also, for every 1000-foot increase in elevation above approximately 2000 feet above sea level, the gauge readings will decrease by about one inch of mercury.

As an example, you would use a vacuum gauge to diagnose a restricted exhaust system with a vacuum gauge. To hook up the gauge, connect the flexible connector hose to the intake manifold, air intake plenum, or any vacuum port below the throttle body. On some models, you can simply remove a plug from the manifold or throttle body; on others, you'll have to disconnect a vacuum hose or line from the manifold or throttle body and hook up the gauge inline with a tee fitting (included with most vacuum gauge kits).

A good vacuum reading is about 15 to 20 in-Hg (50 to 65 kPa) at idle (engine at normal operating temperature). Low or fluctuating readings can indicate many different problems. For instance, a low and steady reading may be caused by retarded ignition or valve timing. A sharp vacuum drop at intervals may be caused by a burned intake valve.

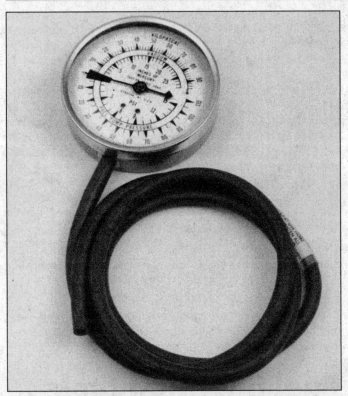

3.11 A vacuum gauge can tell you whether the engine is producing good intake vacuum, help you determine whether the catalytic converter is blocked and help you diagnose a wide variety of engine-related problems

Refer to the Chapter 4 for the troubleshooting chart showing the possible causes of various vacuum gauge readings.

Vacuum pump/gauge

Two tools are indispensable for troubleshooting engine control systems. One is a digital multimeter; the other is a hand-operated vacuum pump equipped with a vacuum gauge (see illustration 3.12).

Many underhood emission control system components are either operated by intake manifold vacuum, or they use it to control other system components. Devices such as check valves, dashpots, purge control valves, solenoids, vacuum control valves, vacuum delay valves, vacuum restrictors, etc. - all these devices control vacuum in some way, or are controlled by it. They amplify, block, delay, leak, reroute or transmit vacuum. Some of them must control a specified amount of vacuum for a certain period of time, or at a certain rate. A vacuum pump applies vacuum to such devices to test them for proper operation.

Suitable vacuum pump/gauges are sold by most specialty tool manufacturers. Inexpensive plastic-bodied pump/gauges - available at most auto parts stores - are perfectly adequate for diagnosing vacuum systems. Make sure the scale on the pump gauge is calibrated in "in-Hg" (inches of mercury). And buy a rebuildable pump (find out whether

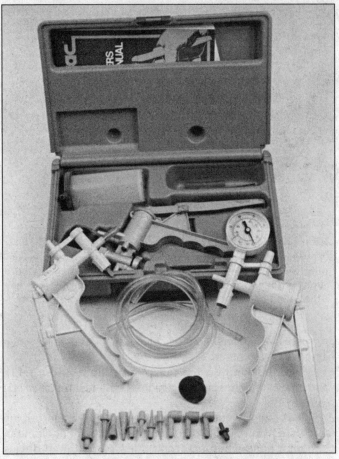

3.12 A hand-operated vacuum pump and gauge tool is indispensable for troubleshooting engine control systems - it can help you track down vacuum leaks and test all vacuum-operated devices; Mityvac pumps (shown) are inexpensive plastic models, like the two in the foreground (one of which can be purchased without a gauge), and sturdier metal units like the one in the box; they come with a variety of fittings and adaptors, and can be used for a host of applications

replacement piston seals are available). When the seals wear, the pump won't hold its vacuum and vacuum measurements will be inaccurate. At this point, you'll have to rebuild the pump.

Using a vacuum pump is simple enough. Most pump kits include an instruction manual that describes how to use the pump in a variety of situations. They also include a selection of adapters (tee-fittings, conical fittings which allow you to connect two lines of different diameters, etc.) and some vacuum hose, to help you hook up the pump to vacuum, hoses, lines, fittings, pipes, ports, valves, etc. Manufacturers also sell replacements for these adapters and fittings in case they wear out, or you lose them. Sometimes, you may need to come up with a really specialized fitting for a more complicated hook-up. A good place to find weird fittings is the parts department of your local dealer. A well-stocked parts department has dozens of special purpose vacuum line fittings designed for various makes and models. Draw a picture of what you want for the parts man and chances are, he'll have the fitting you need.

3.13 When connecting a vacuum pump/gauge to a component (such as the Corvette EGR solenoid in this photo), make sure you've got airtight connections at the pump (arrow) and at the fitting or pipe of the device (arrow), or the test results won't mean much

Here are a few simple guidelines to keep in mind when using a vacuum pump:

1   When hooking up the pump **(see illustration 3.13)**, make sure the connection is airtight, or the test result will be meaningless.

2   Most factory-installed vacuum lines are rubber tubing (some are nylon). Make sure you're using the right-diameter connector hose when hooking up the pump to the device you wish to test. When you attach a connector hose with a larger inside diameter (I.D.) than the outside diameter (O.D.) of the fitting, pipe, port, etc. to which you're attaching it, the vacuum reading will be inaccurate, or you may not get a vacuum reading. If you use a hose or line with a smaller I.D. than the O.D. of the fitting, pipe, port, etc. to which you're hooking up the pump, you'll stretch your connector hose and it will be useless in future tests.

3   In general, use as few pieces as possible to hook up the pump to the device or system being tested. The more hoses, adapters, etc. you use between the pump and the device or system being tested, the more likely the possibility of a loose connection, and a leak.

4   Don't apply more vacuum than necessary to perform a test, or you could damage something. If the pump won't build up the amount of vacuum specified for the test, or won't hold it for the specified period of time because the piston seal is leaking, discontinue the test and rebuild the pump.

5   When you're done with the test, always release the vacuum in the pump before you detach the line or hose from the system. Breaking a connection while vacuum is still applied could cause a device to suck dirt or moisture into itself when exposed to the atmosphere.

6   Always clean the fitting, pipe or port to which you've hooked up the pump and reattach the factory hose or line. Inspect the end of the factory hose or line. It it's flared, frayed or torn, cut off the tip before you reattach it. Make sure the connection is clean and tight.

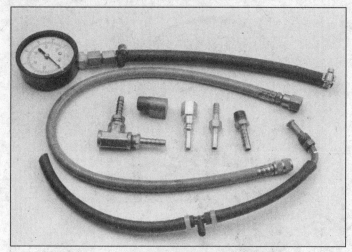

3.14 A fuel pressure gauge is a necessary tool for diagnosing the fuel injection system

7   Clean your pump, adapter fittings and test hose, and put them away when you're done. Don't leave the pump laying around where it could be dropped and damaged.

Fuel injection tools

You don't need a lot of special tools to service fuel injection systems. Most parts and components can be removed and installed with the same tools you use to work on the rest of your vehicle. But there are a few special diagnostic tools that you will need. Here are some of the important ones.

Fuel pressure gauge

Fuel pressure is one of the important operating variables in any electronic fuel injection system. So one of the most important tools you'll need for troubleshooting is a good fuel pressure gauge designed for use with fuel injection systems.

A typical fuel pressure gauge **(see illustration 3.14)** for fuel injection work has a range of 0 to 100 psi. The finest quality gauges are available from OEM suppliers such as Kent-Moore, OTC and Miller, and from professional-quality tool manufacturers such as Mac or Snap-On. However, less expensive units are available at most auto parts stores. These gauges will work just fine for the do-it-yourselfer. They're just not designed for the same level of abuse as a more expensive unit. When buying a gauge, try to verify that at least one of the adapters included with the kit will enable you to hook up the gauge to the system you're going to diagnose. Because Murphy's Law is always an important element of every "adapter search," you'll probably discover that none of the adapters included will fit your system! But don't despair! You can usually find or make something that will work for far less than the difference between a factory gauge and a good aftermarket gauge.

Many fuel injection systems provide a test port, pres-

3.15 Tools like these are necessary for disconnecting the spring-lock or duckbill type fuel line connectors used on some later models

3.16 A 'noid light provides a quick and easy way to check the electrical signal to the fuel injector

sure tap, or pressure relief valve of some sort. The test port, which is usually a Schrader valve, looks just like a tire valve. It's usually located somewhere on the fuel rail. A screw-off cap keeps out dirt when the port's not in use. To hook up your fuel pressure gauge to a test port, simply remove the cap and screw on the adapter attached to the gauge test hose. Most gauges are sold with a variety of adapters. But that doesn't mean you won't have to buy a special adapter or make your own. If possible, try to obtain the correct adapter for your vehicle when you purchase a gauge.

Adapters

In theory, there should be enough adapters available to provide some means of hooking up virtually any aftermarket fuel pressure gauge to any fuel injection system test port. In practice, this isn't always the case. Test ports are not yet standardized, nor are they even included on every system. Every manufacturer, it seems, has its own way of letting you tap into the system.

Some fuel injection systems have no test port. If the system you're servicing has no port, your only option is to relieve the system fuel pressure, disconnect a fuel line from the fuel rail and hook up the fuel pressure gauge with a "T" type fitting. This can be tricky on vehicles equipped with spring-lock couplings or other types of quick-connect fittings. If you're servicing one of these models, you'll have to obtain a T-fitting with the special spring-lock couplings or quick-connect fittings on either end, either from the manufacturer or from a specialized tool company that makes its own line of specialized adapters.

Special tools for disconnecting special connections

The fuel lines on many newer fuel injection systems are now attached to each other and to other components in the fuel injection system with spring lock couplings or other

kinds of quick-connect fittings. If you're servicing a system with funny-looking fuel line connections, do NOT try to disconnect them without a special fuel line disconnect tool **(see illustration 3.15)**.

Injector harness testers ("noid" lights)

Noid (short for [injector] solenoid) lights **(see illustration 3.16)** tell you whether an injector harness is working properly or not. To use one, simply unplug the harness connector from the injector, plug the noid light into the connector and run the engine. The noid light will flash on and off as the computer sends pulses to the injector. Or it won't, if there's something wrong with the injector driver or the harness for that injector. Quick and simple. Noid lights are available in a wide variety of configurations for various injectors.

Stethoscope

An automotive stethoscope **(see illustration 3.17)** looks similar to the one your doctor uses, except that it's equipped

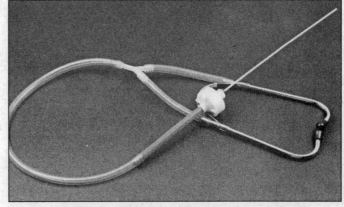

3.17 Use a mechanic's stethoscope to isolate and check the sound made by fuel injectors and other mechanical components

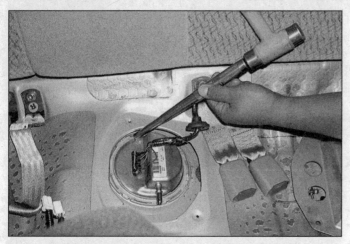

3.18 Use a *brass* punch and hammer to turn the lock-ring counterclockwise

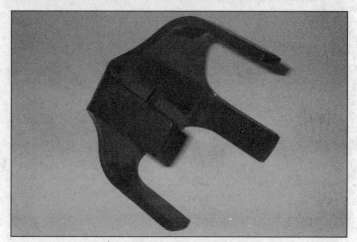

3.19 A wrench like this greatly simplifies lock ring removal

with a probe on the end. When you want to isolate the sound of one injector, listen to a fuel pump, an idle speed control motor, etc., a stethoscope is the only way to go.

Fuel tank lock ring wrenches

Fuel pump/sending unit assemblies are usually mounted inside the tank. To remove a defective pump and install a new unit, you must work through a smallish hole in the top of the tank. This hole is sealed with a circular base plate, the flange of which uses a bayonet-type locking ring that must be turned counterclockwise to unlock it before you can remove the fuel pump/sending unit assembly. If you don't mind dropping the fuel tank, this is a fairly simply procedure. In fact, you can knock the locking ring loose with a hammer and a brass punch (never use a steel punch on one of the lock rings - you don't want to create any sparks around the gas tank!) **(see illustration 3.18)**. Nowadays, many vehicles are equipped with an access plate in the floor of the trunk, or under the seat or hatch area that allows you to get at this lock ring/baseplate without dropping the fuel tank. Which

means you can replace a fuel pump/sending unit without dropping the tank! The trouble is, on many of these vehicles with an access plate, the distance between the access plate and the lock ring/baseplate makes it virtually impossible to knock that ring loose with a hammer and punch. In order to loosen the lock ring through the hole in the trunk, you'll need a special wrench **(see illustration 3.19)**. These lock-ring wrenches are available at most auto parts stores.

Diagnosing and correcting circuit faults

The goal of electrical diagnosis is to find the faulty component which prevents current from flowing through the circuit as originally designed. As fuel injection systems are equipped with more and more electrical and electronic components, devices and subsystems, the potential for electrical and electronic problems increases dramatically. Because of the complexity of these electrical parts and subsystems, and because of the high cost of replacing them, a "hit-and-miss" approach to troubleshooting is expensive. An organized and logical approach to diagnosis is essential to repair fuel injection electrical circuits in a prompt and cost-effective manner.

You'll need a few pieces of specialized test equipment to trace circuits and check components. Accurate methods of measuring current, voltage and resistance are essential for finding the problem without unnecessary parts replacement and wasted time.

Jumper wires

Jumper wires **(see illustration 3.20)** are used mainly for finding open circuits and for finding excessive resistance by bypassing a portion of an existing circuit. They can also be used for testing components off the vehicle. You can pur-

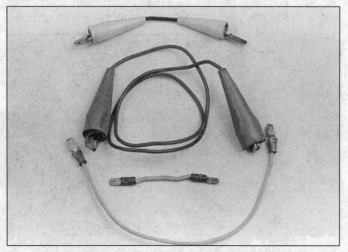

3.20 Jumper wires are a simple yet valuable tool for checking circuits

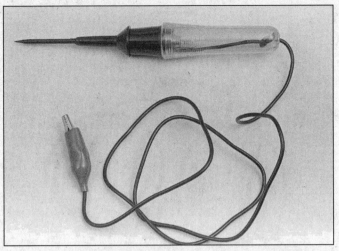

3.21 A test light is an economical and easy to use tool for making sure there is voltage in a powered circuit

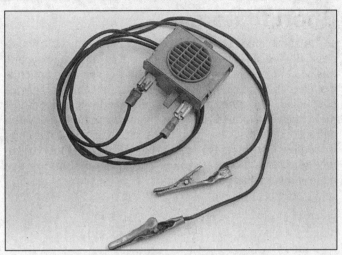

3.22 A test buzzer does the same job as a test light, but gives you the option of remote operation

chase them in completed form, or you can fabricate your own from parts purchased at an automotive or electronics supply store.

Jumper wires can be equipped with various types of terminals for different uses. If you're jumping current from the battery to a component, make sure your jumper wire is equipped with an inline fuse to avoid a current overload, and make sure it has insulated boots over the terminals to prevent accidental grounding. **Warning:** *Never use jumpers made of wire that is thinner (of lighter gauge) than the wiring in the circuit you are testing. Always use a fuse with the same (or lower) rating as the circuit had originally.*

Test lights

Test lights are handy for verifying that there's voltage in a powered circuit. A test light **(see illustration 3.21)** is one of the cheapest electrical testing devices available; it should be the first thing you purchase for your electrical troubleshooting tool box. Test lights can also be fabricated from parts purchased at an automotive or electronics supply store. Test lights come in several styles, but all of them have three basic parts: a light bulb, a test probe and a wire with a ground connector. Six, 12, or 24-volt systems may be tested by changing the bulb to the appropriate voltage. Although accurate voltage measurements aren't possible with a test light, large differences can be detected by the relative brightness of the glowing bulb. **Note:** *Before using a test light for diagnosis, check it by connecting it to the battery, ensuring the bulb lights brightly.*

Test buzzers

A test buzzer **(see illustration 3.22)** works the same way as a test light, but it offers the advantage of remote operation. For example, one person working alone may test a fuel pump circuit by turning the key to On and listening for the sound of the buzzer connected to the fuel pump circuit. A test buzzer can be fabricated at home from parts purchased

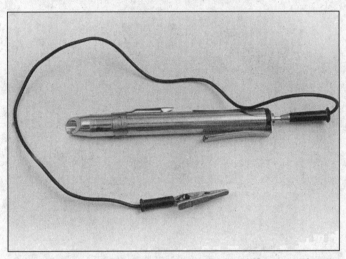

3.23 Use a continuity tester (also called a self-powered test light) to check for open or closed circuits - never use one on circuits with solid state components; it could damage them

at an electronics store or made with jumper wires and a key reminder buzzer. Test buzzers are used in the same manner as described for test lights. Additionally, they can be used to find shorts to ground.

Continuity testers

A continuity tester **(see illustration 3.23)**, also known as a self-powered test light, is used to check for open or short circuits. The typical continuity tester is nothing more than a light bulb, a battery pack and two wires combined into one unit. These parts can be purchased from any auto parts or electronics store. Continuity testers must be used only on non-powered circuits; battery voltage will burn out a low-voltage tester bulb.
Caution: *Never use a self-powered continuity tester on circuits that contain solid state components, since damage to these components may occur.*

Short finders

A short finder **(see illustration 3.24)** is an electromagnetic device designed to trace short circuits quickly and easily. One part of the short finder is a pulse unit, which is installed in place of the fuse for a circuit in which a short is suspected. The other part of the short finder is a hand-held meter which is moved along the faulty wiring harness. Meter deflections indicate the area in the harness where the short is located. Short finders are available from most tool manufacturers for a moderate price. The savings from one use usually offsets the purchase price.

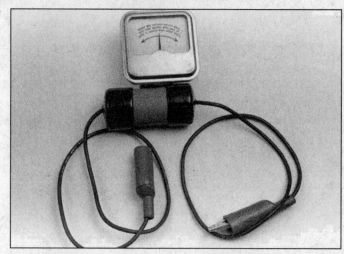

3.24 A short finder simplifies the job of tracing a short circuit

4 Basic troubleshooting

Contents

1 General information

A malfunctioning fuel injection system or component can cause a variety of problems. While some may be obvious, others are not. The obvious symptoms might include a vehicle that won't start or stay running, sluggish performance or a lack of power, pinging, backfiring or excessive exhaust smoke. Symptoms that are more difficult to diagnose include an occasional fuel smell, an intermittent misfire or decreased fuel mileage.

Many of the symptoms described can also be caused by malfunctions of the basic fuel, ignition or mechanical

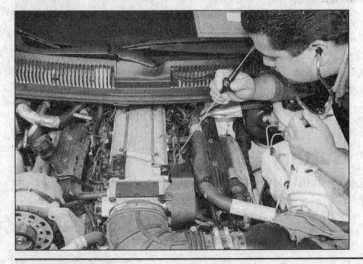

systems of the vehicle. More often than not, the cause of a problem can be found through inspecting and testing one of these basic systems. You may actually find that performing the basic troubleshooting procedures found in this Chapter may correct the symptoms thought to be fuel injection or computer related.

This Chapter provides a guide to the most common problems, and their corrections, diagnosed with the basic tools common to today's automotive industry.

The fundamentals of all basic engine and fuel systems being dealt with in this Chapter are similar enough, among manufacturers, that the basic tests and specifications given will help you correctly track down the reason(s) for the problem(s) being experienced.

2 Safety precautions

Regardless of how enthusiastic you may be about getting on with the job at hand, take the time to ensure that your safety is not jeopardized. A moment's lack of attention can result in an accident, as can failure to observe certain simple safety precautions. The possibility of an accident will always exist, and the following points should not be considered a comprehensive list of all dangers. Rather, they are intended to make you aware of the risks and to encourage a safety-conscious approach to all work you carry out on your vehicle.

Essential DOs and DON'Ts

DON'T rush or take unsafe shortcuts to finish a job.

DON'T allow children or pets in or around the vehicle while you are working on it.

DON'T start the engine without first making sure that the transmission is in Neutral (or Park where applicable) and the parking brake is set.

DON'T touch any part of the engine or exhaust system until it has cooled sufficiently to avoid burns.

DON'T use poorly maintained trouble lights/shop lights that may have exposed wiring, broken insulation or a bad ground

DON'T open any connection in the fuel system without properly releasing the pressure

DON'T siphon toxic liquids such as gasoline, antifreeze and brake fluid by mouth, or allow them to remain on your skin.

DON'T remove the radiator cap from a hot cooling system - let it cool sufficiently, cover the cap with a cloth and release the pressure gradually.

DON'T attempt to drain the engine oil until you are sure it has cooled to the point that it will not burn you.

DON'T use loose fitting wrenches or other tools which may slip and cause injury.

DON'T push on wrenches when loosening or tightening nuts or bolts. Always try to pull the wrench toward you. If the situation calls for pushing the wrench away, push with an open hand to avoid scraped knuckles if the wrench should slip.

DO keep loose clothing and long hair well out of the way of moving parts.

DO get someone to check on you periodically when working alone on a vehicle.

DO carry out work in a logical sequence and make sure that everything is correctly assembled and tightened.

DO keep chemicals and fluids tightly capped and out of the reach of children and pets.

DO remember that your vehicle's safety affects that of yourself and others. If in doubt on any point, seek professional advice.

Gasoline and fuel injection cleaners

Warning: *Gasoline and fuel injection cleaners are extremely flammable, so take extra precautions when you work on any part of the fuel system or hook up external connections to clean the system. Don't smoke or allow open flames or bare light bulbs near the work area, and don't work in a garage where a gas-type appliance (such as a water heater or a clothes dryer) is present. Since gasoline and fuel injector cleaners are carcinogenic, wear latex gloves when there's a possibility of being exposed to fuel, and, if you spill any fuel on your skin, rinse it off immediately with soap and water. The vapors are harmful. Avoid prolonged breathing of vapors or contact with eyes or skin. Use with adequate ventilation. Follow all additional instructions and warning on the product being used. Mop up any spills immediately and do not store fuel-soaked rags where they could ignite. The fuel system on fuel-injected models is under constant pressure, so, if any fuel lines are to be disconnected, the fuel pressure in the system must be relieved first. When you perform any kind of work on the fuel system, wear safety glasses and have a Class B type fire extinguisher on hand.*

Fire

Warning: *We strongly recommend that a fire extinguisher suitable for use on fuel and electrical fires be kept handy in the garage or the workshop at all times. Never try to extinguish a fuel or electrical fire with water. Post the phone number for the nearest fire department in a conspicuous location near the phone.*

A spark caused by an electrical short circuit, by two metal surfaces contacting each other, or even by static electricity built up in your body under certain conditions, can ignite gasoline or battery vapors, which in a confined space are highly explosive. Do not, under any circumstances, use gasoline for cleaning parts. Use an approved safety solvent.

Fumes

Warning: *Certain fumes are highly toxic and can quickly cause unconsciousness and even death if inhaled to any extent. Gasoline vapor falls into this category, as do the vapors from some cleaning solvents. Any draining or pouring of such volatile fluids should be done in a well ventilated area.*

When using cleaning fluids and solvents, read the instructions on the container carefully. Never use materials from unmarked containers.

Never run the engine in an enclosed space, such as a garage. Exhaust fumes contain carbon monoxide, which is extremely poisonous. If you need to run the engine, always do so in the open air, or at least have the rear of the vehicle outside the work area.

If you are fortunate enough to have the use of an inspection pit, never drain or pour gasoline and never run the engine while the vehicle is over the pit. The fumes, being heavier than air, will concentrate in the pit with possibly lethal results.

In the event of an emergency, be sure to post the phone number for poison control in a conspicuous location near the phone.

Battery

Warning: *Never create a spark or allow a bare light bulb near a battery. They normally give off a certain amount of hydrogen gas, which is highly explosive.*

Always disconnect the battery ground/negative(-) cable at the battery before working on the fuel or electrical systems. If disconnecting both cables for any reason, always disconnect the ground/negative cable first, then disconnect the positive cable.

If possible, loosen the filler caps or cover when charging the battery from an external source (this does not apply to sealed or maintenance-free batteries). Do not charge at an excessive rate or the battery may burst.

Take care when adding water to a non maintenance-free battery and when carrying a battery. The electrolyte, even when diluted, is very corrosive and should not be allowed to contact clothing or skin.

Always wear eye protection when using compressed air.

Always wear eye protection when cleaning the battery to prevent the caustic deposits from entering your eyes.

Household current

When using an electric power tool, inspection light, etc., which operates on household current, always make sure that the tool is correctly connected to its plug and that, where necessary, it is properly grounded. Do not use such items in damp conditions and, again, do not create a spark or apply excessive heat in the vicinity of fuel or fuel vapor.

Secondary ignition system voltage

A severe electric shock can result from touching certain parts of the secondary ignition system (such as the spark plug wires, coil, etc.) when the engine is running or being cranked, particularly if components are damp or the insulation is defective. In the case of an electronic ignition system, the secondary system voltage is much higher and could prove fatal.

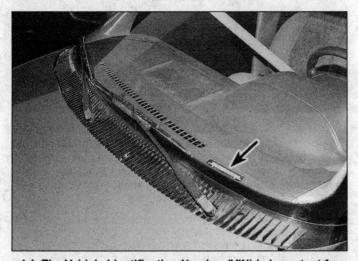

4.1 The Vehicle Identification Number (VIN) is important for identifying the vehicle and engine type - it is on the front of the dash, visible from outside the vehicle, looking through the windshield on the driver's side.

3 Vehicle identification

Changes, modifications and corrections are a continuing process in vehicle and replacement parts manufacturing. Don't rely on information that is 'thought' to be correct, always find the **correct** specification and procedure. It may have been correct for one model year and not the next, even if everything in the vehicle appears the same in all other respects.

Since spare parts manuals and lists are compiled on a numerical basis. The individual vehicle numbers are essential to correctly identify the part needed when going to the local parts store or when checking the specifications to be used.

Vehicle Identification Number (VIN)

This very important identification number is stamped on a plate attached to the left side of the dashboard just inside the windshield on the driver's side of the vehicle **(see illustration 4.1)**. The VIN also appears on the Vehicle Certificate of Title and Registration. It contains information such as where and when the vehicle was manufactured, the model year and engine codes.

Finding the correct information is the usual starting point and two important pieces to find first are the model year and engine codes. On most current vehicles the year of manufacture is the 10th digit in the VIN (reading from the left). On some cars it may be a letter, but since the year 2001, the code is a numeral that correlates directly to the year, i.e. a 1 in the 10th position indicates the car is a 2001 model, a 4 indicates a 2004 model. The engine code is the 8th place in the VIN, and it is most often a letter. You can call a dealer of your brand of vehicle and they can tell you which engine you have based on this letter code. Engines also have their own serial number stamped somewhere on the engine, and again a dealer can help you determine from this number if your engine is the original one for your year of vehicle. **Caution:** *It's possible the original engine may have been swapped for a different engine sometime during the life of the vehicle. This information may or may not have been passed on from owner to owner. If the engine has been replaced it will be necessary to know what engine (year, size, emissions, etc.) is in the vehicle, in order to find the correct specifications to use for repairs, adjustments and fitting the correct replacement parts.*

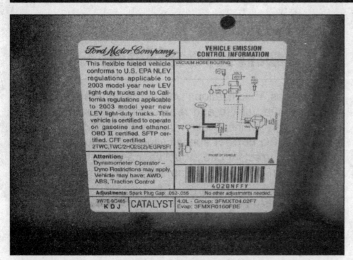

4.2 Here's a typical Vehicle Emission Control Information (VECI) label (this one's from a Chrysler) - note the warning against ignition timing adjustments and the schematic-style vacuum diagram that shows the major emission control components and their relationship to each other, but not their location.

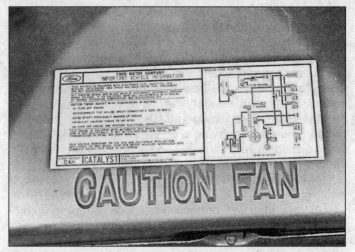

4.3 The Vehicle Emission Control Information (VECI) label, normally located on the top of the cooling fan shroud or on the underside of the hood, contains essential and specific information that applies to the emissions-related devices on your vehicle

The Vehicle Emissions Control Information (VECI) label

The VECI label (see illustrations 4.2, 4.3 and 4.4) identifies the engine, the fuel system and the emission control systems used on your specific vehicle. It also provides essential tune-up specifications, such as the spark plug gap, idle speed, initial ignition timing setting (if adjustable) and components that originally came on the vehicle such as Exhaust Gas Recirculation (EGR), Three Way Catalyst (TWC) converter, Fuel Injection (FI), etc.

Most labels also provide a simplified vacuum diagram of the emissions control devices used on your vehicle and the vacuum lines connecting them to each other and to engine vacuum. You won't find everything you need to know on the VECI label, but it's a very good place to start.

The information on the VECI label is specific to your vehicle. Any changes or modifications authorized by the manufacturer will be marked on the label by a technician making the modification. He may also indicate the change with a special modification decal and place it near the VECI label.

It can't be emphasized enough, DON'T make substitutions for parts or specifications. If the vehicle doesn't run well with all the manufacturer designated parts and specifications used, there is still an unrepaired problem. Trying to compensate by changing spark plug heat ranges or altering timing doesn't correct the problem and in some cases may actually mask a problem and allow damage to other engine components.

What does a VECI label look like?

The VECI label is usually a small, white, adhesive-backed, plastic-coated label about 4 X 6 inches in size, located somewhere in the engine compartment. It's usually affixed to the underside of the hood, the radiator support, the firewall or one of the inner fender panels.

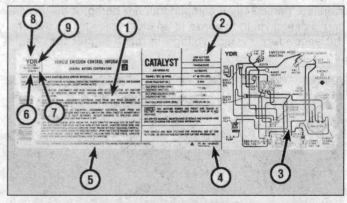

4.4 The Vehicle Emission Control Information (VECI) label provides information regarding engine size, exhaust emission system used, engine adjustment procedures and specifications and an emission component and vacuum hose schematic diagram

1   Adjustment procedures
2   Engine adjustment specifications
3   Emission component and vacuum hose routing
4   Label part number
5   Area of certification (California, Federal or Canada)
6   Evaporative emission system
7   Exhaust emission system
8   Label code
9   Engine size

What if you can't find the VECI label?

If you're not the original owner of your vehicle, and you can't find the VECI label anywhere, chances are it's been removed, or the body part to which it was affixed has been repaired or replaced. Don't worry - you can buy a new one at a dealer parts department. **Note:** *They normally have to be ordered from the assembly plant where the vehicle was manufactured.*

Be sure to give the parts department the VIN number, year, model, engine, etc. of your vehicle; be as specific as possible. For instance, if it's a high-altitude model, a 49-state model or a California model, be sure to tell them, because each of these models may have a different fuel system and a unique combination of emission control devices.

Don't just forget about the VECI label if you don't have one. Intelligent diagnosis of the engine management system on your vehicle begins here. Without the VECI label, you can't be sure every component is still installed and connected as originally manufactured.

4 Problem identification

Identifying the problem, or symptom, is the first step in using your time wisely, getting to the basis for the problem quickly and dealing with it effectively.

In most cases the fastest and most precise method of locating engine management problems is to check the trouble codes of the OBD system. As the other Chapters in this book address, using a simple code reader can give the direction in which to start troubleshooting. If the code has to do with the ignition, check those components first, and likewise if the code is fuel-related, EGR-related, etc., you can narrow down your diagnostic and troubleshooting time considerably. To take that a step further, using a full-fledged scan tool will allow you to monitor the performance of the various sensors and output actuators, and to even view "freeze frame" data. This is a snapshot of the events taking place at the very moment a Diagnostic Trouble Code (DTC) is set. It's stored in the PCM's memory and is the most valuable information you can have when troubleshooting a problem that caused the Malfunction Indicator Lamp (MIL) to come on.

The most inexpensive and easiest way to keep your vehicle operating properly is simply to check it over on a regular basis. This is the best to way spot individual problems before other component problems occur and compound the symptoms. When maintenance is ignored, over a period of time, multiple repairs usually become necessary. This makes diagnosing the symptoms more difficult than if they had been discovered individually during periodic checks.

The emissions, fuel, ignition, and engine management systems are interrelated, a minor problem in one can have a ripple effect on others. These minor malfunctions among several systems can eventually lead to a breakdown which could have been avoided by a simple check and maintenance program.

When you've taken a vehicle to a dealership or auto shop in the past, you'll probably remember how difficult it was to make the service advisor clearly understand the problem being experienced. Sometimes the written repair order described something completely different than what you were trying to convey. So the explanation and problem, many times, was mis-diagnosed or the problem may not have been addressed completely. A return visit to the shop now becomes necessary. This example of poor communication is the stuff that the highly advertised Customer Satisfaction Index (CSI) ratings are made of. Repeat repairs and return visits to a shop don't make for a happy customer.

Follow simple guidelines like:

- Don't ignore the basics! (spark, fuel, air, etc.).
- Don't overlook the simple or obvious problems that can be found upon visual inspection (vacuum line disconnected, air intake hose cracked, etc.).
- Never assume that someone else's diagnosis is correct.
- Start out the repair procedure correctly by questioning yourself, or the driver that experienced the symptoms, these essential pieces of information:
- **WHAT are the problems or symptoms being experienced?**
- Does the engine stall, surge, misfire, or does it idle rough? . . . etc.
- **WHEN are these symptoms experienced?**
Is the engine hot or cold? Does the problem happen immediately, or only after an extended drive? Is the vehicle moving at a constant speed or idling at a stop when the problem occurs? Does the problem occur under easy or hard acceleration? Is the weather wet or dry ? . . . etc.
- **WHERE do the symptoms seem to be most obvious or severe?**
- Are they most severe under a load (possibly pulling a trailer or boat), going up a grade, at sea level or high altitude (such as Denver, Albuquerque, etc.)?
- Did the vehicle emit any out-of-the-ordinary noises or unusual smells at the time the problem was being experienced? Noises from pre-ignition (pinging) or the smell of sulfur (rotten eggs) could help pinpoint the problem system or component.
- Has another shop or person worked on the vehicle recently? If so, what problems was the vehicle taken in for? What was the diagnosis? What was actually done to repair the vehicle?

Everyone has heard, at one time or another, that there is no such thing as a dumb question. Getting all the information possible to repair a problem, in a timely and effective manner, is an instance when that old saying really holds true. Ask all the questions necessary that will help clarify the problem. This can only help narrow the search for the cause of the problem. Even ask questions like; is tire inflation correct? . . . was the parking brake applied? . . . what is the quality of gasoline used? . . . when was the last time the vehicle was serviced, and what was done? . . . etc. If you think these questions sound dumb, see how sluggish a vehicle feels with tires at half pressure, or with a parking brake that is partially applied.

5 Basic system checks

General engine condition

The term "tune-up" is used in this manual to represent a combination of individual operations rather than one specific procedure.

If, from the time the vehicle is new, the routine maintenance schedule is followed closely and frequent checks are made of fluid levels and high wear items, as suggested throughout this manual, the engine will be kept in relatively good running condition and the need for additional work will be minimized.

More likely than not, however, there will be times when the engine is running poorly due to lack of regular maintenance. This is even more likely if a used vehicle, which has not received regular and frequent maintenance checks, is purchased. In such cases, an engine tune-up will be needed outside of the regular routine maintenance intervals.

The following general list of components and tests are those most often needed to bring a generally poor running engine back into a proper state of tune:

Air intake system
Cooling system
Underhood hoses
Check all engine-related fluids
Adjustment of the drivebelts
Check engine vacuum and hoses
Clean, inspect and test the battery, cables and starter
Charging system output
Primary ignition system
Secondary ignition system
Computer power and grounds
Emissions related components
Fuel pump pressure

Any of these areas or components found to be excessively worn, damaged or out of specifications should be repaired replaced before proceeding with other diagnosis.

The vehicle being worked on may have a problem with one or more of these items or systems, so take the time to be thorough and use the procedures in the following Sections.

Since you are now at this point in the repair procedure, questions should have been asked and the visual inspection should have been completed. If the symptom or problem still exists, follow the procedures described to more closely examine the individual components making up the fundamental engine systems.

Disable the ignition system by disconnecting the primary (low voltage) wires from the coil(s), so that the vehicle won't start. **Note:** *On most vehicles, it's easy to keep the engine from starting by removing the fuel pump relay or fuse from the underhood fuse/relay box. Start the engine and it will shortly run out of fuel in the system. When the engine quits, it will not start again as long as the fuel system is disabled. You can also disconnect the electrical connector at the coil pack (or all of the individual coils on systems with coil-on-plug ignitions). This will stop the engine from starting, yet still allow fuel pressure when making tests of the fuel supply.*

Crank the engine over and listen to the sound it is making. A smooth, even rhythm to the engine's rotation, with no slowing at spots during cranking, is a good general indicator that there is even compression in all cylinders. High or low compression, in comparison to other cylinders, would cause individual piston strokes to be harder or easier than others, thereby causing uneven rotating speed.

Now this isn't, by any stretch of the imagination, as accurate as actually performing a compression test. For purposes of saving time, finding the source and correcting the problem, this quick check will indicate whether more time should be spent on this area or should you go on to look elsewhere for the source of the driveability problem being experienced.

A good general rule of thumb would be, if fluctuations or surging are noted of more than 40 or 50 rpm, then there may be a significant difference between the compression of the cylinders. A more in-depth look at each individual cylinder should be taken with a compression gauge to more accurately determine the cause for the compression differences.

Airflow, filters, hoses and connections

Inspect the outer surface of the filter element. Even if the surface looks fairly clean it needs to checked further. Place a shop light on one side of the element and see if light can be see when looking through the filter towards the light. If it is dirty, replace it. If it is only moderately dusty, it can be reused by blowing it clean, from the back to the front surface, with compressed air. If it is a pleated paper type filter, it cannot be washed or oiled. If it cannot be cleaned satisfactorily with compressed air, discard and replace it.

High temperatures in the engine compartment can cause the deterioration of the rubber and plastic components and/or hoses used for engine, accessory and emission systems operation. Periodic inspection should be made for soft deteriorating hoses, cracks, loose clamps, material hardening and leaks.

Some, but not all, hoses are secured to the fittings with

clamps. Where clamps are used, check to be sure they haven't lost their tension, allowing the hose to leak. If clamps aren't used, make sure the hose has not expanded and/or hardened where it slips over the fitting.

Air-leak check

The term "air-leak" refers to outside air that has entered into the system downstream (after) from the airflow meter or mass airflow sensor (where the airflow is metered and fuel flow is calibrated accordingly). This un-metered air makes the correct air/fuel calculations difficult, if not impossible. The computer can't measure the additional air so it's unable to compensate for the change, which results in a lean air/fuel mixture. Although the oxygen sensor does send a signal to adjust for what is indicated by the exhaust gas, it can't command a large enough adjustment to overcome the problem.

Look for air inlet hoses and flexible ductwork that has broken, split or cracked from age and/or underhood heat. One other possibility may be from a previous repair. Sometimes connections don't always get aligned or reassembled quite right. Handling of original hoses or lines sometimes causes them to crack because they have become so brittle with age and heat.

Check for leaks in the air intake system by spraying water or carburetor cleaner in the area of suspected leaks and listen for a change in engine rpm. **Warning:** *Carburetor cleaner spray is flammable and can ignite if sprayed on hot manifolds or comes in contact with an open spark. For the sake of safety, it's recommended that water be used to check for air leaks.*

Oil level and condition

The proper level of good clean oil must be maintained in the engine at all times for a number of reasons. Everyone knows that the first and foremost reason is lubrication, which prevents engine damage. But dirty oil has an affect on other systems as well.

Poorly maintained engine oil will allow sludge and moisture to build up within the lubrication system. Over a period of time this can lead to blockages in the oil passageways or PCV systems. This can increase crankcase pressure and, as a result, increase blow-by gases. Excessive blow-by combined with marginal ignition parts can combine to create an engine misfire that may be hard to locate.

Many modern vehicles have protection built into the engine management system. If for any reason oil pressure drops below a set lower limit, the oil pressure switch will indicate this lack of pressure and the computer will shut the engine off. Hopefully before any damage can take place.

The lubrication system could often be overlooked as a cause of a stalling problem. Here again, regular maintenance and awareness of the overall condition of the engine may help find a simple solution to a problem, rather than allowing matters to become more complicated than they really are.

Coolant level, condition and circulation

The level, condition and circulation of the coolant has a direct affect on engine operation. Of course, the engine must not be allowed to overheat, but it must also reach the correct operating temperature for proper fuel control to take place. Therefore, a thermostat that operates within the temperature range the vehicle was originally designed for, must be installed in the vehicle at all times. Never install a "cooler" thermostat in your engine in an attempt to solve an overheating problem, and never, ever, completely remove the thermostat. With the thermostat removed, the engine may remain in the "open loop" mode (no computerized fuel control) and fuel economy and performance will suffer.

The cooling system must be maintained properly to keep the engine from overheating. Overheating the engine can cause many problems, none of which would seem to be fuel system related. But when an engine is overheated it can not only damage the engine mechanically, it can also damage sensors, electrical solenoids and output actuators, all of which have a impact on how the computer senses the operating condition of the engine. The damaged condition of these components and the ECM's attempt to manage all the systems, without accurate information, will cause a driveability problem. This is one of those items that, although unrelated, can indirectly affect other systems, such as fuel control, of the vehicle.

The cooling system should be checked with the engine cold. Do this before the vehicle is driven for the day or after the engine has been shut off for at least three hours. Remove the cooling system cap and inspect the condition of the coolant. **Note:** *Some later vehicles no longer have a cap on the radiator itself. In these systems the coolant expansion tank/reservoir is a part of the pressure system. The pressure cap is located on the expansion tank.* If you hear a hissing sound (indicating there is still pressure in the system), wait until it stops before proceeding with the cap removal.

The coolant inside the radiator will have some color, probably light green or pink, but should be relatively transparent. If it's rust colored, the system should be drained and refilled. If the coolant level isn't up to the proper level, add additional antifreeze/coolant mixture until it is.

Thoroughly clean the cap, inside and out, with clean water. Pressure check the radiator cap to be sure it maintains the specified pressure (14-to-18 lbs, and is usually stamped on the cap). Pressurizing the system allows the operating temperature of the coolant to reach a temperature above the normal boiling point of 212-degrees.

Make sure that all hose clamps are tight. A small leak in the cooling system, if not large enough to have a noticeable drip, will usually show up as white or rust colored deposits on the areas adjoining the leak. If older style wire-type clamps are used at the ends of the hoses, it may be a good idea to replace them with more secure screw-type clamps.

If rust or corrosion is excessive, or if the coolant is due to be replaced, consider flushing the cooling system at this time. If corrosion is found at the connections or at the radiator cap it is an indication that the coolant should be flushed from the engine, and refilled with a fresh coolant/water mixture. Flushing kits and/or cooling system additives to clean the inside of the system, are available at local auto parts stores.

Vacuum hoses, fittings and connections

The fuel control and engine emission systems often use engine vacuum to operate various switches and control devices on the engine. Accessories such as power brake boosters and heating-ventilation-air conditioning air distribution systems also use engine vacuum to operate their various systems. A vacuum leak in any one of these systems could seriously affect engine performance.

Most emission control systems depend on vacuum for proper operation. These systems use numerous vacuum-operated devices that respond to vacuum to activate and deactivate output actuators which control emissions by altering engine operation in accordance with changing loads and operating temperatures.

It's quite common for vacuum hoses, especially those in the emissions system, to be color coded or identified by colored stripes. Various systems require hoses with different wall thickness, collapse resistance and temperature resistance. When replacing hoses, be sure the new hoses meet the same specifications as the original.

Often, because the routing of the hose may be under other components, the only effective way to check a hose is to remove it completely from the vehicle. If more than one hose is removed, be sure to label the hoses and fittings to ensure correct installation. When checking vacuum hoses, be sure to include all plastic connectors and T-fittings in the inspection. Look at the fittings for cracks, and check the hose where it fits over the fitting for distortion, hardening or cracking, which could cause leakage. Check the entire hose, but especially at spots where the hose may make contact with hot engine components and/or oil leakage areas. A hot engine can melt through or bake a hose until it crumbles, likewise oil leakage will rot a hose until it disintegrates.

The major cause of vacuum-related problems is damaged or disconnected vacuum hoses, lines or tubing. Vacuum leaks can cause many engine performance related problems. It can cause an engine to idle rough or erratic, or misfire. Vacuum leaks in the emission system can cause spark knock or "pinging", or cause an engine to backfire. If a large enough leak is present, the engine may stall repeatedly and of course, fuel economy will suffer drastically.

If you suspect a vacuum problem because one or more of the above symptoms occurs, the following visual inspection may get you to the source of the problem with no further testing:

Make sure all the vacuum hoses are routed correctly - kinked lines block vacuum flow at first, then cause a vacuum leak when they crack and break.

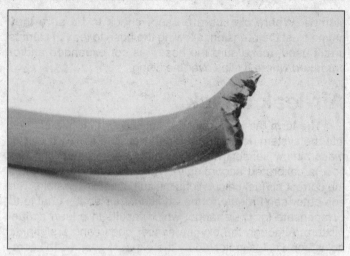

4.5 This vacuum hose was routed too close to an exhaust manifold - after being overheated repeatedly, it finally cracked and broke.

Make sure all connections are tight. Look for loose connections and disconnected lines. Vacuum hoses and lines are sometimes accidentally knocked loose by an errant elbow during an oil change or some other maintenance.

Inspect the entire length of every hose, line and tube for breaks, cracks, cuts, hardening, kinks and tears (**see illustration 4.5**). Replace all damaged lines and hoses.

When subjected to the high underhood temperatures of a running engine, hoses become brittle (hardened). Once they're brittle, they crack more easily when subjected to engine vibrations. When you inspect the vacuum hoses and lines, pay particularly close attention to those that are routed near hot areas such as exhaust manifolds, EGR systems, reduction catalysts (often right below the exhaust manifold on modern front-wheel drive vehicles with transverse engines), etc.

Inspect all vacuum devices for visible damage (dents, broken pipes or ports, broken tees in vacuum lines, etc.)

Make sure none of the lines are coated with coolant, fuel, oil or transmission fluid. Many vacuum devices will malfunction if any of these fluids get inside them.

If none of the above steps eliminates the vacuum leak problem, using a vacuum pump, apply vacuum to each suspect area, then watch the gauge for any loss of vacuum.

And if you still can't find the leak? Well, maybe it's not in the engine control system - maybe it's right at the source, at the intake manifold or the base gasket between the carburetor or throttle body. To test for leaks in this area, spray aerosol carburetor cleaner along the gasket joints with the engine running at idle. If the idle speed smoothes out momentarily, you've located your leak. Tighten the intake manifold or the throttle body fasteners to the specified torque and recheck. If the leak persists, you may have to replace the gasket.

A small piece of vacuum hose (1/4-inch inside diameter) can be used as a stethoscope to detect vacuum leaks. Hold one end of the hose to your ear and probe around vacuum hoses and fittings, listening for the "hissing" sound charac-

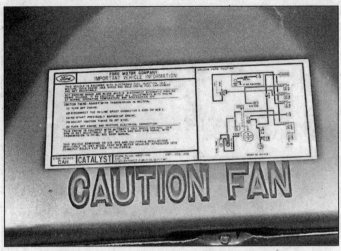

4.6 Raise the hood and find your VECI label - many manufacturers place the vacuum diagram right on the VECI label

teristic of a vacuum leak. **Warning:** *When probing with the vacuum hose stethoscope, watch where you are placing your hands! Be very careful not to come into contact with moving engine components such as the drivebelts, cooling fan, etc.*

Where can you find vacuum diagrams?

The quickest way to determine what vacuum devices are used on your vehicle is to refer to the Vehicle Emission Control Information (VECI) label located in the engine compartment. Most vehicles have a vacuum diagram (or "schematic") located on or near the label. The label is usually affixed to the radiator core support, inner fender panel, engine air cleaner assembly or the underside of the hood for

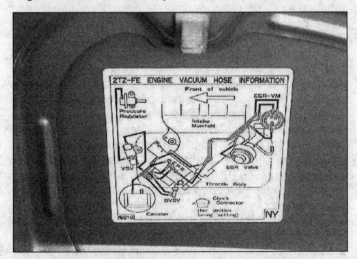

4.7 Some manufacturers put the vacuum schematic on a decal by itself and place it near the VECI label

convenient reference when working on your vehicle.

Raise the hood and find your VECI label. Most manufacturers place the vacuum diagram right on the VECI label **(see illustration 4.6)**. Some put it on a separate label, near the VECI label **(see illustration 4.7)**. **Note:** *The diagrams in this manual are typical examples of the type you'll find on your vehicle's VECI label, in a Haynes Automotive Repair Manual or in a factory service manual. But they're instructional - they DON'T necessarily apply to your vehicle. When you're working on emission control systems, if you notice differences between the vacuum diagram affixed to your vehicle and those in the owner's manual, a Haynes Auto Repair Manual for the specific vehicle or a factory manual, always go with the one on the vehicle. It's always the most accurate diagram.*

If the VECI label has been removed from your vehicle, replacement labels are available at your authorized dealer parts department. (Of course, as mentioned above, sometimes the vacuum diagram is part of the VECI label, sometimes it's not.)

Repairing and replacing vacuum hose and/or plastic lines

Replace defective sections one at a time to avoid confusion or misrouting. If you discover more than one disconnected line during an inspection of the lines, refer to the vehicle vacuum schematic to make sure you reattach the lines correctly. Route rubber hoses and nylon lines away from hot components, such as EGR tubes and exhaust manifolds, and away from rough surfaces which may wear holes in them.

Most factory-installed vacuum lines are rubber, but some are nylon. Connectors can be plastic, bonded nylon or rubber. Nylon connectors usually have rubber inserts to provide a seal between the connector and the component connection.

Replacing nylon vacuum lines can be expensive and tricky. Using rubber hose may not be as aesthetically pleasing as the OEM nylon tubing, but it's perfectly acceptable, as long as the hoses and fittings are tightly connected and correctly routed (away from rough surfaces and hot EGR tubes, exhaust manifolds, etc.).

Here are some tips for repairing nylon vacuum hoses and lines:

If a nylon hose is broken or kinked, and the damaged area is 1/2-inch or more from a connector, cut out the damaged section (don't remove more than 1/2-inch) and install a rubber union.

If the remaining hose is too short, or the damage exceeds 1/2-inch in length, replace the entire hose and the original connector with rubber vacuum hoses and a tee fitting.

If only part of a nylon connector is damaged or broken, cut it apart and discard the damaged half of the harness. Then replace it with rubber vacuum hoses and a tee.

4.8 Battery terminal corrosion usually appears as light, fluffy powder

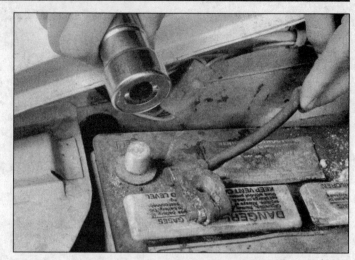

4.9 Regardless of the type of tool used on the battery posts, a clean, shiny surface should be the result

Battery, cables, electrical connections and grounds

Battery warnings and precautions:

a) Batteries give off hydrogen gas constantly. During charging, they give off even more. Hydrogen gas is highly explosive.

b) Always disconnect the battery cable from the negative battery terminal **first,** and hook it up **last**.

c) Sulfuric acid is the active ingredient in battery electrolyte (the fluid inside the battery). It's a powerful acid that will corrode all common metals, destroy paint finishes and clothing and inflict serious burns when it contacts skin and eyes.

d) If you spill electrolyte on your skin, rinse it off immediately with water.

e) If you get electrolyte in your eyes, flush them with water for 15 minutes and get prompt medical attention.

f) If you accidentally ingest electrolyte, immediately drink large amounts of water or milk. Do NOT induce vomiting. Call a doctor immediately.

g) When you service, charge or jump start a battery, make sure the area is well ventilated.

h) Never allow flames, cigarettes or any device that might cause a spark anywhere near a battery being charged or jump started.

i) When inspecting or servicing the battery, always turn the engine and all accessories off.

j) Never break a live circuit at the battery terminals. An arc could occur when the battery, charger or jumper cables are disconnected, igniting the hydrogen gas.

k) Always wear safety goggles when performing any work on the battery.

l) When loosening cables or working near a battery, keep metallic tools away from the battery terminals. The resulting short circuit or spark could damage the battery or ignite the hydrogen gas around the battery.

m) Never move a battery with the vent caps removed. Electrolyte can easily splash out.

n) Always use a battery carrier when lifting a battery with a plastic case or place your hands at the bottom and end of the battery. If you're not careful, too much pressure on the ends can cause acid to spew through the vent caps.

o) Use fender covers to protect the vehicle from acid spillage.

p) Keep sharp objects out of the battery tray to avoid puncturing the case, and don't over-tighten the battery holddown.

Maintenance

All batteries, although later batteries are called "maintenance free", do require some attention. Poor battery and cable connections **(see illustration 4.8)** can cause starting problems and poor operation of the electrical system. The high current requirement of the starting system means that voltage loss through the cables (voltage drop) must be minimized. The voltage drop, caused by the resistance in the cable, the ends and all their connections, reduces the amount of available voltage for cranking, starting and computer functions. Inspect the entire length of each battery cable. Inspect the clamps and all connections. Examine the positive and negative terminals and cables for corrosion or loose connections (usually these two problems are found together, so check for both). Clean and/or replace the cables as necessary.

Clean the cable clamps thoroughly with a battery brush or a terminal cleaner **(see illustrations 4.9 and 4.10)** and a solution of warm water and baking soda. Wash the terminals and the top of the battery case with the same solution but make sure that the solution doesn't get into the battery. When cleaning the cables, terminals and battery top, wear safety goggles and rubber gloves to prevent any solu-

4.10 When cleaning the cable clamps, all corrosion must be removed (the inside of the clamp is tapered to match the taper on the post, so don't remove too much material)

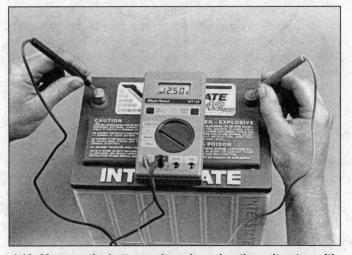

4.11 Use a hydrometer to measure the specific gravity of each individual cell

tion from coming in contact with your eyes or hands. Wear old clothes too - even diluted, sulfuric acid splashed onto clothes will burn holes in them. If the terminals have been extensively corroded, clean them with a terminal cleaner. Thoroughly wash all cleaned areas with plain water. **Note:** *Although cables can be repaired and replacement ends are available, it is a good suggestion to replace the entire cable. Replacement cables have connections that are sealed and resist corrosion much better, and thereby give the cable a longer life than repaired connections.*

Earlier batteries, with removable vent caps, must be checked periodically for low electrolyte (battery fluid) in each of the cells. **Note:** *If you have a maintenance free battery with removable caps, it's a good idea to occasionally check the electrolyte level, regardless of the manufacturer's recommendations. If any of the cells are found to be low, water can be added to bring them up to the correct level.*

Battery condition

On models not equipped with a sealed battery, check the electrolyte level of all six battery cells. Remove the filler caps and check the level of each individual cell - they must be at or near the split ring. If the level is low, add distilled water. Install and securely re-tighten the caps.

Use a hydrometer **(see illustration 4.11)**, that can be purchased at local automotive parts stores, and the accompanying chart **(see illustration 4.12)**, to check the state of charge of each battery cell.

If the battery has a sealed top and no built-in hydrometer to check the state of the batteries charge, you can hook up a digital voltmeter across the battery terminals to check the charge **(see illustration 4.13)**. A fully charged battery should read 12.6 volts or higher (engine off). If the voltage is less than 12.6 volts, charge the battery fully and retest.

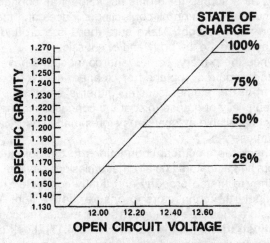

4.12 Use the specific gravity to determine the state of charge of the battery

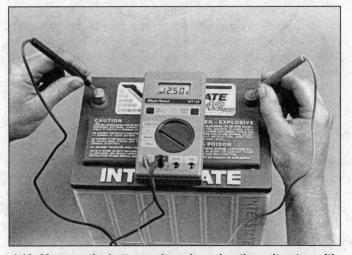

4.13 Measure the battery voltage by using the voltmeter, with a test lead at each battery post, Place the positive lead to the positive post and the negative lead to the negative post

Battery charging

Warning: *Battery handling and servicing involves two hazardous substances: sulfuric acid and hydrogen gas. When batteries are being charged, sulfuric acids creates hydrogen gas, which is very explosive and flammable, is produced. Do not smoke or allow open flames near a charging or a recently charged battery. Wear eye protection when near the battery during charging. Also, make sure the charger is unplugged before connecting or disconnecting the battery from the charger.*

Slow-rate charging is the best way to restore a battery that's discharged to the point where it will not start the engine. It's also a good way to maintain the battery charge in a vehicle that's only driven a few miles between starts. Maintaining the battery charge is particularly important in the winter when the battery must work harder to start the engine and electrical accessories that drain the battery are in greater use.

It's best to use a one or two-amp battery charger (sometimes called a "trickle" charger). They are the safest and put the least strain on the battery. They are also the least expensive. For a faster charge, you can use a higher amperage charger, but don't use one rated more than 1/10th the amp/hour rating of the battery. Rapid boost chargers that claim to restore the power of the battery in one to two hours are hardest on the battery and can damage batteries not in good condition; this type of charging should only be used in emergency situations.

The average time necessary to charge a battery should be listed in the instructions that come with the charger. As a general rule, a trickle charger will fully charge a battery in 12 to 16 hours.

Remove all the cell caps (if equipped) and cover the holes with a clean, damp cloth to prevent spattering electrolyte. Disconnect the negative battery cable and hook the battery charger leads to the battery posts (positive to positive, negative to negative), then plug in the charger. Make sure it is set at 12 volts, if it has a selector switch.

If you're using a charger with a rate higher than two amps, check the battery regularly during charging to make sure it doesn't overheat. If you're using a trickle charger, you can safely let the battery charge overnight after you've checked it regularly for the first couple of hours.

If the battery has removable cell caps, measure the specific gravity with a hydrometer every hour during the last few hours of the charging cycle. Hydrometers are available inexpensively from auto parts stores - follow the instructions that come with the hydrometer. Consider the battery charged when there's no change in the specific gravity reading for two hours and the electrolyte in the cells is gassing (bubbling) freely. The specific gravity reading from each cell should be very close to the others. If not, the battery probably has a bad cell or cells.

Some batteries with sealed tops have built-in hydrometers on the top that indicate the state of charge by the color displayed in the hydrometer window. Normally, a bright-colored hydrometer indicates a full charge and a dark hydrom-

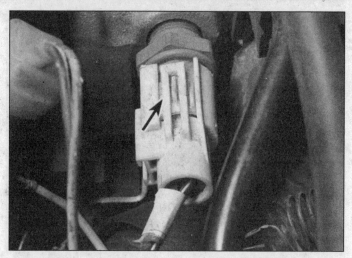

4.14 Most connectors have one or more tabs like this (arrow) that must be lifted before the halves can be separated

eter indicates the battery still needs charging. Check the battery manufacturer's instructions to be sure you know what the colors mean.

Cables

Battery cables can be deceptive by their appearance. The obvious signs of cracks or corrosion may not be evident, but the cable can still need replacement. Feel the cable. Has it become extremely hard? Is it no longer flexible? Cut back the insulation at little, near the ends and examine the cable. If it shows signs of corrosion that weren't showing on the outside, replace the cable(s). **Note:** *It is recommended that battery cables be replaced in pairs. If one is bad the other is probably very close to the same condition, or shortly will be.*

Connections and electrical grounds

The electrical grounds, both the battery-to-engine block and the engine block-to-body/chassis, are usually overlooked as a source for problems. Inspect all connections, they must be clean on all contacting surfaces and the connection must be tight. Make sure there is a ground strap from the engine to the body and/or chassis.

Once the battery, cables and connections have been checked, repaired, replaced or cleaned, seal the connections from the elements using either a small amount of petroleum jelly or grease to coat the connections. There are products available at local parts stores made specifically for this purpose.

Check the electrical connections to the computer, all sensors and actuators and all other emissions devices. Make sure they're mated properly and tightly connected. Shake and wiggle the connectors to ensure they're tight. Loose connectors should be unplugged and inspected for corrosion **(see illustrations 4.14, 4.15, 4.16 and 4.17)**. Look closely at the connector pins and tabs. If corrosion is present, clean it off with a small wire brush and electrical contact cleaner. Some connectors might require use of a special conductive grease to prevent corrosion.

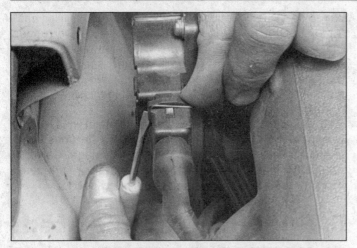

4.15 Some connectors, such as this one on a Toyota throttle position sensor, have a spring clip that must be pried up before the connector can be unplugged

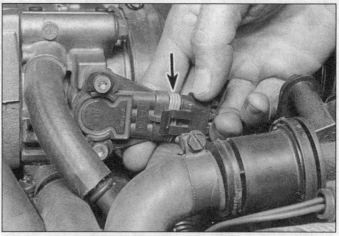

4.16 Many modern engine management system connectors have flexible seals (arrow) to keep moisture off the terminals and prevent corrosion - make sure the seal isn't damaged in any way

Charging system

Check the alternator drivebelt tension and condition. Replace the belt if it's worn or deteriorated. If the drivebelt tension is correct, try turning the alternator pulley with your hand to see if the belt is slipping **(see illustration 4.18)**. If it slips, replace the belt. When replacing a belt, adjust the tension, then make sure the alternator mounting bolts are tight.

Inspect the alternator wiring harness and the connectors at the alternator. They must be in good condition, tight and have no corrosion.

Start the engine and check the alternator for abnormal noises (a shrieking or squealing sound indicates a bad bearing).

If the alternator is to be replaced, consider a rebuilt unit from the local parts store. Older alternators are rebuildable and most parts are readily available at auto parts stores. Some later model vehicles use alternators, referred to by the manufacturer, and aftermarket parts books, as "non-serviceable". This usually means that parts are only available to an authorized rebuilder. Many times parts are soldered or

crimped in place. Some fasteners may even be the type that must be broken to disassemble the unit, requiring the same type fastener for reassembly. Don't just blindly start overhauling your alternator. Check for the availability of parts first!

For specific voltage and amperage tests see Section 8 of this Chapter.

Fuel system

Warning 1: *Gasoline is extremely flammable, so take extra precautions when you work on any part of the fuel system. Don't smoke or allow open flames or bare light bulbs near the work area, and don't work in a garage where a gas-type appliance (such as a water heater or a clothes dryer) is present. Since gasoline is carcinogenic, wear fuel-resistant gloves when there's a possibility of being exposed to fuel, and, if you spill any fuel on your skin, rinse it off immediately with soap and water. Mop up any spills immediately and do not store fuel-soaked rags where they could ignite. The fuel*

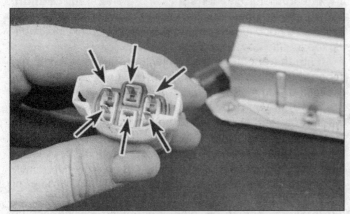

4.17 Check the terminals (arrows) in each connector for corrosion that will cause excessive resistance in the circuit, or even an open circuit

4.18 With the engine off, try turning the pulley by hand to see if the belt slips

system on fuel injected models is under constant pressure, so, if any fuel lines are to be disconnected, the fuel pressure in the system must be relieved first (see Chapter 4 for more information). When you perform any kind of work on the fuel system, wear safety glasses and have a Class B type fire extinguisher on hand.

Warning 2: *Many of the flexible fuel lines/hoses used for fuel injection systems are* **high-pressure** *lines with special crimped-on connections. When replacing a hose, use only hose that is specifically designed for your fuel-injection system.*

This Section is to be used as a preliminary check of the fuel system before any disassembly or repairs. For more specifics on inspection, depressurization, disconnection, removal and testing refer to other Chapters in this book.

If you smell gasoline while driving or after the vehicle has been sitting in the sun, inspect the fuel system immediately.

Remove the gas filler cap and inspect it for damage and corrosion. The gasket should have an unbroken sealing imprint. If the gasket is damaged or corroded, remove it and install a new one.

Inspect the fuel feed and return lines for cracks. Make sure that all the fittings and connectors, which secure the metal fuel lines to the fuel injection system, and the in-line fuel filter (if equipped), are properly connected and/or tightened correctly.

Since some components of the fuel system - the fuel tank and part of the fuel feed and return lines, for example - are underneath the vehicle, they can be inspected more easily with the vehicle raised on a hoist. If that's not possible, raise the vehicle and support it securely on jackstands.

Check all rubber fuel lines for deterioration and chafing. Check especially for cracks in areas where the hose bends and just before fittings, such as where a hose attaches to the fuel filter.

With the vehicle raised and safely supported, inspect the fuel tank and filler neck for punctures, cracks and other damage. The connection between the filler neck and the

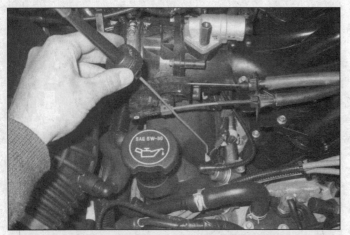

4.19 Use a stethoscope or long screwdriver to determine if the injectors are working properly - they should make a steady clicking sound that rises and falls as engine speed changes

tank is particularly critical. Sometimes, a rubber filler neck will leak because of loose clamps or deteriorated rubber. These are problems a home mechanic can usually rectify. **Warning:** *Do not, under any circumstances, try to repair a fuel tank (except rubber components). A welding torch or any open flame can easily cause fuel vapors inside the tank to explode.*

Carefully check all rubber hoses and metal lines leading away from the fuel tank. Check for loose connections, deteriorated hoses, crimped lines and other damage. Carefully inspect the lines from the tank to the fuel rail or carburetor. Repair or replace damaged sections as necessary.

6 Fuel injection system general checks

Note: *The following procedure is based on the assumption that the fuel pump is working and the fuel pressure is adequate.*

1   Check to see that the battery is fully charged, as the PCM and sensors depend on an accurate supply voltage in order to properly meter the fuel.

2   Check all electrical connectors that are related to the system. Check the ground wire connections for tightness. Loose connectors and poor grounds can cause many problems that resemble more serious malfunctions.

3   Check the air filter element. A dirty or partially blocked filter will severely impede performance and economy.

4   Check the fuses. If a blown fuse is found, replace it and see if it blows again. If it does, search for a wire shorted to ground in the harness.

5   Check the air intake duct to the intake manifold for leaks, which will result in an excessively lean mixture. Also check the condition of all vacuum hoses connected to the intake manifold and/or throttle body.

6   Remove the air intake duct from the throttle body and check for dirt, carbon, varnish, or other residue in the throttle body, particularly around the throttle plate. If it's dirty, clean it with carburetor cleaner spray and a shop rag. **Caution:** *Many throttle bodies are treated with an anti-stick coating, so it isn't a good idea to use a brush of any kind when cleaning the throttle body.*

7   With the engine running, place an automotive stethoscope against each injector, one at a time, and listen for a clicking sound that indicates operation **(see illustration 4.19)**. If you don't have a stethoscope, you can place the tip of a long screwdriver against the injector and listen through the handle. If you hear the injectors operating but there is a misfire condition present, the electrical circuits are functioning, but the injectors may be dirty or fouled from carbon deposits - commercial cleaning products may help, or the injectors may require replacement.

8   If you can't hear the injector operating, disconnect the injector electrical connector and measure the resistance across the terminals of each injector with an ohmmeter **(see illustration 4.20)**. The resistance of most injectors will be in

4.20 Measure the resistance of each injector. It should neither be open nor shorted

4.21 Install the 'noid light into the fuel injection harness electrical connector and confirm that it blinks while the engine is running

the 10 to 20-ohm range. If you encounter an injector that is either open (infinite resistance) or shorted (zero resistance), you know it's faulty.

9   If the injector is not operating, but the resistance reading is within specifications, the PCM or the circuit between the PCM and the injector might be faulty. Purchase a special injector test light (sometimes called a 'noid light - short for solenoid) and install it into the injector harness electrical connector **(see illustration 4.21)**. Start the engine and check to see if the light flashes. If it does, the injector is receiving proper voltage. If it doesn't flash, check the circuit between the injector and the PCM. if the circuit and all connectors are OK, further diagnosis should be performed by a dealer service department or other qualified repair shop.

Key components of the fuel injection system include the fuel pump and the fuel pressure regulator. Incorrect fuel pressure could cause such symptoms as an engine that is hard to start or won't start, to one that hesitates, surges, or misfires. Any basic troubleshooting procedures should include a fuel pump pressure check. Fuel pump pressures and testing procedures are covered in the *Haynes Automotive Repair Manual* for your particular vehicle, and also in the *Haynes Fuel Injection Manual*.

7 Troubleshooting with a vacuum gauge

General information

A vacuum gauge provides valuable information about what is going on inside the engine at a low cost. You can check for many internal engine problems such as rings and valves, leaking intake manifold gaskets, restricted exhaust, improper ignition or valve timing and ignition problems.

Vacuum system problems can produce or contribute to numerous driveability problems. These include, but aren't limited to:

    Deceleration backfiring
    Detonation
    Hard to start
    Knocking or pinging
    Overheating
    Poor acceleration
    Poor fuel economy
    Rich or lean stumbling
    Rough idling
    Stalling
    Won't start when cold

Unfortunately, vacuum gauge readings are easy to misinterpret, so they should be used in conjunction with other tests to confirm the diagnosis.

Both the absolute readings and the rate of needle movement are important for accurate interpretation. Most gauges measure vacuum in inches of mercury (in-Hg). The following typical vacuum gauge readings assume the diagnosis is being performed at sea level. As elevation increases (or atmospheric pressure decreases), the reading will decrease. From sea level to approximately 2,000 feet, the gauge readings will the remain the same. For every 1,000 foot increase in elevation, above 2,000 feet, the gauge readings will decrease about one inch of mercury. **Example:** *Let's say a vehicle, at sea level, has engine vacuum of 17 to 18 in-Hg. This would be a "normal" reading and not be any indication of internal engine trouble. Now, suppose the same vehicle was driven to Denver, Colorado (5,280 feet above sea level). The vacuum reading would be approximately 14 to 15 in-Hg. This reading would be a concern at sea level, but at a mile above sea level this is an indication of "normal" internal engine vacuum.*

Connect the vacuum gauge directly to intake manifold vacuum, not to ported vacuum. You want to read full engine vacuum, uncontrolled by the throttle body or carburetor. Be sure no hoses are left disconnected during the test or false readings will result.

Before you begin the test, allow the engine to warm up completely. Block the wheels and set the parking brake. With the transmission in neutral (or Park, on automatics), start the engine and allow it to run at normal idle speed. **Warning:** *Keep your hands, the vacuum tester and hose clear of the fan and do not stand in front of the vehicle or in line with the fan when the engine is running.*

Read the vacuum gauge and as a general rule apply the following guidelines:

What is "normal" vacuum?

Internal combustion engines, regardless of four, six or eight cylinders, all have the approximately the same range for acceptable vacuum of about 15 to 20 in-Hg.

At wide-open-throttle (WOT) the vacuum reading will be 0 in-Hg, and on deceleration, vacuum may go as high, very briefly, as 25 to 29 in-Hg.

Vacuum diagnostic checks

The following guidelines for vacuum are approximate and will be affected by the overall condition of the engine and related systems:

Cranking vacuum

Disable the ignition system and hold the throttle in the wide open position. Take a reading of the engine vacuum while only cranking the engine, don't start the engine at this time. There should be approximately 1-to-4 in-Hg during cranking.

Operating readings

Start the engine and read the gauge. A healthy engine should produce approximately 15-to-20 in-Hg at idle, with a fairly steady needle.

Raise the engine speed to about 2500 rpm and hold rpm steady, a reading of approximately 19-to-21 in-Hg should be seen on the gauge.

Rev the engine up and down, watch the gauge during both increasing and decreasing rpm. At wide open throttle (hard acceleration), vacuum approaches zero. While on deceleration, the vacuum should jump up to somewhere around 21-to-27 in-Hg as the throttle is released.

If the readings you are seeing aren't at the appropriate level or steady, refer to the following vacuum gauge readings and what they indicate about the engine **(see illustrations 4.22a through 4.22g)**:

4.22a Low, steady reading

Low steady reading

This usually indicates a leaking gasket between the intake manifold and throttle body, a leaky vacuum hose, late ignition timing or incorrect camshaft timing **(see illustration)**. Check ignition timing with a timing light and eliminate all other possible causes, utilizing the tests provided in this Chapter before you remove the timing chain cover to check the timing marks.

4.22b Low, fluctuating needle

Low, fluctuating reading

If the needle fluctuates about three to eight inches below normal **(see illustration)**, suspect an intake manifold gasket leak at an intake port or a faulty injector(s).

4.22c Regular drops

Regular drops

If the needle drops about two-to-four inches at a steady rate **(see illustration)**, the valves are probably leaking. Perform a compression or leakdown test to confirm this.

Irregular drops

An irregular down-flick of the needle (see illustration) can be caused by a sticking valve or an ignition misfire. Perform a compression or leakdown test and read the spark plugs.

4.22d Irregular drops

Rapid vibration

A rapid four in-Hg vibration at idle (see illustration) combined with exhaust smoke indicates worn valve guides. Perform a leak down test to confirm this. If the rapid vibration occurs with an increase in engine speed, check for a leaking intake manifold gasket or head gasket, weak valve springs, burned valves or ignition misfire.

4.22e Rapid vibration

Slight fluctuation

A slight fluctuation, say one inch up-and-down, may mean ignition problems. Check all the usual tune-up items and check for stored trouble codes (see Chapters 7 and 8). If necessary, run the engine on an ignition analyzer.

Large fluctuation

If this occurs (see illustration), perform a compression or leakdown test to look for a weak or dead cylinder or a blown head gasket.

4.22f Large fluctuation

Slow hunting

If the needle moves slowly through a wide range, check for a clogged PCV system, Idle Air Control (IAC) valve problem, throttle body or intake manifold gasket leaks.

Slow return after revving

Quickly snap the throttle open until the engine reaches about 2,500 rpm and let it shut. Normally the reading should drop to near zero, rise above normal idle reading (about 5 in.-Hg over) and then return to the previous idle reading (see illustration). If the vacuum returns slowly and doesn't peak when the throttle is snapped shut, the rings may be worn. If there is a long delay, look for a restricted exhaust system (often the muffler or catalytic converter). An easy way to check this is to temporarily disconnect the exhaust ahead of the suspected part and redo the test.

4.22g Slow return after revving

Restricted or blocked exhaust

When an exhaust system becomes restricted, usually the catalytic converter, it typically causes a loss of power and backfiring through the throttle body or carburetor. A vacuum gauge can be used to check a restricted exhaust by checking for excessive exhaust backpressure and observing any vacuum variation. Follow the steps described:

1   Block the wheels and set the parking brake.
2   Disconnect a vacuum line connected to an intake manifold port and plug the line, so you don't create your own vacuum leak, and install a vacuum gauge to the intake manifold port.
3   Start the engine and record the vacuum at idle. If the vacuum reading slowly drops toward zero, there is a restriction.
4   Gradually increase speed to 2,000 rpm with the transmission in Neutral or Park. The reading from the vacuum gauge should quickly rise above the level recorded at idle, somewhere around 16 in-Hg. If not, there could be excessive backpressure in the exhaust system.
5   While at approximately 2000 rpm, quickly close the throttle. The vacuum reading should return to normal idle vacuum as quickly as it rose above it in the previous step.
6   If the vacuum reading is 5 in-Hg or more higher than the normally observed reading, there is an exhaust restriction.

Once it has been determined that the exhaust system is the cause of the problem, the exact cause must be pinpointed. Perform the following:

7   Turn the ignition key OFF.
8   Disconnect the exhaust system at the exhaust manifold.
9   Start the engine (despite the loud exhaust roar) and gradually increase the engine speed to 2,000 rpm.
10   The reading from the exhaust manifold vacuum gauge should be above 16 in-Hg.
11   If 16 in-Hg. is not reached, the exhaust manifold may be restricted (or the valve timing or ignition timing may be late, or there could be a vacuum leak).
12   If 16 in-Hg. is reached, the blockage is most likely in the muffler, exhaust pipes, or catalytic converter. Also, if the catalytic converter debris has entered the muffler, have it replaced also.

8 Starting and charging circuits

Battery

Warning: *Certain precautions must be followed when checking and servicing the battery. Hydrogen gas, which is highly flammable, is always present in the battery cells, so keep all open flames and sparks away from the battery. The electrolyte inside the battery is actually diluted sulfuric acid, which will cause injury if splashed on your skin or in your eyes. It will also ruin clothes and painted surfaces. See additional warnings and precautions in Section 5 of this Chapter.*

Caution: *Overfilling the cells may cause electrolyte to spill over during periods of heavy charging, causing corrosion or damage. When removing the battery cables, always detach the negative cable first and hook it up last!*

Charging and maintenance

See Section 5 of this Chapter.

Cranking voltage

The next check is cranking voltage. Cranking voltage is used to determine if the battery has enough reserve capacity.

1   Disable the ignition.
2   Hook up a voltmeter across the battery. Now, crank the engine for a few seconds and watch the battery voltage. This will use the starter, cranking the engine, as the load for the battery. **Note:** *In a shop the technicians would use a machine to place an artificial load on the battery to duplicate the starter's effect.*
3   The low limit for this test is 9.6 volts. If the voltage falls to the 9.6 volts, or lower, it doesn't have enough reserve power and will never keep up with the demands of the starting system. Replace the battery. **Note:** *The low limit of 9.6 volts is based upon a outside temperature of approximately 70 degrees Fahrenheit. The acceptable voltage goes down as the temperature drops. If, when testing a battery, the temperature is less than 70 degrees F, refer to the table* (**see illustration 4.23**) *for the correct minimum voltage.*

Battery ground circuit check

1   The other value to check, while cranking, is the voltage of the battery ground circuit. Hook up the voltmeter positive lead to the battery ground at the engine block or starter and the negative lead to the negative terminal of the battery. **Note:** *Be sure to touch the voltmeter probe directly to the battery post, not the clamp. If touched to the clamp, any additional resistance at that connection to the post would not be measured.* With the ignition still disabled, crank the engine for a few seconds and note the reading on the voltmeter.
2   Readings will probably be somewhere between 0.1 and 0.3 volts. Anything above 0.3 volts is an indication of a bad ground connection. Inspect, clean and replace parts as necessary.

Approximate temperature (degrees Fahrenheit)	Minimum voltage
70	9.6
60	9.5
50	9.4
40	9.3
30	9.1
20	8.9
10	8.7
0	8.5

4.23 Follow this chart to determine the acceptable minimum battery voltage, adjusting for the outside side temperature

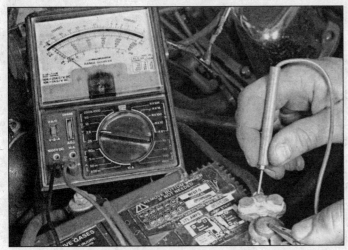

4.24 Here's a battery cable connection being checked for a voltage drop that could be caused by corrosion or a loose connection

Voltage drops

1   The next concern is the voltage drop (the amount voltage lost from one point to another in an electrical circuit) in the battery terminals, cables, starter and connections. Hook up a voltmeter so the meter is connected across the connection where the voltage drop is to be checked, example: If the voltage loss between the battery post and connecting clamp is to be checked, the voltmeter probes should be connected to the post and the clamp **(see illustration 4.24)**.

2   Have the meter set on the volt scale and read the amount of voltage drop on the gauge, it should be 0.2 volts maximum, across any of the individual connections tested.

3   A greater reading than this would indicate an excessive voltage drop. Caused by a loose connection, corroded end or cable, rusty connection, etc. If found, repair any of these conditions and recheck the connections to be sure the problem has been corrected.

Starter

Cranking amperage (starter draw)

1   Checking the amount of cranking amperage required to operate the starter, will require the use of an inexpensive inductive amp gauge **(see illustration 4.25)** which can be found at most auto parts stores.

2   Disable the ignition system, if not already done from previous tests.

3   Place the gauge directly on the battery cable **(see illustration 4.26)**. **Note:** *In order for the reading to be accurate, the use of this gauge requires that it placed directly on the battery cable with about three-to-four inches of clearance from all other components to avoid magnetic interference.*

4   Crank the starter and take a reading after the starter reaches a steady cranking speed. This usually takes about two-to-three seconds. **Caution:** *Don't continuously operate the starter for more than 15 seconds, it can be damaged by overheating.* Compare your readings to these general guidelines:

> Four cylinder engine - 120-to-180 amps
> Six cylinder engine - 150-to-200 amps
> Eight cylinder engine - 180-to-220 amps

Note: *Large cubic inch or high compression eight cylinder engines, as well as engines using high performance starters, may normally use 300-to-350 amps.*

Alternator

1   If a malfunction occurs in the charging circuit, do not immediately assume that the alternator is causing the problem. First, check the following items:

a) Make sure the battery cable clamps, where they connect to the battery, are clean and tight.

b) Test the condition of the battery as described previously. If it does not pass all the tests, replace it with a new battery.

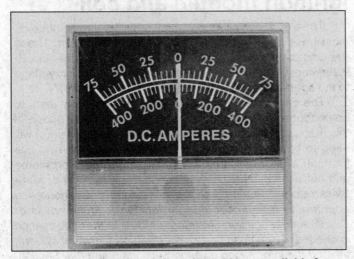

4.25 Simple inductive ammeters like this are available from auto parts stores at reasonable prices

4.26 This is another simple inductive ammeter being used to check starter draw while cranking the engine

4.27 To find out whether there's a drain on the battery, simply disconnect the negative battery cable and hook up a test light between the cable clamp an the battery post - if the light comes on brightly, with all the accessories off, there's an electrical drain (the light will glow dimly due to the current draw of the computer, clock and radio memories).

4.28 This is a typical example of how the identifying information will look on an alternator

c) Check the external alternator wiring and connections.
d) Check the drivebelt condition and tension.
e) Check the alternator mounting bolts for tightness.
f) Run the engine and check the alternator for abnormal noise.
g) Check the fusible links in the wiring harness between the alternator and the battery junction box (which is located in the engine compartment fuse box). If they're burned, determine the cause and repair the circuit.
h) Check the charge light on the dash. It should illuminate when the ignition key is turned ON (engine not running). If it does not, check the circuit from the alternator to the charge light on the dash.
i) Check all the fuses that are in series with the charging system circuit.

2   With the ignition key turned to OFF, remove the cable from the negative terminal of the battery. Connect a test light between the disconnected negative cable clamp and the battery post to check for a drain on the battery (see illustration 4.27). Reconnect the cable to the battery post.

3   With the ignition key turned to OFF, check the "standing" battery voltage with no accessories operating. It should be approximately 12.66 volts. It may be slightly higher if the engine had been operating within the last hour.

4   Start the engine, let it warm up and, with the engine at idle, check the battery voltage again. It should now be greater than the voltage recorded in Step 2, but not more than 14.5 volts. Then turn on all the vehicle accessories (air conditioning, blower motor, rear window defogger, sound system, etc.) and increase the engine speed to 2,000 rpm; the voltage should not drop below the voltage recorded in Step 2.

5   If the indicated voltage is greater than the specified charging voltage, replace the voltage regulator (which, on these models, means replacing the alternator, because the voltage regulator is not serviceable separately).

6   If the indicated voltage reading is less than the specified charging voltage, the alternator is probably defective. Have the charging system checked at a dealer service department or other properly equipped repair facility. **Note:** *Some auto parts stores will bench test an alternator off the vehicle. Some of them will perform this service for free; before taking the alternator to a dealer service department, consult your local auto parts store regarding its policy on bench testing alternators.*

7   When replacing an alternator, make sure the new one has the same specifications as the old one **(see illustration)**.

9 Ignition system

Ignition module and coil

1   While some OBD-II-compliant vehicles use distributors, most have gone to distributorless ignition systems. These systems use either a coil pack or one individual coil per cylinder, controlled by the PCM, to deliver high-tension voltage to the spark plugs **(see illustrations 4.29 and 4.30)**.

2   The condition of the coil and module and any tests to be conducted, although important, are beyond the scope of this manual. If there is no voltage reading the problem(s) will need to be diagnosed further. The primary concern of this manual is engine management system-related problems and corrections. **Note:** *There are many variations of manufacturers wiring, connections, components, locations and appropriate test procedures for ignition modules, coils or Distributorless Ignition Systems (DIS). If further information is needed to diagnose or repair the vehicle electrical system, beyond the information given in Sections 5 and this Section, refer to the specific Haynes Automotive Repair Manual for the vehicle being repaired.*

4.29 Most engines without distributors have a coil-pack like this, where all the spark plug wires are attached - when replacing wires, first mark each wire and terminal if they're not already factory-marked

4.30 Some vehicles have a separate coil for each spark plug - each coil mounts directly over the spark plug so there are no secondary plug wires

Spark plug wires

1   The spark plug wires should be checked at the recommended intervals and whenever new spark plugs are installed in the engine.

2   Using a clean rag, wipe the entire length of the wire to remove built-up dirt and grease. Once the wire is clean, check for burns, cracks and other damage. Do not bend the wire sharply, because the conductor might break.

3   Make a visual check of the spark plug wires while the engine is running. In a darkened garage (make sure there is adequate ventilation) start the engine and observe each plug wire. Be careful not to come into contact with any moving engine parts. If there is a break in the wire, you will see arcing or a small spark at the damaged area. If arcing is noticed, stop the engine, allow the engine to cool and replace the necessary parts.

4   The wires should be further inspected, if necessary, one at a time to prevent mixing up the order, which is essential to proper engine operation.

5   Disconnect the plug wire from the spark plug. A removal tool can be used for this purpose or you can grasp the rubber boot, twist the boot half a turn, to break it loose from the spark plug, and pull the boot free (see illustration 4.31). Do not pull on the wire itself.

6   Disconnect the wire from the distributor, or coil pack. Again, pull only on the rubber boot.

7   Check inside the boot for corrosion, which will look like a white crusty powder. Note: *Don't mistake white, dielectric grease, for corrosion. Many manufacturers use this grease during assembly to prevent corrosion.*

Spark plug wire resistance check

8   Spark plug wires, sometimes referred to as ignition cables, should be checked for continuity to determine if they need replacement. Note: *Spark plug wires can be replaced*

separately. It sometimes is all that is needed to correct a problem. But it is suggested that if any need replacement, they all be replaced as a set. Even if not all wires test bad, their condition is probably very similar to the ones that are already in need of replacement.

9   There are some general resistance (ohms) values used to test spark plug wires. Remove each spark plug wire, one at a time, and hook up an ohmmeter (see Chapter 2). Measure the resistance of each wire. Use the following guidelines for interpreting your vehicle's resistance readings:

a) When measuring the resistance value of the spark plug wires there should be approximately 1K (1,000) ohms per inch of length.

b) There should not be a resistance of more than 30K (30,000) ohms for any complete spark plug wire, regardless of length.

10   These resistance values are for new or used spark plug wires. If your test values are outside these ranges, replace the spark plug wires.

11   Inspect the remaining spark plug wires, making sure that each one is securely fastened at the distributor, or coil pack, and spark plug when the check is complete.

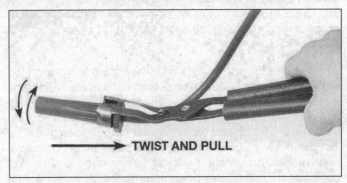

TWIST AND PULL

4.31 When removing the spark plug wires, pull only on the boot and twist it back-and-forth - a spark plug wire removal tool makes this job easier and safer

12 Push the wire and boot back onto the end of the spark plug. It should fit tightly onto the end of the plug and 'snap' into place, indicating a proper connection. If it doesn't, remove the wire and use pliers to carefully crimp the metal connector inside the wire boot until the fit is correct.

13 If new spark plug wires are required, purchase a set for your specific engine model. Pre-cut wire sets with the boots already installed are available or spark plug cable and terminal ends of many different angles can be purchased for anyone that wants to route the wires to fit a custom application. Remove and replace the wires one at a time to avoid mix-ups in the firing order.

Spark plugs

Removal

14 The spark plugs provide a sort of window into the combustion chamber and can give a wealth of information about engine operation to a savvy mechanic. Fuel mixture, heat range, oil consumption and detonation all leave their mark on the tips of the spark plugs.

15 Before you begin the check, drive the vehicle at highway speed, allowing it to warm up thoroughly without excessive idling. Shut the engine off and wait until it cools sufficiently so you won't get burned if you touch the exhaust manifolds.

16 Whether you are replacing the plugs at this time, or just removing to inspect, and intend to re-use the old plugs, compare the condition and color of each old spark plug with those shown on the inside of the back cover of this manual. **Note:** *If a spark plug is worn to the extent that replacement is necessary, it's recommended that all spark plugs be replaced at the same time.*

17 If compressed air is available, blow any dirt or foreign material away from the spark plug area before proceeding (a common bicycle pump will also work).

18 Check the spark plug wires to see if they have the cylinder numbers on them. Label them if necessary so you can reinstall them on the correct spark plugs.

19 Never remove the spark plug wire connector from the spark plug by pulling the wire. Be sure, even when grabbing the boot, that the connector is being grasped before pulling it off the plug. There are some helpful spark plug removal tools available at local automotive parts stores.

20 Once the spark plug wires have been disconnected, proceed with removing the spark plug(s).

Heat range

21 Remove the spark plugs and place them in order on top of the air cleaner or on the work bench. Note the brand and number on the plugs. Compare this to the VECI label, which is the manufacturer's recommendation for that vehicle, to determine if the correct type and heat range is being used.

22 Spark plug manufacturers make spark plugs in several heat ranges for different vehicle applications and driving conditions. These have been determined by working with the vehicle manufacturers to come up with the proper match of spark plug to engine requirements.

23 The engine must have the correct heat range spark plugs before you can read the tips accurately. Plugs that are too hot will mask a rich fuel mixture reading; conversely, cold plugs will tend to foul on a normal mixture. On most European and Japanese spark plugs, the higher the number, the colder the heat range. American plugs are just the opposite.

24 There are several "old mechanic's tales" about heat range that need to be dispelled. Hotter heat range plugs don't make the engine run hotter, they don't make a hotter spark and they don't increase combustion chamber temperature (unless the colder plug wasn't firing).

25 If a change in spark plug heat range is being considered, first ask - what is causing the engine to run in a way that necessitates a change? Manufacturers go to a great deal of trouble to determine the correct plug type, heat range and gap for every vehicle on the market. It's recommended that the spark plug requirements, found on the VECI label under the hood, should be followed at all times. After the conditions are corrected that were causing the spark plug to fire poorly, the original spark recommendation will work as it was intended. **Note:** *Non-resistor spark plugs can add electrical interference or "noise" to the ECM and/or sensor circuits. This is sometimes referred to as "spark echo" (think of all that static that solid, non-resistor, plug wires caused on the radio of your old hot rod). This can have a direct affect on the low amperage current used by computer control vehicles to monitor and control engine functions, such as fuel ratios, spark timing, etc. or any circuit that is controlled by low voltage impulses.*

Reading spark plugs

26 Examine the plugs for hints about the engine's internal condition and state of tune. If any of the plugs are wet with oil, engine repairs are needed right away. If the plugs have significant gray or white deposits, it means that a moderate amount of oil is seeping into the cylinders and repairs will be needed soon, or you've been doing a lot of short trip driving.

27 Late-model emission-controlled engines run very lean. Normally, the plugs range from almost white to tan on the porcelain insulator cone and the ground electrode should be light brown to dark gray.

28 Excessively rich fuel mixtures cause the spark plug tips to turn black, and lean mixtures result in light tan or white tips. You can tell by the color if the fuel mixture is in the ballpark by reading the plugs (compare your plugs with the photos shown on the inside back cover of this manual).

29 If the engine has a misfire and one or more plugs are carbon fouled, look for an ignition problem or low compression in the affected cylinder(s). Sometimes the spark plugs will vary among each other in color because of improper mixture distribution. Look for a leaky intake manifold gasket if one or more adjoining cylinders are running very lean. If the plugs are burning unevenly, you may have a vacuum leak, or a fuel distribution problem in the fuel injection system (perhaps a dirty or inoperative fuel injector).

30 Detonation, preignition and plugs that are too long can result in physical damage to the tip. Check the photos on the inside of the back cover of this manual to help identify these problems.

4.32 An example of a wire-type gauge for checking the gap - if the wire does not slide between the electrodes with a slight drag, adjustment is required

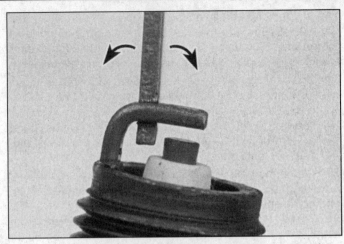

4.33 To change the gap, bend the side electrode as shown to specification, be careful not to chip or crack the porcelain insulator

31   You will also need a gauge, different types are available, to check and adjust the spark plug gap and a torque wrench to tighten the new plugs to the specified torque.

32   If you are replacing the plugs, purchase the new plugs, adjust them to the proper gap and then replace each plug one at a time. **Caution:** *When buying new spark plugs, it's essential that you obtain the correct plugs for your specific vehicle. Don't substitute spark plugs, use what was designed for the vehicle. This information can be found in the Haynes Automotive Repair Manual for your vehicle or in the owner's manual. Many people, even professionals, sometimes substitute heat ranges for the ones called for by the manufacturer. This is a mistake and misses the underlying reason for the condition of the spark plugs. If the spark plug change is to correct a problem (not just a tune-up) the new plug may mask the real cause of the driveability problem, which still exist. Correct the cause and the recommended spark plugs will work as they were originally designed. Incorrect spark plug selection can cause engine damage.*

33   Inspect each of the new plugs for defects. If there are any signs of cracks in the porcelain insulator of a plug, don't use it. Check the electrode gaps of the new plugs. Check the gap by inserting the gauge of the proper thickness between the electrodes at the tip of the plug **(see illustration 4.32)**. The gap between the electrodes should be identical to the manufacturers specifications, which are listed on the VECI label. If the gap is incorrect, use the adjuster, on the feeler gauge to bend the curved side electrode slightly.

34   If the side electrode is not exactly over the center electrode, use the notched adjuster to align them **(see illustration 4.33)**. **Caution 1:** *If the gap of a new plug must be adjusted, bend only the base of the side electrode, do not touch the tip.* **Caution 2:** *Most spark plug manufacturers recommend against adjusting the gap on platinum or iriduim-tipped spark plugs. Doing so could scrape the platinum or iridium plating from the electrodes, which would severely shorten the spark plug's life.*

Installation

35   Prior to installation, apply a light film of anti-seize compound or a drop of oil on the spark plug threads **(see illustration 4.34)**. It's often difficult to insert spark plugs into their holes without cross-threading them. To avoid this possibility, fit a short piece of rubber hose, or an old spark plug boot, over the end of the spark plug **(see illustration 4.35)**. The flexible hose, or boot, acts as a universal joint to help align the plug with the plug hole. Should the plug begin to cross-

4.34 Apply a very thin coat of anti-seize compound, or a few drops of oil, to the spark plug threads ease in installation and prevent the spark plug from seizing in the cylinder head

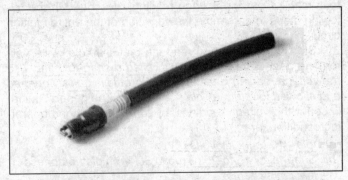

4.35 A length of rubber hose will save time and prevent damaged threads when installing the spark plugs

thread, the hose will slip on the spark plug, preventing thread damage. Follow the manufacturers recommendations for torque when tightening the plugs on installation. If that information isn't readily available, use the following guidelines:

a) Spark plugs with a gasket require only 1/4 additional turn, after the gasket makes contact with the cylinder head, to seal properly.

b) Tapered seat spark plugs, ones that have no gasket, require only 1/16 additional turn, after the spark plug seat contacts the cylinder head, to seal properly.

36 Attach the plug wire to the new spark plug, again using a twisting motion on the boot until it is firmly seated on the end of the spark plug.

37 Follow the above procedure for the remaining spark plugs, replacing them one at a time to prevent mixing up the spark plug wires.

Available spark plug firing voltage

Warning 1: *Before starting these procedures, make sure the vehicle is in park or in neutral with the parking brake set. Always perform all tests while standing to the side of the vehicle - never from the front.*

Warning 2: *To avoid electrical shock,* **always use** *insulated pliers* **(see illustration 4.31)** *when it's necessary to grasp the high voltage spark plug wire, with the engine running, in order to perform tests.*

Note: *The purpose of the following voltage tests are to verify that the ignition system is functioning properly, which must be done before a proper engine management diagnosis can be continued. Although this test would normally be performed on an Engine Analyzer or Oscilloscope, they can successfully be performed with a far less expensive hand-held digital K-V tester with an inductive pick-up.*

1 Spark plug firing voltage is a measurement of the available output of the entire ignition circuit, checked at the spark plugs. Checking for the correct end result, such as the firing voltages within their specifications, is a quick confirmation, of all the parts of the primary and secondary ignition circuits are functioning properly.

2 Using an inductive digital K-V tester, attach the meter to each individual spark plug wire, one at a time, perform the tests and record the voltage readings described in the following steps to determine the condition of the entire ignition circuit.

3 Start the vehicle and read the meter at idle while performing a "snap-test". **Note:** *It's called a snap-test because the voltage reading is taken as the throttle is quickly opened and allowed to return to idle ("snapped").* The general guidelines for the voltage readings, of an engine in good operating condition, are:

a) Idle - 10-to-12 kilovolts (kV)

b) Snap-test - 15-to-25kV (up to 30kV on distributorless ignition systems)

4 Look for consistency between cylinders at idle and on the snap-test. Variations would indicate the ignition system components are worn to different degrees. Inspect the components in question and repair or replace as necessary.

5 If there is no voltage reading the problem will need to be diagnosed further, which is beyond the scope of this manual. The primary concern of this manual is engine management related problems and corrections. If further information is needed to diagnose or repair the electrical system beyond the information given in Section 5 and this Section of this manual, refer to the specific *Haynes Automotive Repair Manual* for the vehicle being repaired.

6 Another simple test to check for sufficient voltage is using a "calibrated ignition tester" tool available at auto parts stores **(see illustration 4.36)**.

Available coil voltage

1 This test will check the available coil voltage to verify the condition of the coil(s).

2 Attach the inductive K-V tester to one of the spark plug wires as in the previous tests. Disconnect the spark plug wire from the spark plug and secure it away from the engine.

Caution: *Never pull the on the spark plug wire itself, it can be internally damaged. Grasp the boot over the tip of the spark plug. The open created by disconnecting the spark plug wire causes the build up of voltage that the coil is trying to send to ground through the spark plug. The available coil voltage goes to maximum buildup when this open in the circuit is made.*

3 Disable the fuel system so the engine won't start (see Chapter 4) and crank the engine over long enough to take the reading.

4.36 To use a calibrated ignition tester, simply remove one plug's spark plug wire (or ignition coil) and push it onto the tester, then clip the tester to a convenient ground on the engine - if there is enough power to fire the test plug while cranking or running the engine, you'll see blue sparks between the electrode tip and the tester

4   A general guideline of 30-to-50 kilovolts (kV) (30,000-to-50,000 volts) of available coil voltage indicates a coil with sufficient reserve capacity for times of greater demand.

5   If there is no voltage reading the problem will need to be diagnosed further, which is beyond the scope of this manual. The primary concern of this manual is engine management related problems and corrections. If further information is needed to diagnose or repair the electrical system beyond the information given in Section 5 and this Section of the manual, refer to the specific *Haynes Automotive Repair Manual* for the vehicle being repaired.

10 EGR (Exhaust Gas Recirculation) system

General information

To reduce oxides of nitrogen emissions, a small amount of exhaust gas is recirculated through the EGR valve **(see illustration 4.37)** into the intake manifold. The introduction of the inert gas lowers the combustion temperatures, which reduces the oxides of nitrogen. The EGR system **(see illustration 4.38)** typically consists of the EGR valve, the EGR modulator, vacuum switching valve, the Electronic Control

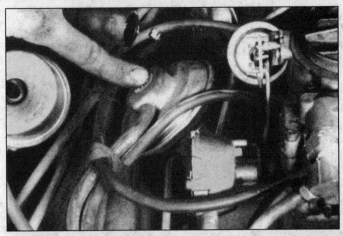

4.37 On most models, the EGR valve is located on the intake manifold, adjacent to the throttle body

Module (ECM) and the EGR gas temperature sensor.

On most vehicles there are additional sensors and actuators included in the EGR system. The EGR valve acts on direct command from the computer after it (the computer) has determined that all the working parameters (air temperature, coolant temperature, EGR valve position, fuel/air mixture etc.) are correct.

Later model vacuum operated EGR valves are often controlled by a computer-controlled solenoid in line with the valve and vacuum source **(see illustration 4.39)**. Some

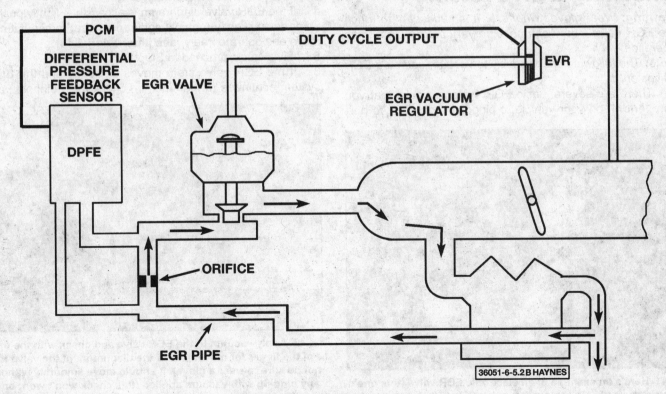

4.38 Schematic of a typical EGR system

4.39 Some EGR solenoids (left arrow) are installed on a bracket near the EGR valve, such as this on a Nissan Maxima (the arrow on the right points to the air injection system solenoid). Some EGR solenoids are installed on the firewall

4.40 Some EGR valves are also equipped with a position sensor like this unit on a Ford Thunderbird - the position sensor is almost always mounted on top of the EGR valve

models also often have a position sensor on the EGR valve that informs the computer what position the EGR valve is in (see illustration 4.40).

Electronic EGR valves are becoming increasingly popular (see illustration 4.41). These types of valves are under complete control of the PCM and don't rely on a vacuum source for operation.

Checking EGR systems

Warning: *Wear gloves whenever it is necessary to touch the EGR valve - they can become very hot during engine operation.*

Note: *The following checks apply to vacuum-operated EGR valves only.*

1   There are several basic EGR system checks that you can perform on your vehicle to pinpoint problems. To per-

form these checks you will need a vacuum pump (see illustration 4.42) and a vacuum gauge.

2   Check for a vacuum source (see illustration 4.43) by hooking up a vacuum gauge to the line going to the EGR valve.

3   If no vacuum if found, the vehicle may have computer controlled solenoids, which regulate the vacuum to the EGR valve, depending upon conditions such as the transmission being in drive, engine at operating temperature, open or closed loop computer operation, etc.

4   If the EGR valve diaphragm is accessible, lightly push it up or down slightly (against spring pressure) to see if it can move and operate freely (see illustration 4.44).

5   If it is stuck, proceed to Step 13.

6   If the EGR valve stem moves smoothly and the EGR system continues to malfunction, check for a pinhole vac-

4.41 Here's an example of an electronic EGR valve (this one's on a Saturn V6). To remove it, unplug the electrical connector and unscrew the bolts

4.42 Apply vacuum to the EGR valve and check with the tip of the finger for movement of the diaphragm (if the valve is hot be sure to wear a glove). It should move smoothly without any binding with vacuum applied (this check won't work on a positive backpressure type valve unless the engine is running and the exhaust system is artificially restricted).

4.43 With the engine running, check for vacuum to the EGR valve

4.44 Use your finger to check for free movement of the diaphragm within the EGR valve

uum leak in the diaphragm of the EGR valve. Obtain a can of spray carburetor cleaner and attach the flexible "straw" to the tip. Aim carefully into the diaphragm areas of the EGR valve and spray around the actuator shaft while the engine is running. Listen carefully for any changes in engine rpm. If there is a leak, the engine rpm will increase and surge temporarily. Then it will smooth back out to a constant idle. The only way to properly repair this problem is to replace the EGR valve with a new unit.

7   After the engine has been warmed up to normal operating temperature, open the throttle to approximately 2,500 rpm and observe the EGR valve stem as it moves with the rise in engine rpm. Use a mirror or even a finger placed on the diaphragm to feel movement, if necessary. If it doesn't move, remove the vacuum hose and check for vacuum with a gauge. Reconnect the hose, raise the rpm of the engine and see or feel if the valve opens up and/or flutters approximately 1/8 inch. Larger abrupt, jerky movements and/or opening all the way will cause a driveability problem and is not indicative of correct operation. Replace the EGR valve. **Warning:** *A computer-controlled EGR valve needs to have the vehicle placed into gear in order for the computer to signal the valve to work. Block the wheels, have an assistant sit in the vehicle and apply the parking brake **and** press firmly on the brake pedal before placing the vehicle in gear for this check.*

8   This test will tell you if the gas flow passages are open and if the gas flow is proper. Remove the vacuum line from the EGR valve and plug the line. Attach a hand-held vacuum pump to the EGR valve. With the engine idling, slowly apply approximately 8-to-10 in-Hg to the valve and watch the valve stem for movement. **Note:** *If the valve is a positive backpressure type, it will be necessary to create an exhaust restriction. This can be done by folding a thick towel over a few times, soaking it in water then having an assistant hold it over the end of the exhaust pipe (don't do this any longer than necessary to perform the test).* If the gas flow is good, the engine will begin to idle rough or it may even stall. If the stem moves but the idle does not change, there is a

restriction in the valve spacer plate or passages in the intake manifold (see *Cleaning the EGR valve*). If the valve stem does not move or the EGR valve diaphragm does not hold vacuum, replace the EGR valve with a new part.

9   The thermostatic vacuum switch (TVS) should also be checked, if equipped. This switch is usually regulated by a bimetal core that expands or contracts according to the temperature. The valve remains closed and does not operate as long as the coolant temperature is below 115 to 129-degrees F. As the coolant temperature rises, the valve will open and the EGR system will operate. Remove the switch and place it in a pan of cool water and check the valve for vacuum - vacuum should not pass through the valve. Heat the water to the specified temperature (over 129-degrees F) and make sure the valve opens and allows the vacuum to pass. If the switch fails the test, replace it with a new part.

EGR vacuum modulator valve (if equipped)

10   Remove the valve.

11   Pull the cover off and check the filters **(see illustrations 4.45 and 4.46)**.

12   Replace the filters or clean them with compressed air, reinstall the cover and the modulator.

4.45 To remove the EGR vacuum modulator filters (if equipped) for cleaning, remove the cap . . .

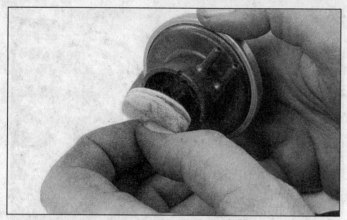

4.46 . . . then pull out the filter(s) and blow it out with compressed air - be sure the coarse side of the outer filter faces the atmosphere (out) when reinstalling the filters

Cleaning the EGR valve

13 The bottoms of EGR valves often get covered with carbon deposits **(see illustration 4.47)**, causing them to restrict exhaust flow or leak exhaust. The valve must be removed so the bottom of the valve and the passages in the manifold can be cleaned **(see illustration 4.48)**. **Caution:** *When removing the EGR valve be sure to replace the gasket upon reassembly* **(see illustration 4.49)**. *There is generally more heat at this location, because of exhaust gases, and the gasket deteriorates quickly. If not replaced, the gasket can be the source of an exhaust leak after reassembly.*

14 There are important points that must be observed when cleaning EGR valves:

a) Never use solvent to dissolve deposits on EGR valves unless you are extremely careful not to get any on the diaphragm.

b) Clean the pintle and valve seat with a dull scraper and wire brush and knock out loose carbon by tapping on the assembly.

c) Some EGR valves can be disassembled for cleaning, but be sure the parts are in alignment before assembly.

4.47 Depress the EGR valve diaphragm and inspect the full length of the pintle and the seat at its base for carbon deposits

11 Evaporative emissions control (EVAP) system

General description

The evaporative emissions control system **(see illustration 4.50)** stores fuel vapors generated in the fuel tank in a charcoal canister when the engine isn't running. When the engine is started, the fuel vapors are drawn into the intake manifold and burned. The crankcase emission control system works like this: When the engine is cruising, the purge control valve (bypass valve) is opened slightly and a small amount of blow-by gas is drawn into the intake manifold and burned. When the engine is started cold or idling, the bypass valve prevents any vapors from entering the intake manifold, since that would cause an excessively rich fuel mixture.

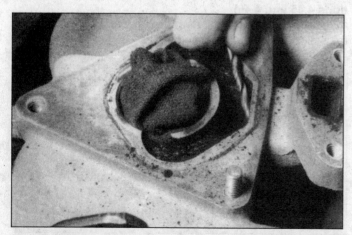

4.48 With a rag in the passage opening, the exhaust gas passages can be scraped clean of deposits

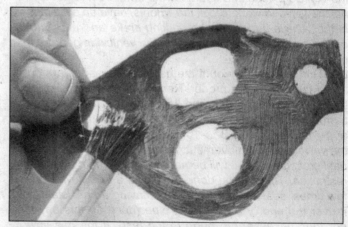

4.49 Coat the new EGR base gasket with a lithium-based grease to help preserve the gasket

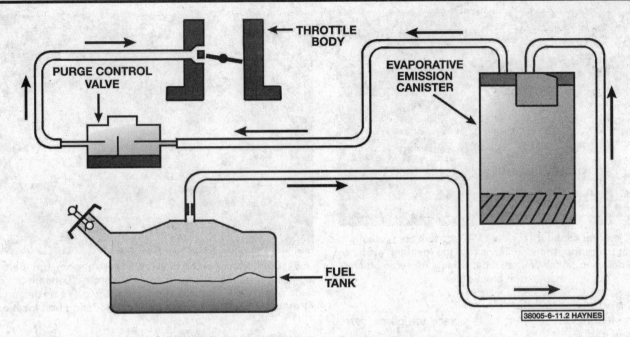

4.50 Typical Evaporative Emission Control System flow diagram

Two types of purge valves or bypass valves are used on these models; an electrically operated valve or a vacuum-operated valve. To find out which type is on your vehicle, follow the hose from the charcoal canister until you locate the purge valve. Some are located on the intake manifold and others near the charcoal canister. Look for an electrical connector **(see illustration 4.51)** to the purge valve (electrically operated) or a vacuum line running between the valve and the throttle body (vacuum-operated).

A faulty EVAP system affects the engine driveability only when the temperatures are warm. The EVAP system is not usually the cause of hard cold starting or any other cold running problems.

Check

Vacuum-operated purge valve

1   Remove the vacuum lines from the purge valve and blow into the larger port of the valve. It should be closed and not pass any air. **Note:** *Some models are equipped with a thermo-vacuum valve that prevents canister purge until the coolant temperature reaches approximately 115-degrees F. Check this valve to make sure that vacuum is controlled at the proper temperatures. The valve is usually located in the intake manifold, near the thermo-time switch and the coolant temperature sensor.*

2   Disconnect the small vacuum hose from the purge valve and apply vacuum with a hand-held vacuum pump **(see illustration 4.52)**. The purge valve should be open and air

4.51 A common location for the canister purge solenoid valve is on the firewall or an inner fender panel, where it's often installed as part of an array of other solenoids

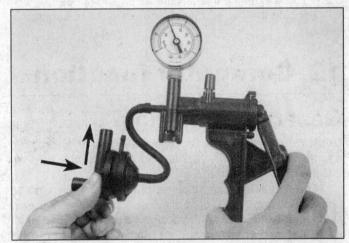

4.52 Apply vacuum and blow air through the purge control valve - air should pass through

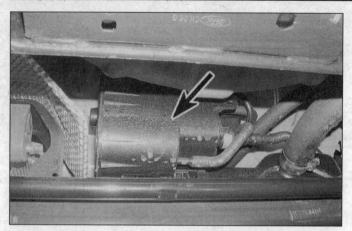

4.53 Charcoal canisters for the EVAP system are typically located at the rear of the vehicle, next to the fuel tank - refer to the Haynes manual for your specific vehicle for removal and installation procedures

4.54 Computers can be anywhere there's room, but there are some common locations: Many are installed beneath the right side of the dash - usually right under the glove box as on this Pontiac Grand Am (arrows point to mounting bolt locations)

should be able to pass through.

3   If the test results are incorrect, replace the purge valve with a new part.

Electrically operated purge valve

1   Disconnect any lines from the purge valve and without disconnecting the electrical connector, place the valve in a convenient spot for testing. Check that the valve makes a "click" sound as the ignition key is turned to the On position.

2   If the valve does not "click", disconnect the valve connector and check for power to the valve using a test light or a voltmeter.

3   If there is battery voltage, replace the purge valve. If there is no voltage present, check the control unit and the wiring harness for any shorts or faulty components.

Canister

1   Label, then detach all hoses to the canister **(see illustration 4.53)**.

2   Slide the canister out of its mounting clamp.

3   Visually examine the canister for leakage or damage.

4   Replace the canister if you find evidence of damage or leakage.

12 Computer function

General information

Note: *For more information and testing on this, or other engine management sensors and components, refer to Chapter 8.*

The actual internal functions of the computer can't be checked without expensive diagnostic equipment. Dealerships have the luxury of "replacing with a known good unit", a popular step in factory service manuals, but for practical diagnosis it really doesn't matter. Even dealerships don't "fix" computers, they check power, grounds and closed loop

operation. There are simple checks to verify that the computer is functioning properly.

The electronic fuel injection and engine management components are really quite reliable. There are actually many more problems with wiring, vacuum hoses and connections. Even very small amounts of rust, oxidation or corrosion can, and will, interfere with the small milliamp current that is used in computer circuits.

When first assembled and run as a new vehicle, any computer problems would have normally shown up at that time. But over the years, and miles, sometimes failures can occur. Heat, moisture, vibration, corrosive salt air, previous inspections, repair or maintenance could all have an affect on the condition of the computer and related systems.

Locate the computer **(see illustrations 4.54, 4.55, 4.56 and 4.57)** and check the harness connections and electrical grounds. If necessary, take the connectors apart and check

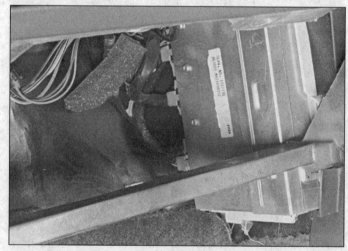

4.55 Another likely location is behind the kick panel (usually the right side) just ahead of the door and underneath the dash

4.56 In recent years manufacturers have been placing the computer in the engine compartment (BMW shown here) for ease of access and actually cooler operation than when sandwiched inside an insulated body panel with no air flow

4.57 The PCM on this Chevrolet Trailblazer is mounted right on the intake manifold

for corrosion or a bent pin. Clean the connectors with electrical contact cleaner and reconnect the computer, making sure that all the terminals are securely seated in the connectors. Check all the computer grounds for corrosion and make sure they're clean, tight and secure.

Refer to Chapter 8 for the oxygen sensor checking procedure, which is a good quick-check to conform that the computer is operating in the closed-loop mode when the engine reaches normal operating temperature.

13 Symptom-based troubleshooting

Note: *The problem symptoms and driveability complaints listed in this Section are primarily related to the fuel, emissions and engine management systems. For other possible causes of vehicle problems, refer to the* Haynes Automotive Repair Manual *for your specific vehicle.*

This Section provides an easy reference guide to the more common problems that may occur during the operation of your vehicle. Various symptoms and their probable causes are grouped under headings denoting components or systems, such as Engine, Cooling system, etc.

Remember that successful troubleshooting isn't a mysterious art practiced only by professional mechanics, it's simply the result of knowledge combined with an intelligent, systematic approach to a problem. Always use a process of elimination starting with the simplest solution and working through to the most complex - and never overlook the obvious. Anyone can run the gas tank dry or leave the lights on overnight, so don't assume that you're exempt from such oversights.

Finally, always establish a clear idea why a problem has occurred and take steps to ensure that it doesn't happen again. If the electrical system fails because of a poor con-

nection, check all other connections in the system to make sure they don't fail as well. If a particular fuse continues to blow, find out why - don't just go on replacing fuses. Remember, failure of a small component can often be indicative of potential failure or incorrect functioning of a more important component or system. If, and/or when, a check engine light should appear on the instrument panel of your vehicle, don't automatically assume that the faulty component is the computer. A majority of the driveability related complaints so often turn out to be corrected by simply attending to the basics. Concentrate on fundamental items such as air flow, fuel flow, adequate voltage and good grounds to operate the ignition system and sensor/relay systems, good engine mechanical condition - i.e. good vacuum, minimal blow by gases, good maintenance schedule for oil and coolant changes, etc. All these items make up the whole picture upon which the computer bases the system operations.

The following is a list of symptoms and driveability complaints, to be used as a guide, most often experienced with engine management systems. The list has been put together to try and cover the majority of all engine management systems. Not all the possibilities listed may apply to all types of systems. Following each symptom are the components and/or general systems to more closely look at in order to correct the problem being experienced:

1 Engine noise

Hiss - vacuum leak(s) (see Section 5)
Electrical arcing (snapping noise) (see Section 9).

2 Engine cranks but won't start

Charcoal canister full of fuel (see Section 11).
Faulty MAP, MAF (if equipped) or coolant sensor or circuit (see Chapters 9 and 10).
EGR valve stuck open (see Section 10).
Faulty canister vent valve (see Section 11).

Lack of or incorrect fuel pressure (see the *Haynes Fuel Injection Manual* or the *Haynes Automotive Repair Manual* for your particular vehicle).

Fuel tank empty.

Water in fuel.

Battery discharged (engine rotates slowly) (see Section 8).

Battery terminal connections loose or corroded (see Section 8).

Fouled spark plugs or bad spark-plug wires (see Section 9).

Faulty ignition module.

Severe vacuum leak (see Sections 5 and 7).

Severely restricted injectors (see Chapter 10)

Broken, loose or disconnected wires in the starting circuit (see Section 8).

Faulty airflow sensor (see Chapters 9 and 10)

Idle Air Control (IAC) valve defective (see Chapters 9 and 10)

3 Engine is hard to start - cold

Leaking injectors (see Chapters 9 and 10)

4 Engine is hard to start - hot

Battery discharged or low (see Section 8).

Air filter clogged (see Section 5).

PCV valve stuck open.

Vacuum/air leak (see Section 5).

Defective coolant sensor or circuit (see Chapter 8).

Defective intake air temperture sensor or circuit (see Chapters 9 and 10).

Defective MAF (if equipped) sensor or circuit (see Chapters 9 and 10).

Defective MAP (if equipped) sensor or circuit (see Chapters 9 and 10).

Faulty TPS or circuit (see Chapters 9 and 10).

Corroded battery connections (see Section 8).

Bad engine ground connection (see Section 8).

Spark plugs fouled (see Section 9).

Fuel pressure incorrect (see the *Haynes Automotive Repair Manual* for your particular vehicle).

Insufficient residual fuel pressure (see the *Haynes Automotive Repair Manual* for your particular vehicle).

Airflow sensor faulty (see Chapters 9 and 10).

5 Engine starts but won't run

Faulty canister vent valve (see Section 11).

EGR valve stuck open (see Section 10).

Loose or damaged electrical connections at the coil or alternator (see Section 9).

Intake manifold vacuum leaks (see Section 7).

Insufficient fuel flow (see the *Haynes Automotive Repair Manual* for your particular vehicle).

6 Engine 'lopes' while idling, rough idle or idles erratically (cold or warm)

Clogged air filter (see Section 5).

Dirty throttle plate or throttle bore.

EGR valve stuck open or leaking (see Section 10).

Vacuum leak (see Section 5).

Air leak in intake duct and/or manifold ("false air") (see Section 5).

IAC faulty (see Chapters 9 and 10)

Lean injector(s) (see Chapters 9 and 10).

Rich injector(s) (see Chapter 8).

Fuel pump not delivering sufficient pressure (see the *Haynes Automotive Repair Manual* for your particular vehicle).

Cold only:

PCV valve stuck open or closed.

Warm only:

TPS or circuit malfunctioning or out of adjustment (see Chapter 8).

MAF (if equipped) sensor or circuit out of adjustment or malfunctioning (see Chapters 9 and 10).

7 Engine misses at idle speed

Spark plugs fouled, faulty or not gapped properly (see Section 9).

Faulty spark plug wires (see Section 9).

Sticking or faulty EGR valve (see Section 10).

Clogged fuel filter and/or foreign matter in fuel (see the *Haynes Automotive Repair Manual* for your particular vehicle).

Vacuum leaks at intake manifold or hose connections (see Section 5).

Incorrect ignition timing (see Section 9).

Low or uneven cylinder compression (see the *Haynes Automotive Repair Manual* for your particular vehicle).

8 Excessively high idle speed

Vacuum leak (see Section 5).

Sticking throttle linkage (see Section 5).

9 Engine misses throughout driving speed range

Fuel filter clogged and/or impurities in the fuel system (see the *Haynes Automotive Repair Manual* for your particular vehicle).

Low fuel pump pressure (see the *Haynes Automotive Repair Manual* for your particular vehicle).

Fouled, faulty or incorrectly gapped spark plugs (see Section 9).

Spark plug wires shorting to ground (see Section 9).

Low or uneven cylinder compression pressures (see the *Haynes Automotive Repair Manual* for your particular vehicle).

Weak or faulty ignition system (see Section 9).

Vacuum leaks (see Section 5).

Leaky EGR valve (see Section 10).

Lean injector(s) (see Chapters 9 and 10).

10 Hesitation, stumbles or stalls on acceleration

Spark plugs fouled (see Section 9).

Fuel filter clogged (see Section 5).

Faulty TPS or circuit (see Chapter 8).

Malfunctioning air temperature sensor or circuit (see Chapters 9 and 10).

MAP (if equipped) sensor or circuit faulty (see Chapters 9 and 10).

Air leak in intake duct and/or manifold ("false air") (see Section 5).

Faulty MAF (if equipped) sensor or circuit (see Chapters 9 and 10).

Dirty throttle plate or throttle bore

Faulty spark-plug wires or ignition coil(s) (see Section 9).

Low fuel pump pressure (see the *Haynes Automotive Repair Manual* for your particular vehicle).

Lean injector(s) (see Chapters 9 and 10).

11 Engine lacks power or has sluggish performance

Clogged air filter (see Section 5).

Restricted exhaust system (most likely the catalytic converter) (see Section 7).

Vacuum leak (see Sections 5 and 7).

EGR valve stuck open or not functioning properly (see Section 10).

MAP (if equipped) sensor or circuit malfunctioning (see Chapters 9 and 10).

Faulty or incorrectly gapped spark plugs (see Section 9).

Fuel filter clogged and/or impurities in the fuel system (see the *Haynes Automotive Repair Manual* for your particular vehicle).

Vacuum leak at the intake manifold (see Section 7).

Lean injector(s) (see Chapters 9 and 10).

12 Stalls on deceleration or when coming to a quick stop

EGR valve stuck or leakage around base (see Section 10).

TPS misadjusted or defective (see Chapters 9 and 10).

Idle Air Control valve malfunctioning (see Chapters 9 and 10).

Fuel filter clogged and/or water and impurities in the fuel system (see the *Haynes Automotive Repair Manual* for your particular vehicle).

Faulty or incorrectly gapped spark plugs. Also check the spark plug wires (see Section 9).

Vacuum leak (see Section 5).

13 Surging at steady speed

Clogged air filter (see Section 5).

Vacuum leak (see Sections 5 and 7).

Air leak in intake duct and/or manifold (false-air) (see Section 5).

EGR valve stuck or leakage around base (see Section 10).

Problem with oxygen sensor or circuit (see Chapters 9 and 10).

Defective TPS or circuit (see Chapters 9 and 10).

Defective Mass Air Flow (MAF) (if equipped) sensor or circuit (see Chapters 9 and 10).

Defective MAP (if equipped) sensor or circuit (see Chapters 9 and 10).

Loose fuel injector wire harness connectors.

Torque Converter Clutch (TCC (if equipped) engaging/disengaging (may feel similar to fuel starvation).

Fuel pressure incorrect (see the *Haynes Automotive Repair Manual* for your particular vehicle).

Fuel pump faulty (see the *Haynes Automotive Repair Manual* for your particular vehicle).

Lean injector(s) (see Chapters 9 and 10).

Defective computer or information sensors (see Chapters 9 and 10).

14 Engine diesels (runs on) when shut-off or idles too fast

Vacuum leak (see Sections 5 and 7).

EGR valve not operating properly (see Section 10).

Excessive engine operating temperature, check for causes of overheating (see Section 5).

Incorrect spark plug selection (see Section 9).

15 Backfiring (through the intake or exhaust)

Vacuum leak in the PCV or canister purge line (see Section 11).

Vacuum leak at fuel injector(s), intake manifold, air control valve or vacuum lines (see Section 5).

Faulty secondary ignition system, (cracked spark plug insulators, bad plug wires) (see Section 9).

EGR system not functioning properly (see Section 10).

Emission control system not operating properly.

Faulty air valve (see the *Haynes Automotive Repair Manual* for your particular vehicle).

Valve clearances incorrectly set (on some vehicles this is a required maintenance item or is done during tune-up procedures).

Damaged valve springs, sticking or burned valves - a vacuum gauge check will often reveal this problem.

16 Poor fuel economy

Clogged air filter (see Section 5).

PCV problem - valve stuck open or closed, or dirty PCV filter (see Section 11).

Defective oxygen sensor (see Chapters 9 and 10).

Incorrect ignition timing (see Section 9).

Fuel leakage (see Section 5).

Fuel injectors worn or damaged (see Chapters 9 and 10).

Sticking/dragging parking brake.

Low tire pressure.

17 Pinging (spark knock)

EGR valve inoperative (see Section 10).

Vacuum leak (see Sections 5 and 7).

Incorrect or damaged spark plugs, coils or wires (see Section 9).

Problem with knock sensor or circuit (see Chapters 9 and 10).

Poor quality fuel.

18 Exhaust smoke

Black (overly rich fuel mixture) - Dirty air filter or restricted intake duct (see Section 5).

Blue (burning oil) - PCV valve stuck open or PCV filter dirty.

19 Fuel smell

Fuel tank overfilled.

Fuel tank cap gasket not sealing.

Fuel lines leaking.

Fuel injector(s) stuck open (see Chapters 9 and 10).

Fuel injector(s) leaks internally (see Chapters 9 and 10).

Fuel injector(s) leaks externally (see Chapters 9 and 10).

EVAP canister filter in Evaporative Emissions Control system clogged (see Section 11).

Vapor leaks from Evaporative Emissions Control system lines (see Section 11).

5 Powertrain management basics

Fuel injection system operation

Why fuel injection?

Today, every new vehicle sold in this country is fuel injected. But it wasn't always that way. For over 75 years, virtually every manufacturer equipped all but a tiny handful of limited production models with carburetors. Even after the original Clean Air Act in 1963, the Big Three stuck with the carburetor. By the mid-Eighties, pushed by increasingly stringent emissions legislation, electronic feedback carburetors had reached a degree of refinement unthinkable in the Sixties. But, despite undeniable progress, time finally ran out for the venerable carburetor. It simply couldn't meet state or Federal emissions standards. There were five major problems with carburetors:

1   The venturi constriction limited the amount of mixture available at higher engine speeds, which caused power to fall off. The solutions were twofold. Manufacturers could have employed multiple carburetors, which would have resulted in an excessively rich mixture at lower engine speeds. Or they could have employed a progressively linked *secondary*. (The secondary is that part of a staged carburetor that is only used to supply extra fuel and air for increased power. The secondary system doesn't open until the primary system has already opened a certain amount.) The second solution was a better strategy, but the result was a more complicated carburetor.

2   The distance between the carburetor and the combustion chambers resulted in a poorly distributed and uneven mixture. The problem was compounded by the limited amount of space usually available for the intake manifold. So the shape of the intake manifold was usually less-than-ideal for getting the air-fuel mixture to the combustion chamber.

3   Cold starts - particularly in cold weather - were sometimes difficult on carburetor-equipped vehicles. The choke mechanism helped, but because its opening angle was never a perfectly accurate response to the actual operating conditions of the engine during warm-up, it always wasted fuel and diminished driveability. The use of a choke mechanism also necessitated the addition of a fast idle cam, which opened the throttle plate slightly while the engine was on choke. The fast idle cam promoted a slightly faster idle during warm-up; without it, a cold engine was more likely to stall.

4   Transient enrichment during acceleration was poor. When the throttle was opened suddenly, it leaned out the mixture because fuel flow didn't keep up with air velocity. The addition of an accelerator pump alleviated this problem by squirting extra fuel into the throat of the carburetor, but the pump wasted fuel and increased emissions.

5   During hard cornering, the fuel in the float bowl might try to climb the walls of the bowl, lowering the fuel level in the bowl, raising the float, closing the float valve and blocking fuel delivery. Properly-designed baffles installed in the float bowl mitigated this tendency, but again the result was a more complicated carburetor.

Vehicles with fuel-injection systems have none of these problems. Fuel is metered much more precisely under all operating conditions because it's sprayed out of each injector under pressure, instead of being drawn through carburetor tubes and passages by pressure differential. When fuel is sprayed under pressure, instead of being sucked by pressure differential, the amount of fuel delivered can be increased or decreased much more rapidly. In other words, a fuel injection system responds to changes in engine operating conditions more quickly than a carburetor. And that's why it has totally replaced the carburetor.

Fuel injection: A brief history

Fuel injection has been around longer than most people think. It was actually experimented with in the late 1800's and then used on diesel engines in the early 1900's. During WW-II, Bosch began developing fuel injection for German military aircraft. In the USA, Bendix developed a fuel injection system for the Patton tank and, by the end of the war, was also developing fuel injection for American military aircraft. In the late Forties, Stuart Hillborn designed, built and installed an indirect fuel injection system on an Offenhauser engine for the 1949 Indianapolis 500. In 1957, General Motors debuted what was probably the first widely available production fuel injection system, the Rochester Ramjet mechanical injection system, on the 1957 Pontiac Bonneville. The 1957 Corvette got the same system. Pontiac discontinued the Ramjet system in 1959 due to lack of interest. It was available on Corvettes until 1965.

Meanwhile, across the Pond, Germany's Kugelfischer and Robert Bosch were working on mechanical fuel injection systems of their own. In the mid-Fifties, Kugelfischer developed the first mechanical injection system for the famous Mercedes-Benz 300 Gull Wing and roadster. The Kugelfischer system was used in numerous Mercedes vehicles during the early Sixties. Kugelfischer's system was also used on BMW 2002tii models.

Bosch developed two totally different systems, one mechanical and one electronic. Bosch debuted its Electronically Controlled Gasoline Injection (ECGI) in 1967. In 1969, the ECGI system was renamed Bosch D-Jetronic and installed in the VW Type 3 (fastback, notchback and squareback). For the next six years, the D-Jet system was installed on a wide variety of European vehicles. It was last used on the 1975 Volvo 164E and the 1975 Mercedes-Benz 450. The next year, both manufacturers switched to the other new Bosch system, Continuous Injection System (CIS), or K-Jetronic, as it was marketed to the public. It would be awhile before European cars went back to electronic injection.

CIS was the first widespread production mechanical injection system. It's been out of production since the early Nineties, but CIS was installed in over 6,000,000

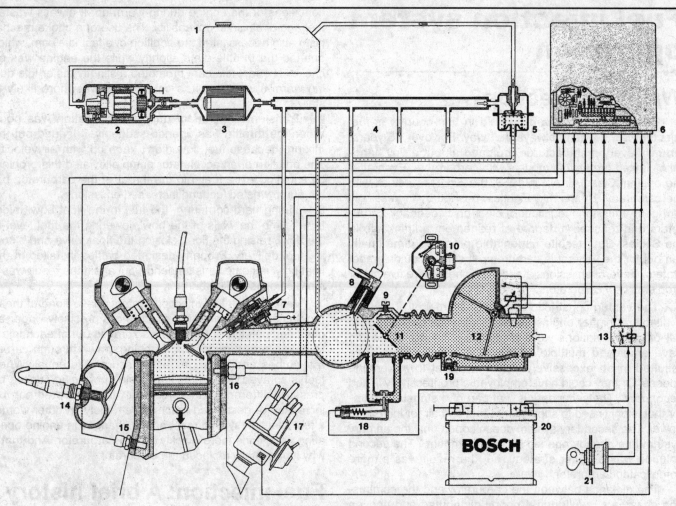

5.1 Schematic of a typical electronic port fuel injection system

1	Fuel tank	*9*	Idle speed adjusting screw	*16*	Thermo-time switch
2	Electric fuel pump	*10*	Throttle valve switch	*17*	Distributor
3	Fuel filter	*11*	Throttle valve	*18*	Auxiliary air valve
4	Distributor pipe	*12*	Airflow sensor	*19*	Idle mixture adjusting screw
5	Pressure regulator	*13*	Relay combination	*20*	Battery
6	Control unit	*14*	Lambda (oxygen) sensor	*21*	Ignition switch
7	Injector	*15*	Engine coolant temperature		
8	Cold start injector		sensor		

British, French, German, Italian and Swedish cars (including Audi, BMW, Ferrari, Lotus, Mercedes-Benz, Peugeot, Porsche, Rolls-Royce, Saab, Volkswagen and Volvo) before its demise. CIS was a huge improvement over carburetors, but - as its name implies - fuel was sprayed from (strictly mechanical) injectors continuously, which meant that there was still a lot of room for improvement in terms of fuel control. By the early Nineties, it was obvious that CIS simply wasn't capable of controlling the air/fuel mixture ratio accurately enough for the emissions regulations that were looming ahead. If you're the owner of an older vehicle equipped with a Bosch CIS system and are interested in a detailed look at CIS and its many variants, refer to the Haynes Techbook *Fuel Injection Manual - 1986 thru 1999* (ARM 10220).

The other system developed by Bosch during this period, L Jetronic **(see illustration 5.1)** was probably the first mass-produced electronic fuel injection system, and incorporated most of the components still in use today in most modern fuel injection systems. It first saw use in BMWs in the late Seventies and by the early to mid-Eighties was used on Alfa-Romeos, Citroens, Jaguars, Lancias, Morgans, Opels, Rovers and Vauxhalls.

Back in the States again, GM introduced the first modern electronic multiport fuel injection system in 1975, on the 1976 Cadillac Seville. Jointly developed by Bendix, Bosch and GM, it featured an analog computer, a fuel rail and eight fuel injectors. In 1980, Cadillac also introduced the first digital fuel injection system, known as - what else? - Digital Fuel Injection (DFI). Though GM engineers designed DFI as a true multiport system, it fell victim to the bean counters and debuted as a two-injector Throttle Body Injection (TBI) system. In 1981, Chrysler introduced its first modern fuel injection system, on the Imperial, but discontinued it after 1983. In 1982, Pontiac debuted its own version of TBI on its "Iron Duke" 2.5L inline four. Chevrolet and other GM divisions also used the Pontiac TBI system on various "A" and "X"-body platforms, including the Celebrity, Citation, Omega, Phoenix and Skylark.

The ultimate TBI system debuted in 1983 as Cross Fire Injection on the new 1984 Corvette. Cross Fire consisted of two throttle bodies with two injectors in each unit, with the throttle bodies mounted in a staggered fashion on a common manifold. The Cross Fire-equipped 5.7L V8 on the 1984 Corvette had 20 more horsepower than the 1982 carbureted Vette. GM quickly added Cross Fire to the 5.0L V8 used in Camaros and Firebirds.

In 1985, GM debuted two more new fuel injection systems that, in retrospect, were perhaps the harbingers of things to come in the fuel injection world. The first new system was Multiport Fuel Injection (MFI), which was available on the 2.8L V6 used in the Camaro, Cavalier, Celebrity, Citation and many other vehicles. The second new system was the Tuned Port Injection (TPI) system available on the Camaro 5.0L V8 and on the Corvette 5.7L V8. TPI was good for 40 more horsepower on the 5.7L V8! Though both the MFI and TPI systems are now over 20 years old, they would be recognizable as modern fuel injection systems to anyone reading this book. They were equipped with an in-tank electric fuel pump, a fuel rail and an injector for each intake port. Most significantly, they were equipped with an Electronic Control Module (ECM) that received data from an array of information sensors, compared this information to its map, made command decisions, then altered the operating conditions of the engine as necessary to keep everything humming along smoothly. It was the beginning of modern powertrain management, which we'll get to in a moment. But first, let's look at fuel injection itself. Because once you understand how fuel injection works, you'll be able to more easily grasp why it needs a sophisticated management system to keep it running smoothly.

What is fuel injection?

There are many types of fuel injection systems on the road today. Some of the components differ from one system to another, but the principle is always the same. Pressurized fuel is squirted into the bore of a throttle body by one or two injectors, such as GM's TBI system, or directly into each intake port by an injector like GM's MFI system. We're not going to get into TBI systems in this book because no TBI system was in production by the time that the OBD-II era began. If you own a vehicle equipped with a TBI system and want to take a closer look at TBI, refer to the Haynes Techbook *Fuel Injection Manual 1978 to 1985* (ARM 10215) or to the Haynes Techbook *Fuel Injection Manual 1986 thru 1999* (ARM 10220).

Most of the other components used on one injection system are found on all fuel injection systems. We'll look at each of those components in detail in a moment. But first, let's look at what happens in all fuel injected engines: Fuel is pumped from the fuel tank by an electric fuel pump, through the fuel lines and fuel filter, then through the fuel injectors into the air being drawn through the intake ports into the combustion chambers. Each injector contains a tiny valve that's opened and closed by a small solenoid. A small computer fires the injector by closing the ground path for this solenoid, which lifts the valve and allows the pressurized fuel to exit the injector through a precisely machined nozzle that sprays the fuel in a manner similar to the nozzle on your garden hose. When the computer opens the ground path for the solenoid, the valve closes, shutting off the spraying fuel. This cycle of operation occurs over and over, many times a second, as long as the engine is running. You would think that, given the amount of abuse to which they're subjected, injectors would be the weak link in any fuel injection system. Amazingly, just the opposite is true. Manufactured to a high degree of precision, the injectors are rugged little workhorses that usually last 100,000 miles or more. Now let's look at the typical multiport fuel injection system in more detail.

Why port fuel injection?

Unlike a TBI system, which sprays fuel into the throttle body through one or two injectors, a port fuel injection system sprays pressurized fuel through an injector at each intake port. Because no fuel is lost in the intake manifold, port injection systems offer more power, better mileage and lower emissions than throttle body injection systems. Now let's look at the typical components in an electronic fuel injection system.

The air induction system

The air induction system consists of the air filter housing, the air intake duct, the resonator(s), if equipped, the throttle body and the intake manifold.

Air filter housing

The air filter housing **(see illustration 5.2)** contains the air filter element, a pleated paper-type filter that must be replaced at specified intervals. The air filter housing is always located in the engine compartment, usually in a corner where it can be attached to one of the fenders and where it's somewhat isolated from engine heat. Cooler air is denser air and denser air has more oxygen in it. Most modern air filter housings employ some sort of ambient air intake duct that brings air from somewhere outside the engine compartment - a wheel well or a void behind the bumper cover - to the filter housing.

The air filter housing assembly is also a convenient location for various information sensors that monitor the mass, volume and/or temperature of the incoming air. Nearly all Mass Air Flow (MAF) sensors and Volume Air Flow (VAF) sensors are located at the air filter housing. And manufacturers often mount Intake Air Temperature (IAT) sensors on the air filter housing as well.

Air intake duct

The air intake duct **(see illustration 5.3)** is the black plastic tube that connects the air filter housing to the throttle body. The air intake duct is also a handy place to locate certain types of information sensors, such as the Intake Air Temperature (IAT) sensor or the Mass Air Flow (MAF) sensor.

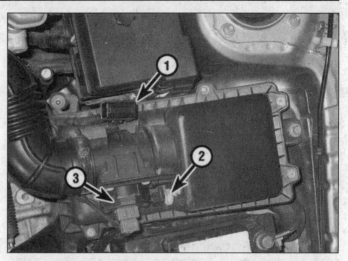

5.2 Typically, the air filter housing is a convenient place to locate various fuel injection components. On this particular filter housing (a 1999 Kia Sephia), that would include the DIAGNOSTIC connector (1), the Intake Air Temperature (IAT) sensor (2) and the Mass Air Flow (MAF) sensor (3)

Resonators

On some modern fuel-injected vehicles, manufacturers are attaching one or more odd-looking boxes to either the air filter housing or the air intake duct, or to both components. These mysterious-looking devices are generally referred to as resonators **(see illustrations 5.4a, 5.4b and 5.4c)**. Resonators perform several functions. First, they act as baffles to muffle engine noises that would otherwise escape through the induction system. Second, they expand the interior volume of the induction system, which means that more intake air is available to prevent air starvation during heavy acceleration.

Throttle body

The throttle body **(see illustration 5.5a)** is an aluminum casting which is always located between the air intake

5.3 The air intake duct is a good source of filtered outside air for emission control hoses such as the PCV fresh air intake hose (A) and the intake air bypass control thermal valve (B) on this 2003 Honda Accord

5.4a Some air intake duct resonators, such as this unit, are simply secured to the underside of the intake duct and connected to the incoming air by a hose-clamped tube

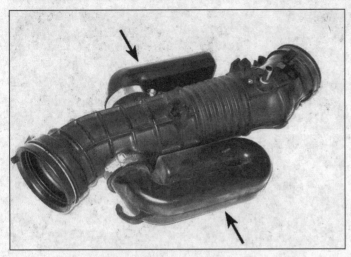

5.4b Some air intake ducts are equipped with multiple resonators

5.4c Ambient air resonators are mounted upstream from the air filter housing, like this one, which is located in the void behind the bumper cover and ahead of the left wheel well (this is a favorite spot for ambient air resonators because the air here is calm and cool)

duct and the intake manifold. It houses a throttle plate that opens and closes in response to the position of the accelerator pedal. In conventional setups, the accelerator pedal is connected to the throttle plate by the accelerator cable. The throttle body also serves as the mounting point for various information sensors such as the Throttle Position (TP) sensor and (on some vehicles) the Manifold Absolute Pressure (MAP) sensor, and for output actuators such as the Idle Air Control (IAC) valve.

On many newer electronically actuated throttle bodies (see illustration 5.5b) there is no direct mechanical connection between the accelerator pedal and the throttle plate linkage. Instead, an information sensor known as an Accelerator Pedal Position (APP) sensor, which is located at the top of the accelerator pedal (or, on some vehicles, mounted in the engine compartment and actuated by a cable) monitors the angle of the accelerator pedal and puts out a variable voltage signal that's proportional to the pedal angle. This signal is processed by the Powertrain Control Module (PCM), which commands a motor on the throttle body to open or close the throttle plate accordingly.

Intake manifold

The intake manifold is an aluminum or composite component (see illustrations 5.6a and 5.6b) that consists of the

5.5a The typical mechanically-actuated throttle body has a number of components connected to it:

A Vacuum hoses, such as this PCV fresh air inlet hose pipe (the hose is disconnected in this photo)
B Accelerator cable
C Throttle Position (TP) sensor
D Coolant hoses (to help warm up the throttle body and prevent icing)
E Idle Air Control (IAC) valve

5.5b The typical electronically-actuated throttle body has no accelerator cable, TP sensor or IAC valve connected to it. Most electronic throttle bodies usually have a single electrical connector

5.6a A typical cast aluminum intake manifold

5.6b A typical composite intake manifold is made of nylon, plastic or some other synthetic material

air intake plenum, which is a large accumulator or reservoir for incoming air, and an intake runner from the plenum to each intake port. Most intake manifolds are one-piece castings. Some manifolds are a two-piece design, consisting of an upper and lower manifold. The intake manifold is also the mounting point for the throttle body and for various information sensors, such as the Intake Air Temperature (IAT) sensor and/or the Manifold Absolute Pressure (MAP) sensor. The intake manifold also provides a convenient mounting point for the fuel rail and the fuel injectors, which are inserted into machined holes in the intake ports.

The fuel delivery system

The fuel delivery system consists of the fuel tank, the fuel pump, the fuel filter, the fuel pressure regulator, the fuel pulsation damper (if equipped), the fuel rail, the fuel injectors and the fuel lines and hoses connecting these components.

Return-type vs. returnless-type fuel delivery systems

Before we look at the various components of the fuel delivery system, it's important that you understand the difference between a conventional return-type fuel delivery system and the newer *returnless*-type system that is now being employed by more and more manufacturers. At the current rate at which returnless systems are replacing the older return-type systems, it will only be a matter of years until the return-type system is obsolete.

Return-type systems

In a conventional return-type fuel delivery system, pressurized fuel is pumped through the fuel lines and fuel filter, then into the fuel rail and out the injector nozzles. Because the pump delivers more fuel than the injectors can use, particularly at idle and during deceleration, excess fuel is returned to the fuel tank via the fuel pressure regulator and a return line. When you remove your foot from the accelerator pedal during idle or deceleration, intake manifold vacuum

is high. A vacuum hose connecting the intake manifold to a vacuum chamber in the upper part of the fuel pressure regulator pulls a spring-loaded diaphragm off its seat, allowing excess fuel to flow through the regulator, then through a return line back to the fuel tank. The return-type system was pretty standard until a few years ago when manufacturers began replacing this setup with a returnless system.

Returnless-type systems

There are two problems with a conventional, return-type system: First, there's a lot of hose and line and connections through which fuel leaks can develop as the vehicle ages. Second, all that unused fuel that keeps getting pumped back to the fuel tank soaks up engine heat each time it does a lap through the fuel rail. While there's little danger of vapor lock occurring, warmer fuel evaporates, which means that the EVAP system has to work overtime to soak up all those unburned hydrocarbons. The solution? Eliminate the return line to the tank.

In a returnless-type system, the fuel pressure regulator is located back at the fuel pump instead of at the fuel rail. When the fuel pump's output exceeds the upper threshold of the specified operating pressure range, the spring-loaded regulator opens, dumping the excess fuel back into the tank. A few returnless systems even eliminate the fuel pressure regulator by using the fuel pump itself to control the fuel pressure by altering its speed, which is controlled by the Powertrain Control Module (PCM). At the time this manual was written, returnless systems were becoming more widespread. Within several years they will likely be the norm.

Electric fuel pumps

Fuel must be delivered to the fuel injectors at the right pressure, in the right volume and within a fairly consistent temperature range. There must be no fuel vapor or air bubbles in the fuel at the point of delivery. The electric fuel pump **(see illustration 5.7)**, with a little help from the fuel pressure regulator, makes all this happen.

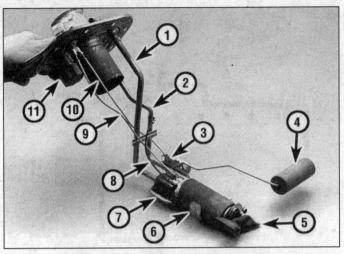

5.7 A typical in-tank fuel pump assembly

1   Fuel feed line
2   Fuel return line
3   Fuel gauge sending unit
4   Fuel gauge sending unit float
5   Fuel pump intake strainer (sometimes referred to as a "sock")
6   Fuel pump
7   Pulsation damper
8   Fuel pump ground wire
9   Fuel pump electrical lead
10 Fuel gauge sending unit electrical lead
11 Splash cup liquid vapor separator

Electric fuel pumps offer several significant advantages over the mechanical pumps used on carbureted vehicles:

1   A mechanical pump is driven by the camshaft, so it must be bolted to the cylinder head or block. An electric fuel pump can be located anywhere. Most electric pumps are located inside the fuel tank, which puts them right at the fuel supply, muffles their operating noise - a high-pitched whirring sound - and protects them from exposure to the elements.

2   The speed at which a mechanical pump operates is determined by engine speed; it pumps more slowly at idle, more quickly at higher rpm. Electric pumps run at a constant speed that's high enough to provide more than enough fuel pressure for any conceivable condition. (Some modern variable-speed pumps, in response to a command from the Powertrain Control Module, can change speed virtually instantaneously to keep fuel pressure within the specified operating range. On these systems there is no need for a fuel pressure regulator.)

3   Engine heat is transferred through a mechanical pump to the fuel; this doesn't happen with an electric pump, which is actually cooled and lubricated by the fuel passing through it. Keeping the fuel as cool as possible is a critical factor in controlling evaporative emissions.

4   A mechanical pump must create a strong enough vacuum to draw the fuel from the tank, through the fuel filter, through the fuel lines, and into the float bowl of the carburetor. An electric pump pushes fuel to the injectors.

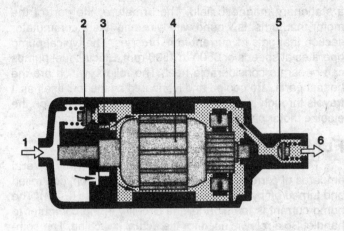

5.8 Cutaway of a typical electric fuel pump

1 Fuel inlet	4	Electric motor
2 Pressure relief valve		armature
3 Roller cell pump	5	Non-return valve
	6	Fuel outlet

How does an electric fuel pump work?

Now, let's look at how a typical electric fuel pump works: Most electric pumps are the *roller vane* type, consisting of an electric motor and a rotor inside an integral housing **(see illustration 5.8)**. The rotor has pockets (slots) machined into its outer circumference. A roller (something like a roller bearing) is installed in each pocket. The diameter of the roller is only a few thousandths of an inch less than the distance between the walls of the pocket. Which means the roller is free to move up and down - but not sideways - in its pocket. As the rotor is turned by the electric motor, the rollers are forced outward by centrifugal force, and roll along the inside wall of the pump housing. Because the bearing surfaces (the sides) of the rollers contact both the pump housing wall and the pocket walls, they create a seal. The rotor itself is round; but the pump housing is an oblong shape, which allows the rollers to move out farther from the rotor on the suction side than they do on the pressure side. In other words, the space between the rotor and the pump housing on the suction side is larger than the space between the rotor and the housing on the pressure side. So as the rotor turns, a pressure differential, or vacuum, is created on the suction side of the pump.

Air pressure inside the top of the fuel tank is pushing against the surface of the fuel. This is what forces the fuel into that low-pressure area at the suction side of the pump. As the rotor continues to rotate, fuel is trapped in the space between the two adjacent rollers, the rotor and the housing. As this space moves closer to the pressure side, it gets smaller and smaller, raising the pressure of the fuel, which is finally forced out the pump outlet. Of course, when this little sequence is repeated 3500 to 4500 times per minute (the speed of the typical pump), a good deal of pressure can be created.

The electric motor uses permanent magnets to create

a stationary magnetic field. The armature, the part of the motor that turns, is wound with wire and has a commutator section that gets its current from brushes. The typical pump operates at speeds of 3500 to 4500 rpm. Electric fuel pumps can generate considerable heat. The rollers, which are the hottest parts, are cooled and lubricated by the fuel itself as it travels through the pump. Fuel is even pumped through the electric motor part of the pump to help cool the motor.

Fuel pump relay

The electric motor in a fuel pump draws several amperes of current. The pump motor is turned on, controlled and turned off by the Powertrain Control Module (PCM). The pump current is too high for the circuitry in the computer to handle. So a relay is used for the actual switching. The computer simply controls the relay. A relay is an electrically operated switch with an input magnetic coil, an armature (spring arm) and output switch contacts. Fine wire is wound around the laminated iron core of the input coil. The laminated core increases the coil's magnetic field strength. The armature is a spring-loaded iron bar in close proximity to the electromagnet. The armature arm itself is usually the spring. The armature is electrically insulated from the relay base.

One electrical output contact is attached to the armature; the other output contact is mounted on a stationary arm. Power from the battery is always available to the stationary arm contact. When the computer sends a small current through the electromagnet coil, its magnetic field pulls down the armature arm, the two contacts close and the large current needed to run the fuel pump moves through the contacts. The relay allows battery current to go to the fuel pump without going through the ignition switch or computer.

Fuel pump relays are usually located in the engine compartment fuse and relay box, but they can be located almost anywhere in the engine compartment or in the passenger area. If you can't find the fuel pump relay, check your owner's manual, or refer to Chapter 4 or Chapter 12 in the *Haynes Automotive Repair Manual* for your vehicle.

Fuel accumulator

The accumulator (**see illustration 5.9**) is a small reservoir that stores pressure in the fuel system. The accumulator can be installed anywhere in the fuel line between the fuel pump and the injectors. The typical accumulator consists of a housing with a bladder and spring inside. The housing is a two-piece metal stamping. The bladder is a balloon-like container made of rubber or plastic-covered fabric. A metal plate is fastened to the back side of the bladder for the spring to push against. Some accumulators have a single port which serves as the inlet as well as the outlet, while others have two ports.

When the fuel pump is energized, the accumulator fills with pressurized fuel in about one second. As fuel pressure in the fuel line builds, fuel flows into the accumulator and pushes the bladder back, compressing the spring. Once the accumulator is full, it remains filled and under pressure, even after the system is turned off (unless the pressure in the system bleeds down).

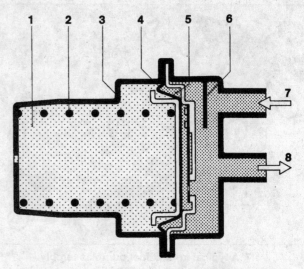

5.9 Cutaway of a typical fuel accumulator assembly

1	Spring chamber	5	Accumulator volume
2	Spring	6	Baffle plate
3	Stop	7	Fuel inlet
4	Diaphragm	8	Fuel outlet

Think of the fuel stored in the accumulator as an emergency reservoir. Should the need arise - for instance, the engine suddenly consumes more fuel than the pump can deliver - fuel at the right pressure and in sufficient volume is available. As soon as this event is over, the pump pressure recharges the accumulator (the accumulator is never actually empty, but constantly fluctuating to maintain the desired system pressure). Accumulators can also smooth out pulsations in the fuel system caused by the fuel pump.

Finally, it should be noted that the accumulator also serves as an anti-vapor lock device by maintaining high residual pressure in the fuel lines, after the vehicle has been turned off, long enough for the fuel to cool off.

Fuel filter

There are actually two types of fuel filters. The first type (**see illustration 5.10**) is a woven nylon or plastic screen located on the inlet (suction) end of the in-tank fuel pump. This filter is generally referred to as the inlet strainer or sock. Filters must have a known, uniform porosity. In other words, they must possess a specified ability to stop materials down to a certain size. That size is usually expressed in microns. A micron is 4/1,000,000 of an inch (0.00000394 inch). The screen/strainer/sock type filter has a porosity of about 70 microns. It can filter larger dirt particles and can stop water from passing through unless completely submerged. This type of filter isn't usually replaced as a maintenance item, but it could become clogged. If this happens, the filter must be removed and cleaned, or replaced.

The other type of fuel filter (**see illustration 5.11**) is a replaceable metal canister that must be changed at the interval specified by the manufacturer. This filter contains a porous material that allows fuel - but not solid particles

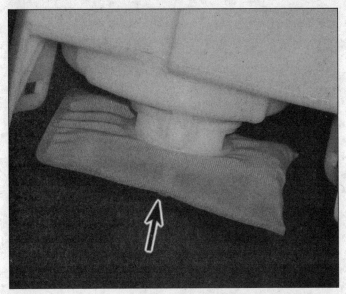

5.10 A typical fuel pump inlet filter (also known as an inlet strainer or sock)

- to pass through. The filter element in a fuel filter is usually a fibrous or paper-like material; some filters even use a porous metal. A filter must be able to do several things. It must let the fuel pass through, yet it must catch all particles of dirt above a certain size, and it must prevent these particles from working their way through the filter for the service life of the filter.

The engine can't run without the proper supply of fuel at the right pressure. So the size of the filter pores must be large enough to allow fuel to flow through easily. Yet the pores must be small enough to trap dirt that will damage or clog the fuel injectors. Typically, the best compromise is around 10 to 20 microns.

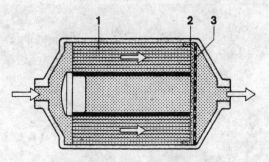

5.11 Cutaway of a typical fuel filter

1   Paper element   3   Supporting plate
2   Strainer

Filters hold on to the dirt by using a chemically-treated porous paper. The chemical treatment makes the paper sticky. When a particle of dirt contacts the paper, it's unable to break free. The filter element is also folded into an accordion shape to increase the surface area of the filter and help trap dirt particles in the folds so they can't break loose. The increased surface area afforded by the accordion arrangement also means fuel can pass through easily even if part of the filter becomes clogged.

Fuel pulsation damper

The fuel pulsation damper (see illustration 5.12a) is virtually identical in appearance to a fuel pressure regulator, except that it doesn't have a vacuum hose connecting it to the intake manifold. The pulsation damper is mounted on the fuel rail, usually - but not always - near the fuel supply line fitting. A spring-loaded diaphragm inside the damper smooths out the rhythmical pressure surges from the fuel pump (see illustration 5.12b). Think of it as a shock absorber for fuel pump pulsations.

5.12a A typical fuel pulsation damper. This unit is bolted to one end of the fuel rail, but pulsation dampers aren't always this accessible or easy to find. For example, the pulsation damper shown in illustration 5.14a is on the underside of the fuel rail, and can't be accessed, removed or replaced without removing the fuel rail

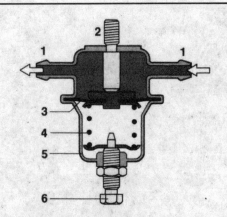

5.12b Cutaway of a typical fuel pulsation damper:

1   Fuel inlet and outlet pipes
2   Mounting stud
3   Diaphragm
4   Compression spring
5   Damper housing
6   Adjusting screw (not all dampers are adjustable)

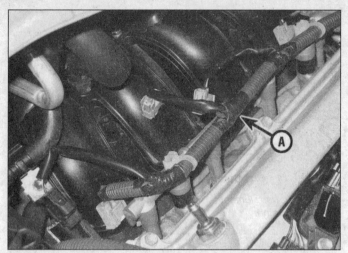

5.13a The fuel rail assembly on a four-cylinder model can be difficult to locate, either because it's buried under the intake plenum, or because it's obscured by the fuel injector wiring harness (A). But disconnect the fuel injector electrical connectors and detach the injector harness . . .

Fuel rail

The fuel rail (see illustrations 5.13a, 5.13b, 5.13c and 5.13d) is a pressurized reservoir for delivering fuel to the injectors. The pressure rapidly rises and falls inside the fuel rail as the injectors open and close. If the volume inside the fuel rail is too small, this rapidly fluctuating pressure can affect the amount of fuel injected. On older tubular type fuel rails - they look sort of like big fuel lines - the fuel pressure fluctuates wildly as the injectors open and close because the interior volume of these units is so small. As manufacturers have learned more about this phenomenon, fuel rails have grown larger. On these newer, larger units, pressure is steadier at the injectors.

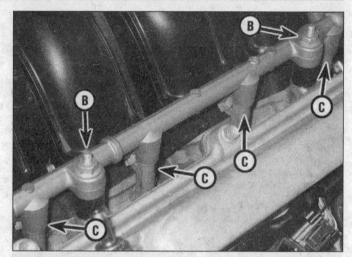

5.13b . . . and there it is! Now the fuel rail mounting bolts (B) and the fuel injectors (C) are plainly visible

Fuel injectors

The fuel injectors (see illustrations 5.14a, 5.14b and 5.14c) are installed between the fuel rail and the intake port. The upper end of each port injector is press-fitted into the fuel rail. An O-ring forms a seal between the injector and the fuel rail. The lower end of each injector, which is inserted into a hole in the intake manifold and protrudes into the intake port, is also fitted with an O-ring to prevent air leaks and protect the injector from heat and vibration. Many injectors are protected by an inlet fuel screen in the injector itself.

Fuel injectors are opened and closed by a solenoid inside each injector. A solenoid is an electromagnetic device consisting of a coil winding surrounding a movable metal

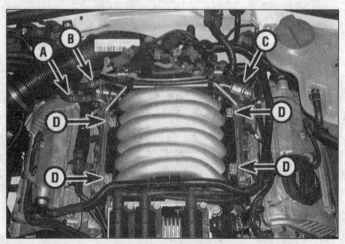

5.13c A typical fuel rail assembly on a V6 engine (1999 VW Passat)

A	Fuel supply line fitting	D	Fuel rail mounting bolts
B	Fuel return line fitting		
C	Fuel pressure regulator		

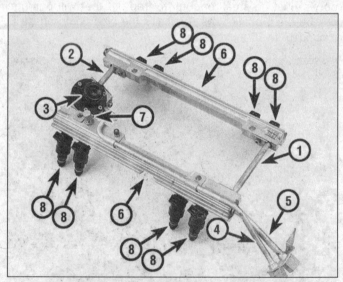

5.13d A typical V8 fuel rail/fuel injector assembly, removed for clarity (from a Corvette)

1	Front crossover tube	5	Fuel inlet pipe
2	Rear crossover tube	6	Fuel rails
3	Fuel pressure regulator	7	Schrader valve test port
4	Fuel outlet pipe	8	Fuel injectors

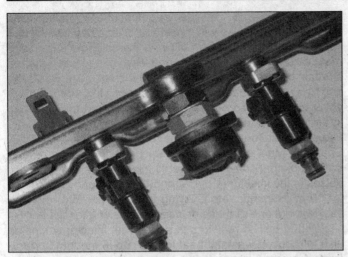

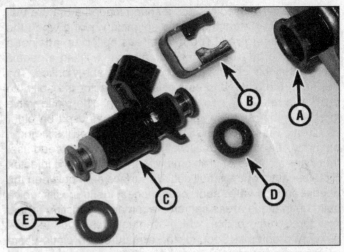

5.14a A pair of typical port-type fuel injectors, still installed in the fuel rail (fuel rail removed for clarity). Most modern injectors are secured to the fuel rail by some sort of retainer clip (by the way, that device between the two injectors is a fuel pulsation damper)

5.14b One of the same two injectors, removed for clarity:

A   *Injector mounting bore in fuel rail - upper end of injector is inserted into this bore*
B   *Injector retainer clip*
C   *Fuel injector (no further disassembly is possible)*
D   *Upper injector O-ring (seals the injector in the fuel rail)*
E   *Lower injector O-ring (seals the injector in the intake manifold)*

armature. (Think of the armature as a small plunger that moves when the coil winding is energized.) When the engine is running, the voltage supply wire to each injector solenoid is always hot. The Powertrain Control Module (PCM) opens and closes the ground path for the injector solenoid in response to inputs from information sensors such as the Camshaft Position (CMP) sensor, the Crankshaft Position (CKP) sensor, the Engine Coolant Temperature (ECT) sensor, the oxygen sensor(s) and the Throttle Position (TP) sensor. Each time that the PCM closes the ground path for an injector, current flows through the solenoid winding, creating a strong magnetic field, which pulls up the armature. When the armature moves up (about 0.1 mm), it lifts the needle valve, which is attached to the lower end of the armature, off its seat. When the needle valve is lifted off its seat, the pressurized fuel inside the injector sprays out through the orifice or nozzle. A pintle on the tip of the needle valve helps to atomize and distribute the fuel. (The shape of the needle, the valve seat, the pintle and the nozzle all help determine the size and shape of the spray pattern.) When the PCM cuts the current to the injector coil winding, the field collapses and a helical spring shuts the armature and needle valve.

An injector might be held open by the PCM for as long as 20 milliseconds. Fuel is delivered to the injector at a virtually constant pressure, so the longer the valve is open, the more fuel it sprays into the intake port. Early injector solenoids had to lift up the armature and needle valve about 10 to 30 thousandths of an inch to open the valve and deliver a squirt of fuel, and they took about 2 milliseconds to do so. The typical injector in use today opens its armature and needle about 6 thousandths of an inch, and the opening time on one of these low-lift units is about 1 millisecond. Because the distance that it must travel is so short, a modern fuel injector can respond *very* quickly. Obviously, *very* precise fuel delivery control is possible with injectors.

Types of fuel injectors

Electronic solenoid injectors all work the same way. Their differences are primarily in the area of valve design, so that's how injectors are usually classified. Three basic types of injector valves have emerged as the most common on modern vehicles.

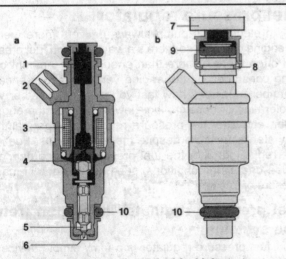

5.14c Cutaway of a typical fuel injector:

a	Fuel injector cross-section	4	Solenoid armature
		5	Needle valve
b	Fuel injector mounting details	6	Pintle
		7	Fuel rail
1	Strainer	8	Injector retainer clip
2	Electrical connector	9	Upper injector O-ring
3	Solenoid winding	10	Lower injector O-ring

Pintle-valve injectors use a spring-loaded armature that is magnetically attracted by the solenoid winding when the winding is energized. The armature is pulled up against a return spring by electro-magnetic attraction, lifting a needle valve and finely-ground pintle out of a tiny spray orifice. The design of the pintle and seat gives the injector the ability to provide a relatively narrow spray pattern. The pintle-valve injector is the original injector design; it was used on older Electronic Fuel Injection (EFI) engines. But you'll still find it on many newer vehicles as well. Despite its widespread use, there are a couple of problems with the pintle-valve injector. First, because of the small contact surface area between the needle and the valve seat, even modest fuel deposits which build up in those areas can create a major restriction to fuel flow through the orifice, which eventually leads to lean fuel delivery problems. Second, the armatures on pintle-valve injectors are usually heavier and larger than the valves used in other injector designs. So their response time is slower. And wear is greater, so the service life of the typical pintle valve injector is shorter than that of other designs.

In *ball-type* injectors, the electrical part is similar to the electrical portion of a pintle-valve injector. But its armature is smaller and has a rounded valve tip that mates with a conical seat. The ball-type injector has several things going for it. The smaller armature design of the ball-type injector allows quicker response time and means less seat wear and fuel fouling. The spray pattern is typically wider. The multiple-orifice design (as many as six orifices in some units) also allows a higher fuel flow rate for a given firing time. And more fuel can be delivered while the valve is open. But ball-type injectors are typically used primarily in Throttle Body Injection (TBI) systems, where their added bulk isn't as much a hindrance to automotive engineers as it is in port fuel injection systems.

A *disk-type* injector looks similar to pintle-valve and ball-type injectors, but it doesn't have an armature. The magnetic field produced by the coil is directed toward the valve area by the shape of the injector core. The valve itself is a disk-and-seat arrangement with the spray orifice in the center of the seat. The disk in this type of injector is a much smaller mass to move with a magnetic field, so it's able to respond more quickly. Because of its lighter weight, less spring tension is needed to return the disk to the seat to stop fuel flow. Which means the disk doesn't slam down with as much force when the coil is de-energized. And the greater contact surface area between the disk and the seat reduces point-to-point contact pressure. This design seems to resist the build-up of fuel deposits better than other injector designs. And even when such deposits do occur, they don't restrict fuel flow as significantly as in other designs.

Current-limited injector-driver circuitry

Finally, a few words of warning about injector-driver circuitry: Older electronic fuel injection systems used battery voltage to operate the injector solenoids. And most fuel injection driver circuits used ballast resistors wired in series with the fuel injectors. The combination of these resistors and redesigned injector circuitry produced a pretty good

injector for the time. The injector solenoid coil winding used a larger-diameter wire with fewer turns, so it had less electrical resistance. This design allowed the solenoid to respond more quickly when energized. And less voltage was required to attain optimal current flow through the solenoid. That's the good news. The bad news was that applying direct battery voltage to this type of injector could burn out the windings in as little as a tenth of a second. Professional technicians use electronic fuel injector testers from (available from OTC, Snap-On, Mac, etc.) to activate each injector from a remote switch box that could be preset to allow a precise number of pulses to the injector (1 pulse for 500 milliseconds; 50 pulses for 10 milliseconds; etc.). Trying to test an injector dynamically without one of these devices was asking for trouble.

Wiring ballast resistors in series with injector solenoids also introduced wasteful heat losses. So in modern *current-limited* injector-driver circuit designs, these resistors have been eliminated with no apparent loss in response time. How did they do it? The driver current rises rapidly to a level sufficient to open the injector, then it's reduced to the minimum level of current necessary to keep the injector valve open. The current rise time, from the moment at which the valve opens to the moment at which the current reaches the maximum safe level (about 6 to 8 amps), is very quick, about 1.2 milliseconds, and it's fixed, i.e. it's always about 1.2 milliseconds. The phase of the pulse width that's altered occurs during the second, current-limited (to about .5 amp) phase. So, once again, don't apply battery voltage to a current-limited injector (unless you plan to do so for less than 1.2 milliseconds!). So again, to be on the safe side, always use an electronic fuel injector tester from one of the specialty tool manufacturers.

Fuel pressure regulator

An electric fuel pump always delivers more fuel than the engine can use, so there's always enough fuel pressure. And often there is *more* than enough. The amount of fuel being consumed by the engine varies in accordance with a number of factors: how fast you're going, whether you're accelerating or decelerating, how much load the engine is under, etc. The fuel pressure regulator helps maintain a fairly stable pressure despite these deviations. Fuel pressure regulators alter the fuel pressure in accordance with engine operating conditions, such as changes in manifold pressure or vacuum.

Fuel pressure regulator operation (return-type systems)

A fuel pressure regulator is a fairly simple device **(see illustrations 5.15a and 5.15b)**. It consists of a metal housing with a spring-loaded diaphragm and a valve attached to the fuel side of the diaphragm. A fuel inlet pipe directs fuel to the valve. The inlet pipe and the fuel side of the housing are usually an integral piece. An outlet pipe extends into the fuel side of the housing and serves as the seat for the valve. When the valve is seated, fuel is blocked; when it's open, fuel flows through the outlet pipe. A vacuum or pressure reference pipe connects the back (spring) side of the

5.15a A typical return-type fuel pressure regulator:

1   *Vacuum line (from intake manifold)*
2   *Banjo bolt and sealing washers for fuel return line*
3   *Fuel return line*
4   *Pressure regulator mounting clamp screw*
5   *Fuel pressure regulator*

diaphragm housing to the intake manifold.

Here's how it works: Fuel from the pump fills the fuel lines, the fuel rail, the fuel injectors and the fuel side of the pressure regulator. The diaphragm spring that holds the valve against its seat is designed to compress when the pressure against the diaphragm reaches the upper limit of the operating range of the system. When fuel pressure exceeds this upper limit, the diaphragm is pushed back against the compressed spring, the valve, which is attached to the diaphragm, is lifted off its seat, fuel flows through the outlet pipe and returns to the fuel tank. As fuel flows out of the regulator, the fuel pressure in the fuel rail and the regulator drops back within its operating range, and below spring pressure. The spring pushes the diaphragm back to its normal position, seating the valve and blocking fuel flow.

A vacuum hose is attached to a port on the regulator on the spring side of the diaphragm. During periods of high intake manifold vacuum (steady cruising, deceleration), when less fuel is required by the injectors, the vacuum present in the regulator counteracts the spring pressure on the diaphragm, which allows fuel to bleed off through the valve. The result is reduced fuel pressure in the fuel rail. During periods of low intake manifold vacuum (heavy acceleration), when more fuel is demanded by the injectors, vacuum in the regulator is reduced. The spring in the regulator is now able to exert more force on the diaphragm and valve, which seals the regulator, causing fuel pressure to rise.

Fuel pressure regulator operation (returnless-type systems)

On a returnless-type system, the fuel pressure regulator is located back at the in-tank fuel pump (**see illustration 5.15c**), not up at the fuel rail, as it is on return-type systems. So, there is no need for a return line from the fuel rail back to the fuel tank. When the fuel pressure exceeds

5.15b Cutaway of a typical fuel-rail-mounted, return-type fuel pressure regulator assembly:

1   *Fuel inlet pipe*
2   *Fuel return pipe (back to the fuel tank)*
3   *Valve*
4   *Valve holder*
5   *Diaphragm*
6   *Compression spring*
7   *Intake manifold vacuum pipe*

the upper threshold of the specified fuel pressure range, the spring inside the regulator compresses, the regulator opens and the fuel is dumped back into the fuel tank. There is no vacuum hose connecting the intake manifold to a returnless-type pressure regulator. Think of the returnless-type fuel pressure regulator as a "pop-off" valve.

Fuel hoses and lines

Pressurization of the fuel provides a nice spray pattern at each injector nozzle, but it poses special problems for fuel hoses and lines. The pressure was no more than 4 to 6 psi in a carbureted system and around 9 to 15 psi in a throttle body injection system. But in a port fuel injection system fuel pressure can be anywhere from 25 to as high as 70 psi on some systems. Which is why fuel injection systems use specially designed fuel hoses and lines to connect components such as the fuel pump, fuel filter and fuel rail.

Steel tubing

Fuel injected vehicles use rigid steel tubing under the vehicle, which can be securely attached to the frame or floor-pan. Steel lines can withstand high pressure easily. They're also coated or plated to resist corrosion. If you ever have to replace metal fuel lines, don't substitute copper or aluminum - they'll crack.

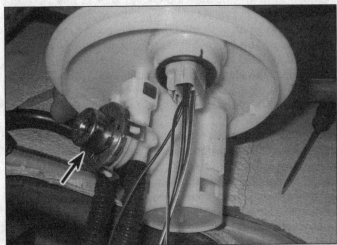

5.15c Typically, returnless-type fuel pressure regulators are part of the fuel pump assembly back at the fuel tank

5.16a Spring-type hose clamps are still used on some vehicles to secure fuel filler neck hoses to the filler pipe at the fuel tank and to connect some EVAP hoses to EVAP metal lines

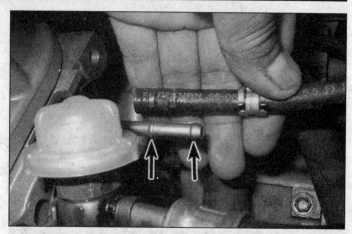

5.16b Spring-type hose clamps are also still used to connect fuel return hoses to the fuel pressure regulator. When securing a fuel or EVAP hose to a metal pipe, slide the hose onto the pipe up to the second ridge (left arrow), then center the clamp between the two ridges (the ridges will create bulges in the rubber hose that indicate the location of the ridges)

Because fuel lines used on fuel-injected vehicles are under fairly high pressure, it is critical that they be replaced with lines of equivalent specification. If you have to replace a fuel line, use only steel tubing that meets the manufacturer's specifications. Don't use copper or aluminum tubing to replace steel tubing. These materials cannot withstand normal vehicle vibration.

Some steel fuel lines have threaded fittings. When loosening these fittings to service or replace components:

a) Always hold the stationary fitting with a wrench while turning the tube nut (this will prevent the line from twisting).

b) If you're going to replace one of these fittings, use original equipment parts or parts that meet original equipment standards.

Flexible hoses

Flexible synthetic hoses are used for bridging the gap between the rigidly mounted steel fuel lines and the fuel injection system. Because the engine shakes and vibrates, it's not feasible to run metal lines directly to the fuel injection system. Two types of flexible hoses are used. One type has three layers: The inner layer is a fuel-resistant, rubber-like, synthetic material made by DuPont™. This material, known commercially as Neoprene™, doesn't swell or dissolve when it comes in contact with fuel the way rubber does. The next layer is a woven polyester fabric that gives the hose strength against pressure and flexing. The outer layer of the hose is another synthetic rubber material, such as Hypalon™, which allows it to resist abrasion and weathering. The other type of hose is really an extruded plastic (nylon) tubing. Nylon tubing is commonly found on fuel-injected vehicles because of its ability to withstand higher pressures.

There are many types of hoses designed for different applications on automobiles. When servicing a fuel-injected vehicle, NEVER substitute hoses or lines designed for use on carbureted vehicles. Carburetor hoses will not stand up to the higher operating pressures of fuel injection systems.

Always use the same type and size hose or line specified by the manufacturer. When installing new fuel hoses, don't route hoses (or metal lines) within four inches of the exhaust system or within ten inches of the catalytic converter. Make sure that no rubber hoses are installed directly against the vehicle, particularly in places where there is any vibration. If allowed to touch some vibrating part of the vehicle, a hose can easily become chafed and it might start leaking. A good rule of thumb is to maintain a minimum of 1/4-inch clearance around a hose (or metal line) to prevent contact with the vehicle underbody.

Plastic tubing

Some fuel lines - between the fuel supply and return pipes of the fuel pump and the front of the fuel tank, for example - are plastic. If you ever have to replace either line, use only the original equipment plastic tubing. **Caution:** *When removing or installing plastic fuel line tubing, be careful not to bend or twist it too much, which can damage it. And damaged fuel lines MUST be replaced! Also, be aware that the plastic fuel tubing is NOT heat resistant, so keep it away from excessive heat. Nor is it acid-proof, so don't wipe it off with a shop rag that has been used to wipe off battery electrolyte. If you accidentally spill or wipe electrolyte on plastic fuel tubing, replace the tubing.*

Fuel line connections

There are many types of fittings used to connect fuel injection lines and hoses. You won't see too many conventional screw-type hose clamps on the fuel injection hoses of most modern vehicles, because they don't have a lot of fuel hoses anymore. But *spring-type* hose clamps **(see illustration 5.16a)** are still used to connect the fuel filler neck hose to the filler pipe on the fuel tank. Spring-type clamps are also still used on the return hoses of some vehicles with conventional return-type systems **(see illustration 5.16b)**.

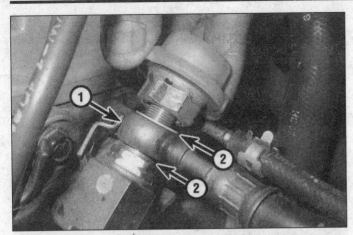

5.17 Banjo fittings provide a virtually leak-proof connecting between fuel lines. When you remove a banjo fitting (1), be sure to discard the old sealing washers (2) and replace them with new washers when you reconnect the fitting (or the connection might spring a leak)

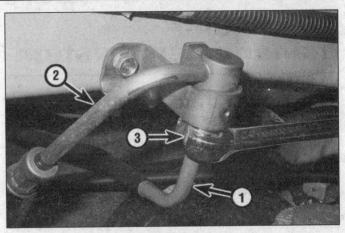

5.18 A typical threaded fitting assembly on a firewall:

1   Fuel supply line from fuel tank
2   Fuel supply line from firewall to fuel rail
3   Threaded fitting (use a flare-nut wrench, as shown, to protect the corners of the nut from stripping)

After disconnecting a spring-type clamp, always verify that it's still stiff enough to re-use. If it's lost its tensile memory, replace it, or you'll have a leak in no time.

Banjo-type fittings (**see illustration 5.17**) are used on some vehicles to connect the fuel supply line to the fuel rail. Banjo fittings are robust enough to withstand the high-pressure of the fuel delivery system, but you should replace the sealing washers every time you disconnect a banjo fitting, or you could wind up with a leak.

Threaded fittings (**see illustration 5.18**) are also used on some vehicles to connect fuel supply line fittings. Be sure to use flare-nut wrench to loosen and tighten the nut on a threaded fitting to protect the nut. If you round-off the corners of the nut on one of these fittings, you'll have to replace the entire fitting.

Quick-connect fittings (**see illustration 5.19**) are by far the most common type of fitting used on modern fuel-injected vehicles. They're usually easier to disconnect and reconnect than banjo and threaded fittings, and are just as leak-proof. The only drawbacks? Sometimes you need a special tool to disconnect and reconnect the quick-connects used by some manufacturers. (Special tools for all of the common types of quick-connect fittings are available at most auto parts retailers.) And on many quick-connects, you must replace the *retainer*, which is the part that locks the male and female sides of the fitting together. Haynes manuals covering late-model vehicles provide easy-to-follow, step-by-step instructions and photos depicting how to disconnect and reconnect the quick-connect fittings used on your vehicle, so study those photo sequences carefully before tearing into quick-connects.

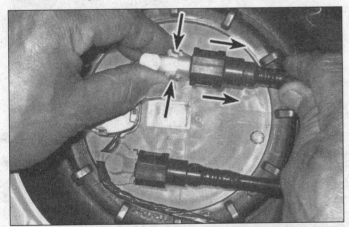

5.19 A couple of typical quick-connect fittings being used to connect the fuel supply and return lines to the supply and return pipes on top of the fuel pump. To disconnect this particular type of quick-connect fitting, squeeze the retainer tabs on the white part of the fitting and pull on the black part of the fitting until the two halves are separated (some quick-connects require a special tool for disconnection and reconnection)

Warning: *Gasoline is extremely flammable, so take extra precautions when you work on any part of the fuel system. Don't smoke or allow open flames or bare light bulbs near the work area, and don't work in a garage where a gas-type appliance (such as a water heater or a clothes dryer) is present. Since gasoline is carcinogenic, wear fuel-resistant gloves when there's a possibility of being exposed to fuel, and, if you spill any fuel on your skin, rinse it off immediately with soap and water. Mop up any spills immediately and do not store fuel-soaked rags where they could ignite. The fuel system is under constant pressure, so, if any fuel lines are to be disconnected, the fuel pressure in the system must be relieved first. When you perform any kind of work on the fuel system, wear safety glasses and have a Class B type fire extinguisher on hand.*

The engine management system

The Powertrain Control Module (PCM)

Think of the PCM **(see illustration 5.20)** as the brain of the engine management system. The PCM monitors signals from an array of information sensors, processes this information in accordance with its program, then controls ignition timing and fuel delivery to maximize performance and fuel efficiency. It also controls the various emissions control systems. Despite its complexity, the PCM is one of the most reliable components in the entire engine management system. The failure rate of PCMs is remarkably low, which means it should be the last component you suspect in the event there's a problem with your fuel injection system.

Without computers, modern vehicles could not have complied with increasingly stringent government-mandated emission reductions nor could they have achieved the current level of operating efficiency that allows us to have horsepower and fuel economy at the same time. Automobiles first began using engine control computers in the Seventies. Those early units were designed to control the timing of the ignition system, the fuel injection system and/or the idle control system. But computers did those jobs so easily and so well that manufacturers were soon using them to control other aspects of vehicle operation as well. By the mid- to late-Nineties, computers were controlling automatic transmissions, anti-lock brake systems, traction control systems, airbag systems, climate control systems, cruise control systems and theft deterrent systems. The application of computer controls to modern cars and trucks has, in short, revolutionized the automobile.

Early computers were referred to as the Engine Control Unit (ECU) or the Electronic Control Module (ECM). Some had wackier names like Single Board Engine Controller (SBEC) or Single Module Engine Controller (SMEC). In 1996 (the year in which all new vehicles had to meet OBD-II requirements), the now ubiquitous engine control computer was given its most recent terminology upgrade. It's now referred to as the Powertrain Control Module (PCM). In part, this was a formal acknowledgment that the computer didn't just control the fuel injection and ignition systems; it controlled nearly every aspect of powertrain operation.

The Environmental Protection Agency (EPA) and the Federal government require all automobile manufacturers to warranty their major emissions components for eight years or 80,000 miles, whichever comes first, and for two years or 24,000 miles on emissions-related components (see Chapter Two for more details). And some states - California, Massachusetts, Maine, Vermont and others - mandate extended emissions warranties as well (again, see Chapter Two). If your vehicle is still covered by a Federal and/or state extended emissions warranty, your dealer will service

5.20 A typical Powertrain Control Module (PCM) unit

or replace the PCM at not cost to you. Keep this in mind when diagnosing and/or repairing any system problems.

Location

The PCM is usually located under the dashboard or behind one of the kick panels, those triangular-shaped trim panels that cover up the small area next to the footwell, where you put your feet when you're sitting in the vehicle. Some manufacturers even locate the PCM in the engine compartment (which underscores the fact that these little black boxes are tougher than they look). A PCM that's located under the dash can be difficult to access because you might have to remove the center console and some trim panels from the dash. The good news is that once you've reached the PCM, it's usually very easy to remove. Most PCMs are secured by nothing more than one or two small brackets.

Construction

Early engine management computers, or electronic control units, were usually encased in metal housings. Many still are, but some are now housed inside plastic housings. It depends where the manufacturer locates the PCM. If it's in the engine compartment it's more likely to be made of metal; if it's inside the vehicle, it might be plastic instead. Open up the housing of a typical PCM and the circuit board(s) inside will look just like any computer board, with a couple of printed circuit boards that look just like the boards inside the PC on your desktop, except smaller. On these boards are hundreds of electronic components. We're not going to get into what each of these components does. Instead, let's look at the important functions shared by all PCMs. The first thing you notice about a PCM is that one or two large, sometimes very large, electrical connectors are plugged into it. The wiring harnesses leading to these connectors carry voltage signals from an array of information sensors to the PCM, carry voltage signals from the PCM to various output actuators and even to some sensors and bring battery voltage to power the PCM itself.

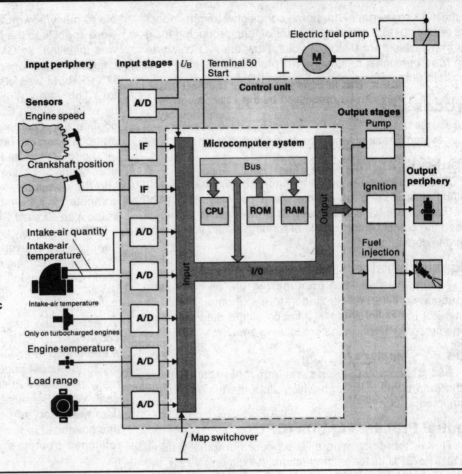

5.21 Simplified data-flow schematic of a typical PCM

A quick lap through the PCM

The PCM constantly adjusts things like the ignition timing and the pulse width (on-time) of the injectors while the engine is running, by comparing the stream of data from various information sensors with its own three-dimensional map (the operating instructions, or program). The map consists of two types of information: fixed and variable. The fixed values include computer system operating instructions and vehicle constants such as the number of cylinders, the types of emissions equipment used on the vehicle, and transmission gear ratios. Variable information is specific to vehicle operation at a given moment. Engine speed, vehicle speed, intake airflow, throttle angle, ignition timing, engine coolant temperature, intake air temperature, manifold absolute pressure, etc. are all variable information.

While a PCM is capable of lightning-fast decision making, it can't actually do anything by itself, such as finding out what is going around it or changing the operating conditions of the engine, transmission or some other system. For that, the computer needs a wide array of information sensors to feed it information, and almost as many output actuators to carry out its commands. But before we get to the sensors and actuators, let's look at some of the important functions of the typical PCM. We'll divide our discussion into three parts: input stages, processing, and output stages (**see illustration 5.21**).

Input stages

The input stages convert input voltage signals from all the information sensors to a format that the PCM can process.

Analog-to-digital (A/D) converters

Most of the information sensors keeping the PCM up to date produce an analog (continuously variable) voltage signal. For example, an oxygen sensor produces an analog voltage output between 0 and 1.1 volts. (Unlike oxygen sensors, most other sensors don't actually produce any voltage - they are supplied a voltage by the PCM and their resistance changes with temperature or movement. The PCM then uses the voltage drop to calculate the temperature or position of the sensor it is monitoring.) But the PCM cannot process an analog voltage input, so the input is routed through an A/D converter, which converts it to a 10-bit digital format. Every analog voltage input must run through an A/D converter before it can be processed by the PCM.

Signal conditioners (pulse shapers)

The voltage signals for some inputs and outputs need to be adjusted to an appropriate level before they can be processed. For example, suppose that an A/D converter that is designed to read a 0-volt-to-5.volt signal must convert a 0-volt-to-1.1-volt output from an oxygen sensor. The PCM routes such a signal through a signal conditioner on its way to the A/D converter. The signal conditioner might "boost" this anemic 0- to 1.1-volt by a factor of four, producing a signal that varies from 0- to 4.4 volts. Now the A/D converter can read the signal better and will produce a cleaner, more accurate output for processing by the PCM.

Processing

This is the area in the PCM where the actual microcomputer systems reside. All processing takes place here.

Input-output (I/O) unit

The I/O unit handles all incoming and outgoing data traffic. Input signals are read at the frequency and speed at which they arrive. Output signals are always at whatever speed the computer is capable of running at and in the most suitable sequence.

Clock generator

To prevent the PCM from locking up, all computing sequences must be controlled in terms of time. The clock generator is the timekeeper. It keeps all the data humming along smoothly through the processing area.

Bus

Bus is a computer geek slang term for busbar. The bus is the data corridor through which all of the main units are connected.

Central Processing Unit (CPU)

This is the place where all processing actually takes place. The CPU includes the arithmetic-logic unit (ALU), the Read-Only Memory (ROM) and the Random Access Memory (RAM) chips.

Arithmetic-logic unit (ALU)

The ALU is the "calculator" that performs all arithmetic (addition, subtraction, multiplication and division) and logical operations (and, or, no) on all stored data. The ALU gets whatever programming and theoretical values it needs from Read-Only Memory (ROM) and measures operating data from Random-Access Memory (RAM). The results of these calculations (Bosch calls them "instantaneous intermediate values") from the ALU are stored in the accumulator. All of these computations are handled by a logic program that controls the processing sequence, orders the steps, reads the necessary data and controls the input-output.

Read-Only Memory (ROM)

ROM consists of the map (the program software), plus characteristic values, characteristic curves and theoretical values that are unique to the vehicle powertrain that the PCM is managing. This data is "burned" into the ROM integrated circuit when ROM is produced. On older computers, ROM could not be altered. On later computers, it could be altered, either by replacing ROM or "flashing" it.

On older General Motors and some other older vehicles, the permanent part of the computer map (program) was located inside the computer, on the motherboard. The map contained those instructions that were universally applica-

ble to many powertrain combinations. But other instructions were specific to the make and model in which the computer was installed, so GM put that code on a separate memory chip called a Programmable Read Only Memory (PROM). (The PROM was also sometimes referred to as a calibrator.) This strategy allowed a manufacturer to save money by using a single computer in a wide range of vehicles. To configure the computer so that it would be vehicle specific and could run the engine management system of a particular model, the manufacturer inserted a PROM with the necessary specific code. The PROM chip was simply plugged into the computer, so programming or reprogramming the computer was a simple matter of replacing the PROM. This setup also allowed GM and other manufacturers to configure a PROM to comply with different air quality regulations in different states or even in foreign markets. And if a bug in the PROM was causing driveability problems, the manufacturer could simply install a new PROM. But PROM chips were fragile, so GM introduced an erasable PROM (EPROM). On an EPROM, the memory was erased by exposing it to ultraviolet light and then it was reprogrammed. Later versions, known as EEPROMs (electrically erasable PROM), allowed a dealership to easily update or change the PROM's memory to the latest specification. Today nobody but old timers really refers to PROMs, EPROMs and EEPROMs as a big deal. Why? Because even if they can be removed, it's seldom necessary to do so anymore now that the technology has advanced to the point at which almost any PCM can be reflashed (reprogrammed) electronically without removing it.

Random-Access Memory (RAM)

RAM is the operating-data memory. The data produced and delivered by the information sensors is stored in RAM until it's processed by the CPU or is "updated" (overwritten). The data in RAM must be continuously updated during operation. And it's erased every time that the system is turned off. RAM is also the temporary memory storage place for any calculated values that the PCM needs for any calculations that it's getting ready to process.

Adaptive memory

Adaptive memory adjusts for variables such as component wear, fuel quality and production inconsistencies. Most PCMs have had adaptive memory since the beginning of OBD-II. This adaptive memory feature allows the computer to make minor operating adjustments to compensate for these types of factors, and to maintain driveability when certain operating values are outside the program parameters. The adaptive memory changes are stored in the computer Random Access Memory (RAM), but are lost whenever the battery is disconnected. When this happens, the driver simply drives the vehicle for about 20 miles until the computer "relearns" the adaptive memory program changes. Today's OBD-II PCMs still have adaptive memory, and a lot of other features that are unique to OBD-II. We'll look at those features in Chapter 6.

Output stages

High-level digital outputs

Some of the more important functions of the PCM are to fire the spark plugs and fuel injectors, turn the engine cooling fan on and off, turn the Exhaust Gas Recirculation (EGR) valve on and off, turn the Evaporative Emission Control (EVAP) system purge valve on and off, etc. Note that all of these functions are "On/Off" type operations, like a light switch. For example, when the PCM turns on the cooling fan, it needs to provide 12 volts and perhaps half an amp or slightly more. But the PCM isn't capable of putting out this kind of power because it runs on low voltage. So it energizes the digital output for the fan instead. A transistor inside the digital output turns on a 12-volt circuit that powers the fan. In other words, a digital output works like a relay (except that it's a solid state device instead of an electro-mechanical one). There are similar high-level digital outputs for each output actuator that is simply turned on and off, such as the ignition coils and the injectors.

Digital-to-analog (D/A) converters

Some output actuators require an analog rather than a digital voltage output, but the digital PCM can't speak analog, so it sends a digital command through a D/A converter to translate.

Communication chips

The PCM also need some chips that can implement the various communications standards currently being used on modern vehicles. Several communications standards are used on motor vehicles. The most popular standard right now is the Controller Area Network (CAN). CAN was specifically developed by Robert Bosch GmbH for the automotive market as a vehicle bus for the proliferation of engine control units (ECUs) located all over the vehicle. CAN is much faster than earlier communications standards. It can handle speeds between 500 kilobits per second and 1 megabit per second, which allows the various computers on a vehicle to communicate with each other hundreds of times a second. One benefit of a communications bus between the PCM and the other modules on a vehicle is that it allows the other modules to send fault codes to the PCM, which can store the codes and communicate them to a scan tool. Being able to access all the fault codes from a single computer makes it easier for a professionals and amateurs alike to diagnose a problem more quickly.

Computer precautions

Computers have delicate internal circuitry that is easily damaged when subjected to excessive voltage, static electricity or magnetism. When diagnosing any electrical problems in a circuit connected to the computer, remember that most computers operate at a relatively low voltage (about 5 volts).

Observe the following precautions whenever working on or around the computer and/or engine control system circuits:

1) Do not damage the wiring or any electrical connectors in such a way as to cause it to ground or touch another source of voltage.
2) Do not use any electrical testing equipment (such as an ohmmeter) that is powered by a six-or-more-volt battery. The excessive voltage might cause an electrical component in the computer to burn or short. Use only a ten mega-ohm impedance multimeter when working on engine control circuits.
3) Do not remove or troubleshoot the computer without the proper tools and information, because any mistakes can void your warranty and/or damage components.
4) All spark plug wires should be at least one inch away from any sensor circuit or control wires. An unexpected problem in computer circuits is magnetic fields that send false signals to the computer, frequently resulting in hard-to-identify performance problems. Although there have been cases of high-power lines or transformers interfering with the computer, the most common cause of this problem in the sensor circuits is the position of the spark plug wires (too close to the computer wiring).
5) Use special care when handling or working near the computer. Remember that static electricity can cause computer damage by creating a very large surge in voltage (see *Static electricity and electronic components below*).

Static electricity and electronic components

Caution: *Static electricity can damage or destroy the computer and other electronic components. Read the following information carefully.*

Static electricity can cause two types of damage. The first and most obvious is complete failure of the device. The other type of damage is much more subtle and harder to detect as an electrical component failure. In this situation the integrated circuit is degraded and can become weakened over a period of time. It might perform erratically, or it might manifest itself as an intermittent failure of some other component.

The best way to prevent static electricity damage is to drain the charge from your body by grounding your body to the frame or body of the vehicle and then working strictly on a static-free area. A static-control wrist strap properly worn and grounded to the frame or body of the vehicle will drain the charges from your body, thereby preventing them from discharging into the electronic components. Consult your dealer parts department for a list of the static protection kits available.

Remember that it is often not possible to feel a static discharge until the charge level reaches 3,000 volts! It is very possible to be damaging the electrical components without even knowing it!

Information sensors

An information sensor is an input device that converts one form of energy to another. Information sensors transform the operating conditions of the engine into electrical signals that can be translated into workable parameters for the PCM. Since a PCM can only read voltage signals, an information sensor must convert motion, pressure, temperature, light and other forms of energy to voltage. There are many types of Information sensors - switches, timers, resistors, thermistors, transformers and generators. Information sensors monitor engine operating conditions such as air flow, air mass, air temperature, coolant temperature, exhaust oxygen content, manifold absolute pressure, throttle position, etc. and transmit this information to a computer in a low-voltage analog or digital format. Some information sensors are simply digital switches; i.e. they're on-off devices. They send no signal to the computer until a certain threshold in coolant temperature, throttle position, etc. has been exceeded. Most information sensors are analog devices; that is, they react to changes in the condition they're monitoring by altering a continuous voltage signal to the computer.

Many important information sensors are resistors. A resistor can send an analog signal that's proportional to temperature, pressure, motion or other variables. A resistor, however, cannot generate its own voltage. It can only modify a voltage applied to it. Therefore, automobile resistive sensors must operate with a reference voltage from the PCM. This is a fixed voltage applied by the PCM to the resistor. To prevent inaccurate sensor signals, the reference voltage must be less than the minimum battery voltage. Some of the older engine management systems operated with a nine-volt reference voltage (Ford EEC-I, II and III, for example). But all modern engine management systems use a five-volt reference voltage.

Each information sensor is specifically designed to gather data from one particular operating aspect of the engine. For example, the Mass Air Flow (MAF) sensor is positioned inside the air intake system, where it measures the volume and density of the incoming air to help the computer calculate how much fuel is needed to maintain the correct air/fuel mixture. Let's look at how a typical sensor works: The computer sends a reference voltage to the sensor. As sensor resistance changes, so does the return voltage. Okay. Now, let's assume that a temperature sensor can be calibrated to send a 0-volt return signal at 0 degrees F. and a 5.volt return signal at 250 degrees F. Every 1-degree temperature change causes a 0.02-volt change in the return voltage. The computer reads these 20-millivolt increments and correlates them to air temperature or engine coolant temperature.

Diagnosing information sensor problems can be tricky because of the interrelationship between various engine management systems and components. For example, a fuel-injected engine develops an intake manifold vacuum leak (known as "false air" because it's not part of the measured air entering the manifold). The PCM displays a Diag-nostic Trouble Code (DTC) indicating a permanently lean condition (excessive oxygen in the exhaust stream) output from the oxygen sensor. Your first thought might be "Well, I'd better change my oxygen sensor." Actually, the intake leak is allowing more air into the combustion chamber than it can burn up, producing an excessively lean exhaust stream. The oxygen sensor detects excess oxygen in the exhaust and sends this information to the PCM, which cannot compensate for the excessive level of oxygen and therefore stores and displays a DTC for the oxygen sensor.

Yogi Berra once said "When you get to a fork in the road, take it!" Part of the difficulty experienced by home mechanics when trying to track down and identify the actual cause of a symptom is that it's easy to take a wrong turn when you get to a fork in the road. The first step, therefore, is to *know the territory*. Study the engine management system on your vehicle. Learn what all the information sensors *do*. Learn what they measure or monitor. Then think about the various implications of a DTC set by the PCM. Is it really a malfunctioning sensor or its circuit? Or is it an aberrant operating condition that's causing the sensor circuit to go haywire?

Okay, let's get that first step out of the way. Let's look at the important information sensors on your vehicle. Please bear in mind that the photos accompanying each brief description are intended as typical examples to familiarize you with each sensor's general appearance and location. If you want to know *exactly* what each sensor looks like and where it's located on *your* vehicle, refer to the *Haynes Automotive Repair Manual* for your vehicle.

Accelerator Pedal Position (APP) sensor

The APP sensor (see illustration 5.22a), which is located at the top of the accelerator pedal, is part of the elec-

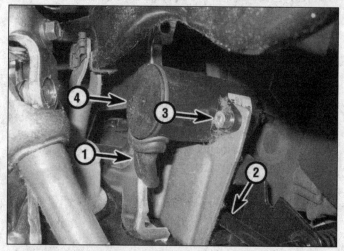

5.22a A typical Accelerator Pedal Position (APP) sensor, located at the top of the accelerator pedal:

1	Electrical lead	3	Mounting bolts (other bolt not visible)
2	Linkage rod	4	APP sensor

tronic accelerator control system used on more and more OBD-II vehicles. On vehicles equipped with an APP sensors, there is no accelerator cable. The APP sensor monitors the angle of the accelerator pedal and sends this data to the PCM, which controls an output actuator known as the *throttle plate solenoid* or *throttle control module* (located on or inside the throttle body). The throttle solenoid opens and closes the throttle plate, in accordance with commands from the PCM, to an opening angle that's directly proportional to the angle of the accelerator pedal. In other words, as you depress the accelerator pedal, the throttle plate inside the throttle body opens accordingly. It's just that it's done electronically instead of mechanically.

The typical APP sensor consists of a couple of identical *potentiometers*, which are variable resistors that receive a reference voltage from the PCM and return a voltage signal to the PCM that's proportional to the angle of the accelerator pedal. One of the potentiometers is redundant, and serves as a back-up in the event that the primary potentiometer fails. The PCM compares the signal outputs from both potentiometers to assess the accuracy of the primary potentiometer's signal.

On some vehicles the APP sensor is located inside the engine compartment, on the firewall or even under the battery tray (**see illustration 5.22b**). On these vehicles, there is an "accelerator cable," but it only connects the accelerator pedal to the APP sensor. This type of APP sensor is a *linear* potentiometer, i.e. it measures the linear movement of the accelerator cable instead of the angular change of the accelerator pedal.

Barometric Pressure (BARO) sensor

The Barometric Pressure sensor, or BARO sensor, measures atmospheric pressure. The PCM uses this data to determine air density and altitude. At one time, the BARO sensor was a stand-alone unit located somewhere in the engine compartment, often on the firewall. But most manufacturers have integrated the BARO sensor, along with the Intake Air Temperature (IAT) sensor, into the Mass Air Flow (MAF) sensor or the Volume Air Flow (VAF) sensor. If there's a problem with the BARO sensor you have to replace the MAF or VAF sensor.

Brake Pedal Position (BPP) switch

The BPP switch (**see illustration 5.23**) is located at the top of the brake pedal. It's a normally open switch that closes when the brake pedal is applied and sends a signal to the PCM, which interprets this signal as its cue to disengage the torque converter clutch. The BPP switch is also used to disengage the brake shift interlock system on some vehicles.

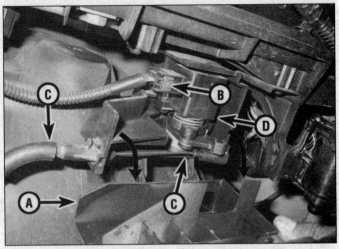

5.22b A less typical *linear*-type APP sensor, located on the underside of the battery tray (on some vehicles equipped with type of APP sensor, the sensor is located on the firewall):

A	Swing-down door	C	"Accelerator" cable
B	Electrical connector	D	APP sensor

Camshaft Position (CMP) sensor

The CMP sensor produces a signal that the PCM uses to identify the number 1 cylinder and to time the firing sequence of the fuel injectors. On OHC engines, the CMP sensor is

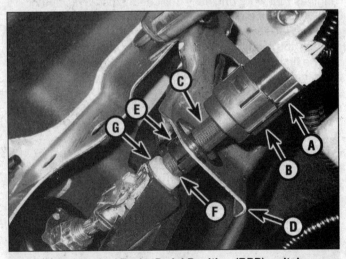

5.23 A typical Brake Pedal Position (BPP) switch

A Electrical connector
B BPP switch
C Plunger barrel (note serrations on surface of barrel for adjusting switch)
D Switch mounting bracket
E Switch holder
F Plunger tip (not visible because it's inside plunger barrel; tip touches pad at top of brake pedal arm)
G Pad at top of brake pedal arm

5.24a On an OHC engine, the Camshaft Position (CMP) sensor is typically located on the cylinder head, near the camshaft. If it's a DOHC engine, the CMP sensor might be near either camshaft. On some DOHC OBD-II engines, there are *two* CMP sensors, one for each camshaft

5.24b On some OHC and DOHC engines, the CMP sensor is located under the timing belt cover, which means you'll have to remove the cover to access the CMP sensor

A   Electrical harness (if you see a harness disappearing into the upper end of the timing belt cover, and haven't yet located the CMP sensor, this is a hint that it's probably under the timing belt cover)
B   Electrical connector
C   CMP sensor mounting bolt

Crankshaft Position (CKP) sensor

located on the cylinder head(s) near the camshaft(s) **(see illustration 5.24a)**. On some OHC engines, the CMP sensor is located at the timing belt end of the engine. On others, it's located under the timing belt cover **(see illustration 5.24b)**. On OHV engines, the CMP sensor is usually located in one of two spots. On some OHV engines, usually those engines that were originally designed to use a distributor, it's either inside the distributor, or inside a distributor-like housing **(see illustration 5.24c)** that's installed at the same location as the distributor. On other OHV engines, it's located on the timing chain cover at the front of the engine, near the camshaft **(see illustration 5.24d)**.

The CKP sensor is a magnetic pick-up coil or Hall Effect device that produces a signal that the PCM uses to determine the position and speed of the crankshaft. A CKP sensor works in a fashion similar to an ignition pick-up coil and trigger wheel in an electronic distributor. The difference between a CKP sensor and a pick-up coil/trigger wheel is

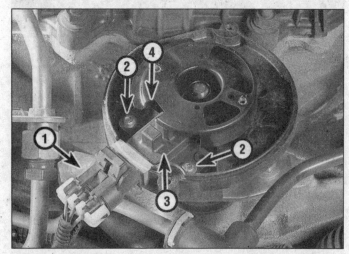

5.24c On some older OHV engine designs, the CMP sensor is inside a distributor-like housing

1   Electrical connector
2   CMP sensor mounting screws
3   CMP sensor
4   Reluctor

5.24d On newer OHV engines, the CMP sensor is mounted somewhere on the timing chain cover, near the front end of the camshaft

A   Electrical connector
B   CMP sensor mounting bolt

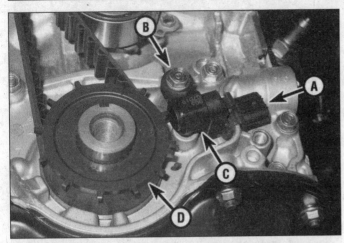

5.25a On some engines, the Crankshaft Position (CKP) sensor is mounted at the front end of the block, near the crankshaft pulley. On this type of installation, the trigger wheel is mounted right behind the crankshaft damper pulley or on the face of the timing belt sprocket

A *Electrical connector (already disconnected)*
B *CKP sensor mounting bolt*
C *CKP sensor*
D *Trigger wheel*

that, instead of reading the ignition-timing signal from a trigger wheel mounted on the distributor shaft, a CKP sensor reads it off a trigger wheel mounted directly on the crankshaft, timing belt sprocket, harmonic balancer or flywheel. This eliminates any timing variations that might result from backlash in the timing chain or distributor shaft freeplay. CKP sensors are used in all distributorless ignition engines. Basically, the CKP sensor reads the position of the crankshaft by detecting when pulse rings on the crankshaft, timing belt sprocket, harmonic balancer or flywheel pass by it. The CKP sensor is located near the crankshaft pulley **(see illustration 5.25a)**, on the side of the block **(see illustration**

5.25b On other engines, the CKP sensor is mounted at the rear of the block, near the flywheel or driveplate (but this one here takes its reading off of a trigger wheel on the crankshaft, not the flywheel or driveplate)

A *Electrical connector*
B *CKP sensor mounting bolt*
C *CKP sensor*

5.25b), or on the transmission bellhousing. If the CKP sensor is mounted on the side of the block, the trigger wheel is located on the crankshaft **(see illustration 5.25c)** and cannot be serviced without removing the crank.

Electronic Load Detector (ELD)

The ELD **(see illustration 5.26)**, which is used on many Honda vehicles (and, likely, on many other vehicles in the future) monitors the electrical load on the system and keeps the PCM informed. The PCM controls the voltage output of the alternator in response to the data conveyed by this signal. The ELD is located in the engine compartment fuse and relay box.

5.25c On engines with the CKP sensor mounted on the side of the block, the trigger wheel (A) is located inside the engine, on the crankshaft. The business end of the CKP sensor (B), which protrudes through the block, is located so that it can sense the teeth of the trigger wheel as they rotate past it

5.26 A typical Electronic Load Detector (ELD) unit

1 *80-amp fuse*
2 *40-amp fuse*
3 *ELD unit*
4 *Fuse/ELD mounting screws*

5.27a On a four-cylinder engine, the Engine Coolant Temperature (ECT) sensor is typically mounted on the thermostat housing, on the opposite end of the cylinder head from the timing belt or chain, or somewhere on the intake manifold

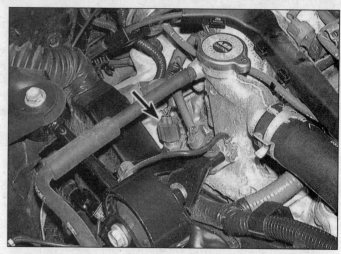

5.27b On a V6 or V8 engine, the ECT sensor is usually located on the intake manifold or on the thermostat housing

Engine Coolant Temperature (ECT) sensor

The ECT sensor (see illustrations 5.27a and 5.27b) is a thermistor (temperature-sensitive variable resistor) that sends a voltage signal to the PCM, which uses this data to determine the temperature of the engine coolant. The ECT sensor helps the PCM control the air/fuel mixture ratio and ignition timing, and it also helps the PCM determine when to turn the Exhaust Gas Recirculation (EGR) system on and off. Most ECT sensors are located on the intake manifold, the thermostat housing or the cylinder head. The ECT sensor is often located near or right next to the coolant temperature sending unit for the coolant temperature gauge on the dash. Don't confuse the two. An ECT sensor has two wires and a coolant-temperature sending unit has one wire (because it's grounded through the engine).

All fuel injection systems use thermistor-type temperature sensors to measure engine coolant (and air) temperature because temperature affects intake air density and air-fuel mixture ratio. A thermistor (see illustration 5.27c),

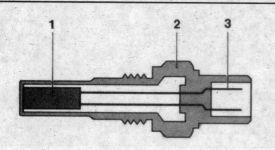

5.27c Cutaway of a typical ECT sensor

1   Thermistor
    (NTC resistor)
2   ECT body
3   Electrical terminal

also known as a Negative Temperature Coefficient (NTC) resistor, is a special kind of variable resistor whose resistance decreases as the temperature increases. The bimetal element used in a thermistor has a highly predictable and repeatable property: The amount of current and voltage it conducts at a certain temperature is always the same. This characteristic makes the thermistor an excellent analog temperature sensor. As the temperature increases, the resistance decreases, and the current and voltage increase. The PCM uses this rising voltage signal, along with signals from other sensors, to alter the injector pulse width or the fuel pressure as the engine warms up.

Fuel Tank Pressure (FTP) sensor

The fuel tank pressure sensor (see illustration 5.28) measures the fuel tank pressure when the PCM tests the EVAP system, and it's also used to control fuel tank pressure by signaling the EVAP system to purge the tank when the pressure becomes excessive. The fuel tank pressure sensor is typically located somewhere on top of the fuel tank or on the fuel pump/fuel gauge sending unit mounting flange.

Input Shaft Speed (ISS) and Output Shaft Speed (OSS) sensors

The Input Shaft Speed (ISS) and Output Shaft Speed (OSS) sensors are magnetic pick-up coils used on OBD-II automatic transaxles and transmissions. The PCM uses the analog voltage signal from the OSS to calculate shift points, torque converter lock-up and release, etc. Prior to OBD-II, automatics were equipped with a Vehicle Speed Sensor (VSS), which functioned as the sending unit for the speedometer and, in more sophisticated applications, as the

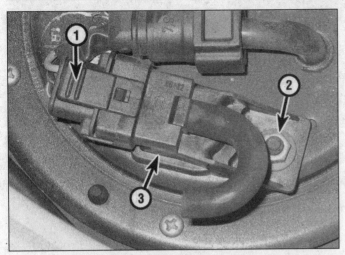

5.28 A typical Fuel Tank Pressure (FTP) sensor, installed on top of the fuel tank, on the fuel pump/fuel gauge sending unit mounting flange (some FTP sensors are mounted directly on top of the fuel tank instead of the fuel pump/fuel gauge sending unit flange)

1   *Electrical connector*
2   *FTP sensor mounting bolt*
3   *FTP sensor*

device that sent a vehicle speed signal to the engine management computer. But OBD-II requires that the PCM must have some way of verifying that the transaxle or transmission is operating correctly. So manufacturers began installing *two* speed sensors, one at the input shaft and another one at the output shaft (where the VSS had been installed). The PCM compares the signals from both sensors to monitor wear and slippage inside the transmission, and sets a DTC when things start to get too loose. And just like a conventional VSS, the OSS sensor monitors the rotational

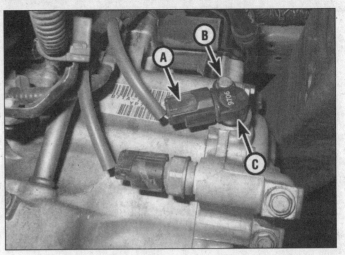

5.29a A typical Input Shaft Speed (ISS) sensor on an automatic *transaxle*

A   *Electrical connector*
B   *ISS sensor mounting bolt*
C   *ISS sensor*

speed of the output shaft and provides an analog voltage signal to the PCM, which uses this information to control the torque converter and to calculate speed scheduling and the correct operating pressure for the transaxle.

The ISS and OSS sensors are located, respectively, near the input shaft and the output shaft (**see illustrations 5.29a and 5.29b**). ISS and OSS sensors can be difficult to locate on automatic transaxles because they can be on the front, the top, the end, or the back, as long as they're near the input and output shafts. ISS and OSS sensors are easier to find on automatic transmissions because both of them are nearly always located on the left or right side of the transmission (**see illustration 5.29c**).

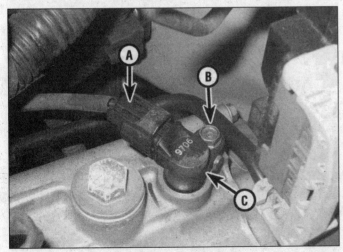

5.29b A typical Output Shaft Speed (OSS) sensor on an automatic *transaxle*

A   *Electrical connector*
B   *OSS sensor mounting bolt*
C   *OSS sensor*

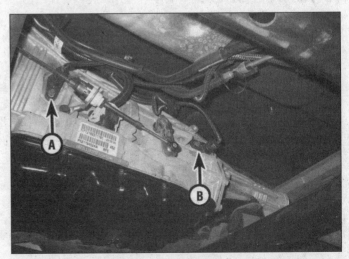

5.29c Typical Input Shaft Speed (ISS) and Output Shaft Speed (OSS) sensors on an automatic *transmission*

A   *Input Shaft Speed (ISS) sensor*
B   *Output Shaft Speed (OSS) sensor*

5.30a Some Intake Air Temperature (IAT) sensors are an integral component of the Mass Air Flow (MAF) sensor

5.30b A typical Air Intake Air Temperature (IAT) sensor mounted on the air intake duct. IAT sensors that are installed in the air intake duct are usually just pushed into place and sealed by some sort of rubber grommet

1   *Electrical connector*
2   *IAT sensor*
3   *Rubber insulator grommet (inspect these grommets for cracks and deterioration)*

Intake Air Temperature (IAT) sensor

The IAT sensor monitors the temperature of the air entering the engine and sends a signal to the PCM. The IAT sensor, like the ECT sensor, is a thermistor. For a description of how thermistors work, see *Engine Coolant Temperature* (ECT) sensor above. On some vehicles, the IAT sensor is located on the air filter housing **(see illustration 5.2)**. On other vehicles, it's an integral component of the Mass Air Flow (MAF) sensor **(see illustration 5.30a)**. On others, it's located on the air intake duct or on the intake manifold plenum **(see illustrations 5.30b and 5.30c)**.

Knock sensor

The knock sensor is a "piezoelectric" crystal that oscillates in proportion to engine vibration. (The term *piezoelectric* refers to the property of certain crystals that produce a voltage when subjected to a mechanical stress.) The oscillation of the piezoelectric crystal produces a voltage output that is monitored by the PCM, which retards the ignition timing when the oscillation exceeds a certain threshold. When the engine is operating normally, the knock sensor oscillates consistently and its voltage signal is steady. When detonation occurs, engine vibration increases, and the oscillation of the knock sensor exceeds a design threshold. (Detonation is an uncontrolled explosion, after the spark occurs at the spark plug, which spontaneously combusts the remaining air/fuel mixture, resulting in a "pinging" or "slapping" sound.) If allowed to continue, the engine could be damaged. When the knock sensor is working properly, the maximum timing advance for all driving conditions is achieved.

Knock sensors can be difficult to locate because they're often buried under intake or exhaust manifolds and miscellaneous engine plumbing and wiring. A good rule of thumb for finding the knock sensor(s) is that they're usually located

between a pair of cylinders, where they'll "hear" any knocking sounds better. For example, on four-cylinder engines, the knock sensor is usually installed in the side of the block, between either cylinders 1 and 2, 2 and 3 or 3 and 4 **(see illustration 5.31a)**. On some V6 and V8 engines the knock sensors are threaded into the side of the engine block, one per cylinder bank. On most late model V6 and V8 engines, the knock sensor(s) is usually located below the intake manifold, in the valley between the cylinder heads **(see illustration 5.31b)**. On many V6 and V8 engines there are *two* knock sensors, one for each cylinder bank.

5.30c A typical Intake Air Temperature (IAT) sensor mounted on the air intake plenum. IAT sensors installed in the intake manifold plenum are usually screwed into place, so they offer a better seal against vacuum leaks than do sensors installed in the air intake duct

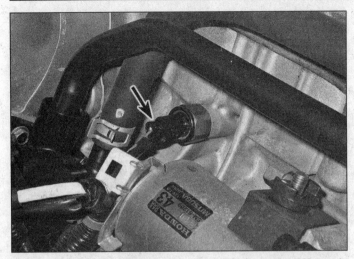

5.31a On a four-cylinder engine (and even on some V6s and V8s) the knock sensor is installed on the block (in the case of a V engine, there's usually one on each cylinder bank)

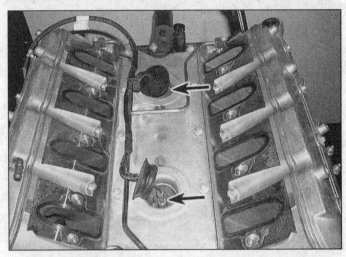

5.31b On some V6 and V8 engines the knock sensors are installed in the valley between the cylinder heads - you'll have to remove the intake manifold to access them

Manifold Absolute Pressure (MAP) sensor

The MAP sensor (see illustrations 5.32a and 5.32b), which is located on the intake manifold plenum or on top of the throttle body, monitors the pressure or vacuum downstream from the throttle plate, inside the intake manifold. The MAP sensor measures intake manifold pressure and vacuum on the absolute scale, i.e. from zero instead of from sea-level atmospheric pressure (14.7 psi). The MAP sensor converts the absolute pressure into a variable voltage signal that changes with the pressure. The PCM uses this data to determine engine load so that it can alter the ignition advance and fuel enrichment.

Manifold Absolute Pressure (MAP) sensors are used on many fuel injection systems as an alternative to, and sometimes in addition to, Volume Air Flow (VAF) or Mass Air Flow (MAF) sensors.

The idea behind a MAP sensor is that manifold absolute pressure is an indication of engine load. How does it work? A pressure sensor is connected to the intake manifold between the throttle plate and the intake valves. The sensor houses two diaphragm cells that expand and contract in accordance with changing pressure. The inside of one diaphragm cell is vented to the atmosphere; the space surrounding both cells is vented to intake manifold pressure. When manifold pressure goes up, the cells compress, and pull an iron core armature into a coil, changing the electrical signal to the PCM. A rising manifold-pressure indicates an increasing load, so the PCM increases the pulse-width of the injectors. This signal is an analog one, so it must be digitized by an A/D converter inside the PCM before it makes sense to the computer. When manifold pressure goes down, as it does at idle, for example, the diaphragm cells expand, pushing the core out of the coil. Now the analog voltage signal tells the PCM to reduce pulse-width, reducing the amount of fuel injected.

5.32a The Manifold Absolute Pressure (MAP) sensor is located somewhere on the intake manifold on most vehicles

5.32b Some MAP sensors are located right on the throttle body

5.33a The Mass Air Flow (MAF) sensor is located either on the air filter housing . . .

1	Electrical connector	3	MAF sensor
2	Mounting screws		

5.33b . . . between the air filter housing and the air intake duct . . .

1	Electrical connector	3	MAF sensor
2	Hose clamps		

Most manifold pressure sensors have a couple of corrective features to account for differences in temperature and altitude. The Intake Air Temperature (IAT) sensor signals the PCM to correct injector pulse width for colder, denser air. Altitude compensation is achieved by venting one cell to the atmosphere. In a part-load range, both manifold pressure and atmospheric pressure are reduced as the altitude increases, so the fuel injection signal must be adjusted for thinner air.

Some manufacturers no longer regard manifold-pressure sensing as a sufficiently accurate measurement of engine load. Many modern systems now measure airflow or air mass instead. But manifold pressure sensing is still widely used by GM, Chrysler, Honda, Toyota and other manufacturers. And some manufacturers equip their engine management systems with both MAP *and* MAF sensors.

Mass Air Flow (MAF) sensor

The MAF sensor **(see illustrations 5.33a, 5.33b and 5.33c)**, also known as a hot-wire sensor, is a black plastic or cast aluminum housing located in the intake tract somewhere between the air filter housing and the throttle body. (Some manufacturers, such as Mitsubishi, refer to the MAF sensor as the Volume Air Flow (VAF) sensor, but it's the same device.) If you remove the sensor for a better look, you'll see small platinum resistance wires suspended inside the cylinder. The wires are smaller in diameter than a human hair - about 70 micrometers, or less than 1/10 of a millimeter. Each wire looks - and is - delicate. It looks like it could break rather easily just from normal vibration. But in actual service, this type of sensor has proven more reliable than the old Bosch vane-type airflow sensor. An ingenious suspension system prevents the wires from snapping in two and a pair of mesh protective screens at either end of the sensor cylinder protect the wires from damage from incoming particulate matter as well as from backfires. In the unlikely event that a

5.33c . . . or somewhere in the air intake duct itself

1	Electrical connector	3	MAF sensor
2	Hose clamps		

wire should break, the engine will run - albeit in a limp-home mode - well enough to get you home. (You can simulate limp-home mode by unplugging the air-mass sensor connector on a warmed-up engine, then driving the vehicle).

The MAF sensor is completely electronic - there are no moving parts. It measures airflow as a function of the amount of current flowing through heated wires. It gets its hot-wire name from this heated-wire design. The MAF sensor has several significant advantages over the vane-type airflow sensor used on pre-OBD-II systems.

First, it measures air mass, or weight (in physics, mass and weight aren't exactly the same thing, but they're proportional, so for the purposes of this discussion, we'll use them more or less interchangeably). The air-fuel mixture ratio is really the ratio of the masses of the substances involved. A certain mass of fuel is mixed with a certain mass of air.

Unlike a MAP sensor, which measures the absolute pressure inside the intake manifold, measuring the air mass also eliminates the need for compensation sensors for air temperature and altitude. And eliminating compensation corrections simplifies the PCM program.

An air-mass sensor has no moving parts. The system monitors the cooling effect of intake air as it moves across the heated wires. Imagine a fan blowing across an electric heater. If the fan motor is set to its Low position, the cooling effect on the heater wires is minimal; turn the fan motor to its High position and the cooling effect increases. The control circuit uses this effect to measure how much air is passing over the hot wires. The wires are heated to a specific temperature differential that is 180-degrees F. above the incoming air when the ignition is turned on. As soon as air begins to flow over the wire, the wire cools. The control circuit applies more voltage to keep the wire at its original temperature differential. This creates a voltage signal that the PCM monitors. The greater the air flow, the more the wire cools and the greater the voltage signal.

A hot-wire sensor responds much more quickly than the hinged flap inside a vane-type airflow sensor. Changes in air mass are followed by corrected measurements within 1 to 3 milliseconds. The wire in a MAF sensor offers virtually zero resistance to the air moving past it. Even at maximum airflow, the drag on the wire, measured in milligrams, is insignificant. Air mass measurement by hot wire improves driveability, stability and reliability. Even racers use it!

Output shaft speed sensor

See *Input Shaft Speed (ISS) and Output Shaft Speed (OSS) sensors.*

Oxygen sensors

The oxygen sensor **(see illustration 5.34a)**, once referred to as a Lambda sensor (Bosch), an exhaust gas oxygen (EGO) sensor (US manufacturers) or simply an O_2 sensor, is the most important information sensor on a fuel-injected vehicle. The oxygen sensor compares the difference between the amount of oxygen in the exhaust and the amount of oxygen in the ambient air, and it expresses the results of this comparison as an analog voltage signal that varies between 0 and 1 volt.

An oxygen sensor is a galvanic battery that generates a small variable voltage signal in proportion to the difference between the oxygen content in the exhaust stream and the oxygen content in the ambient air. The PCM uses the voltage signal from the upstream oxygen sensor to maintain a "stoichiometric" air/fuel ratio of 14.7:1 by constantly adjusting the "on-time" of the fuel injectors. There are *two* oxygen sensors for each catalytic converter: one *upstream* sensor (ahead of the catalyst) and a *downstream* oxygen sensor (on or right behind the catalyst).

The oxygen sensor is based on the Lambda concept pioneered by the Robert Bosch Corporation. Lambda is the Greek symbol which engineers use to indicate the ratio of one number to another. When discussing the control of the air-fuel ratio, lambda refers to the ratio of excess air to stoichiometric air quantity. (That's why Bosch calls the oxygen sensor a lambda sensor).

When the maximum amount of available air is combined with fuel at the stoichiometric (ideal) air-fuel ratio of 14.7:1, there's no air left over, and there's no shortage of air. Lambda, therefore, equals 1. But if the mixture ratio is lean, say 15, 16 or 17:1, there's air left over after combustion. The lambda ratio of excess air to the ideal amount of air is now

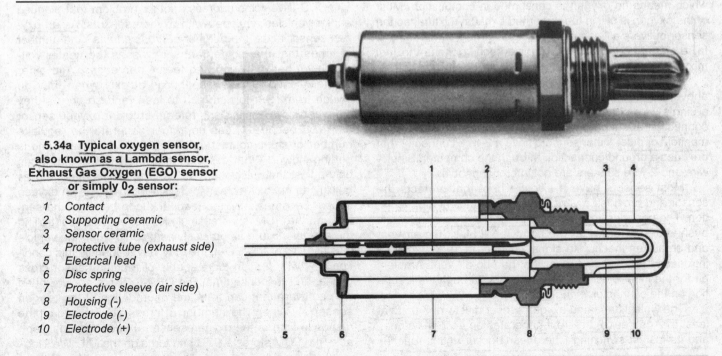

5.34a Typical oxygen sensor, also known as a Lambda sensor, Exhaust Gas Oxygen (EGO) sensor or simply O_2 sensor:

1   Contact
2   Supporting ceramic
3   Sensor ceramic
4   Protective tube (exhaust side)
5   Electrical lead
6   Disc spring
7   Protective sleeve (air side)
8   Housing (-)
9   Electrode (-)
10 Electrode (+)

greater than 1, say, 1.05, 1.09, 1.13, etc. And if the mixture is rich, say 12, 13 or 14.1, there's a shortage of air, so the lambda ratio is less than 1, say, 0.95, 0.91, 0.87, etc. If the air-fuel ratio is richer than 11.7:1 or leaner than 18:1 (lambda ratios of less than 0.8 or greater than 1.20, respectively) the engine won't run.

The oxygen sensor is really a galvanic battery that generates a low-voltage signal between 0.1 and 0.9 volt (100 to 900 millivolts). When oxygen content in the exhaust is low (rich mixture), sensor voltage is high (450 to 900 millivolts). When exhaust oxygen content is high (lean mixture), sensor voltage is low (100 to 450 millivolts). The oxygen sensor voltage changes fastest near a lambda ratio of 1 (air-fuel ratio of 14.7:1), making it ideal for maintaining a stoichiometric ratio.

The oxygen sensor consists of two platinum electrodes separated by a zirconium dioxide (ZrO_2) ceramic electrolyte. ZrO_2 attracts free oxygen ions, which are negatively charged. One electrode is exposed to ambient (outside) air through vents in the sensor shell and collects many O_2 ions, becoming a more negative electrode. The other electrode is exposed to exhaust gas and it too collects O_2 ions. But it collects fewer ions and becomes more positive, compared to the other electrode. When there's a large difference between the amount of oxygen in the exhaust and the amount of oxygen in the air (rich mixture), the negative oxygen ions on the outer electrode move to the positive inner electrode, creating a direct current. The sensor then develops a voltage between the two electrodes. When there is more oxygen in the exhaust (lean mixture), there is less difference between O_2 ions on the electrodes and a lower voltage.

The important thing to remember here is that an oxygen sensor measures oxygen; it doesn't measure air-fuel ratio. Which is one reason why the sensor, and the PCM, can be fooled. For example, let's say the engine misfires, which means no oxygen is consumed in combustion. Most of the oxygen is still in the unburned exhaust mixture, so the sensor delivers a "lean mixture" signal. The PCM reads this false signal and logically, but mistakenly, richens the fuel mixture!

All oxygen sensors work on the principle explained above, but construction details differ. Some sensors have a single-wire connector for the output signal. The ground connection exists between the sensor shell and the exhaust manifold or pipe. Other sensors have a 2-wire connector that provides a ground connection through the computer. Single-wire and 2-wire sensors are not interchangeable.

Most sensors have a silicone boot that protects the sensor and provides a vent opening for ambient air circulation. The boot position is important for these sensors. If it is pushed too far down on the body, it will block the air vent and create an inaccurate signal voltage. In 1986, Chrysler introduced an oxygen sensor that had no air vent. Ambient air for the inner electrode was absorbed through the insulation on the connector wiring.

The typical unheated oxygen sensor must warm up to at least 572-degrees F before it generates an accurate signal, and its fastest switching time doesn't occur until it reaches

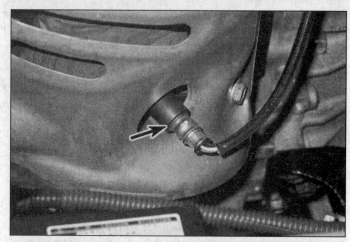

5.34b If you're lucky, the upstream oxygen sensor is screwed right into the exhaust manifold, where it's easy to reach

a temperature of about 1472-degrees F. This is why the engine management system must remain in open-loop fuel control when the engine is cold. Manufacturers solved this problem by installing heated oxygen sensors. Heated sensors have an extra wire that delivers 1 ampere or less current to the sensor electrodes whenever the ignition switch is turned to ON. Heated sensors warm up more quickly during cold-engine starts and they stay warm enough to provide an accurate voltage signal regardless of operating conditions. Heated oxygen sensors are a must on turbocharged vehicles, where the oxygen sensor is installed downstream from the turbo. The turbo absorbs so much of the heat energy in the exhaust that it prolongs sensor warm-up on a cold engine. On turbo vehicles, an unheated oxygen sensor can also cool off to a temperature below its minimum operating temperature during long periods of idling and low-speed operation. A heated oxygen sensor solves these problems.

OBD-II vehicles address another problem that plagued earlier vehicles equipped with oxygen sensors: As an oxygen sensor ages, the number of *cross counts* - the number of times that the oxygen sensor crosses the center voltage level between rich and lean - decreases. And older oxygen sensors don't respond as quickly when they do switch from lean to rich, rich to lean, and so on, as they did when new. Technicians refer to an older oxygen sensor as "lazy" because it can no longer generate the requisite number of cross counts and because its response time is getting slower. What this means to the PCM is that it can only adjust the pulse-width of the injectors as often and as quickly as the oxygen sensor tells it to do so. As an oxygen sensor becomes lazy, the feedback loop between the sensor and the PCM is increasingly less effective at controlling the air/fuel mixture as precisely as it could when the vehicle was new. Prior to OBD-II, the only way to identify this condition was with a scan tool capable of reading sensor cross counts and response time. But OBD-II PCMs are equipped with software that can track the degradation of the oxygen sensor(s). When the number of cross counts and/or the response time of the oxygen sensor(s) becomes unacceptable, the PCM stores a DTC and turns on the MIL. We'll look

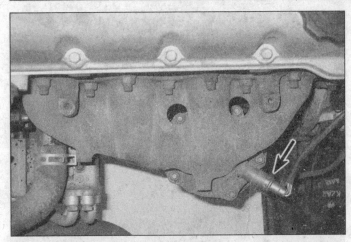

5.34c Some upstream oxygen sensors are located slightly below the exhaust manifold (but still above or on the upstream catalytic converter)

5.34d This is the post-catalyst oxygen sensor for an upstream catalyst, which on this vehicle is actually an integral component of the exhaust manifold. As you can see, this sensor would not be accessible from above; you'd have to raise the front of the vehicle to access it

at how it does this in more detail in the next chapter.

Each pre-catalyst oxygen sensor is installed in the exhaust manifold or in the exhaust pipe right below the exhaust manifold, but still above or on the upstream catalyst **(see illustrations 5.34b and 5.34c)** and each post-catalyst oxygen sensor is installed somewhere after of the upstream catalyst **(see illustration 5.34d)**. The pre-cat and post-cat oxygen sensors are usually easier to find and access on vehicles that *don't* use upstream catalysts because the catalysts are underneath the vehicle, where there's plenty of room to work **(see illustrations 5.34e and 5.34f)**.

Power Steering Pressure (PSP) switch

The PSP switch **(see illustrations 5.35a and 5.35b)** monitors the pressure inside the power steering system. When the pressure exceeds a certain threshold at idle or during low speed maneuvers, the switch sends a signal to

5.34e Here's a typical pre-catalyst oxygen sensor on a V6 that's using just one catalyst (and therefore just two oxygen sensors) . . .

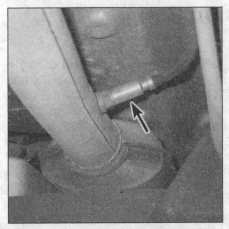

5.34f . . . and the post-catalyst sensor for the same V6 with one catalyst

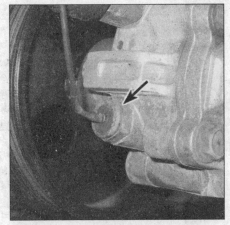

5.35a On some vehicles the Power Steering Pressure (PSP) switch is located right on the power steering pump

5.35b On other vehicles the PSP switch is located on the power steering high-pressure line

5.36 The Throttle Position (TP) sensor (A) is always mounted on the opposite side of the throttle body from the throttle linkage (B), and it's always installed concentric to the throttle plate shaft

the PCM, which raises the idle slightly to compensate for the extra load on the engine. The PSP switch is located on the power steering pump or on the power steering pressure line.

Throttle Position (TP) sensor

The TP sensor **(see illustration 5.36)** is a potentiometer that receives a constant voltage input from the PCM and sends back a voltage signal that varies in relation to the opening angle of the throttle plate inside the throttle body. This voltage signal tells the PCM when the throttle is closed, half-open, wide open or anywhere in between. The PCM uses this data, along with information from other sensors, to calculate injector pulse width (the interval of time during which an injector solenoid is energized by the PCM). The

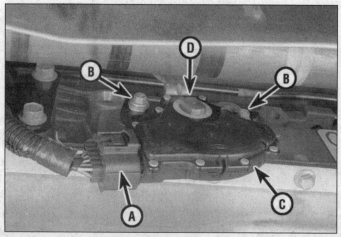

5.37b A typical Transmission Range (TR) sensor on an automatic transmission:

A	Electrical connector	C	TR sensor
B	Mounting bolts	D	Manual lever shaft

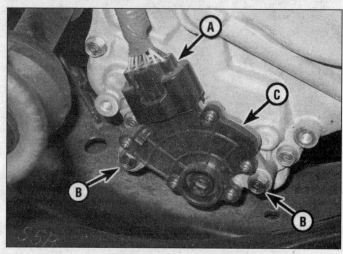

5.37a A typical Transmission Range (TR) sensor on an automatic transaxle:

A	Electrical connector	C	TR sensor
B	Mounting bolts		

TP sensor is located on the throttle body, on the end of the throttle plate shaft.

A potentiometer is a variable resistor with three terminals. A reference voltage is applied to one end of the resistor, and the other end is grounded. The third terminal is connected to a movable wiper, or contact, that slides across the resistor. Depending on the position of this sliding contact - near the supply end or the ground end of the resistor - return voltage will be high or low. Since the current through the resistor remains constant, so does the temperature. So the resistance doesn't change because of variations in temperature. The result is a constant voltage drop across the resistor so that the return voltage changes only in relation to sliding contact movement. A potentiometer-type TP sensor is both a load and a speed sensor. It tells the PCM not only the position of the throttle, but the speed at which it's being opened or closed.

Transmission Range (TR) sensor

The TR sensor **(see illustrations 5.37a and 5.37b)** is located at the manual lever on automatic transaxles and transmissions. The TR sensor functions like a conventional Park/Neutral Position (PNP) switch: it prevents the engine from starting in any gear other than Park or Neutral, and it closes the circuit for the back-up lights when the shift lever is moved to Reverse. The PCM also sends a voltage signal to the TR sensor, which uses a series of step-down resistors that act as a voltage divider. The PCM monitors the voltage output signal from the TR sensor, which corresponds to the position of the manual lever. Thus the PCM is able to determine the gear selected and is able to determine the correct pressure for the electronic pressure control system of the transaxle or transmission.

5.38a On manual transaxles, you'll find the Vehicle Speed Sensor (VSS) on top of the differential (which is located at the rear of the transaxle, where the axleshafts are connected to the transaxle)

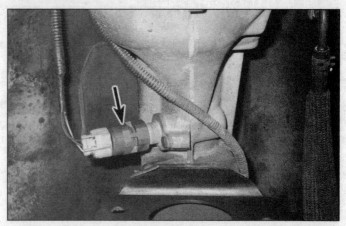

5.38b On manual transmissions, the Vehicle Speed Sensor (VSS) is usually located on the extension housing

Vehicle Speed Sensor (VSS)

The VSS **(see illustrations 5.38a and 5.38b)** is a magnetic pick-up coil or Hall Effect type switch that is driven by the differential. The VSS receives a 5.volt reference signal from the PCM and generates a pulsed output that the PCM uses to determine vehicle speed (the number of pulses per minute rises and falls in proportion to the speed). On many vehicles, the VSS is also the sending unit for the speedometer on the instrument cluster. The VSS is used on all manual transaxles and transmissions, and on some automatics. The VSS is located on top of the differential part of a transaxle or on the extension housing of a transmission.

Output actuators

The output actuators of an electronic engine management system - air injection system, EGR valve, EVAP canister purge valve, fuel injectors, idle air control system, ignition coil(s), etc. - are used by the PCM to keep everything running smoothly. These PCM-controlled devices are constantly adjusted by the PCM in order to keep the air/fuel ratio in the ideal stoichiometric ratio of 14.7:1 and to manage or minimize emissions such as unburned hydrocarbons and oxides of nitrogen. Using its information sensors, the PCM constantly monitors the operating conditions of the engine - load, speed, air density, temperature, etc. It processes this information, then commands its output actuators to come on, or go off, or change the frequency or duration of their on or off time, etc.

Air injection system

The air injection system, also known as the Air Injection Reaction (AIR) system, reduces carbon monoxide (CO) and hydrocarbon (HC) content in the exhaust gases by pumping fresh air into the hot exhaust gases leaving the exhaust ports. When outside air is mixed with the hot exhaust gases,

oxidation is increased, reducing the concentration of HC and CO. Oxidation is a process by which oxygen is added to certain harmful emissions (like CO and HC) in order to transform them into harmless substances like carbon dioxide (CO_2) and water (H_2O). This process takes place inside the *oxidation* catalyst, which is one of the two catalysts inside a Three-Way Catalyst (TWC). Some of the oxygen for this process is provided by the other half of the TWC, known as the *reduction* catalyst. The rest of the oxygen is supplied by the air injection system.

There are several typical versions of air injection used by various manufacturers. One system consists of a belt-driven air pump, a control valve **(see illustration 5.39a)**, one or two check valves and the rubber hoses connecting all of these components. Air is drawn into the pump, compressed, then expelled from the pump and routed to the control valve, which is actually a couple of valves inside the same housing (the diverter valve and the switching valve). When no additional air is needed in the exhaust manifold(s) and/or in

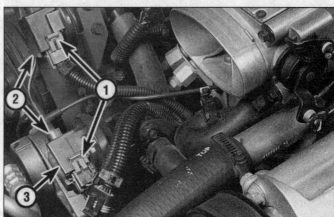

5.39a In some air injection systems, the PCM directs the control valve, which houses the diverter valve and the switching valve, to either dump air into the atmosphere through the diverter valve, or to send air through the switching valve to the check valves

1 Electrical connectors	3 Control valve
2 Vacuum lines	

5.39b Some air injection systems use an electric air pump instead of a belt-driven pump. In a conventional belt-driven air injection system, the pump runs all the time and the PCM decides when to send air to the exhaust manifold(s) or to the catalyst(s). On an air injection system with an electric pump, the air pump itself is turned on and off by the PCM

the oxidation catalyst(s), the PCM directs the diverter valve to dump the air into the atmosphere or into the air induction system. When air is needed for oxidation (during open-loop), the diverter valve sends the air to the switching valve, which routes the air through the check valve(s) to the exhaust manifold(s) or to the oxidation catalyst(s), depending on operating conditions. The check valves are designed so that air can only go through them in one direction; it cannot travel backward. As you might guess, the check valves are the first components to inspect if the air injection system malfunctions. Because they're the last line of defense against hot exhaust gases, they are usually the first parts to break in this system.

Some air injection systems use an air pressure relief valve instead of a control valve. In this type of system, holes in the air pressure relief valve prevent excess downstream pressure. When the pressure at the relief valve becomes excessive, it's vented into the atmosphere. The rest of the time, air goes through the pressure relief valve, then through the check valve(s), etc. just like the system previously described.

Some air injection systems use an electric air pump **(see illustration 5.39b)** instead of a belt-driven pump. This type of system consists of the air pump, an air pump solenoid, a shutoff valve, a couple of check valves and the hoses connecting these components. The air pump is an electrically driven device, the circuit for which is controlled by the air pump relay, which in turn is controlled by the PCM. When the PCM determines that engine coolant temperature, air temperature and engine rpm are all within the appropriate range, it energizes the air pump relay, which closes the circuit to the air pump and the air pump solenoid simultaneously. The air pump solenoid controls vacuum to the shutoff valve. When the PCM turns on the relay, a valve inside the air pump solenoid opens and intake manifold vacuum pulls up the shutoff valve diaphragm. When the shutoff valve diaphragm moves up, low-pressure air from the air pump

5.40a A typical EVAP canister purge valve installation on a four-cylinder engine (canister mounting bracket detached from cylinder head):

1	Electrical connector	4	EVAP canister purge
2	Hose clamps		valve
3	Mounting screws		

is pumped through a one-way check valve into the exhaust manifold. Another check valve, between the manifold vacuum supply pipe and the air pump solenoid, maintains vacuum to the solenoid for a specified interval of time when manifold vacuum decreases. This type of system never operates for more than a couple of minutes at a time, so it seldom malfunctions.

EVAP canister purge control solenoid valve

The EVAP canister purge control solenoid valve **(see illustrations 5.40a and 5.40b)**, or simply the purge valve, is located in the engine compartment, usually near the intake manifold. The EVAP purge valve is normally closed. But when ordered to do so by the PCM, it allows the fuel vapors

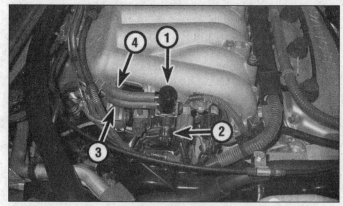

5.40b A typical EVAP canister purge valve installation on a V6 engine:

1	EVAP canister purge	3	EVAP hose
	valve	4	EVAP hose
2	Electrical connector		

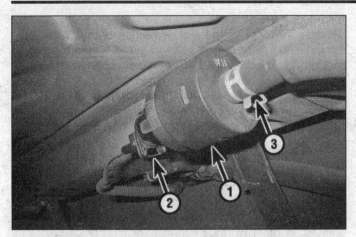

5.41a A typical EVAP canister vent shut valve (also referred to as a vent close valve) that's located near the EVAP canister, underneath the vehicle

1   *EVAP canister vent shut valve*
2   *Electrical connector*
3   *EVAP hose*

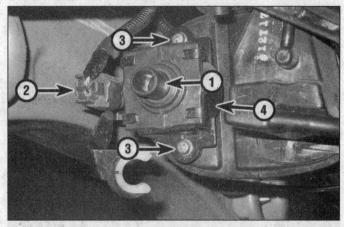

5.41b On most current EVAP systems, the canister vent shut valve is located right on the canister itself:

1   *EVAP hose pipe (hose disconnected for clarity)*
2   *Electrical connector*
3   *Mounting screws*
4   *EVAP canister vent shut valve*

that are stored in the EVAP canister to be drawn into the intake manifold, where they're mixed with intake air, then burned along with the normal air/fuel mixture, under certain operating conditions. Earlier purge valves were simply off or on, i.e. they were either turned off or, when turned on by the PCM, they allowed whatever vapors that were stored in the canister to be drawn into the intake manifold until they were gone. But the PCM *controls* the flow of vapors on most current purge valves so that EVAP vapors are admitted into the intake manifold only when it's appropriate and at a rate that doesn't upset the air/fuel mixture.

EVAP canister vent shut valve

The EVAP canister vent shut valve (see illustrations 5.41a and 5.41b) is located underneath the vehicle, usually near or on the EVAP canister. The PCM-controlled vent shut valve is normally closed but it opens to allow fresh outside air to enter the EVAP canister when the canister is being purged. On OBD-II vehicles with the ability to perform leak and pressure tests, the vent shut valve also closes and seals off the EVAP system whenever the tests are being conducted by the PCM. (We'll look at the OBD-II EVAP system monitor in more detail in the next chapter.)

Exhaust Gas Recirculation (EGR) valve

When the engine is put under a load (hard acceleration, passing, going up a steep hill, pulling a trailer, etc.), combustion chamber temperature increases. When combustion chamber temperature exceeds 2500-degrees Fahrenheit, excessive amounts of oxides of nitrogen (NOx) are produced. NOx is a precursor of photochemical smog. When combined with hydrocarbons (HC), other "reactive organic compounds" (ROCs) and sunlight, it forms ozone, nitrogen

dioxide, nitrogen nitrate and other nasty stuff. The PCM-controlled EGR valve allows exhaust gases to be recirculated back into the intake manifold where they dilute the incoming air/fuel mixture, which lowers the combustion chamber temperature and decreases the amount of NOx produced during high-load conditions. The EGR valve is connected to the exhaust manifold by an external tube or by an internal passage in the cylinder head that routes a small portion of exhaust gases to the valve (see illustrations 5.42a and 5.42b). The EGR valve is usually located on or near the

5.42a A typical Exhaust Gas Recirculation (EGR) valve installation that's connected to the exhaust manifold by an external pipe

1   *Electrical connector*
2   *EGR valve mounting bolts*
3   *EGR valve*
4   *Threaded fitting for external pipe connecting exhaust manifold to EGR valve mounting base (part of upper intake manifold on this vehicle)*

5.42b An EGR valve installation that *doesn't* use an external EGR pipe. Instead, the EGR valve sits right on top of a coolant casting with an internal passage from the exhaust manifold that admits exhaust gases directly into the EGR valve from underneath. Another internal passage routes the exhaust gases to the intake manifold

1   *Electrical connector*
2   *EGR valve mounting bolts*
3   *EGR valve*

intake manifold, where it needs to send recirculated exhaust gases. But it can be mounted on the intake manifold, on a mounting bracket adjacent to the intake manifold, on an engine coolant casting or directly on the cylinder head.

Fuel injectors

The fuel injectors **(see illustrations 5.14a, 5.14b and 5.14c)**, which spray a fine mist of fuel into the intake ports, where it is mixed with incoming air, are turned on and off under PCM control. The injector solenoids are the most important output actuators in an electronic fuel injection system. Two factors influence the quality and accuracy of their delivery: *when they're opened* and *how long they're open*. For more information about the injectors, see *Fuel injectors* earlier in this chapter.

Timing the injection system

Manufacturers have employed several different methods of firing (opening) the fuel injectors. In the non-electronic Bosch Continuous Injection System (CIS), also referred to as K-Jetronic, the injectors were *not* timed - they simply sprayed fuel all the time. How much fuel they sprayed was determined by the control pressure of the fuel delivery system, which was continuously adjusted in proportion to the amount of air entering the engine. Effective, but not particularly efficient.

Early electronic fuel injection systems employed a strategy known as *group injection*. In this type of system, half of the injectors were fired at the same time. For example, on a four-cylinder engine, two injectors were fired during one crankshaft revolution, and then the other two injectors were

fired during the next crank revolution. On a V8 engine, four injectors fired during the first revolution of the crank; then the other four fired on the next go-round. When a group of two, or four, injectors fired, they fired simultaneously. When a group of injectors fires in a group injection system, clouds of injected fuel vapor waited momentarily in each intake port for the intake valve to open because not all the intake valves served by that group were going to be opening at the same time.

Another early injection timing system was known as *simultaneous double-fire* injection. In a simultaneous double-fire system, all the injectors were fired together as one big group every crankshaft revolution. But only half of the fuel needed by each cylinder was injected each time its injector opened. In other words, each injector fired twice before its corresponding intake valve opened to admit the air/fuel mixture. Again, as in a group injection system, the injected fuel vapors formed a cloud outside their respective valve while they wait for it to open. Simultaneous double-fire systems used less computer power than sequential systems, yet still managed to deliver very good performance and response. The only disadvantage to this system was that the fuel pressure in the fuel rail had a tendency to drop when all the injectors opened at once. The addition of a fuel accumulator to the system usually solved this problem.

All modern electronic fuel injection systems fire (open) the injectors in firing order sequence. This system, which is the only type of system you will encounter on an OBD-II vehicle, is known as *sequential* fuel injection. In a sequential system, the injectors are fired one at a time, in the spark plug firing order. Each fuel injector delivers fuel just outside its assigned intake valve. Fuel delivery is timed to occur immediately before, during or after intake valve opening, depending on engine rpm and intake manifold air velocity. This system currently produces the highest performance and fuel efficiency and the lowest emissions.

Fuel injector pulse width and duty cycle

The PCM controls injector on-time, known as *pulse width* **(see illustration 5.43)**, by opening and closing the ground path for each injector solenoid. Pulse width is the length of time - measured in milliseconds - during which the injector solenoid is energized. The PCM alters injector pulse width in relation to the amount of fuel that the engine needs. It takes into account such factors as airflow, air temperature, throttle position, coolant temperature, oxygen content in the exhaust, crankshaft position, vehicle speed, and even fuel temperature. The PCM samples these conditions many times a second, so the pulse width changes constantly. A short pulse width delivers less fuel, a longer pulse width, more. Basically, when the oxygen sensor detects a rich condition in the exhaust gas stream, the PCM shortens the pulse width to lean out the air-fuel mixture; when a lean condition is detected, the PCM lengthens the pulse width to enrich the mixture. But keep in mind that this basic feedback loop is also influenced by the other variables mentioned above.

T = Complete Cycle Time
t = Duty Cycle Time (Pulse Width)

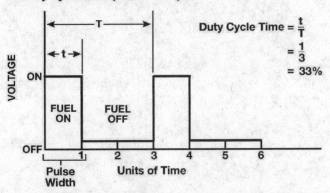

$$\text{Duty Cycle Time} = \frac{t}{T}$$
$$= \frac{1}{3}$$
$$= 33\%$$

SHORT DUTY CYCLE (PULSE WIDTH), MINIMUM FUEL INJECTION

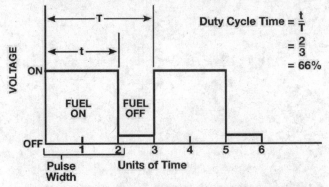

$$\text{Duty Cycle Time} = \frac{t}{T}$$
$$= \frac{2}{3}$$
$$= 66\%$$

LONG DUTY CYCLE (PULSE WIDTH), MAXIMUM FUEL INJECTION

10206-5-43 HAYNES

5.43 Pulse width is the length of time - measured in milliseconds - during which the injector solenoid is energized. The pulse width is controlled by the PCM, which turns the ground path for the solenoid on and of

The pulse width is related to the *duty cycle*. The duty cycle is the ratio of injector on-time to total on-and-off time. In other words, it's a variable percentage of one complete injector operating cycle. A simple example will make this relationship clearer: Let's say that the pulse width is 1 millisecond and the total cycle time is 3 milliseconds. Therefore, the duty cycle is the pulse width divided by the total cycle time, or 1/3, or 33 percent. Another example: The pulse width is 2 milliseconds and the total cycle time is 3 milliseconds. So the duty cycle is 2/3, or 66 percent. The duty cycle changes in response to changes in engine loads and in response to the amount of oxygen present in the exhaust stream. The pulse width and the total cycle time change in relation to engine speed. The higher the engine rpm, the higher the frequency of the pulse width and the total cycle time. In other words, as engine rpm goes up, the time available for pulse width and total cycle time shortens. To keep from getting confused, just remember that pulse width and total cycle times are always expressed as units of time (milliseconds), while duty cycle is always expressed as a percentage of the total cycle time.

Idle Air Control (IAC) valve

The IAC valve (**see illustrations 5.44a and 5.44b**) controls the amount of air allowed to bypass the throttle plate when the throttle plate is at its (nearly closed) idle position. The IAC valve is controlled by the PCM. When the engine is placed under an additional load at idle (high power steering pressure or running the air conditioning compressor during low-speed maneuvers, for example), the engine can run roughly, stumble and even stall. To prevent this from happening, the PCM opens the IAC valve to increase the idle speed enough to overcome the extra load imposed on the engine.

Ignition coils

The ignition coils are under the control of the Powertrain Control Module (PCM). There is no separate ignition control module on an OBD-II vehicle. Instead, "coil drivers" (transistors) inside the PCM turn the ground path for the primary side of the coils on and off.

5.44a Some Idle Air Control (IAC) valves are mounted remotely, somewhere near the throttle body and the intake manifold plenum

5.44b Some IAC valves are mounted directly on the throttle body

Notes

6 OBD-II monitors

The monitors are what makes OBD-II different from OBD-I

The OBD-II system is far more complex than its OBD-I predecessor, not because of its hardware but because of its software. Pop the hood on any vehicle built to comply with OBD-II regulations and see if you can find any differences between it and your last OBD-I vehicle. Other than the phrase "OBD-II certified" on the Vehicle Emission Control Information (VECI) decal or label, you probably didn't find much, right? That's because what makes a vehicle OBD-II compliant isn't about the hardware, it's about the program inside the PCM. Sure, if you look carefully, you might notice that there's one or more additional oxygen sensors. So, yeah, there is a little more hardware on an OBD-II vehicle than there was on an OBD-I vehicle, but most of the information sensors are the same ones used on older vehicles. Each sensor still monitors some engine condition: coolant temperature, airflow, engine speed, throttle position, etc.

But OBD-II makes greater utilization of the sensors because it also uses their inputs to calculate whether or not they are functioning properly and whether or not the engine's emissions are within the range mandated by the federal government. Think of OBD-II as an on-board emission analyzer. It analyzes the engine management system by comparing the inputs from various sensors, looking up and comparing these inputs to what the program says that they should be, then calculates whether or not those values are logical. In other words, do they make sense when the PCM compares them to each other, and to the overall operation of the engine management system? It also directly analyzes the emissions of the engine by measuring the oxygen content of the exhaust gas downstream of the catalytic converter(s). The PCM uses *monitors*, which are a series of tightly controlled tests, conducted under very specific criteria, to determine whether all the sensors are functioning correctly and working together to keep the engine within the government-mandated limits of allowable emissions. In this chapter we'll look at the monitors, but first let's summarize the different strategies employed by OBD-I and OBD-II, so that you can see why the PCM needs monitors. Before we look at OBD-II monitors, let's summarize the differences between OBD-I and OBD-II.

OBD-I

OBD-I was a passive system. Designed to detect circuit malfunctions in the engine management system that caused driveability problems, OBD-I waited patiently for a sensor circuit to go out of range. If a monitored sensor produced a low-voltage, high-voltage, out-of-range or flat (steady) electrical input to the PCM, or if it produced no signal voltage at all, the PCM would set one or more Diagnostic Trouble Codes (DTCs) and turn on that Check Engine or Service Engine Soon light. When the Check Engine light came on, you had to extract, then look up, any stored DTC(s), grab your multimeter, track down the cause of the problem, repair it and erase the DTC(s). As soon as the problem was fixed, the engine ran smoothly again and driveability was restored. Some of the more sophisticated OBD-I systems also monitored the amount of fuel *trim* (correction) needed to maintain closed-loop operation. If fuel trim became so excessive that it suggested an extremely rich or lean condition, the system set a code. OBD-I was an impressive engineering achievement, and it lives on today in every OBD-II vehicle. Nevertheless, there were some problems with OBD-I.

Even when it worked just as it was supposed to, OBD-I really only monitored *electrical* malfunctions. For example, the engine could be running fine during closed-loop operation, with the oxygen sensor measuring the amount of oxygen in the exhaust stream and the PCM making the necessary adjustments to keep the air/fuel ratio at the stoichiometric ratio of 14.7:1. But the computer is only looking at the electrical activity in the feedback loop between the oxygen sensor and itself. At some point down the road - usually after *many* miles - a catalytic converter can become so contaminated that it no longer functions *chemically*. When the catalyst finally ceases to function on an OBD-I vehicle, the engine may continue to run well, so the driver is blissfully unaware that the tailpipe emissions have gone *way* up. But OBD-I is unable to detect catalyst deterioration. It just looks at the voltage signal from the oxygen sensor. Now suppose that the catalyst fails just after a biennial smog inspection. If no other malfunction brings the vehicle into a dealer service department or independent garage in the meantime, it will be almost *two years* before the defective catalyst is diagnosed and replaced.

OBD-II

An OBD-II PCM can also detect system electrical glitches just like an OBD-I computer, but it does far more than that. Because it was designed to detect system malfunctions that cause *emission* problems, it has to be able to detect *chemical* and *mechanical* problems as well. The information sensors and output actuators employed in OBD-II systems aren't that different from the hardware used in OBD-I systems. There are a few more information sensors on an OBD-II vehicle. For example, a four-cylinder OBD-II vehicle has at least two heated oxygen sensors, and a V6 or a V8 has at least three (one in each exhaust manifold, ahead of the catalytic converter, and one behind the catalyst) **(see illustration 6.1)**. But as we said earlier, it's the *software* that really distinguishes OBD-II from OBD-I.

Let's look at the dead catalyst scenario. On an OBD-II vehicle, there are two oxygen sensors for each catalyst, one upstream from the catalyst and another downstream from the cat. The upstream catalyst serves the same function as an oxygen sensor on an OBD-I vehicle. It produces a low-voltage signal (between 0 and 0.9 volts) that the PCM uses to determine whether there is too little or too much oxygen

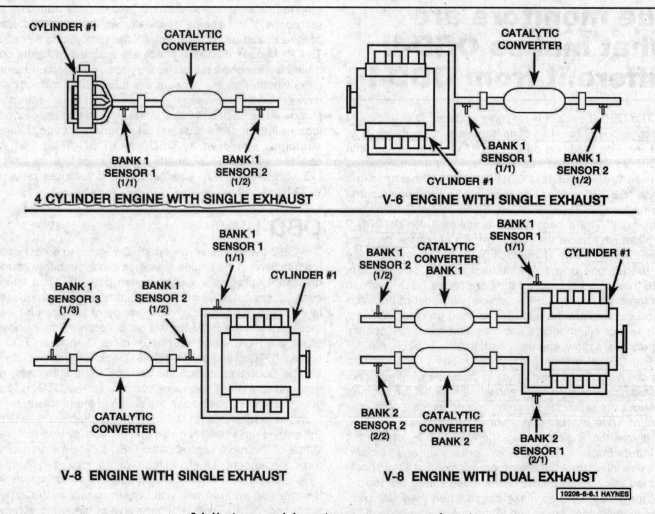

4 CYLINDER ENGINE WITH SINGLE EXHAUST

V-6 ENGINE WITH SINGLE EXHAUST

V-8 ENGINE WITH SINGLE EXHAUST

V-8 ENGINE WITH DUAL EXHAUST

10206-6-6.1 HAYNES

6.1 Upstream and downstream oxygen sensor layouts

in the exhaust gases so that the PCM can alter the pulse-width of the fuel injectors accordingly. The downstream oxygen sensor also works just like a conventional oxygen sensor, except that its signal, when put on an oscilloscope, looks very, very "lazy." In fact, if the catalyst is doing its job, the output from the downstream oxygen sensor should look almost like a flat line. Why? Because the catalyst is converting harmful substances in the exhaust gases (HC, CO and NOx) into less harmful substances like CO_2 and H_2O, so the downstream sensor shouldn't be detecting too much or too little oxygen. The PCM compares the voltage inputs from the upstream and downstream oxygen sensors to determine how well the catalyst is working. When the catalyst eventually begins to deteriorate, the frequency of cross-counts from the downstream sensor will begin to increase (for an explanation of "cross-counts," see *Oxygen sensor monitor* later in this Chapter). The PCM's program or map has a threshold "line in the sand" with respect to the number of cross-counts that it will accept from the downstream sensor. When the cross-counts from the downstream sensor exceed that threshold, the PCM sets a Diagnostic Trouble Code (DTC) and turns on the Malfunction Indicator Light (MIL). In other words, by comparing the input signals from two sensors, an OBD-II PCM can infer a *chemical* problem. So instead of belching HC, CO and NOx out the tailpipe for a year or two, the owner takes the vehicle to a repair facility, has the catalyst replaced and gets that annoying MIL turned off. Or, if the owner is a confident Do-It-Yourselfer, he/she will attempt the diagnosis and carry out the repair. With the current generation of code readers and scan tools available, it's entirely possible.

Note that OBD-II arrives at the cause of the problem *indirectly*. Using the logic of its map (program), it infers the cause of the problem by comparing data from two or more different sensor signals. This is another difference between OBD-I and OBD-II. OBD-I was a *passive* system that just sat there and waited until some sensor electrical circuit jumped out of range at which point it set and code and turned on the Check Engine light. Unlike OBD-I, OBD-II is an *active* system. It doesn't just sit there and wait for the phone to ring like OBD-I. Instead, it constantly compares the voltage signals from various sensors and decides whether they make sense in the context of the Big Picture. And if they don't, it sets a DTC and turns on the MIL.

OBD-II has the capability of recognizing and storing intermittent faults or glitches in sensor data that falls outside of the expected data range, and will store this information as a *pending* or *maturing* code. If the questionable event happens again within a certain amount of time (or *drive cycles*), a full-on DTC will set in the PCM's memory.

Another OBD-II feature is its ability to store and retrieve *freeze frame data*. With the use of a scan tool, the data stored in this single frame lets you view the conditions under which a fault occurs and will help you determine why a DTC was set. When one of the PCM's monitors detects a fault in some monitored component or system, it sets a Diagnostic Trouble Code (DTC). And it also saves in memory a freeze frame or *snapshot* of the important engine operating condi-

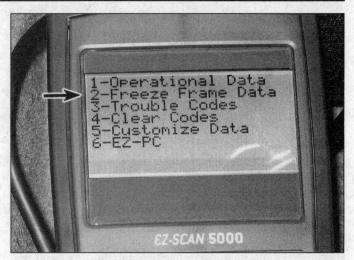

6.2 A scan tool like this one allows you to view freeze frame data

tions (sensor circuit voltage, for example) at the moment the DTC was set **(see illustration 6.2)**. This freeze frame data is extremely helpful when diagnosing what might be wrong with an engine management component or circuit because it can help you pinpoint which component, sensor, circuit, etc. jumped out of range, shorted, grounded, went open, etc. at the moment that the DTC was set.

Okay, now that you know what OBD-II can do, let's look at how it does it.

Monitor terminology and concepts

The *monitors* are PCM-conducted tests, which are carried out under very specific conditions to verify that all of the sensors in a subsystem are working together to keep tailpipe emissions legal. The OBD-II monitors are:

- Catalyst efficiency monitor
- Comprehensive Component Monitor (CCM)
- Evaporative emissions system (EVAP) monitor
- Exhaust Gas Recirculation (EGR) system monitor
- Fuel system monitor
- Heated catalyst monitor
- Heated oxygen sensor monitor
- Misfire detection monitor
- Secondary Air Injection (AIR) monitor

Three of the monitors - the comprehensive component, fuel system and misfire detection monitors - run continuously. These three monitors are always running as long as the vehicle is being operated under manufacturer-specified conditions known as *enabling criteria*. The other monitors - catalyst, evaporative emissions, exhaust gas recirculation, oxygen sensor and secondary air - are run once per *trip*. When they run during each trip depends, again, on certain enabling criteria, specified by the manufacturer, which must be present. Before we get into the monitors in more detail, let's look more closely at these two terms and some other terms and concepts related to the monitors.

Enabling criteria

The monitors are designed to run only under conditions very specifically defined by the manufacturer. These conditions are known as the enabling criteria. The conditions that must be present for each monitor to run are specific to each test. For example, the heated oxygen sensor monitor cannot test the oxygen sensor voltage or cross-counts until the engine is warm enough to enter closed-loop operation. The EGR monitor can't test the EGR system at idle because the EGR is closed at idle. The catalyst monitor can't test the efficiency of the catalytic converter until the upstream and downstream oxygen sensors, and the catalytic converter, are warmed up and the engine is in closed-loop operation. And so on.

The PCM cannot run a monitor on a component or system until it is up and running, nor can it monitor that component or system when the engine operating conditions are unacceptable. Otherwise, the component or system might flunk the test, either because the test is inaccurate or because the engine operating conditions aren't conducive to running the monitor at that time. So the PCM doesn't run the monitor until *all* of the enabling criteria are present. When we look at the monitors in more detail in a moment, you'll notice that some enabling criteria are universal, i.e. they apply to all vehicles. Other enabling criteria are manufacturer-specific, i.e. they apply only to a specific make and model.

Trips

The monitors are run by the PCM at some point during a *trip*, which in "OBD-II talk" means something quite different than an OBD-I trip. In OBD-I, a trip simply consisted of starting the engine, running it for a certain amount of time, then turning it off. In OBD-II, the definition of a trip depends on which monitor the PCM is going to run. So we could say that an OBD-II trip consists of starting the engine, running it in such a manner and under such conditions that all of the enabling criteria are present to run the particular monitor that the PCM wants to run, then turning off the engine. Again, always keep in mind that *the trip definition depends on the monitor that the PCM wants to run*. It's entirely possible that during a short trip to the store, the enabling criteria might be present for some monitors but not for others.

Certain types of failures can turn on the MIL in one trip. For example, the instant that the misfire monitor detects a serious misfire, or the CCM detects an electrical malfunction in a sensor circuit, the PCM turns on the MIL immediately. Other monitors won't turn on the MIL on the first trip. If they detect a failure, they store it in PCM memory. When the PCM stores the first occurrence of a two-trip fault in its memory, this is known as a "maturing" fault. A maturing fault doesn't reach maturity - and the MIL won't come on - unless the fault is detected again during the next consecutive trip.

If the fuel and misfire monitors detect a failure, the PCM notes the failure but it doesn't automatically set a DTC. Instead, it watches and waits for a repeat performance to occur under similar conditions (same load, engine temperature, engine speed, etc.). Some OBD-II technicians refer to this second similar set of circumstances as a "similar conditions window." If the same fuel or misfire failure occurs *even one more time during the next 80 trips*, the PCM will set a DTC. As soon as the PCM stores at DTC and turns on the MIL, it also turns on a *trip counter*, then it keeps track of the number of trips made once the fault has been noticed. If the fault isn't detected again during the next three trips, the PCM turns off the MIL. However, if the requisite enabling criteria for the fuel or misfire monitor are not present during the next three trips, the MIL stays on. In other words, the PCM is looking for three consecutive trips with the enabling criteria present - and the fault absent - before it will turn off the MIL.

Just because the MIL goes out doesn't mean that any stored DTCs are erased. The DTC and its freeze frame remain in PCM memory - and can be extracted from memory with a scan tool - even when the PCM turns off the MIL. However, if you erase any stored DTC(s) with a scan tool, the DTC(s) and freeze frame data are gone forever.

The Diagnostic Executive

At the beginning of this chapter, we summarized the differences between OBD-I and OBD-II. In that summary we mentioned that OBD-II arrives at the cause of a problem *indirectly* using the logic of its program to infer the cause of the problem by comparing the signals from two or more different sensors. For example, even though OBD-II doesn't actually *know* that a catalyst is contaminated, it can infer this conclusion indirectly by comparing the voltage signals from the upstream and downstream oxygen sensors. Of course, if the PCM were to run a monitor of these sensors before either of them was fully warmed up or before the engine was fully warmed up and in closed loop, it would be a meaningless test. So neither the oxygen sensor monitor nor the catalyst monitor can be run by the PCM until *all* of the conditions needed to run these monitors are present.

It's the job of the *Diagnostic Executive* to make sure that the enabling criteria necessary to run each monitor are present and to decide the order in which the monitors are to be run and the correct time to run them. It must also make sure that the monitors don't interfere or conflict with each other or affect the vehicle's performance. Think of the Diagnostic Executive as the dispatcher for the OBD-II system.

One of the things that the Diagnostic Executive *doesn't* want to do is to store a DTC and turn on the MIL frivolously. Most people have better things to do with their time than taking their vehicle to the dealer every other week to have the MIL turned off, only to find that it came on because someone forgot to screw the gas cap on the fuel filler neck. So even when the Diagnostic Executive does have to store a DTC and turn on the MIL, it also works hard to get that light turned off as quickly as possible. After three good trips, the Diagnostic Executive will ask the PCM to turn off the MIL. When that happens, the PCM fires up the *warm-up counter*. Once the warm-up counter starts, it adds one to the current number of warm-ups every time that the PCM verifies another completed *warm-up* (see below). As long as the fault doesn't reoccur during - let's say - the next 40 warm-ups, the DTC (and freeze frame data) is erased when the warm-up counter reaches 40. Some faults - fuel and misfire faults, for example - must not reoccur for 80 consecutive successful warm-ups before the DTC and freeze frame data are erased. (40 and 80 warm-ups are typical targets, but keep in mind that these numbers will vary from one manufacturer to another.)

Warm-ups

In OBD-II talk, warm-up doesn't just mean starting the engine and warming it up. A warm-up is characterized by two specific requirements: After the engine is started, the coolant temperature must reach 160-degrees Fahrenheit AND the PCM must see an increase of 40-degrees or more in coolant temperature. In other words, if you started an

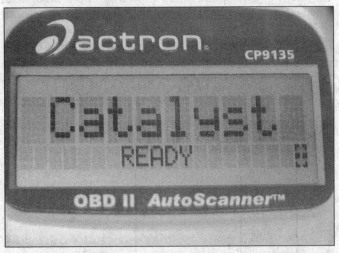

6.3a This handy code reader is small, but is capable of displaying the readiness status of the monitors

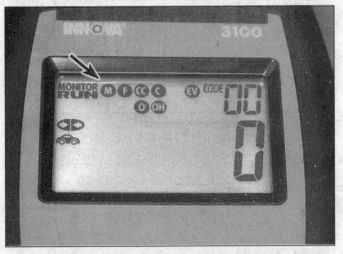

6.3b This code reader displays monitor readiness status in the form of small icons

engine that was already 130-degrees and drove the vehicle until the engine coolant temperature was 160-degrees, that would not constitute a bona fide warm-up in OBD-II, because even though the engine reached the 160-degree threshold, it didn't increase at least 40-degrees. But if you started an engine that was 120-degrees and drove the vehicle until the coolant temperature reached 160-degrees, that would be a legitimate warm-up.

The Diagnostic Executive has its priorities

The PCM must run some of the monitors in a very specific sequence because it often needs information from one monitor before it can run another monitor. So it establishes test priorities using the following three strategies:

Pending

If the PCM finds that a sensor that it needs to run a certain monitor is defective for some reason, the Diagnostic Executive won't run the test *pending* the repair or replacement of the sensor or sensor circuit. For example, if a DTC for one of the oxygen sensors is already stored in the PCM, the Diagnostic Executive won't run the catalyst monitor until the sensor is replaced.

Conflict

The Diagnostic Executive realizes that if two monitors are running at the same time, there could be a *conflict*. So, it prevents one monitor from running while allowing the other monitor to run first. For instance, the catalyst monitor will not run if the EGR monitor is already in progress, because the EGR monitor energizes the EGR solenoid valve, which dilutes the intake charge, which affects the normal stoichiometric air/fuel ratio of 14.7:1. The Diagnostic Executive will wait until the EGR monitor has completed its testing, and then and *only* then will it run the catalyst monitor.

Suspend

The Diagnostic Executive might *suspend* one monitor until another monitor has been run and has received a passing grade. If the Diagnostic Executive knows that it needs a correctly functioning oxygen sensor before it can run the catalyst monitor, it will suspend the catalyst monitor until the oxygen sensor monitor has run successfully.

Readiness flags

IF the vehicle is started and driven in such a manner that it satisfies all of the enabling criteria needed to run all of the monitors, and IF it passes all of the tests, the Diagnostic Executive puts a "check mark" next to each monitor to indicate that they've passed. These check marks are often referred to as *readiness flags*.

Before OBD-II can pass as a system, each monitored subsystem must run and pass. Good code readers and scan tools can display the *readiness status* of the monitors **(see illustrations 6.3a, 6.3b and 6.3c)**. The readiness status display lists all of the monitors and indicates which ones have run successfully, which ones are pending, etc. If

6.3c This scan tool is showing that not all of the monitors have been run yet. It's either time for another drive cycle, or a problem in the OBD-II system is preventing a monitor from being run

from running and passing. For example, if the readiness status display indicates that the catalyst and oxygen sensor monitors are both pending, it could indicate a problem that's preventing the oxygen sensor monitor from running, which you can quickly verify by noting whether an oxygen sensor DTC has been set by the PCM. (As we said earlier, the catalyst monitor can't run until the oxygen sensor monitor has run and passed.)

Scan tools that can display the readiness status of the monitors can also reset (erase) the monitor readiness flags. Powering down the system will also erase all readiness flags from the PCM's memory. In either case, the system will then need to see an entire *Drive Cycle* (see below) in order to run all of the monitors successfully.

The OBD-II Drive Cycle and the Federal Test Procedure (FTP)

In order to run all of the monitors and set all of the readiness flags, the vehicle must be driven through a complete OBD-II *Drive Cycle* **(see illustration 6.4)**. The drive cycle is similar, though not identical, to the Federal test Procedure (FTP). However, both tests share some important features. If you're unfamiliar with the FTP, the following brief overview

you're trying to troubleshoot or repair the system, the readiness status display on your scan tool is a helpful diagnostic tool because the status of the monitors can offer clues about some conflict that might be preventing a particular monitor

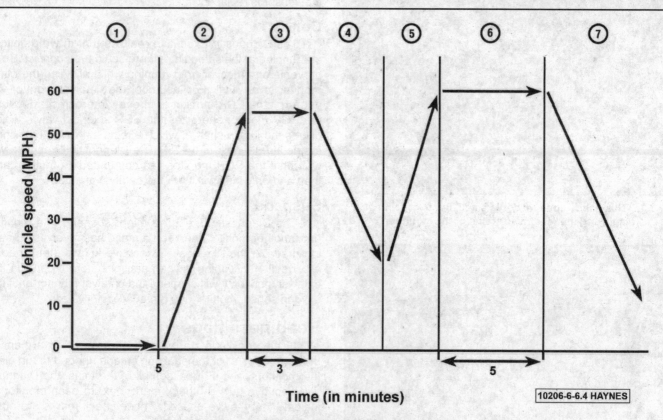

6.4 Example of a "typical" OBD-II drive cycle

1 Cold start (coolant below 122-degrees F), followed by a 5 to 8 minute warm-up at idle
2 Accelerate to 55 mph at 1/2 throttle
3 Steady cruise at 55 mph for 3 minutes
4 Coast down to 20 mph without touching the brake or clutch
5 Accelerate to 60 mph at 3/4 throttle
6 Steady cruise at 60 mph for 5 minutes
7 Second deceleration, no brake or clutch

will familiarize you with how it works - and will demonstrate why the OBD-II Drive Cycle is important.

The Federal Test Procedure (FTP)

In the FTP, the vehicle is driven and its fuel efficiency is measured. Then it's refueled and the Evaporative Emissions Control (EVAP) system is tested. Then the vehicle's emissions are recorded under a full range of engine speed and load combinations while the vehicle is driven on a dynamometer. (If you live in a state that requires that all vehicles be tested biennially on a dyno with a pair of rollers in the floor onto which you place the drive wheels (see illustration 6.5), then you're probably already familiar with this test.) Finally, the vehicle is put inside a climate-controlled, sealed room where other tests are conducted, most predominantly the effectiveness of the EVAP system.

The dynamometer test is of particular relevance to the OBD-II Drive Cycle because it simulates the same sort of driving conditions - acceleration, cruise and deceleration - that the vehicle will encounter in the real world. This type of test is referred to as a "loaded-mode" drive cycle because the dyno rollers make the engine work against resistance forces similar to those it will face when the vehicle is actually driven.

The FTP is an important step in verifying the compliance of new vehicles. Unfortunately, it's a one-time test conducted on a random sampling of new makes and models. So even if a vehicle is certified to meet certain emission standards at the time that it's sold, there's no guarantee that every emission system and component will keep running smoothly until the first smog test, which, depending on the state, could be two to four years after the vehicle is purchased. What was needed was some way to test the vehicle continuously during those long intervals between smog tests.

The OBD-II drive cycle

With the advent of OBD-II it became possible to *test each vehicle every time that it was driven.* The OBD-II Drive Cycle is similar, though not identical, to the Federal Test Procedure (FTP). Both are designed to test the system under a wide range of operating conditions that are considered a part of normal vehicle operation. It takes about 12 to 15 minutes to complete the entire Drive Cycle. A typical OBD-II Drive Cycle consists of:

1) Cold start (coolant below 122 degrees F.)
2) Five to eight-minute warm-up and idle period
3) First acceleration to 55 mph at half-throttle with the air conditioning turned off
4) First steady cruise at 55 mph for three minutes
5) First deceleration to 20 mph
6) Second acceleration, this time at 3/4-throttle to 60 mph
7) Second steady cruise at 60 mph for five minutes
8) Second deceleration (without applying the clutch or brake pedal)

During an OBD-II drive cycle all of the conditions will be present for the Diagnostic Executive to run all of the monitors. In the tests listed above, note that the engine is warmed up and driven under the typical conditions that it would encoun-

6.5 Typical smog station dyno

ter in daily driving. This allows the monitors to test all of the following:

During a **cold start**, the PCM examines the intake air and engine coolant temperature signals to verify that the engine is indeed cold (typically 122-degrees F or less).

During the **idle and warm-up** phase, the PCM monitors those components - such as the Engine Coolant Temperature (ECT) sensor and the oxygen sensor heaters - that go into operation as soon as the engine starts running. On some vehicles, it might also monitor fuel control and misfire during warm-up. And the Comprehensive Component Monitor (CCM) watches out for problems that could set a DTC and prevent some monitors from running.

Once the vehicle has warmed up and the system has entered closed loop, the vehicle is accelerated at half-throttle with no accessory loads turned on. During this first **acceleration** phase, the misfire monitor is still running. Now that the engine is under a load, the misfire monitor might discover a problem that wasn't detectable at idle. (This is an example of how OBD-II repeatedly looks at the same system and/or component under different operating conditions.) EGR purge flow, EVAP purge flow and/or fuel trim might also be monitored during this initial acceleration phase, if the conditions are right to do so.

During the first **steady cruise** phase, the PCM watches out for problems with the oxygen sensor, fuel trim and misfire, canister purge and, on some systems, the EGR.

During the first **deceleration** phase, the fuel monitor notes whether fuel delivery is shut off during closed throttle deceleration. The Diagnostic Executive might also decide to run the EGR and EVAP monitors during this first deceleration.

During the second **acceleration** phase, the vehicle is accelerated under a greater load, and the same tests that were run during the initial acceleration phase are run again, just to see how those same components and systems do when they have to work harder.

The second **steady cruise** phase is a little longer than the first one. The catalyst monitor will most likely run, as by now it's likely that it's fully warmed up.

The second **deceleration** phase is a mirror image of the first one, but some systems have certain criteria, like neither the brake pedal nor the clutch pedal can be depressed (the monitor wants this to happen under more of a "coasting" condition).

The OBD-II Drive Cycle is complete when the vehicle engine management system has satisfied the enabling criteria for *all* of the monitors. If all of the monitors have run successfully, the readiness status display on your scan tool will mark them with the word "DONE" or with some similar terminology.

The monitors: a closer look

Now that we've given you a general overview of the monitors, and the terminology and concepts that you need to be familiar with in order to understand how the monitors work, let's look at each of the individual monitors in more detail. We'll start with the three monitors - the misfire monitor, the fuel monitor and the Comprehensive Component Monitor (CCM) - that run continuously, then we'll move on to the other monitors.

Misfire monitor

The first of the three continuous monitors that we want to discuss is the misfire monitor, which is arguably the most important of all the monitors because it protects the catalytic converter(s) from the serious damage that can be caused by misfires. If an engine misfires, the unburned fuel that inevitably accompanies the misfire will destroy the catalytic converter(s).

How does the misfire monitor work? Every time that a spark plug ignites the air/fuel mixture inside its combustion chamber, the crankshaft accelerates. Conversely, every time that the spark plug fails to ignite the air/fuel mixture inside the combustion chamber, the crankshaft decelerates. If the next spark plug in the firing order ignites the air/fuel mixture, the crankshaft accelerates again. The Crankshaft Position (CKP) sensor sends an analog (sine wave) signal to the PCM that's proportional in frequency and amplitude to the rotating speed of the crankshaft. In other words, the CKP sensor on a healthy engine should produce a sine wave that's consistent (symmetrical) in frequency and amplitude. But if the misfire monitor detects a *decrease* in the frequency and/or amplitude of the CKP sensor's signal, the misfire monitor assumes this change is a misfire.

The misfire monitor ignores bad advice

The trouble is, a misfire isn't the only possible cause of a change in crankshaft speed, so OBD-II software had to filter out false alarms. For example, a cold engine doesn't always run that smoothly until it's fully warmed up, and every little

hiccup produces a slight change in crankshaft speed. So OBD-II doesn't allow the misfire monitor to run under cold start conditions, because it might cause the misfire monitor to mistakenly identify a change in crank speed as a misfire. And even when an engine is warmed up, the driver might blip the throttle, which will also produce a brief change in crankshaft speed. But the OBD-II software measures and compares inputs on vehicle speed, load and throttle position, which enables the misfire monitor to filter out throttle blips. Another example: On rough roads, OBD-II designers feared that backfeed through the driveshaft (RWD vehicles) or the driveaxles (FWD vehicles) might confuse the misfire monitor. OBD-II addresses this problem with a couple of strategies: First, on some ABS-equipped vehicles, the signals from the wheel speed sensors are also used to inform the PCM that the road is rough, alerting it to the possibility that the misfire monitor might mistaken driveline/driveaxle backlash as a misfire condition. Second, if a misfire is detected on automatic transmission-equipped vehicles, the lock-up torque converter is temporarily disengaged. By doing this, rough-road vibrations that would be normally be transmitted by the driveshaft/driveaxles to the engine will cease long enough for the PCM to determine whether the misfire monitor is detecting a real misfire or not.

The misfire monitor runs continuously . . . most of the time

The misfire monitor doesn't depend on the test results from any other monitor, so there are no "suspend" conditions. The misfire monitor's test results are sent to the PCM continuously as long as the monitor is running. There are, however, some conditions that cannot be filtered out by the PCM. The misfire monitor will *not* run when one of the following conditions occurs:

- The engine is being cranked over
- The engine is being started when it's cold, or is being started in extremely cold or hot temperatures
- The PCM timer has not yet run out
- The throttle is rapidly opened and closed (blipping)
- The engine is decelerated with a closed throttle
- The engine speed exceeds the specified threshold rpm
- The Manifold Absolute Pressure (MAP) sensor voltage fluctuates temporarily
- The fuel level in the fuel tank drops below 15 percent of its capacity (this is why some manufacturers now refer to their fuel level gauges as fuel level *sensors*, because the PCM needs to know how much fuel is in the tank)

How the misfire monitor operates

The misfire monitor watches for any emission-related failure that will cause an unacceptably dirty exhaust. When it detects something, it tells the PCM to store a DTC. But the PCM classifies the degree of misfire into one of two broad

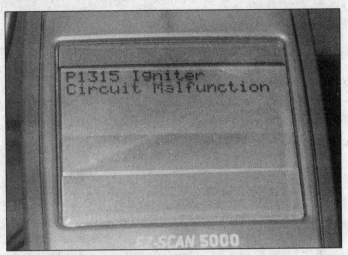

6.6 Diagnostic trouble code and code description shown on a scan tool

categories before it decides whether to just turn on the MIL or to turn on a *flashing* MIL:

- The misfire would cause the engine to fail a state smog test (PCM turns on a steady MIL)
- The misfire is serious enough to damage the catalyst if its severity is not reduced immediately (PCM turns on a flashing MIL)

Enabling criteria

Enabling criteria for the misfire monitor include the following inputs:

- Coolant temperature in the specified range, input from the Engine Coolant Temperature (ECT) sensor
- Engine load input from the Manifold Absolute Pressure (MAP) sensor is at a specified voltage
- Engine speed input from the Crankshaft Position (CKP) sensor at a specified rpm
- Start-to-run condition (the engine has been started and is running)
- Time-in-run (the engine has been running for a specified period of time)
- Vehicle speed in a specified range, input from the Vehicle Speed Sensor (VSS)

The misfire monitor will *not* run, however, if the PCM has stored a DTC that would affect the results.

Pending conditions

The misfire monitor will not run if:

- Vehicle is in "limp-home" mode
- Misfire monitor is waiting for an input signal from one of the sensors - ECT sensor, TP sensor, MAP sensor, CKP sensor or CMP sensor - that it needs to run (of course, if there's a missing signal there will be an accompanying DTC)
- PCM has stored a DTC for the VSS

So if the MIL is on, you'll have to extract the DTC **(see illustration 6.6)**, track down the problem and fix it before the misfire monitor will run again.

Conflicts

If the PCM has stored a one-trip maturing code for a rich or lean fuel system, an EVAP system purge or EGR problem, it won't allow the misfire monitor to run because the monitor could be affected by any of those conditions.

Suspends

There are no suspend conditions under which the misfire monitor won't run because this monitor doesn't depend on successful (passing) test results from the other monitors.

To the PCM, there are misfires . . . and there are *misfires*

The PCM stores a DTC if the misfire monitor discovers a misfire that would increase tailpipe emissions. But the PCM doesn't automatically turn on the MIL the first time that the misfire monitor notes a misfire. If the misfire causes *a 2 percent change in crankshaft speed in a 1000-rpm interval*, a DTC is stored but the MIL isn't turned on. We refer to this type of DTC as a pending, or "maturing" code. If the misfire monitor detects the same emission-related misfire on the next trip, the PCM turns on the MIL. We refer to this second DTC, the one that turns on the MIL, as a matured code.

When an extreme misfire occurs - a misfire so serious that it threatens the catalyst - the MIL doesn't wait for the PCM and the misfire monitor to sort things out the next trip. The PCM responds immediately by turning on the MIL, which *blinks on and off* for the duration that the misfire monitor detects the cat-killing misfire. The blinking MIL is annoying (it's *supposed* to be annoying) because if the problem isn't fixed quickly, you're looking at a new catalyst. Even if the misfire decreases to the point where the blinking stops, the MIL will remain illuminated to remind you that there's a DTC stored.

When does the PCM turn off the MIL for a misfire?

If the misfire monitor runs successfully on three consecutive trips after a DTC has been stored, it will turn off the MIL. But the monitor isn't just looking for a passing score during those three consecutive trips. It's looking for a passing score under driving conditions that mirror the conditions that were present at the time that the DTC was stored. More specifically, the monitor must run under conditions that are within 10 percent of the calculated load value and within 375 rpm of the engine speed at the moment that the misfire was originally detected. If these two conditions are present, and if the PCM sees no recurrence in a 1000-rpm interval, it will record one good trip. After it has recorded *three consecutive good trips with no recurrence* under these specified conditions, the PCM will turn off the MIL. However, the DTC and the freeze frame data that were stored at the moment the misfire monitor detected the misfire will remain in the PCM's

6.7 A damaged spark plug like this will cause misfiring

6.8 Areas to look for excessive wear or damage on the camshafts are the bearing surfaces and the camshaft lobes

memory for the next 40 to 80 warm-up cycles, after which they too will be erased if there are no further misfire incidents.

Typical causes of a misfire

Worn or damaged spark plugs **(see illustration 6.7)** and/or plug wires are the usual suspects when a misfire occurs. But there are many other possibilities besides bad spark plugs or plug wires. A defect or failure of any the following components or systems could also cause a misfire:

- Burned and/or leaking valve(s)
- Clogged fuel injectors
- Contaminated fuel
- Cracked engine block or cylinder head
- Defective CKP sensor
- Defective fuel pressure regulator (stuck open or stuck closed)
- Defective ignition coil(s)
- Disconnected fuel injector
- EGR valve stuck open
- High resistance in spark plug wire(s)
- Incorrect input to PCM from defective ECT sensor
- Incorrect input to PCM from defective MAP sensor
- Incorrectly adjusted valve clearances
- Incorrectly installed timing belt
- Insufficient voltage at the positive primary terminal of the ignition coil(s)
- Insufficient voltage to fuel pump
- Leaking cylinder head gasket
- Leaking fuel injectors
- Loose spark plug(s)
- Low fuel level in fuel tank
- Open or short in fuel injector or in injector harness
- Plugged fuel filter
- Restricted EGR passage(s)
- Restricted exhaust pipe, catalyst or muffler

- Sticking valve(s)
- Worn camshaft lobes **(see illustration 6.8)**
- Worn out fuel pump
- Worn piston rings

Fuel system monitor

Like the misfire monitor, the fuel system monitor also tests continuously. It also has the capability to store freeze frame data in the PCM when it detects a fuel system failure. The fuel system monitor runs only during closed-loop operation. The PCM uses a timer to tell it when enough time has passed to begin running the monitor. On some vehicles, the timer just starts counting down the moment you start the engine. On others, the timer is based on the signal sent from the Engine Coolant Temperature (ECT) sensor.

How the fuel system monitor operates

Before we look at how the fuel system monitor works, you need to know the difference between short- and long-term fuel trim.

Short-Term Fuel Trim (STFT)

Short-Term Fuel Trim (STFT) is a program in the PCM that controls the pulse width (the "on-time") of the injectors in order to keep the system in closed loop operation. STFT starts with a baseline value, then adjusts the system to be richer or leaner from that baseline. But there are upper and lower limits to the corrections that STFT can make. If the engine management system is functioning correctly and if the engine is in good condition mechanically, then the corrections made by the STFT should be fairly benign. But if the system becomes too lean or too rich, then short-term fuel corrections must increase accordingly. When you turn the ignition key to OFF, the STFT values stored in the PCM's memory are erased; i.e. the STFT corrections start at square one the next time you start the engine.

Long-Term Fuel Trim (LTFT)

When STFT corrections run out of room to maneuver, another PCM program, known as Long-Term Fuel Trim (LTFT), kicks in. LTFT shifts the baseline value of STFT from its original starting point to some point closer to the actual corrections that are needed to keep the system in closed loop. The system must be in closed loop before it will store long-term corrections. LTFT values are stored in the PCM's memory even when you turn off the engine.

STFT, LTFT and the fuel system monitor

The PCM combines these STFT and LTFT corrections to calculate the *overall* fuel correction necessary to keep the system in closed loop. If the system becomes too lean or too rich, fault data is stored in the PCM's memory as a maturing fault. If the system goes too lean or too rich on two consecutive trips, the fault matures, at which point a DTC and freeze frame data are stored in memory and the PCM turns on the MIL.

The PCM can also turn off the MIL, but only after it sees three consecutive trips during which the fuel system monitor passes. The catch is that the load and speed conditions during those three trips must be very similar to the load and engine speed conditions present when the DTC was stored in the first place, not unlike the misfire monitor.

Enabling criteria

The enabling criteria for the fuel system monitor include the following inputs:

- Engine is warmed up to normal operating temperature (closed loop)
- Manifold Absolute Pressure (MAP) sensor signal is present
- Engine Coolant Temperature (ECT) sensor signal is present
- Intake Air Temperature (IAT) sensor signal is present
- Throttle Position (TP) sensor signal is present
- Vehicle Speed Sensor (VSS) signal is present
- Barometric Pressure (BARO) signal is present
- Crankshaft Position (CKP) sensor signal is present
- Long Term Fuel Trim (LTFT) data is available
- Short Term Fuel Trim (STFT) data is available

Pending conditions

The fuel system monitor will not run if the Malfunction Indicator Light (MIL) has been turned on by the PCM as a result of a failure of any of the following sensors or monitors:

- EGR monitor or solenoid DTC is stored
- EVAP monitor or solenoid DTC is stored
- Misfire DTC stored
- System is in limp-home mode because of a failed TP, ECT or MAP sensor
- Upstream oxygen sensor - no pass on rationality check
- Upstream oxygen sensor heater - DTC stored

Conflicts

If a maturing code for any of the following events is present, the fuel system monitor probably won't run:

- EGR system
- EVAP system
- Misfire
- Upstream oxygen sensor heater

Suspends

Once all of the enabling criteria have been satisfied, the fuel system monitor runs continuously (although some systems will not allow the fuel system monitor to run if the fuel level is too low).

Typical causes of a fuel system problem

Because the fuel and ignition systems have become so interconnected, refer to the malfunctions listed under the *Typical causes of a misfire* in the previous section on the misfire monitor.

Comprehensive Component Monitor (CCM)

The Comprehensive Component Monitor (CCM) continuously watches over the sensor inputs and control outputs that aren't tested by the other monitors. Depending on the type of sensor being monitored and the design of the system, DTCs are stored after one or two trips.

CCM-monitored sensors must be functional, rational and on time for work

All sensor circuits are monitored for continuity and out-of-range values. This type of test is referred to as a "functionality" test. And some sensor circuits are also monitored to verify that they make sense in the context of the signal inputs from other sensors that the CCM is watching over. This type of test is referred to as a "rationality" test. The rationality test won't receive a passing grade if one sensor input conflicts with another sensor input that has already been verified as an accurate signal.

Electrical failures in monitored components usually result in an illuminated MIL immediately. But some rationality failures take two trips before the MIL is turned on. So if one sensor input contradicts another sensor input, but both sensor inputs are within the specified range of electrical activity, it might take two trips before the MIL comes on. The intention of this strategy is to prevent the MIL from being displayed for some sort of electrical aberration that might - or might not - recur on the next trip.

The PCM also measures the amount of time certain sensors take to respond to changing engine conditions. If a sensor responds within the manufacturer's specified performance threshold, the PCM flags it as satisfactory and it's then eligible to join other enabling criteria needed to run other monitors. But if the sensor doesn't respond within the specified time period, the PCM flags it as unsatisfactory.

The ECT sensor is closely watched by the CCM

To get a better understanding of how the PCM interacts with a timed sensor, let's look at the most obvious example: the Engine Coolant Temperature (ECT) sensor. The ECT sensor, also known as a thermistor or a Negative Temperature Coefficient (NTC) resistor, is a special kind of variable resistor whose resistance decreases as the temperature increases. The bimetal element used in a thermistor has a highly predictable and repeatable property: The amount of current and voltage that it conducts at a certain temperature is always the same. This characteristic makes the thermistor an excellent analog temperature sensor. As the temperature increases, the resistance decreases, and the current and voltage increase. The ECT sensor's first job is to tell the PCM when the engine is warmed up enough to put the engine management system into closed-loop operation. When you start the engine, the PCM puts its stopwatch on the ECT sensor and measures how long it takes the ECT sensor to reach the temperature level necessary for closed-loop operation. If the ECT sensor reaches the closed-loop temperature within the specified time, the PCM flags it as satisfactory. If the ECT sensor doesn't reach this level within the specified time, or doesn't reach it at all, the PCM flags it as unsatisfactory, and any monitor that needs a functioning ECT sensor and/or a warmed-up engine as part of its enabling criteria will not be able to run. (Of course, the ECT sensor itself might be fine. The problem might be caused by a low coolant level or an air bubble inside the cooling system right at the spot where the ECT sensor is installed, either of which would prevent the ECT sensor from reaching the specified closed-loop temperature within the specified time frame.) The PCMs in some OBD-II systems will disable monitoring of the ECT sensor during cold starts in extremely cold weather because the ECT sensor might not register accurate resistance readings in such conditions. The PCMs on some OBD-II systems can also disable the ECT sensor if the Vehicle Speed Sensor (VSS) tells the PCM that the vehicle isn't moving.

Enabling criteria

Some sensors are tested when the ignition key is turned to ON. Other sensors are not tested until the engine operating conditions under which they're designed to work are achieved. Sensor tests vary in accordance with the design of the engine management system and the particular types of sensors used in that system.

Typically monitored inputs

The CCM monitors the following sensor inputs (not all systems use all of the sensors listed below, and some might use sensors not on this list):

- 4WD Low switch (4WD vehicles only)
- Brake switch
- Camshaft Position (CMP) sensor
- Crankshaft Position (CKP) sensor
- Cruise control servo switch
- Engine Coolant Temperature (ECT) sensor
- Evaporative Emissions Control (EVAP) purge solenoid
- Input Shaft Speed (ISS) sensor
- Intake Air Temperature (IAT) sensor
- Knock sensor
- Manifold Absolute Pressure (MAP) sensor
- Manual transmission clutch switch
- Mass Air Flow (MAF) sensor
- Output Shaft Speed (OSS) sensor
- Throttle Position (TP) sensor
- Transmission turbine speed sensor (automatics only)
- Transmission gear position indicator switch (PRNDL switch)
- Transmission fluid pressure switch (automatics only)
- Transmission temperature sensor
- Vacuum sensor
- Vehicle Speed Sensor (VSS)

The CCM also monitors output actuators

Most output actuators are solenoids with inductive windings. The PCM uses parallel testing circuits to monitor certain output actuator circuits. The testing circuits are spliced into the power (hot) sides of the output actuator circuits. When a solenoid winding is energized (turned on), the voltage signal sent to the solenoid winding drops. This is normal, and will result in a favorable check. But if there's bad circuit or solenoid winding (open circuit condition), the voltage sent to the solenoid won't drop. When the CCM detects such an occurrence it knows something must be wrong, so it relays that information to the PCM.

Typically monitored outputs

The CCM monitors the following actuator outputs (not all systems use all of the actuators listed below and some systems might use actuators not on this list):

- EVAP canister purge solenoid
- EVAP purge vent solenoid
- Idle Air Control (IAC) solenoid
- Ignition control system
- Transmission converter clutch solenoid
- Transmission shift control solenoids
- Transmission enable solenoid

Oxygen sensor monitor

Aside from being an instrumental part of fuel delivery and efficiency, the oxygen sensors (see illustration 6.9) on an OBD-II certified vehicle are critical compo-

6.9 Typical oxygen sensor

nents in the war against emissions. The low-voltage signal from each upstream oxygen sensor is the means by which the PCM keeps the air/fuel mixture at the stoichiometric ratio of 14.7:1. The voltage signal from each downstream sensor tells the PCM whether the catalytic converter is working efficiently or whether it needs to be replaced. Aside from the catalytic converter(s) the oxygen sensors are the most important emission control components on the vehicle.

An OBD-II system must infer emissions because it can't measure them directly like the gas analyzer used at a smog station. The oxygen sensor is critical to this strategy because the information that it provides is used by the PCM to determine whether the engine's emissions are within the limits of the law, or not. Oxygen sensor operating parameters are used by the PCM to run other monitors that test fuel correction, catalytic converter operation, the EVAP system and the EGR system. If an oxygen sensor isn't working properly, these other monitors can't run because the results wouldn't make any sense.

What the oxygen sensor monitor looks for in an oxygen sensor

The oxygen sensor monitor looks for several behavioral characteristics that indicate a healthy oxygen sensor. The oxygen sensor must get on-line as soon as possible, operate within a suitable voltage range and have good reflexes. And its signal must not be shorted or open.

The oxygen sensor mustn't be late for work

In the old (OBD-I) days you had to wait for the exhaust gases to warm up the oxygen sensor(s). During that warm-up period, the engine ran in open loop. The PCM used programmed default values in its map to provide an air/fuel mixture that was rich enough to keep the engine running smoothly until it warmed up. During this warm-up period, a fuel-injected engine ran little cleaner than a carbureted engine. During extended idle periods, especially in really cold climates, some oxygen sensors could cool off enough to put the system out of closed loop. In an attempt to shorten

sensor warm-up time and prevent sensors from taking a nap during extended idle periods, some manufacturers began installing *heated* oxygen sensors. Heated sensors shortened the open-loop period significantly and guaranteed that no sensor would fall asleep while on watch. With the advent of OBD-II, heated oxygen sensors became mandatory, and the heater circuit was put under the same scrutiny as the oxygen sensor itself so that the oxygen sensor monitor could determine how long the sensor was taking to warm up.

The oxygen sensor must be able to operate within a suitable voltage range

Technically, an oxygen sensor operates in the 0.1 to 0.9 volt range. In reality, most sensors operate somewhere within a narrower range, typically between 300 and 600 millivolts. When the system is rich (too little oxygen in the exhaust) an oxygen sensor must be able to operate at a suitably high voltage (about 600 millivolts). When the system is lean (too much oxygen in the exhaust) the oxygen sensor must be able to work operate at a suitably low voltage range (about 300 millivolts). The oxygen sensor monitor watches the oxygen sensor circuit to make sure that the sensor is still facile enough to do so. When the day comes that the oxygen sensor can no longer operate within this range, the PCM stores a DTC and freeze frame data and turns on the MIL.

The oxygen sensor must have quick reflexes

Every time the oxygen sensor crosses the center voltage level between rich and lean, its output voltage flips from high (600 millivolts) to low (300 millivolts), and every time it crosses the center voltage level between lean and rich, its output flips from low to high. These little switches from high to low and low to high are referred to as "cross-counts." An oxygen sensor produces the most cross-counts when it's brand new, then it's all downhill from there. As the sensor ages, its cross-counts inevitably decrease in frequency. In order to keep the air/fuel mixture as close as possible to the stoichiometric ideal of 14.7:1, the PCM needs frequent and timely updates on changes in the oxygen content of the exhaust. As the cross-counts start to fall behind the actual changes in oxygen content in the exhaust, the PCM's corrections to the pulse width of the injectors begin to fall behind the actual rich or lean condition in the exhaust. An oxygen sensor afflicted by old age is sometimes referred to by technicians as a "lazy sensor." In the OBD-I era, a lazy sensor usually went undetected until the catalyst was damaged or the vehicle failed a smog test. But the oxygen sensor monitor doesn't tolerate lazy sensors.

An oxygen sensor must not only be able to switch back and forth between 300 and 600 millivolts frequently, it must also be able to do it *quickly* every time that it does so. The switch from high to low and vice versa must occur within a very brief period of time or the transition is unacceptable to the PCM. When the oxygen sensor's switching time becomes too slow, the oxygen sensor monitor will fail and the PCM will store a DTC and freeze frame data and turn on the MIL.

The oxygen sensor signal must not be shorted or open

The PCM watches out for oxygen sensor voltage levels that are constantly high (a short in the sensor or the circuit) or constantly low (high resistance in the sensor or circuit) or don't fluctuate at all. If one of these situations occurs, the PCM stores a DTC and freeze frame data and turns on the MIL.

Enabling criteria

The enabling criteria for the oxygen sensor include the following inputs:

- Engine is warmed up
- EVAP canister purge is not likely to affect the results
- High-pressure power steering switch is OFF
- The specified time interval has elapsed since start-up (according to the PCM timer)
- Throttle Position (TP) sensor is within the specified range
- Transmission Range (TR) sensor indicates that the shifter is in D
- Vehicle Speed Sensor (VSS) indicates that the vehicle has been driven at the specified speed for the certain specified time interval without any interruptions

Pending conditions

The oxygen sensor monitor will not run if the Malfunction Indicator Light (MIL) has been turned on by the PCM as a result of a failure of any of the following sensors or monitors:

- Misfire DTC is stored
- Transmission Range (TR) sensor input fails
- Upstream oxygen sensor DTC is stored
- Vehicle is in limp-home mode because a Manifold Absolute Pressure (MAP) sensor, Throttle Position (TP) sensor or Engine Coolant Temperature (ECT) sensor DTC is stored
- Vehicle Speed Sensor (VSS) DTC is stored

Conflicts

If one or more of the following conflicts are present, the oxygen sensor monitor won't run:

- Fuel system monitor is running an intrusive test
- Insufficient time has elapsed on PCM timer since engine was started
- Misfire DTC is maturing
- High pressure indicated by the Power Steering Pressure (PSP) switch
- Upstream oxygen sensor heater DTC is stored

Suspends

There are no suspends for the oxygen sensor monitor. The results of the oxygen sensor monitor are stored in the

6.10 Typical catalytic converter

PCM's memory (as long as the enabling criteria are present) because other monitors - EVAP, catalyst, fuel correction and EGR - need those results before they can run.

Catalyst monitor

The catalytic converter, or catalyst, is inarguably the most important emission control component on a modern motor vehicle (see illustration 6.10). Catalytic converters are the main reason why gasoline-powered vehicles put out almost 100 percent less HC, CO and NOx than they did before the Clean Air Act. But even though catalysts can continue to neutralize the bad stuff in the exhaust for a hundred thousand or more miles without a problem, they can also go south in a hurry if they're subjected to cat-killers like excessively rich air/fuel mixtures, excessive heat or contamination. Contamination is usually caused by a bad cylinder head gasket (or a cracked cylinder head or block) or leaking valve guides and/or piston rings, any one of which can dump oil or antifreeze into the exhaust stream, which carries the contaminant right into the catalyst. So one of the goals of OBD-II was to devise a scheme that could monitor the condition of the cat without actually putting a tailpipe sniffer in there full-time. But before we look at how they did it, let's review how a catalyst works.

Once it's warmed up, the catalyst converts unburned toxic emissions - hydrocarbons (HC), carbon monoxide (CO) and oxides of nitrogen (NOx) - into harmless substances like carbon dioxide (CO_2) and water vapor (H_2O). A catalyst is some substance that modifies and increases the rate of a chemical reaction without itself being consumed by the reaction. In other words, an automotive catalyst should last indefinitely as long as it's not subjected to something that it was never designed to catalyze, such as raw unburned fuel. That's why an OBD-II system monitors the condition of the catalyst(s), because without a functioning catalyst no modern engine can comply with Federal (or state) government standards for HC, CO and NOx. In short, without a catalyst (or catalysts), the tailpipe HC, CO and NOx emissions of all vehicles would be *way* over the legal limit. But OBD-II won't let this happen because as soon as the catalyst monitor detects tailpipe emissions that are 1.5 times the Federal Test Procedure (FTP) standard, it turns on the MIL. But we're getting ahead of ourselves. First, the PCM has to run the catalyst monitor, so it must determine whether the conditions are right to do so.

Before the PCM will run the catalyst monitor, it looks at the engine coolant temperature, the load on the engine, the position of the throttle plate and the air/fuel ratio, and it looks to see whether the system is in closed-loop. If the PCM finds out that any DTCs are stored that might prevent the catalyst monitor from running correctly, it suspends the test results. It will also postpone running the catalyst monitor if it detects a wide-open throttle, a closed-throttle deceleration or any other condition that might cause the system to leave closed-loop operation.

There are two oxygen sensors for each catalyst on the vehicle. The heated upstream oxygen sensor is identical in design and function to an OBD-I oxygen sensor. It produces a voltage signal that's proportional to the level of oxygen in the exhaust gases, and the PCM uses this signal to alter the injector pulse-width accordingly so that the engine remains in closed loop. But OBD-II certified vehicles use a second heated oxygen sensor that's located downstream in relation to the catalyst. To understand its function, you need to first understand how a catalytic converter works.

How the catalyst works

All OBD-II catalytic converters are the "three-way" type i.e. they reduce hydrocarbons (HC), carbon monoxide (CO) and oxides of nitrogen, or simply nitrogen oxide (NOx). There are actually two catalysts inside each catalytic converter. The first catalyst (the one through which the exhaust gases pass first, before entering the second catalyst) is known as the *reduction* catalyst because it reduces NOx to its harmless constituents, nitrogen and oxygen. The monolithic substrate, which is the honeycomb-like ceramic grid inside the reduction catalyst, is coated with platinum and rhodium. The second catalyst, which is known as the *oxidation* catalyst, reduces HC and CO by oxidizing them into water vapor (H_2O) and carbon dioxide (CO_2). The monolithic substrate inside the oxidation catalyst is coated with platinum and palladium.

Three bad gases

Before we go inside the catalyst, let's review briefly where each of these three gases comes from and why they're bad. Hydrocarbons (HC) are a toxic by-product of incomplete combustion, i.e. incorrect ignition timing, misfires, detonation, preignition, etc. Carbon monoxide (CO), a colorless, odorless and highly toxic gas, is formed when the air/fuel mixture ratio is excessively rich. Nitrogen oxides (NOx) are produced when the temperature inside the combustion chambers reaches or exceeds 2500-degrees Fahrenheit. How bad is NOx? Well, think about it: Even though the sole purpose of the reduction catalyst is to reduce NOx,

many manufacturers also continue to install Exhaust Gas Recirculation (EGR) systems on their vehicles as well, just to minimize the production of NOx in the first place. Why is everyone so afraid of NOx? Because of what it can lead to . . .

NOx is a constituent of ground level ozone *and* photochemical smog. Ozone (O_3) is an *allotrope* (a structurally differentiated form) of oxygen that's derived or formed naturally from *diatomic* (made up of two atoms) oxygen by electric discharge or by exposure to ultraviolet radiation. Ozone is found in two places. Stratospheric ozone is the "good" ozone that forms a belt around the earth about 20 miles up. Because of its unique ability to filter out ultraviolet radiation from the sun, stratospheric ozone is the type of ozone that you heard or read about in the Nineties because it was being depleted by the chlorofluorocarbons (CFCs) in aerosol sprays and certain types of refrigerant. Ground level ozone is the same stuff but it's the "bad" ozone because it's unhealthy for human beings. When ground level ozone and *volatile organic compounds* (VOCs) - the vapors from various industrial solvents emitted by stationary sources - are mixed together with sunlight, you get *photochemical smog*. In short, reducing NOx emissions from automobiles helps to "break the chain" of ingredients needed to make smog.

Oxygen storage ability equals catalyst efficiency

The special coating on the oxidation catalyst's monolithic substrate breaks down HC and CO into CO_2 and H_2O. And it also *captures and stores any excess oxygen that's left over from the catalyzing process*. This allows the oxidation catalyst to continue oxidizing HC and CO *even when the oxygen content in the exhaust gases is low*. It also means that *the amount of oxygen coming out of the catalyst should be low*, as long as the catalyst is operating correctly. Therefore, the *rate of change from high oxygen content to low oxygen content should also be much less at the outlet end than at the inlet end* of the converter.

An automotive engineer might therefore conclude that the ability of the oxidation catalyst to store oxygen could also be used as an indicator of the efficiency of the catalytic converter. As the catalytic converter ages, wouldn't the oxidation catalyst slowly lose its ability to store oxygen? In other words, if you could measure the increasingly larger and larger amount of oxygen coming out the back end of the catalytic converter, could you not infer the condition of the converter? That's exactly what happened with the automotive industry's switch to OBD-II. The downstream oxygen sensor, which is located in the exhaust pipe right behind the catalytic converter, monitors the amount of oxygen in the exhaust gases coming out of the catalyst, or more correctly, it measures the oxygen *not* coming out of the cat. As long as the catalyst is operating correctly, the change from high to low and low to high oxygen content is much smaller at the catalyst outlet than it is at the inlet end of the catalyst. And this is an indication of catalyst efficiency.

But as the catalyst ages, it deteriorates and/or becomes contaminated, and its ability to store oxygen becomes increasingly diminished. So it has no stored reserves of oxygen in the oxidation catalyst for catalyzing HC and CO when the oxygen content in the exhaust gases is too low to support optimal oxidation of these toxic gases. As its oxygen storage ability deteriorates, more oxygen exits the catalyst, and the switching rate of the downstream oxygen sensor starts to look more and more like the switching rate of the upstream oxygen sensor.

The oxygen level in the exhaust gases coming out of the catalyst is measured by the downstream oxygen sensor as a percentage of the upstream oxygen sensor's switching rate. When the switching rate of the downstream sensor approaches a rate similar to that of the upstream sensor's switching rate, the PCM stores a DTC and turns on the MIL. At this point, the results of the catalyst monitor must be suspended, i.e. they will not be recorded with a passing grade in the PCM's memory until the PCM knows that the oxygen sensor monitor has passed. The catalyst monitor must run once per trip and is normally a two- or three-trip failure, i.e. the PCM can turn off the MIL if the catalyst monitor passes on the next three consecutive trips.

Enabling criteria

- Engine is at a specified rpm
- Engine is warmed up and in closed loop
- The voltage from the Manifold Absolute Pressure (MAP) sensor is at a specified level
- Throttle plate is open

Pending conditions

The catalyst monitor won't run if any of the following conditions could cause the test to fail or to provide inaccurate results:

- Downstream oxygen sensor or sensor heater DTC is stored
- Downstream oxygen sensor rationality DTC is stored
- Fuel monitor rich or lean DTC is stored
- Misfire DTC is stored
- Sensor DTC (MAP sensor, TP sensor, ECT sensor, etc.) is stored that has put vehicle into limp-home mode
- Upstream oxygen sensor or sensor heater DTC is stored
- Upstream oxygen sensor rationality DTC is stored

Conflicts

The catalyst monitor won't run if Diagnostic Executive detects any of the following events:

- EGR monitor test is running
- EVAP monitor test is running
- Fuel system intrusive test is running
- PCM start-up timer hasn't counted down to zero yet

The catalyst monitor also won't run if there is a one-trip maturing DTC in the PCM's memory for the following conditions:

- Downstream oxygen sensor heater
- Fuel system too lean
- Fuel system too rich
- Misfire
- Oxygen sensor monitor
- Upstream oxygen sensor
- Upstream oxygen sensor heater

Suspends

The results of the catalyst monitor cannot be recorded into the PCM's memory until the oxygen sensor monitor has completed its testing and has passed.

Evaporative Emissions Control (EVAP) monitor

The typical OBD-I Evaporative Emissions Control (EVAP) system was fairly simple. It had an activated charcoal canister, a computer-controlled (on later systems) purge solenoid valve and a bunch of plastic, nylon and/or neoprene hoses connecting the fuel tank to the canister, the canister to the purge valve and the purge valve to the intake manifold. That was about it. When the engine was warmed up, the computer would open the purge valve and empty the contents of the canister into the intake manifold.

When new vehicles rolled down the assembly line, random samples were administered the Federal Test Procedure (FTP), which included a fuel vapor test. The fuel vapor test was rudimentary but accurate. The vehicle's fuel tank was filled, the vehicle was placed inside a sealed room and the air in the room was monitored for the presence of fuel vapors. The threshold was extremely low, i.e. no leakage was the only acceptable way to pass the test. The trouble is, an OBD-I vehicle never took that test again. If the vehicle was operated in a state with a smog check program, the EVAP "test" consisted of a visual verification that the canister, the purge valve and the lines were installed correctly. And that was about it. There was no meaningful way to functionally *test* the EVAP system or to monitor it during daily operation.

Well, those days, as they say, are over. The FTP is still conducted on random samples of new vehicles, just as it was during OBD-I, but that's just the beginning. State smog check programs have now clamped down hard on the EVAP system because it's been identified as a major source of unburned hydrocarbons (HC) leaking into the atmosphere. The typical state smog check program now includes a test that pressurizes the EVAP system with nitrogen, then monitors the pressure for a specified period of time to verify that the system has no leaks. Even a small leak means that your vehicle flunks the smog test. You have to repair the EVAP system or have it repaired before you can have your vehicle retested. But it's highly unlikely that you'll ever go into a smog test without knowing in advance whether your EVAP system is in good shape because OBD-II has added another line of defense against leaks in the evaporative emissions control system, the EVAP monitor.

If you have ever wondered why the automatic shut-off on the fuel pump nozzle at the gas station clicks off before the tank is actually full, it's because that last 10 percent is baffled in such a way that the tank is considered "full" when the other 90 percent is filled; this is an expansion area for fuel and fuel vapors. Sure, you can squirt maybe another gallon or two into that baffled area, but if you do then you're actually overfilling the tank by putting fuel into that expansion area. And if the vehicle is left outside on a hot day, guess what? Fuel vapors fill the expansion area, then start looking for a way out through some convenient EVAP hose. Most EVAP hoses are already subjected to vibration and pelted by pebbles and other road debris. If the tank is also repeatedly overfilled, those EVAP hoses and lines begin to break down under the effects of pressurized fuel vapors. It's only a matter of time until the EVAP system springs a leak somewhere. But unlike in the days of OBD-I, the EVAP monitor detects these leaks as soon as they occur, at which point the PCM stores a DTC and turns on the MIL. So instead of leaking unburned HC vapors into the atmosphere for another year or two until the next smog test, you can now look for a leak, fix it and erase the DTC. (For a more detailed look at the EVAP system on your vehicle, refer to Chapter 6 in your Haynes manual.)

EVAP monitor strategies

Depending on the manufacturer, EVAP monitors use several different strategies to detect EVAP system leaks. Some manufacturers use a vacuum sensor to monitor the purge lines between the fuel tank and the EVAP canister and between the canister and the intake manifold. Others use an intrusive test that energizes the EVAP canister purge during closed loop and looks for changes in Short Term Fuel Trim (STFT) and in idle air control. Another strategy uses a small pump to pressurize the EVAP system and measures how long it takes to reach a specified pressure. Now let's look at each of these three strategies a little more closely.

Vacuum sensor type EVAP monitor

In vehicles that use this type of EVAP monitor, a vacuum switching valve opens and closes off each EVAP purge line and the intake manifold vacuum line so that the vacuum sensor can test each discrete part of the EVAP system separately. A vacuum switching valve closes the vapor line between the fuel tank and the canister, then the vacuum sensor tests that line for leaks. Then the vacuum switching valve closes the next line in the system and the vacuum sensor tests that line. And so on, until each segment of the EVAP system has been tested. If an EVAP line is broke, cracked or disconnected, the pressure inside the line will be incorrect, the EVAP monitor won't see the values that it's looking for and the PCM will store a DTC and turn on the MIL.

When the PCM energizes the EVAP canister purge valve, intake manifold vacuum pulls any vapors stored inside the canister into the intake manifold. When this occurs the vacuum sensor verifies the change in pressure as the vapors are purged from the canister. If the vacuum sensor doesn't see the pressure change that it's looking for, the PCM knows that the system's integrity has been compromised, at which point it stores a DTC and turns on the MIL.

Pressurizing type EVAP monitor

This type of EVAP monitor uses a small PCM-controlled electric pump to pressurize the EVAP system and a canister vent valve that seals off the system when it's being pressurized. When the PCM runs the EVAP monitor, it turns on the vent valve to seal off the EVAP system, turns on a timer and turns on the pump, which pressurizes the system to a specified pressure. When the system reaches the specified pressure, the PCM turns off the pump and looks at the timer.

If the pump shuts down too soon, the PCM assumes that the interior volume of the EVAP system has been decreased, perhaps by a pinched EVAP line or kinked EVAP hose, either of which would block off part of the system.

If the pump starts up again right after shutting off, the PCM knows that there is a leak in the system. If it's a big leak, the pump might run continuously because it cannot achieve the specified pressure. In either case the PCM knows that there must be a leak somewhere in the EVAP system.

If the pump starts up, runs and stops, starts up, runs and stops, over and over again, it's because there is a small leak. The EVAP monitor watches the pump's cycling rate, then factors in the interior volume of the EVAP system and crunches these numbers to determine the size of the leak. If the leak is large enough, the EVAP monitor fails.

Intrusive type EVAP monitor

When the engine goes into closed loop, the PCM turns on the EVAP canister purge valve and looks for changes in STFT and idle air control. The PCM should get a rich signal (lack of oxygen) from the upstream oxygen sensor(s) if there's a lot of fuel vapor stored in the canister, and should respond by shortening the pulse-width of the fuel injectors. On the other hand, if there is little or no fuel vapor stored in the canister, turning on the purge valve *leans out* the air/fuel mixture ratio, just like a vacuum leak. In either case, the system should respond to the change in the air/fuel mixture by altering the injector pulse-width to restore the stoichiometric ratio of 14.7:1. If your vehicle has this type of EVAP monitor, it won't run until the fuel system and oxygen sensor monitors have run and passed because it needs information from the oxygen sensor and from STFT in order to run.

Exhaust Gas Recirculation (EGR) monitor

Introducing inert exhaust gases into the combustion chambers was tricky on an OBD-I vehicle. First of all, the PCM didn't really know exactly *when to turn on the EGR valve.* It knew the vehicle's speed, the load on the engine, the throttle plate position, the temperature of the engine, etc. It put all these factors together then made an educated guess regarding when to turn on the EGR valve. Then once the PCM turned on the EGR valve it still had to guess with respect to how much exhaust gas to admit into the intake manifold. Too little recirculated exhaust gases meant that the combustion chambers would remain too hot and would continue to produce some NOx; too much recirculated gases meant driveability problems. Then the PCM had to make another educated guess regarding *when to turn off the EGR*. Under OBD-I, the PCM watched over the EGR system's electrical circuit, but that was about it. It had no other diagnostic or monitoring capabilities.

An OBD-II EGR monitor still looks for shorts and opens in the control solenoids and switching valves used in the typical EGR system. If it finds an electrical fault, the PCM stores the DTC and turns on the MIL. In that respect, the EGR monitor isn't that different from OBD-I. And the EGR monitor still has no way to directly measure NOx emissions. But an OBD-II PCM must be able to keep the EGR system functioning correctly because NOx emissions are serious business. So the EGR monitor actively tests the functionality of the EGR system by turning it on during closed loop.

Several different types of EGR valves and special sensors are used on OBD-II vehicles to enable the EGR monitor to run its tests. Some vehicles are equipped with a vacuum-controlled EGR valve, which is regulated by a PCM-controlled vacuum switching valve, which is controlled by a pulse-width modulated signal from the PCM.

Other vehicles use a motorized EGR valve, which is opened and closed by a PCM-controlled solenoid. Motorized EGR valves are equipped with a valve position sensor, which tells the PCM how far the valve is open. Some vehicles are equipped with an exhaust gas temperature sensor, which monitors temperature changes inside the EGR supply pipe or passage. And they might also be equipped with a differential pressure feedback sensor, which is used by the PCM to compare exhaust pressure to EGR flow as the valve is opened. (For a more detailed look at the EGR system on your vehicle, refer to Chapter 6 in your Haynes manual.)

A typical intrusive EGR test

EGR monitors use a number of different strategies to test the EGR system. The following example is typical:

- The engine is fully warmed up and has been running for predetermined time period.
- The PCM waits until the engine rpm is sufficiently high so that driveability won't be affected when the EGR is turned on.
- Using the Short Term Fuel Trim (STFT) data, the PCM determines that any correction being made is not too big (the PCM will use the STFT data to see how it is affected when the EGR valve is activated).
- The three enabling criteria above suggest that the EGR monitor will run during a steady cruising speed, probably around 55 to 60 mph, with little load on the engine.

- When these conditions are met, the PCM will turn the flow of EGR off (the valve would normally be open at this stage). This allows more air (and less inert exhaust gases) into the combustion chambers. The extra air should be sensed immediately by the upstream oxygen sensor(s), at which point the STFT should increase to restore the correct air/fuel ratio. If the PCM sees this increase in STFT, it assumes that the EGR system is functioning correctly. If it doesn't see this change in STFT, the PCM assumes that the EGR system was not making any change i.e. introducing inert exhaust gases into the combustion chambers, so the EGR monitor fails and the PCM stores failure data. If the EGR monitor fails again on the next trip, the PCM stores a DTC and turns on the MIL.

This intrusive type of test not only infers that the EGR valve is functioning, it also infers that the exhaust gas pipe or passage between the exhaust manifold and the EGR valve is open, and that there's a change in STFT when the EGR valve opens and closes. Now let's look at the enabling criteria, pending conditions, conflicts and suspends for the EGR monitor.

Enabling criteria

The enabling criteria for the EGR monitor include the following inputs:

- Engine is warmed up
- Engine load is within the specified range
- Engine speed is within the specified range
- PCM timer indicates that the specified interval of time has elapsed since startup
- Short Term Fuel Trim (STFT) is within the proper range
- Throttle position is within the proper range
- Vehicle speed is within the proper range

Pending conditions

The EGR monitor will not run when any of the following conditions are present:

- Catalyst monitor test is in progress
- EVAP monitor is running
- Fuel system too lean DTC is stored or maturing
- Fuel system too rich DTC is stored or maturing
- Misfire DTC is stored or maturing
- Oxygen sensor monitor DTC is stored or maturing
- PCM timer indicates that not enough time has elapsed since startup
- Upstream oxygen sensor heater DTC is stored or maturing

Conflicts

The EGR monitor will not run if any of the following conditions are present.*

- Camshaft Position (CMP) sensor DTC is stored
- Crankshaft Position (CKP) sensor DTC is stored

- Fuel system DTC is stored
- Misfire DTC is stored
- Upstream oxygen sensor DTC is stored
- Upstream oxygen sensor heater DTC is stored
- Vehicle is in limp-home mode because of a failure of the Engine Coolant Temperature (ECT) sensor
- Vehicle is in limp-home mode because of a failure of the Manifold Absolute Pressure (MAP) sensor
- Vehicle is in limp-home mode because of a failure of the Throttle Position (TP) sensor
- Vehicle Speed Sensor (VSS) DTC is stored

*Note: *The types of component or monitor failures that affect the operation of the EGR monitor vary from one manufacturer to another because not all manufacturers' EGR monitors test EGR systems the same way.*

Suspends

The results of the EGR monitor cannot be stored in the PCM's memory until the oxygen sensor monitor passes.

AIR monitor

Some OBD-II vehicles are equipped with an air pump that pumps filtered ambient air into the exhaust manifold during cold-start warm-ups to help oxidize unburned hydrocarbons before they reach the catalyst. (Instead of pumping air into the exhaust manifold, some systems still pump air directly into the oxidation part of the catalytic converter during warm-ups, which accomplishes the same thing.) On some vehicles the air pump is belt-driven and runs all the time; a diverter valve sends the air to the exhaust manifold or catalyst when it's needed there or to the atmosphere when it's not needed. On other vehicles, the air pump is electric and is controlled directly by the PCM, so there is no need for a diverter valve. (For a more detailed look at the air injection system on your vehicle, if equipped, refer to the *Haynes Automotive Repair Manual* for your vehicle.)

The AIR monitor runs both passive and active tests

The AIR monitor is passive most of the time, but will become active when it has to.

A typical passive AIR test

The passive AIR test monitors oxygen sensor voltage from start-up to closed-loop operation. After you start the (cold) engine, the AIR system pumps air into the exhaust manifold during the warm-up period to help oxidize all those unburned hydrocarbons before they reach the catalyst. As soon as the oxygen sensor has heated up enough to go to work, it starts sending a low-voltage (excess oxygen) signal back to the PCM. When the engine management system enters closed loop, the PCM turns off the air injection system, then it verifies that the oxygen sensor is now switching back and forth between high (600 millivolts) and low voltage (300 millivolts). If the PCM verifies that the oxygen sensor is now switching back and forth the way that it's supposed to in closed loop, it passes the AIR monitor, and doesn't bother with the active test. But if the PCM has any reason to believe that the AIR system has not been pumping air into the exhaust during warm-up, it proceeds to the next test, which is an active test.

A typical active AIR test

An active AIR test is run after the engine management system has already entered closed-loop operation. The AIR monitor uses the oxygen sensor to tell it whether the oxygen content in the exhaust changes as the AIR system is turned on and off by the PCM. And like the EVAP monitor, the AIR monitor is looking for a change in oxygen sensor voltage and in Short Term Fuel Trim (STFT) as air is pumped into the exhaust stream. When extra air is introduced into the exhaust gases during closed loop, the oxygen sensor voltage should go low (around 300 millivolts) and the STFT should indicate that it has richened the air/fuel mixture by increasing injector pulse-width. If the PCM doesn't see this activity, it stores a DTC and turns on the MIL.

Notes

7 Trouble code retrieval

The Federal government's OBD-II program mandates a standard 16-pin diagnostic link connector (DLC) for all vehicles (see illustration 2.1). The DLC is also referred to as a J1962 connector (a designation taken from the physical and electrical specification number assigned by the SAE). Besides its standard pin configuration, the J1962 must also provide power and ground circuits for scan tool hook-up.

The different pins of the plug (see illustration 2.2) are used by different manufacturers in different ways, depending on which communication protocol is used. There are four protocols available:

Protocol	Connector pins used
J1850 VPW	2, 4, 5 and 16
IS0 9141 - 2	4, 5, 7, 15 and 16
J1850 PWM	2, 4, 5, 10 and 16
KWP2000 (ISO14230)	4, 5, 7, 15 and 16

Generally speaking, European and Asian manufacturers use ISO/KWP protocols, while General Motors uses J1850 VPW, and Ford uses J1850 PWM. The plugs pins are configured as follows:

Terminal	Designation
Pin 1	Manufacturer discretion
Pin 2	SAE J1850 Line (Bus +) positive line
Pin 3	Manufacturer discretion
Pin 4	Chassis ground
Pin 5	Signal ground
Pin 6	CAN data Bus, high - ISO 15765-4
Pin 7	K-line - ISO 9141-2/ISO 14230-4
Pin 8	Manufacturer discretion
Pin 9	Manufacturer discretion
Pin 10	SAE J1850 (Bus -) negative line
Pin 11	Manufacturer discretion
Pin 12	Manufacturer discretion
Pin 13	Manufacturer discretion
Pin 14	CAN data bus, low - ISO 15765-4
Pin 15	L-line
Pin 16	Battery positive

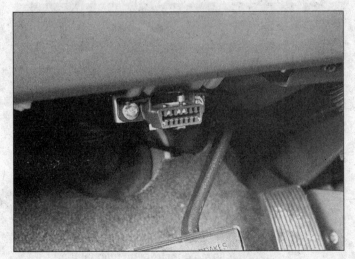

7.1 The 16 pin DLC terminal

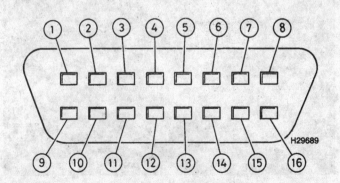

7.2 Terminal designations for the Data Link Connector (DLC)

7.3 The most common location for the DLC is under the driver's end of the dash, just to the left of the steering column

7.4 Sometimes the Data Link Connector (DLC) may be found behind an access panel like this one. The panel shouldn't require a tool to access the connector

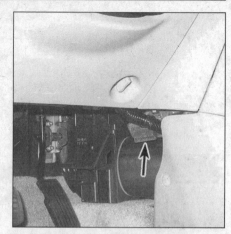

7.5 This Data Link Connector (DLC) is located under the dash, to the right of the steering column, close to the center console

The SAE has also recommended locating the DLC or J1962 connector under the driver's end of the dash (see illustrations 7.3, 7.4 and 7.5). If you can't find the DLC on your vehicle, refer to your owner's manual.

Now that all new vehicles have a standardized connector and a universal set of diagnostic trouble codes, the same scan tool can be used on any vehicle, and any home mechanic can access these codes with a relatively affordable generic scan tool.

All aftermarket generic scan tools include good documentation, so refer to the manufacturer's hook-up instructions in your scan tool manual (see illustrations 7.6 and 7.7). Before plugging a scan tool into the DLC, inspect the condition of the DLC housing; make sure that all the wires are connected and that the contacts are fully seated in the housing. Inside the connector, make sure that there's no corrosion on the pins and that no pins are bent or damaged.

7.6 The Data Link Connector (DLC) on this vehicle is located in the center console behind a plastic access cover

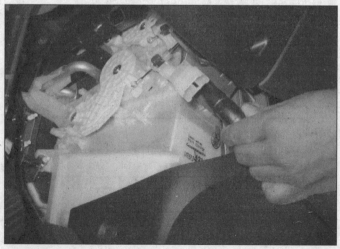

7.7 Connect the scan tool or code reader cable connector to the vehicle's 16-pin Data Link Connector (DLC) . . .

7.8 . . . then follow the instruction manual that came with the tool

8 Trouble codes

Code structure

With the implementation of OBD-II, a standardized code system became one of the major benefits. These five-character alphanumeric codes are made up as follows:

The first character, or letter prefix, defines the system group

B Body
C Chassis
P Powertrain
U Network communications

The second character defines the code type

Body/chassis

0 SAE defined (OBD-II)
1 Manufacturer defined
2 Manufacturer defined
3 For future allocation

Powertrain

0 SAE defined (OBD-II)
1 Manufacturer defined
2 SAE defined (OBD-II)
3 P3000-P3399 - SAE defined (OBD-II), P3400-P3999 - Manufacturer defined

Network communications

0 SAE defined (OBD-II)
1 Manufacturer defined
2 Manufacturer defined
3 For future allocation

The third character defines the system area *(See page 9-3)*

Powertrain - P0/P1 code

0 Fuel, air or emission control
1 Fuel or air

2 Fuel or air
3 Ignition system or misfire
4 Emission control
5 Vehicle speed, idle speed control or auxiliary inputs
6 Computer or auxiliary outputs
7 Transmission
8 Transmission
9 Transmission

Powertrain - P2 code

0 Fuel, air or emission control
1 Fuel, air or emission control
2 Fuel, air or emission control
3 Ignition system or misfire
4 Emission control
5 Auxiliary inputs
6 Computer or auxiliary outputs
7 Transmission
8 For future allocation
A Fuel, air or emission control

Powertrain - P3 code

0 Fuel, air or emission control
1 Fuel, air or emission control
2 Fuel, air or emission control
3 Ignition system or misfire
4 Cylinder deactivation
5 For future allocation
6 For future allocation
7 For future allocation
8 For future allocation
9 For future allocation

Network communications

0 Network electrical
1 Network communications
2 Network communications
3 Network software
4 Network data

P0 - generic codes

Note: *The following list of OBD-II trouble codes is a generic list applicable to all models equipped with an OBD-II system, although not all codes apply to all models.*

P0000   No fault found

P0001   Fuel volume regulator control circuit open

P0002   Fuel volume regulator control circuit range/performance

P0003   Fuel volume regulator control circuit low

P0004   Fuel volume regulator control circuit high

P0005   Fuel shutoff valve (A) control circuit open

P0006   Fuel shutoff valve (A) control circuit low

P0007   Fuel shutoff valve (A) control circuit high

P0008   Engine position system performance (bank 1)

P0009   Engine position system performance (bank 2)

P0010   Intake camshaft position actuator circuit open (bank 1)

P0011   "A" Camshaft position - timing over-advanced (bank 1)

P0012   "A" Camshaft position - timing over-retarded (bank 1)

P0013   "B" Camshaft position - actuator circuit malfunction (bank 1)

P0014   "B" Camshaft position - timing over-advanced (bank 1)

P0015   "B" Camshaft position - timing over-retarded (bank 1)

P0016   Crankshaft position/camshaft position, bank 1, sensor A - correlation

P0017   Crankshaft position/camshaft position, bank 1, sensor B - correlation

P0018   Crankshaft position/camshaft position, bank 2, sensor A - correlation

P0019   Crankshaft position/camshaft position, bank 2, sensor B - correlation

P0020   Intake camshaft position actuator circuit open (bank 2)

P0021   Intake camshaft position-timing over-advanced (bank 2)

P0022   Intake camshaft position-timing over-retarded (bank 2)

P0023   "B" Camshaft position - actuator circuit (bank 2)

P0024   "B" Camshaft position - timing over-advanced or system performance problem (bank 2)

P0025   "B" Camshaft position - timing over-retarded (bank 2)

P0026   Intake valve control solenoid circuit, bank 1 - range/performance problem

P0027   Exhaust valve control solenoid circuit, bank 1 - range/performance problem

P0028   Intake valve control solenoid circuit, bank 2 - range/performance problem

P0029   Exhaust valve control solenoid circuit, bank 2 - range/performance problem

P0030   HO2S heater control circuit (bank 1, sensor 1)

P0031   HO2S heater control circuit low (bank 1, sensor 1)

P0032   HO2S heater control circuit high (bank 1, sensor 1)

P0033   Turbocharger bypass valve control circuit

P0034   Turbocharger bypass valve control circuit low

P0035   Turbocharger bypass valve control circuit high

P0036   HO2S heater control circuit (bank 1 sensor 2)

P0037   HO2S heater control circuit low (bank 1, sensor 2)

P0038   HO2S heater control circuit high (bank 1, sensor 2)

P0039   Turbocharger bypass valve control circuit - range/performance problem

P0040   Upstream oxygen sensors swapped from bank to bank (HO2S - bank 1, sensor 1/ bank 2, sensor 1)

P0041   Downstream oxygen sensors swapped from bank to bank (HO2S - bank 1, sensor 2/ bank 2, sensor 2)

P0042 HO2S heater control circuit malfunction (bank 1, sensor 3)

P0043 HO2S heater control circuit low (bank 1, sensor 3)

P0044 HO2S heater control circuit high (bank 1, sensor 3)

P0045 Turbo/supercharger boost control solenoid - circuit open

P0046 Turbo/supercharger boost control solenoid - circuit range/performance problem

P0047 Turbo/supercharger boost control solenoid - circuit low

P0048 Turbo/supercharger boost control solenoid - circuit high

P0049 Turbo/supercharger turbine - over-speed

P0050 HO2S heater control circuit (bank 2, sensor 1)

P0051 HO2S heater control circuit low (bank 2, sensor 1)

P0052 HO2S heater control circuit high (bank 2, sensor 1)

P0053 HO2S heater resistance (bank 1, sensor 1)

P0054 HO2S heater resistance (bank 1, sensor 2)

P0055 HO2S heater resistance (bank 1, sensor 3)

P0056 HO2S heater control circuit malfunction (bank 2, sensor 2)

P0057 HO2S heater control circuit low (bank 2, sensor 2)

P0058 HO2S heater control circuit high (bank 2, sensor 2)

P0059 HO2S heater resistance (bank 2, sensor 1)

P0060 HO2S heater resistance (bank 2, sensor 2)

P0061 HO2S heater resistance (bank 2, sensor 3)

P0062 HO2S heater control circuit malfunction (bank 2, sensor 3)

P0063 HO2S heater control circuit low (bank 2, sensor 3)

P0064 HO2S heater control circuit high (bank 2, sensor 3)

P0065 Air assisted injector control range/ performance problem

P0066 Air assisted injector control circuit or circuit low

P0067 Air assisted injector control circuit high

P0068 Throttle position (TP) sensor inconsistent with mass air flow (MAF) sensor

P0069 Manifold pressure (MAP) sensor - barometric pressure correlation

P0070 Ambient air temperature sensor circuit problem

P0071 Ambient air temperature sensor range/ performance problem

P0072 Ambient air temperature sensor circuit low input

P0073 Ambient air temperature sensor circuit high input

P0074 Ambient air temperature sensor circuit intermittent

P0075 Intake valve control solenoid circuit (bank 1)

P0076 Intake valve control solenoid circuit low (bank 1)

P0077 Intake valve control solenoid circuit high (bank 1)

P0078 Exhaust valve control solenoid circuit malfunction (bank 1)

P0079 Exhaust valve control solenoid circuit low (bank 1)

P0080 Exhaust valve control solenoid circuit high (bank 1)

P0081 Intake valve control solenoid circuit (bank 2)

P0082 Intake valve control solenoid circuit low (bank 2)

P0083 Intake valve control solenoid circuit high (bank 2)

P0084 Exhaust valve control solenoid circuit malfunction (bank 2)

P0085 Exhaust valve control solenoid circuit low (bank 2)

P0086 Exhaust valve control solenoid circuit high (bank 2)

P0086 Exhaust valve control solenoid, bank 2 - circuit high

P0087 Fuel rail/system pressure - too low

P0088 Fuel rail/system pressure - too high

P0089 Fuel pressure regulator - performance problem

P0090 Fuel metering solenoid - open circuit

P0091 Fuel metering solenoid - short to ground

P0092 Fuel metering solenoid - short to positive

P0093 Fuel system leak detected - large leak

P0094 Fuel system leak detected - small leak

P0095 Intake air temperature (IAT) sensor 2 - circuit malfunction

P0096 Intake air temperature (IAT) sensor 2 - circuit range/performance problem

P0097 Intake air temperature (IAT) sensor 2 - circuit low input

P0098 Intake air temperature (IAT) sensor 2 - circuit high input

P0099 Intake air temperature (IAT) sensor 2 - circuit intermittent/erratic

P0100 Mass air flow or volume air flow circuit malfunction

P0101 Mass air flow or volume air flow circuit, range or performance problem

P0102 Mass air flow or volume air flow circuit, low input

P0103 Mass air flow or volume air flow circuit, high input

P0104 Mass air flow or volume air flow circuit, intermittent

P0105 Manifold absolute pressure or barometric pressure circuit malfunction

P0106 Manifold absolute pressure or barometric pressure circuit, range or performance problem

P0107 Manifold absolute pressure or barometric pressure circuit, low input

P0108 Manifold absolute pressure or barometric pressure circuit, high input

P0109 Manifold absolute pressure or barometric pressure circuit, intermittent

P0110 Intake air temperature circuit malfunction

P0111 Intake air temperature circuit, range or performance problem

P0112 Intake air temperature circuit, low input

P0113 Intake air temperature circuit, high input

P0114 Intake air temperature circuit, intermittent

P0115 Engine coolant temperature circuit

P0116 Engine coolant temperature circuit range/performance problem

P0117 Engine coolant temperature circuit, low input

P0118 Engine coolant temperature circuit, high input

P0119 Engine coolant temperature circuit, intermittent

P0120 Throttle position or pedal position sensor/switch circuit malfunction

P0121 Throttle position or pedal position sensor/switch circuit, range or performance problem

P0122 Throttle position or pedal position sensor/switch circuit, low input

P0123 Throttle position or pedal position sensor/switch circuit, high input

P0124 Throttle position or pedal position sensor/switch circuit, intermittent

P0125 Insufficient coolant temperature for closed loop fuel control

P0126 Insufficient coolant temperature for stable operation

P0127 Intake air temperature too high

P0128 Coolant thermostat (coolant temperature below thermostat regulating temperature)

P0129 Barometric pressure - too low

P0130 O2 sensor circuit malfunction (bank 1, sensor 1)

P0131 O2 sensor circuit, low voltage (bank 1, sensor 1)

P0132 O2 sensor circuit, high voltage (bank 1, sensor 1)

P0133 O2 sensor circuit, slow response (bank 1, sensor 1)

P0134   O2 sensor circuit - no activity detected (bank 1, sensor 1)

P0135   O2 sensor heater circuit malfunction (bank 1, sensor 1)

P0136   O2 sensor circuit malfunction (bank 1, sensor 2)

P0137   O2 sensor circuit, low voltage (bank 1, sensor 2)

P0138   O2 sensor circuit, high voltage (bank 1, sensor 2)

P0139   O2 sensor circuit, slow response (bank 1, sensor 2)

P0140   O2 sensor circuit - no activity detected (bank 1, sensor 2)

P0141   O2 sensor heater circuit malfunction (bank 1, sensor 2)

P0142   O2 sensor circuit malfunction (bank 1, sensor 3)

P0143   O2 sensor circuit, low voltage (bank 1, sensor 3)

P0144   O2 sensor circuit, high voltage (bank 1, sensor 3)

P0145   O2 sensor circuit, slow response (bank 1, sensor 3)

P0146   O2 sensor circuit - no activity detected (bank 1, sensor 3)

P0147   O2 sensor heater circuit malfunction (bank 1, sensor 3)

P0148   Fuel delivery error

P0149   Fuel timing error

P0150   O2 sensor circuit malfunction (bank 2, sensor 1)

P0151   O2 sensor circuit, low voltage (bank 2, sensor 1)

P0152   O2 sensor circuit, high voltage (bank 2, sensor 1)

P0153   O2 sensor circuit, slow response (bank 2, sensor 1)

P0154   O2 sensor circuit - no activity detected (bank 2, sensor 1)

P0155   O2 sensor heater circuit malfunction (bank 2, sensor 1)

P0156   O2 sensor circuit malfunction (bank 2, sensor 2)

P0157   O2 sensor circuit, low voltage (bank 2, sensor 2)

P0158   O2 sensor circuit, high voltage (bank 2, sensor 2)

P0159   O2 sensor circuit, slow response (bank 2, sensor 2)

P0160   O2 sensor circuit - no activity detected (bank 2, sensor 2)

P0161   O2 sensor heater circuit malfunction (bank 2, sensor 2)

P0162   O2 sensor circuit malfunction (bank 2, sensor 3)

P0163   O2 sensor circuit, low voltage (bank 2, sensor 3)

P0164   O2 sensor circuit, high voltage (bank 2, sensor 3)

P0165   O2 sensor circuit, slow response (bank 2, sensor 3)

P0166   O2 sensor circuit - no activity detected (bank 2, sensor 3)

P0167   O2 sensor heater circuit malfunction (bank 2, sensor 3)

P0168   Fuel temperature too high

P0169   Incorrect fuel composition

P0170   Fuel trim malfunction (bank 1)

P0171   System too lean (bank 1)

P0172   System too rich (bank 1)

P0173   Fuel trim malfunction (bank 2)

P0174   System too lean (bank 2)

P0175   System too rich (bank 2)

P0176   Fuel composition sensor circuit malfunction

P0177   Fuel composition sensor circuit, range or performance problem

P0178   Fuel composition sensor circuit, low input

P0179   Fuel composition sensor circuit, high input

P0180   Fuel temperature sensor A circuit malfunction

P0181   Fuel temperature sensor A circuit, range or performance problem

P0182	Fuel temperature sensor A circuit, low input	P0212	Injector circuit malfunction - cylinder no. 12
P0183	Fuel temperature sensor A circuit, high input	P0213	Cold start injector no. 1 malfunction
P0184	Fuel temperature sensor A circuit, intermittent	P0214	Cold start injector no. 2 malfunction
P0185	Fuel temperature sensor B circuit malfunction	P0215	Engine shut-off solenoid malfunction
P0186	Fuel temperature sensor B circuit, range or performance problem	P0216	Injection timing control circuit malfunction
P0187	Fuel temperature sensor B circuit, low input	P0217	Engine overheating condition
P0188	Fuel temperature sensor B circuit, high input	P0218	Transmission overheating condition
P0189	Fuel temperature sensor B circuit, intermittent	P0219	Engine overspeed condition
P0190	Fuel rail pressure sensor circuit malfunction	P0220	Throttle position or pedal position sensor/ switch B circuit malfunction
P0191	Fuel rail pressure sensor circuit, range or performance problem	P0221	Throttle position or pedal position sensor/ switch B, range or performance problem
P0192	Fuel rail pressure sensor circuit, low input	P0222	Throttle position or pedal position sensor/ switch B circuit, low input
P0193	Fuel rail pressure sensor circuit, high input	P0223	Throttle position or pedal position sensor/ switch B circuit, high input
P0194	Fuel rail pressure sensor circuit, intermittent	P0224	Throttle position or pedal position sensor/ switch B circuit, intermittent
P0195	Engine oil temperature sensor malfunction	P0225	Throttle position or pedal position sensor/ switch C circuit malfunction
P0196	Fuel rail pressure sensor circuit, range or performance problem	P0226	Throttle position or pedal position sensor/ switch C, range or performance problem
P0197	Fuel rail pressure sensor circuit, low input	P0227	Throttle position or pedal position sensor/ switch C circuit, low input
P0198	Fuel rail pressure sensor circuit, high input	P0228	Throttle position or pedal position sensor/ switch C circuit, high input
P0199	Fuel rail pressure sensor circuit, intermittent	P0229	Throttle position or pedal position sensor/ switch C circuit, intermittent
P0200	Injector circuit malfunction	P0230	Fuel pump primary circuit malfunction
P0201	Injector circuit malfunction - cylinder no. 1	P0231	Fuel pump secondary circuit, low
P0202	Injector circuit malfunction - cylinder no. 2	P0232	Fuel pump secondary circuit, high
P0203	Injector circuit malfunction - cylinder no. 3	P0233	Fuel pump secondary circuit, intermittent
P0204	Injector circuit malfunction - cylinder no. 4	P0234	Engine overboost condition
P0205	Injector circuit malfunction - cylinder no. 5	P0235	Turbocharger boost sensor A circuit malfunction
P0206	Injector circuit malfunction - cylinder no. 6	P0236	Turbocharger boost sensor A circuit, range or performance problem
P0207	Injector circuit malfunction - cylinder no. 7		
P0208	Injector circuit malfunction - cylinder no. 8		
P0209	Injector circuit malfunction - cylinder no. 9		
P0210	Injector circuit malfunction - cylinder no. 10		
P0211	Injector circuit malfunction - cylinder no. 11		

P0237 Turbocharger boost sensor A circuit, low

P0238 Turbocharger boost sensor A circuit, high

P0239 Turbocharger boost sensor B circuit malfunction

P0240 Turbocharger boost sensor B circuit, range or performance problem

P0241 Turbocharger boost sensor B circuit, low

P0242 Turbocharger boost sensor B circuit, high

P0243 Turbocharger wastegate solenoid A malfunction

P0244 Turbocharger wastegate solenoid A, range or performance problem

P0245 Turbocharger wastegate solenoid A, low

P0246 Turbocharger wastegate solenoid A, high

P0247 Turbocharger wastegate solenoid B, malfunction

P0248 Turbocharger wastegate solenoid B, range or performance problem

P0249 Turbocharger wastegate solenoid B, low

P0250 Turbocharger wastegate solenoid B, high

P0251 Injection pump fuel metering control A, malfunction (cam/rotor/injector)

P0252 Injection pump fuel metering control A, range or performance problem (cam/rotor/injector)

P0253 Injection pump fuel metering control A, low (cam/rotor/injector)

P0254 Injection pump fuel metering control A, high (cam/rotor/injector)

P0255 Injection pump fuel metering control A, intermittent (cam/rotor/injector)

P0256 Injection pump fuel metering control B malfunction (cam/rotor/injector)

P0257 Injection pump fuel metering control B, range or performance problem (cam/rotor/injector)

P0258 Injection pump fuel metering control B, low (cam/rotor/injector)

P0259 Injection pump fuel metering control B, high (cam/rotor/injector)

P0260 Injection pump fuel metering control B, intermittent (cam/rotor/injector)

P0261 Cylinder no. 1 injector circuit, low

P0262 Cylinder no. 1 injector circuit, high

P0263 Cylinder no. 1 contribution/balance fault

P0264 Cylinder no. 2 injector circuit, low

P0265 Cylinder no. 2 injector circuit, high

P0266 Cylinder no. 2 contribution/balance fault

P0267 Cylinder no. 3 injector circuit, low

P0268 Cylinder no. 3 injector circuit, high

P0269 Cylinder no. 3 contribution/balance fault

P0270 Cylinder no. 4 injector circuit, low

P0271 Cylinder no. 4 injector circuit, high

P0272 Cylinder no. 4 contribution/balance fault

P0273 Cylinder no. 5 injector circuit, low

P0274 Cylinder no. 5 injector circuit, high

P0275 Cylinder no. 5 contribution/balance fault

P0276 Cylinder no. 6 injector circuit, low

P0277 Cylinder no. 6 injector circuit, high

P0278 Cylinder no. 6 contribution/balance fault

P0279 Cylinder no. 7 injector circuit, low

P0280 Cylinder no. 7 injector circuit, high

P0281 Cylinder no. 7 contribution/balance fault

P0282 Cylinder no. 8 injector circuit, low

P0283 Cylinder no. 8 injector circuit, high

P0284 Cylinder no. 8 contribution/balance fault

P0285 Cylinder no. 9 injector circuit, low

P0286 Cylinder no. 9 injector circuit, high

P0287 Cylinder no. 9 contribution/balance fault

P0288 Cylinder no. 10 injector circuit, low

P0289 Cylinder no. 10 injector circuit, high

P0290 Cylinder no. 10 contribution/balance fault

P0291 Cylinder no. 11 injector circuit, low

P0292 Cylinder no. 11 injector circuit, high

P0293 Cylinder no. 11 contribution/balance fault

P0294 Cylinder no. 12 injector circuit, low

P0295 Cylinder no. 12 injector circuit, high

P0296   Cylinder no. 12 contribution/balance fault

P0297   Vehicle over-speed condition

P0298   Engine oil over temperature

P0300   Random/multiple cylinder misfire detected

P0301   Cylinder no. 1 misfire detected

P0302   Cylinder no. 2 misfire detected

P0303   Cylinder no. 3 misfire detected

P0304   Cylinder no. 4 misfire detected

P0305   Cylinder no. 5 misfire detected

P0306   Cylinder no. 6 misfire detected

P0307   Cylinder no. 7 misfire detected

P0308   Cylinder no. 8 misfire detected

P0309   Cylinder no. 9 misfire detected

P0310   Cylinder no. 10 misfire detected

P0311   Cylinder no. 11 misfire detected

P0312   Cylinder no. 12 misfire detected

P0313   Misfire detected with low fuel

P0314   Single cylinder misfire (cylinder not specified)

P0315   Crankshaft position system - variation not learned

P0316   Misfire detected during startup - first 1000 revolutions

P0317   Rough road hardware not present

P0318   Rough road sensor signal A - circuit malfunction

P0319   Rough road sensor signal B - circuit malfunction

P0320   Crankshaft position (CKP) sensor/engine speed (RPM) sensor - circuit malfunction

P0321   Crankshaft position (CKP) sensor/engine speed (RPM) sensor - range or performance problem

P0322   Crankshaft position (CKP) sensor/engine speed (RPM) sensor - no signal

P0323   Crankshaft position (CKP) sensor/engine speed (RPM) sensor - circuit intermittent

P0324   Knock control system error

P0325   Knock sensor no. 1 circuit malfunction (bank 1 or single sensor)

P0326   Knock sensor no. 1 circuit, range or performance problem (bank 1 or single sensor)

P0327   Knock sensor no. 1 circuit, low input (bank 1 or single sensor)

P0328   Knock sensor no. 1 circuit, high input (bank 1 or single sensor)

P0329   Knock sensor no. 1 circuit, intermittent (bank 1 or single sensor)

P0330   Knock sensor no. 2 circuit malfunction (bank 2)

P0331   Knock sensor no. 2 circuit, range or performance problem (bank 2)

P0332   Knock sensor no. 2 circuit, low input (bank 2)

P0333   Knock sensor no. 2 circuit, high input (bank 2)

P0334   Knock sensor no. 2 circuit - intermittent (bank 2)

P0335   Crankshaft position sensor "A" - circuit malfunction

P0336   Crankshaft position sensor "A" - range or performance problem

P0337   Crankshaft position sensor "A" - low input

P0338   Crankshaft position sensor "A" - high input

P0339   Crankshaft position sensor "A" - circuit intermittent

P0340   Camshaft position sensor "A" - circuit malfunction (bank 1)

P0341   Camshaft position sensor "A" - range or performance problem (bank 1)

P0342   Camshaft position sensor "A" - low input (bank 1)

P0343   Camshaft position sensor "A" - high input (bank 1)

P0344   Camshaft position sensor "A" - circuit intermittent (bank 1)

P0345 Camshaft position sensor "A" - circuit malfunction (bank 2)

P0346 Camshaft position sensor "A" - range/performance problem (bank 2)

P0347 Camshaft position sensor "A" - low input (bank 2)

P0348 Camshaft position sensor "A" - range/performance problem (bank 2)

P0349 Camshaft position sensor "A" - circuit intermittent (bank 2)

P0350 Ignition coil primary or secondary circuit malfunction

P0351 Ignition coil A primary or secondary circuit malfunction

P0352 Ignition coil B primary or secondary circuit malfunction

P0353 Ignition coil C primary or secondary circuit malfunction

P0354 Ignition coil D primary or secondary circuit malfunction

P0355 Ignition coil E primary or secondary circuit malfunction

P0356 Ignition coil F primary or secondary circuit malfunction

P0357 Ignition coil G primary or secondary circuit malfunction

P0358 Ignition coil H primary or secondary circuit malfunction

P0359 Ignition coil I primary or secondary circuit malfunction

P0360 Ignition coil J primary or secondary circuit malfunction

P0361 Ignition coil K primary or secondary circuit malfunction

P0362 Ignition coil L primary or secondary circuit malfunction

P0363 Misfire detected - fueling disabled

P0365 Camshaft position sensor "B" - circuit malfunction (bank 1)

P0366 Camshaft position sensor "B" - range/performance problem (bank 1)

P0367 Camshaft position sensor "B" - low input (bank 1)

P0368 Camshaft position sensor "B" circuit high input (bank 1)

P0369 Camshaft position sensor "B" circuit intermittent (bank 1)

P0370 Timing reference high resolution signal A malfunction

P0371 Timing reference high resolution signal A, too many pulses

P0372 Timing reference high resolution signal A, too few pulses

P0373 Timing reference high resolution signal A, intermittent/erratic pulses

P0374 Timing reference high resolution signal A, no pulse

P0375 Timing reference high resolution signal B malfunction

P0376 Timing reference high resolution signal B, too many pulses

P0377 Timing reference high resolution signal B, too few pulses

P0378 Timing reference high resolution signal B, intermittent/erratic pulses

P0379 Timing reference high resolution signal B, no pulse

P0380 Glow plug/heater circuit A malfunction

P0381 Glow plug/heater indicator circuit malfunction

P0382 Glow plug/heater circuit B malfunction

P0385 Crankshaft position sensor "B" - circuit malfunction

P0386 Crankshaft position sensor "B" - range or performance problem

P0387 Crankshaft position sensor "B" - low input

P0388 Crankshaft position sensor "B" - high input

P0389 Crankshaft position sensor "B" - circuit intermittent

P0390 Camshaft position sensor "B" - circuit malfunction

P0391 Camshaft position sensor "B" - range/performance problem (bank 2)

P0392 Camshaft position sensor "B" - low input (bank 2)

P0393 Camshaft position sensor "B" - high input (bank 2)

P0394 Camshaft position sensor "B" - circuit intermittent (bank 2)

P0400 Exhaust gas recirculation - flow malfunction

P0401 Exhaust gas recirculation - insufficient flow detected

P0402 Exhaust gas recirculation - excessive flow detected

P0403 Exhaust gas recirculation - circuit malfunction

P0404 Exhaust gas recirculation - range or performance problem

P0405 Exhaust gas recirculation valve position sensor A - circuit low

P0406 Exhaust gas recirculation valve position sensor A - circuit high

P0407 Exhaust gas recirculation valve position sensor B - circuit low

P0408 Exhaust gas recirculation valve position sensor B - circuit high

P0409 Exhaust gas recirculation valve position sensor A - circuit malfunction

P0410 Secondary air injection system malfunction

P0411 Secondary air injection system, incorrect flow detected

P0412 Secondary air injection system switching valve A - circuit malfunction

P0413 Secondary air injection system switching valve A - open circuit

P0414 Secondary air injection system switching valve A - shorted circuit

P0415 Secondary air injection system switching valve B - circuit malfunction

P0416 Secondary air injection system switching valve B - open circuit

P0417 Secondary air injection system switching valve B - shorted circuit

P0418 Secondary air injection system, pump relay A - circuit malfunction

P0419 Secondary air injection system, pump relay B - circuit malfunction

P0420 Catalyst system efficiency below threshold (bank 1)

P0421 Warm-up catalyst efficiency below threshold (bank 1)

P0422 Main catalyst efficiency below threshold (bank 1)

P0423 Heated catalyst efficiency below threshold (bank 1)

P0424 Heated catalyst temperature below threshold (bank 1)

P0425 Catalyst temperature sensor (bank 1)

P0426 Catalyst temperature sensor - range/ performance problem (bank 1)

P0427 Catalyst temperature sensor - low input (bank 1)

P0428 Catalyst temperature sensor - high input (bank 1)

P0429 Catalyst heater - control circuit malfunction (bank 1)

P0430 Catalyst system efficiency below threshold (bank 2)

P0431 Warm-up catalyst efficiency below threshold (bank 2)

P0432 Main catalyst efficiency below threshold (bank 2)

P0433 Heated catalyst efficiency below threshold (bank 2)

P0434 Heated catalyst temperature below threshold (bank 2)

P0435 Catalyst temperature sensor (bank 2)

P0436 Catalyst temperature sensor - range/ performance problem (bank 2)

P0437 Catalyst temperature sensor - low input (bank 2)

P0438 Catalyst temperature sensor - high input (bank 2)

P0439 Catalyst heater - control circuit malfunction (bank 2)

P0440 Evaporative emission control system malfunction

P0441 Evaporative emission control system, incorrect purge flow

P0442 Evaporative emission control system, small leak detected

P0443 Evaporative emission control system, purge control valve circuit malfunction

P0444 Evaporative emission control system, open purge control valve circuit

P0445 Evaporative emission control system, short in purge control valve circuit

P0446 Evaporative emission control system, vent control circuit malfunction

P0447 Evaporative emission control system, open vent control circuit

P0448 Evaporative emission control system, shorted vent control circuit

P0449 Evaporative emission control system, vent valve/solenoid circuit malfunction

P0450 Evaporative emission control system, pressure sensor malfunction

P0451 Evaporative emission control system, pressure sensor range or performance problem

P0452 Evaporative emission control system, pressure sensor low input

P0453 Evaporative emission control system, pressure sensor high input

P0454 Evaporative emission control system, pressure sensor intermittent

P0455 Evaporative emission (EVAP) control system leak detected (no purge flow or large leak)

P0456 Evaporative emission (EVAP) control system leak detected (very small leak)

P0457 Evaporative emission control system leak detected (fuel cap loose/off)

P0458 Evaporative emission control system, purge control valve - circuit low

P0459 Evaporative emission control system, purge control valve - circuit high

P0460 Fuel level sensor circuit malfunction

P0461 Fuel level sensor circuit, range or performance problem

P0462 Fuel level sensor circuit, low input

P0463 Fuel level sensor circuit, high input

P0464 Fuel level sensor circuit, intermittent

P0465 Purge flow sensor circuit malfunction

P0466 Purge flow sensor circuit, range or performance problem

P0467 Purge flow sensor circuit, low input

P0468 Purge flow sensor circuit, high input

P0469 Purge flow sensor circuit, intermittent

P0470 Exhaust pressure sensor malfunction

P0471 Exhaust pressure sensor, range or performance problem

P0472 Exhaust pressure sensor, low

P0473 Exhaust pressure sensor, high

P0474 Exhaust pressure sensor, intermittent

P0475 Exhaust pressure control valve malfunction

P0476 Exhaust pressure control valve, range or performance problem

P0477 Exhaust pressure control valve, low

P0478 Exhaust pressure sensor, high

P0479 Exhaust pressure sensor, intermittent

P0480 Cooling fan no. 1, control circuit malfunction

P0481 Cooling fan no. 2, control circuit malfunction

P0482 Cooling fan no. 3, control circuit malfunction

P0483 Cooling fan rationality check malfunction

P0484 Cooling fan circuit, high current

P0485 Cooling fan power/ground circuit malfunction

P0486 Exhaust gas recirculation (EGR) sensor "B" circuit malfunction

P0487 Exhaust gas recirculation (EGR) system, throttle position control circuit malfunction

P0488 Exhaust gas recirculation (EGR) system, throttle position control range/performance

P0489 Exhaust gas recirculation (EGR) system, circuit low

P0490	Exhaust gas recirculation (EGR) system, circuit high
P0491	Secondary air injection system (bank 1)
P0492	Secondary air injection system (bank 2)
P0493	Fan over-speed (clutch locked)
P0494	Fan speed - low
P0495	Fan speed - high
P0496	Evaporative emission system - high purge flow
P0497	Evaporative emission system - low purge flow
P0498	Evaporative emission system, vent control - circuit low
P0499	Evaporative emission system, vent control - circuit high
P0500	Vehicle speed sensor malfunction
P0501	Vehicle speed sensor, range or performance problem
P0502	Vehicle speed sensor circuit, low input
P0503	Vehicle speed sensor circuit, intermittent, erratic or high input
P0505	Idle control system malfunction
P0506	Idle control system, rpm lower than expected
P0507	Idle control system, rpm higher than expected
P0508	Idle control system circuit low
P0509	Idle control system circuit high
P0510	Closed throttle position switch malfunction
P0511	Idle air control (IAC) system - circuit malfunction
P0512	Starter request circuit
P0513	Incorrect immobilizer key
P0514	Battery temperature sensor circuit range/performance problem
P0515	Battery temperature sensor circuit
P0516	Battery temperature sensor circuit low
P0517	Battery temperature sensor circuit high
P0518	Idle air control (IAC) system, circuit intermittent
P0519	Idle air control (IAC) system, circuit performance
P0520	Engine oil pressure sensor/switch circuit malfunction
P0521	Engine oil pressure sensor/switch circuit, range or performance problem
P0522	Engine oil pressure sensor/switch circuit, low voltage
P0523	Engine oil pressure sensor/switch circuit, high voltage
P0524	Engine oil pressure too low
P0525	Cruise control, servo control - circuit range/performance problem
P0526	Fan speed sensor - circuit malfunction
P0527	Fan speed sensor - circuit range/performance problem
P0528	Fan speed sensor - no signal
P0529	Fan speed sensor - circuit intermittent
P0530	A/C refrigerant pressure sensor, circuit malfunction
P0531	A/C refrigerant pressure sensor, range or performance problem
P0532	A/C refrigerant pressure sensor, low input
P0533	A/C refrigerant pressure sensor, high input
P0534	A/C refrigerant charge loss
P0535	A/C evaporator temperature sensor - circuit malfunction
P0536	A/C evaporator temperature sensor - circuit range/performance problem
P0537	A/C evaporator temperature sensor - circuit low
P0538	A/C evaporator temperature sensor - circuit high
P0539	A/C evaporator temperature sensor - circuit intermittent
P0540	Intake air heater "A" circuit malfunction

P0541   Intake air heater "A" circuit low

P0542   Intake air heater "A" circuit high

P0543   Intake air heater "A" circuit open

P0544   Exhaust gas temperature sensor circuit malfunction (bank 1)

P0545   Exhaust gas temperature sensor circuit low (bank 1)

P0546   Exhaust gas temperature sensor circuit high (bank 1)

P0547   Exhaust gas temperature sensor circuit malfunction (bank 2)

P0548   Exhaust gas temperature sensor circuit low (bank 2)

P0549   Exhaust gas temperature sensor circuit high (bank 2)

P0550   Power steering pressure sensor, circuit malfunction

P0551   Power steering pressure sensor circuit, range or performance problem

P0552   Power steering pressure sensor circuit, low input

P0553   Power steering pressure sensor circuit, high input

P0554   Power steering pressure sensor circuit, intermittent input

P0555   Brake booster pressure sensor - circuit malfunction

P0556   Brake booster pressure sensor - circuit range/performance problem

P0557   Brake booster pressure sensor - circuit - low input

P0558   Brake booster pressure sensor - circuit - high input

P0559   Brake booster pressure sensor - circuit - intermittent

P0560   System voltage malfunction

P0561   System voltage unstable

P0562   System voltage low

P0563   System voltage high

P0564   Cruise control system, multi-function input signal

P0565   Cruise control on signal malfunction

P0566   Cruise control off signal malfunction

P0567   Cruise control resume signal malfunction

P0568   Cruise control set signal malfunction

P0569   Cruise control coast signal malfunction

P0570   Cruise control accel signal malfunction

P0571   Cruise control/brake switch A, circuit malfunction

P0572   Cruise control/brake switch A, circuit low

P0573   Cruise control/brake switch A, circuit high

P0574   Cruise control system - vehicle speed too high

P0575   Cruise control system - input circuit malfunction

P0576   Cruise control system - input circuit low

P0577   Cruise control system - input circuit high

P0578   Cruise control system, multi-function input "A" - circuit stuck

P0579   Cruise control system, multi-function input "A" - circuit range/performance problem

P0580   Cruise control system, multi-function input "A" - circuit low

P0581   Cruise control system, multi-function input "A" - circuit high

P0582   Cruise control system, vacuum control - circuit open

P0583   Cruise control system, vacuum control - circuit low

P0584   Cruise control system, vacuum control - circuit - high

P0585   Cruise control system, multi-function input A/B - correlation

P0586   Cruise control system, vent control - circuit open

P0587   Cruise control system, vent control - circuit low

P0588   Cruise control system, vent control - circuit high

P0589   Cruise control system, multi-function input B - circuit malfunction

P0590   Cruise control system, multi-function input B - circuit stuck

P0591   Cruise control system, multi-function input B - circuit range/performance problem

P0592   Cruise control system, multi-function, input B - circuit low

P0593   Cruise control system, multi-function input B - circuit high

P0594   Cruise control system, servo control - circuit open

P0595   Cruise control system, servo control - circuit low

P0596   Cruise control system, servo control - circuit high

P0597   Thermostat heater control system - circuit open

P0598   Thermostat heater control system - circuit low

P0599   Thermostat heater control system - circuit high

P0600   Serial communication link malfunction

P0601   Internal control module, memory check sum error

P0602   Control module, programming error

P0603   Internal control module, keep alive memory (KAM) error

P0604   Internal control module, random access memory (RAM) error

P0605   Internal control module, read only memory (ROM) error

P0606   PCM processor fault

P0607   Control module performance

P0608   Engine control module (ECM) VSS, output A malfunction

P0609   Engine control module (ECM) VSS, output B malfunction

P0610   Control module - vehicle options error

P0611   Fuel injector control module - performance

P0612   Fuel injector control module - relay control circuit

P0613   Transmission control module (TCM) processor error

P0614   Engine control module (ECM)/transmission control module (TCM) - mismatch

P0615   Starter relay - circuit malfunction

P0616   Starter relay - circuit low

P0617   Starter relay - circuit high

P0618   Alternative fuel control module - KAM error

P0619   Alternative fuel control module - RAM/ROM error

P0620   Generator control circuit malfunction

P0621   Generator lamp L, control circuit malfunction

P0622   Generator lamp F, control circuit malfunction

P0623   Generator lamp control circuit

P0624   Fuel cap lamp control circuit

P0625   Generator field terminal - circuit low

P0626   Generator field terminal - circuit high

P0627   Fuel pump control - circuit open

P0628   Fuel pump control - circuit low

P0629   Fuel pump control - circuit high

P0630   VIN not programmed or mismatch - ECM/PCM

P0631   VIN not programmed or mismatch - TCM

P0632   Odometer not programmed - ECM

P0633   Immobilizer key not programmed - ECM

P0634   ECM/TCM - internal temperature too high

P0635   Power steering control circuit

P0636   Power steering control circuit low

P0637   Power steering control circuit high

P0638   Throttle actuator control range/performance problem (bank 1)

P0639   Throttle actuator control range/performance problem (bank 2)

P0640 Intake air heater control circuit

P0641 Sensor reference voltage A - circuit open

P0642 Engine control module (ECM), knock control - defective

P0643 Sensor reference voltage A - circuit high

P0644 Driver display, serial communication - circuit malfunction

P0645 A/C clutch relay control circuit

P0646 A/C clutch relay control circuit low

P0647 A/C clutch relay control circuit high

P0648 Immobilizer lamp control - circuit malfunction

P0649 Speed control lamp control circuit

P0650 Malfunction indicator lamp (MIL), control circuit malfunction

P0651 Sensor reference voltage B - circuit open

P0652 Sensor reference voltage B - circuit low

P0653 Sensor reference voltage B - circuit high

P0654 Engine rpm output, circuit malfunction

P0655 Engine hot lamp output control, circuit malfunction

P0656 Fuel level output, circuit malfunction

P0657 Actuator supply voltage - circuit open

P0658 Actuator supply voltage - circuit low

P0659 Actuator supply voltage - circuit high

P0660 Intake manifold tuning valve control circuit open (bank 1)

P0661 Intake manifold tuning valve control circuit low (bank 1)

P0662 Intake manifold tuning valve control circuit high (bank 1)

P0663 Intake manifold tuning valve control circuit open (bank 2)

P0664 Intake manifold tuning valve control circuit low (bank 2)

P0665 Intake manifold tuning valve control circuit high (bank 2)

P0666 ECM/TCM internal temperature sensor - circuit malfunction

P0667 ECM/TCM internal temperature sensor - circuit range/performance problem

P0668 ECM/TCM internal temperature sensor - circuit low

P0669 ECM/TCM internal temperature sensor - circuit high

P0670 Glow plug module control - circuit malfunction

P0671 Glow plug, cylinder 1 - circuit malfunction

P0672 Glow plug, cylinder 2 - circuit malfunction

P0673 Glow plug, cylinder 3 - circuit malfunction

P0674 Glow plug, cylinder 4 - circuit malfunction

P0675 Glow plug, cylinder 5 - circuit malfunction

P0676 Glow plug, cylinder 6 - circuit malfunction

P0677 Glow plug, cylinder 7 - circuit malfunction

P0678 Glow plug, cylinder 8 - circuit malfunction

P0679 Glow plug, cylinder 9 - circuit malfunction

P0680 Glow plug, cylinder 10 - circuit malfunction

P0681 Glow plug, cylinder 11 - circuit malfunction

P0682 Glow plug, cylinder 12 - circuit malfunction

P0683 Glow plug control module communication to ECM - malfunction

P0684 Glow plug control module communication to ECM - range/performance problem

P0685 EGM power relay, control - circuit open

P0686 ECM power relay control - circuit low

P0687 Engine, control relay - short to ground

P0688 Engine, control relay - short to positive

P0689 ECM power relay sense - circuit low

P0690 ECM power relay sense - circuit high

P0691 Engine coolant blower motor 1 - short to ground

P0692 Engine coolant blower motor 1 - short to positive

P0693 Engine coolant blower motor 2 - short to ground

P0694 Engine coolant blower motor 2 - short to positive

P0695   Fan 3 control - circuit low

P0696   Fan 3 control - circuit high

P0697   Sensor reference voltage C - circuit open

P0698   Sensor reference voltage C - circuit low

P0699   Sensor reference voltage C - circuit high

P0700   Transmission control system malfunction

P0701   Transmission control system, range or performance problem

P0702   Transmission control system, electrical

P0703   Torque converter/brake switch B, circuit malfunction

P0704   Clutch switch input circuit malfunction

P0705   Transmission range sensor, circuit malfunction (PRNDL input)

P0706   Transmission range sensor circuit, range or performance problem

P0707   Transmission range sensor circuit, low input

P0708   Transmission range sensor circuit, high input

P0709   Transmission range sensor circuit, intermittent input

P0710   Transmission fluid temperature sensor, circuit malfunction

P0711   Transmission fluid temperature sensor circuit, range or performance problem

P0712   Transmission fluid temperature sensor circuit, low input

P0713   Transmission fluid temperature sensor circuit, high input

P0714   Transmission fluid temperature sensor circuit, intermittent input

P0715   Input/turbine speed sensor circuit malfunction

P0716   Input/turbine speed sensor circuit, range or performance problem

P0717   Input/turbine speed sensor circuit, no signal

P0718   Input/turbine speed sensor circuit, intermittent signal

P0719   Torque converter/brake switch B, circuit low

P0720   Output speed sensor malfunction

P0721   Output speed sensor circuit, range or performance problem

P0722   Output speed sensor circuit, no signal

P0723   Output speed sensor circuit, intermittent signal

P0724   Torque converter/brake switch B circuit, high

P0725   Engine speed input circuit malfunction

P0726   Engine speed input circuit, range or performance problem

P0727   Engine speed input circuit, no signal

P0728   Engine speed input circuit, intermittent signal

P0730   Incorrect gear ratio

P0731   Incorrect gear ratio, first gear

P0732   Incorrect gear ratio, second gear

P0733   Incorrect gear ratio, third gear

P0734   Incorrect gear ratio, fourth gear

P0735   Incorrect gear ratio, fifth gear

P0736   Incorrect gear ratio, reverse gear

P0737   TCM engine speed output circuit

P0738   TCM engine speed output circuit low

P0739   TCM engine speed output circuit high

P0740   Torque converter clutch, circuit malfunction

P0741   Torque converter clutch, circuit performance problem or stuck in Off position

P0742   Torque converter clutch circuit, stuck in On position

P0743   Torque converter clutch circuit, electrical problem

P0744   Torque converter clutch circuit, intermittent

P0745   Pressure control solenoid malfunction

P0746   Pressure control solenoid, performance problem or stuck in Off position

P0747   Pressure control solenoid, stuck in On position

P0748 Pressure control solenoid, electrical problem

P0749 Pressure control solenoid, intermittent operation

P0750 Shift solenoid A malfunction

P0751 Shift solenoid A, performance problem or stuck in Off position

P0752 Shift solenoid A, stuck in On position

P0753 Shift solenoid A, electrical problem

P0754 Shift solenoid A, intermittent operation

P0755 Shift solenoid B malfunction

P0756 Shift solenoid B, performance problem or stuck in Off position

P0757 Shift solenoid B, stuck in On position

P0758 Shift solenoid B, electrical problem

P0759 Shift solenoid B, intermittent operation

P0760 Shift solenoid C malfunction

P0761 Shift solenoid C, performance problem or stuck in Off position

P0762 Shift solenoid C, stuck in On position

P0763 Shift solenoid C, electrical problem

P0764 Shift solenoid C, intermittent operation

P0765 Shift solenoid D malfunction

P0766 Shift solenoid D, performance problem or stuck in Off position

P0767 Shift solenoid D, stuck in On position

P0768 Shift solenoid D, electrical problem

P0769 Shift solenoid D, intermittent operation

P0770 Shift solenoid E malfunction

P0771 Shift solenoid E, performance problem or stuck in Off position

P0772 Shift solenoid E, stuck in On position

P0773 Shift solenoid E, electrical problem

P0774 Shift solenoid E, intermittent operation

P0775 Pressure control solenoid "B"

P0776 Pressure control solenoid "B" performance or stuck in Off position

P0777 Pressure control solenoid "B" stuck On

P0778 Pressure control solenoid "B" electrical

P0779 Pressure control solenoid "B" intermittent

P0780 Shift malfunction

P0781 First-to-second shift malfunction

P0782 Second-to-third shift malfunction

P0783 Third-to-fourth shift malfunction

P0784 Fourth-to-fifth shift malfunction

P0785 Shift/timing solenoid malfunction

P0786 Shift/timing solenoid, range or performance problem

P0787 Shift/timing solenoid, low

P0788 Shift/timing solenoid, high

P0789 Shift/timing solenoid, intermittent

P0790 Normal/performance switch circuit malfunction

P0791 Intermediate shaft speed sensor circuit

P0792 Intermediate shaft speed sensor circuit range/performance problem

P0793 Intermediate shaft speed sensor circuit no signal

P0794 Intermediate shaft speed sensor circuit intermittent

P0795 Transmission fluid pressure (TFP) solenoid "C" - circuit malfunction

P0796 Transmission fluid pressure (TFP) solenoid "C" - performance or stuck Off

P0797 Transmission fluid pressure (TFP) solenoid "C" - stuck On

P0798 Transmission fluid pressure (TFP) solenoid "C" electrical malfunction

P0799 Transmission fluid pressure (TFP) solenoid "C" intermittent circuit malfunction

P0800 Transfer case control system, MIL request - circuit open

P0801 Reverse inhibit control circuit malfunction

P0802 Transmission control system, MIL request - circuit open

P0803 First-to-fourth upshift (skip shift) solenoid control circuit malfunction

P0804   First-to-fourth upshift (skip shift) lamp control circuit malfunction

P0805   Clutch position sensor circuit

P0806   Clutch position sensor circuit range/performance problem

P0807   Clutch position sensor circuit low

P0808   Clutch position sensor circuit high

P0809   Clutch position sensor circuit intermittent

P0810   Clutch position control error

P0811   Excessive clutch slippage

P0812   Reverse input circuit

P0813   Reverse output circuit

P0814   Transmission range display circuit

P0815   Upshift switch circuit

P0816   Downshift switch circuit

P0817   Starter disable circuit

P0818   Driveline disconnect switch input circuit

P0819   Up and down shift switch to transmission range - correlation

P0820   Gear lever X - Y position sensor circuit

P0821   Gear lever X position circuit

P0822   Gear lever Y position circuit

P0823   Gear lever X position circuit intermittent

P0824   Gear lever Y position circuit intermittent

P0825   Gear lever Push-Pull switch (shift anticipate)

P0826   Up and down switch - input circuit

P0827   Up an down switch - input circuit low

P0828   Up and down switch - input circuit high

P0829   5-6 shift - mechanical problem

P0830   Clutch pedal switch "A" circuit

P0831   Clutch pedal switch "A" circuit low

P0832   Clutch pedal switch "A" circuit high

P0833   Clutch pedal switch B circuit

P0834   Clutch pedal switch "B" circuit low

P0835   Clutch pedal switch "B" circuit high

P0836   Four wheel drive (4WD) switch circuit

P0837   Four wheel drive (4WD) switch circuit range/performance problem

P0838   Four wheel drive (4WD) switch circuit low

P0839   Four wheel drive (4WD) switch circuit high

P0840   Transmission fluid pressure sensor/switch "A" circuit malfunction

P0841   Transmission fluid pressure sensor/switch "A" circuit range/performance problem

P0842   Transmission fluid pressure sensor/switch "A" circuit low

P0843   Transmission fluid pressure sensor/switch "A" circuit high

P0844   Transmission fluid pressure sensor/switch "A" circuit intermittent

P0845   Transmission fluid pressure sensor/switch "B" circuit malfunction

P0846   Transmission fluid pressure sensor/switch "B" circuit range/performance problem

P0847   Transmission fluid pressure sensor/switch "B" circuit low

P0848   Transmission fluid pressure sensor/switch "B" circuit high

P0849   Transmission fluid pressure sensor/switch "B" circuit intermittent

P0850   Park/neutral position (PNP) switch - input circuit malfunction

P0851   Park/neutral position (PNP) switch- input circuit low

P0852   Park/neutral position (PNP) switch - input circuit high

P0853   Drive switch - input circuit malfunction

P0854   Drive switch - input circuit low

P0855   Drive switch - input circuit high

P0856   Traction control input signal - malfunction

P0857   Traction control input signal - range/performance problem

P0858   Traction control input signal - low

P0859   Traction control input signal - high

P0860   Gear shift module communication circuit - malfunction

P0861   Gear shift module communication circuit - low input

P0862   Gear shift module communication circuit - high input

P0863   Transmission control module (TCM) communication circuit - malfunction

P0864   Transmission control module (TCM) communication circuit - range/performance problem

P0865   Transmission control module (TCM) communication circuit - low input

P0866   Transmission control module (TCM) communication circuit - high input

P0867   Transmission fluid pressure (TFP) sensor

P0868   Transmission fluid pressure (TFP) sensor - low

P0869   Transmission fluid pressure (TFP) sensor - high

P0870   Transmission fluid pressure (TFP) circuit malfunction - sensor/switch C

P0871   Transmission fluid pressure (TFP) sensor C - range/performance problem

P0872   Transmission fluid pressure (TFP) sensor C - circuit low

P0873   Transmission fluid pressure (TFP) sensor C - circuit high

P0874   Transmission fluid pressure (TFP) sensor C - intermittent circuit malfunction

P0875   Transmission fluid pressure (TFP) sensor D - circuit malfunction

P0876   Transmission fluid pressure (TFP) sensor D - range/performance problem

P0877   Transmission fluid pressure (TFP) sensor D - circuit low

P0878   Transmission fluid pressure (TFP) sensor D - circuit high

P0879   Transmission fluid pressure (TFP) sensor D - intermittent circuit malfunction

P0880   Transmission control module (TCM) power input signal malfunction

P0881   Transmission control module (TCM) power input signal range/performance

P0882   Transmission control module (TCM) power input signal low

P0883   Transmission control module (TCM) power input signal high

P0884   Transmission control module (TCM) power input signal intermittent malfunction

P0885   Transmission control module (TCM) power relay - control circuit open

P0886   Transmission control module (TCM) power relay - control circuit low

P0887   Transmission control module (TCM) power relay - control circuit high

P0888   Transmission control module (TCM) power relay sense circuit malfunction

P0889   Transmission control module (TCM) power relay - sense circuit range/performance

P0890   Transmission control module (TCM) power relay - sense circuit low

P0891   Transmission control module (TCM) power relay - sense circuit high

P0892   Transmission control module (TCM) power relay - sense circuit intermittent malfunction

P0893   Multiple gears engaged

P0894   Transmission component slipping

P0895   Shift time too short

P0896   Shift time too long

P0897   Transmission fluid deteriorated

P0898   Transmission control system - MIL request - circuit low

P0899   Transmission control system - MIL request - circuit high

P0900   Clutch actuator - circuit open

P0901   Clutch actuator - circuit range/performance problem

P0902   Clutch actuator - circuit low

P0903   Clutch actuator - circuit high

P0904   Transmission gate select position circuit - malfunction

P0905   Transmission gate select position circuit - range/performance problem

P0906   Transmission gate select position circuit - low

P0907   Transmission gate select position circuit - high

P0908   Transmission gate select position circuit - intermittent circuit malfunction

P0909   Transmission gate select control error

P0910   Transmission gate select actuator - circuit open

P0911   Transmission gate select actuator - circuit range/performance problem

P0912   Transmission gate select actuator - circuit low

P0913   Transmission gate select actuator - circuit high

P0914   Gear shift position circuit - malfunction

P0915   Gear shift position circuit - range/performance problem

P0916   Gear shift position circuit - low

P0917   Gear shift position circuit - high

P0918   Gear shift position circuit - intermittent malfunction

P0919   Gear shift position control - error

P0920   Gear shift forward actuator - circuit open

P0921   Gear shift forward actuator - circuit range/performance problem

P0922   Gear shift forward actuator - circuit low

P0923   Gear shift forward actuator - circuit high

P0924   Gear shift reverse actuator - circuit open

P0925   Gear shift reverse actuator - circuit range/performance problem

P0926   Gear shift reverse actuator - circuit low

P0927   Gear shift reverse actuator - circuit high

P0928   Gear shift lock solenoid - circuit open

P0929   Gear shift lock solenoid - circuit range/performance problem

P0930   Gear shift lock solenoid - circuit low

P0931   Gear shift lock solenoid - circuit high

P0932   Hydraulic pressure sensor - circuit malfunction

P0933   Hydraulic pressure sensor - range/performance problem

P0934   Hydraulic pressure sensor - circuit low input

P0935   Hydraulic pressure sensor - circuit high input

P0936   Hydraulic pressure sensor - circuit intermittent

P0937   Hydraulic oil temperature sensor - circuit malfunction

P0938   Hydraulic oil temperature sensor - range/performance problem

P0939   Hydraulic oil temperature sensor - circuit low input

P0940   Hydraulic oil temperature sensor - circuit high input

P0941   Hydraulic oil temperature sensor - circuit intermittent

P0942   Hydraulic pressure unit

P0943   Hydraulic pressure unit - cycling period too short

P0944   Hydraulic pressure unit - loss of pressure

P0945   Hydraulic pump relay - circuit open

P0946   Hydraulic pump relay - circuit range/performance problem

P0947   Hydraulic pump relay - circuit low

P0948   Hydraulic pump relay - circuit high

P0949   ASM - adaptive learning not done

P0950   ASM control circuit

P0951   ASM control circuit - range/performance problem

P0952   ASM control circuit - low

P0953   ASM control circuit - high

P0954 ASM - intermittent circuit malfunction

P0955 ASM mode circuit - malfunction

P0956 ASM mode circuit - range/performance problem

P0957 ASM mode circuit - low

P0958 ASM mode circuit - high

P0959 ASM mode circuit - intermittent circuit malfunction

P0960 Pressure control (PC) solenoid A - control circuit open

P0961 Pressure control (PC) solenoid A - control circuit range/performance problem

P0962 Pressure control (PC) solenoid A - control circuit low

P0963 Pressure control (PC) solenoid A - control circuit high

P0964 Pressure control (PC) solenoid B - control circuit open

P0965 Pressure control (PC) solenoid B - control circuit range/performance problem

P0966 Pressure control (PC) solenoid B - control circuit low

P0967 Pressure control (PC) solenoid B - control circuit high

P0968 Pressure control (PC) solenoid C - control circuit open

P0969 Pressure control (PC) solenoid C - control circuit range/performance problem

P0970 Pressure control (PC) solenoid C - control circuit low

P0971 Pressure control (PC) solenoid C - control circuit high

P0972 Shift solenoid (SS) A - control circuit range/performance problem

P0973 Shift solenoid (SS) A - control circuit low

P0974 Shift solenoid (SS) A - control circuit high

P0975 Shift solenoid (SS) B - control circuit range/performance problem

P0976 Shift solenoid (SS) B - control circuit low

P0977 Shift solenoid (SS) B - control circuit high

P0978 Shift solenoid (SS) C - control circuit range/performance problem

P0979 Shift solenoid (SS) C - control circuit low

P0980 Shift solenoid (SS) C - control circuit high

P0981 Shift solenoid (SS) D - control circuit range/performance problem

P0982 Shift solenoid (SS) D - control circuit low

P0983 Shift solenoid (SS) D - control circuit high

P0984 Shift solenoid (SS) E - control circuit range/performance problem

P0985 Shift solenoid (SS) E - control circuit low

P0986 Shift solenoid (SS) E - control circuit high

P0988 Transmission fluid pressure (TFP) sensor E - circuit range/performance problem

P0989 Transmission fluid pressure (TFP) sensor E - circuit low

P0990 Transmission fluid pressure (TFP) sensor E - circuit high

P0991 Transmission fluid pressure (TFP) sensor E - circuit intermittent

P0992 Transmission fluid pressure (TFP) sensor F - circuit malfunction

P0993 Transmission fluid pressure (TFP) sensor F - circuit range/performance problem

P0994 Transmission fluid pressure (TFP) sensor F - circuit low

P0995 Transmission fluid pressure (TFP) sensor F - circuit high

P0996 Transmission fluid pressure (TFP) sensor F - circuit intermittent

P0997 Shift solenoid (SS) F - control circuit range/performance problem

P0998 Shift solenoid (SS) F - control circuit low

P0999 Shift solenoid (SS) F - control circuit high

P2 - codes

Note: *The following list of OBD-II trouble codes is a generic list applicable to all models equipped with an OBD-II system, although not all codes apply to all models.*

P2000   Nitrogen oxides (NOx) trap efficiency, bank 1 - below threshold

P2001   Nitrogen oxides (NOx) trap efficiency, bank 2 - below threshold

P2002   Particulate trap efficiency, bank 1 - below threshold

P2003   Particulate trap efficiency, bank 2 - below threshold

P2004   Intake manifold runner control , bank 1 - stuck open

P2005   Intake manifold runner control, bank 2 - stuck open

P2006   Intake manifold runner control, bank 1 - stuck closed

P2007   Intake manifold runner control, bank 2 - stuck closed

P2008   Intake manifold runner control, bank 1 - circuit/open

P2009   Intake manifold runner control, bank 1 - circuit low

P2010   Intake manifold runner control, bank 1 - circuit high

P2011   Intake manifold runner control, bank 2 - circuit/open

P2012   Intake manifold runner control, bank 2 - circuit low

P2013   Intake manifold runner control, bank 1 - circuit high

P2014   Intake manifold runner position sensor/ switch, bank 1 - circuit malfunction

P2015   Intake manifold runner position sensor/switch circuit, bank 1 - range/performance

P2016   Intake manifold air control actuator position sensor/switch, bank 1 - circuit low

P2017   Intake manifold air control actuator position sensor/switch, bank 1 - circuit high

P2018   Intake manifold air control actuator position sensor/switch, bank 1 - circuit intermittent

P2019   Intake manifold air control actuator position sensor/switch, bank 2 - circuit malfunction

P2020   Intake manifold air control actuator position sensor/switch, bank 2 - range/performance

P2021   Intake manifold air control actuator position sensor/switch, bank 2 - circuit low

P2022   Intake manifold air control actuator position sensor/switch, bank 2 - circuit high

P2023   Intake manifold air control actuator position sensor/switch, bank 2 - circuit intermittent

P2024   Evaporative emission (EVAP) fuel vapor temperature sensor - circuit malfunction

P2025   Evaporative emission (EVAP) fuel vapor temperature sensor - range/performance

P2026   Evaporative emission (EVAP) fuel vapor temperature sensor - low voltage

P2027   Evaporative emission (EVAP) fuel vapor temperature sensor - high voltage

P2028   Evaporative emission (EVAP) fuel vapor temperature sensor - circuit intermittent

P2029   Auxiliary heater (fuel fired) - system disabled

P2030   Auxiliary heater (fuel fired) - performance problem

P2031   Exhaust gas temperature (EGT) sensor 2, bank 1 - circuit malfunction

P2032   Exhaust gas temperature (EGT) sensor 2, bank 1 - circuit low

P2033   Exhaust gas temperature (EGT) sensor 2, bank 1 - circuit high

P2034   Exhaust gas temperature (EGT) sensor 2, bank 2 - circuit malfunction

P2035   Exhaust gas temperature (EGT) sensor 2, bank 2 - circuit low

P2036   Exhaust gas temperature (EGT) sensor 2, bank 2 - circuit high

P2037   Reductant injection air pressure sensor - circuit malfunction

P2038 Reductant injection air pressure sensor - range/performance

P2039 Reductant injection air pressure sensor - low input

P2040 Reductant injection air pressure sensor - high input

P2041 Reductant injection air pressure sensor - circuit intermittent

P2042 Reductant temperature sensor - circuit malfunction

P2043 Reductant temperature sensor - range/performance

P2044 Reductant temperature sensor - low input

P2045 Reductant temperature sensor - high input

P2046 Reductant temperature sensor - circuit intermittent

P2047 Reductant injector 1, bank 1 - open circuit

P2048 Reductant injector 1, bank 1 - circuit low

P2049 Reductant injector 1, bank 1 - circuit high

P2050 Reductant injector 1, bank 2 - open circuit

P2051 Reductant injector 1, bank 2 - circuit low

P2052 Reductant injector 1, bank 2 - circuit high

P2053 Reductant injector 2, bank 1 - open circuit

P2054 Reductant injector 2, bank 1 - circuit low

P2055 Reductant injector 2, bank 1 - circuit high

P2056 Reductant injector 2, bank 2 - open circuit

P2057 Reductant injector 2, bank 2 - circuit low

P2058 Reductant injector 2, bank 2 - circuit high

P2059 Reductant injection air pump - open circuit

P2060 Reductant injection air pump - circuit low

P2061 Reductant injection air pump - circuit high

P2062 Reductant supply control - open circuit

P2063 Reductant supply control - circuit low

P2064 Reductant supply control - circuit high

P2065 Fuel gauge tank sensor B - circuit malfunction

P2066 Fuel gauge tank sensor B - performance problem

P2067 Fuel gauge tank sensor B - circuit low

P2068 Fuel gauge tank sensor B - circuit high

P2069 Fuel gauge tank sensor B - circuit intermittent

P2070 Intake manifold tuning (IMT) valve - stuck open

P2071 Intake manifold tuning (IMT) valve - stuck closed

P2075 Intake manifold air control actuator position sensor/switch - circuit malfunction

P2076 Intake manifold air control actuator position sensor/switch - range/performance

P2077 Intake manifold air control actuator position sensor/switch - circuit low

P2078 Intake manifold air control actuator position sensor/switch - circuit high

P2079 Intake manifold air control actuator position sensor/switch - circuit intermittent

P2080 Exhaust gas temperature (EGT) sensor 1, bank 1 - range/performance

P2081 Exhaust gas temperature (EGT) sensor 1, bank 1 - circuit intermittent

P2082 Exhaust gas temperature (EGT) sensor 1, bank 2 - range/performance

P2083 Exhaust gas temperature (EGT) sensor 1, bank 2 - circuit intermittent

P2084 Exhaust gas temperature (EGT) sensor 2, bank 1 - range/performance

P2085 Exhaust gas temperature (EGT) sensor 2, bank 1 - circuit intermittent

P2086 Exhaust gas temperature (EGT) sensor 2, bank 2 - range/performance

P2087 Exhaust gas temperature (EGT) sensor 2, bank 2 - circuit intermittent

P2088 Camshaft position (CMP) actuator A, bank 1 - circuit low

P2089 Camshaft position (CMP) actuator A, bank 1 - circuit high

P2090 Camshaft position (CMP) actuator B, bank 1 - circuit low

P2091 Camshaft position (CMP) actuator B, bank 1 - circuit high

P2092 Camshaft position (CMP) actuator A, bank 2 - circuit low

P2093 Camshaft position (CMP) actuator A, bank 2 - circuit high

P2094 Camshaft position (CMP) actuator B, bank 2 - circuit low

P2095 Camshaft position (CMP) actuator B, bank 2 - circuit high

P2096 Post catalytic converter fuel trim (FT), bank 1 - too lean

P2097 Post catalytic converter fuel trim (FT), bank 1 - too rich

P2098 Post catalytic converter fuel trim (FT), bank 2 - too lean

P2099 Post catalytic converter fuel trim (FT), bank 2 - too rich

P2100 Throttle actuator control (TAC) motor - open circuit

P2101 Throttle actuator control (TAC) motor - range/performance

P2102 Throttle actuator control (TAC) motor - circuit low

P2103 Throttle actuator control (TAC) motor - circuit high

P2104 Throttle actuator control (TAC) system - forced idle mode

P2105 Throttle actuator control (TAC) system - forced engine shut down mode

P2106 Throttle actuator control (TAC) system - forced limited power mode

P2107 Throttle actuator control (TAC) module - processor fault

P2108 Throttle actuator control (TAC) module - performance problem

P2109 Throttle/pedal position sensor A - minimum stop performance

P2110 Throttle actuator control (TAC) system - forced limited rpm mode

P2111 Throttle actuator control (TAC) system - actuator stuck open

P2112 Throttle actuator control (TAC) system - actuator stuck closed

P2113 Throttle/pedal position sensor "B" minimum stop performance

P2114 Throttle/pedal position sensor "C" minimum stop performance

P2115 Throttle/pedal position sensor "D" minimum stop performance

P2116 Throttle/pedal position sensor "E" minimum stop performance

P2117 Throttle/pedal position sensor "F" minimum stop performance

P2118 Throttle actuator control motor current range/performance

P2119 Throttle actuator control throttle body range/performance

P2120 Throttle/pedal position sensor/switch "D" circuit

P2121 Throttle/pedal position sensor/switch "D" circuit range/performance

P2122 Throttle/pedal position sensor/switch "D" circuit low input

P2123 Throttle/pedal position sensor/switch "D" circuit high input

P2124 Throttle/pedal position sensor/switch "D" circuit intermittent

P2125 Throttle/pedal position sensor/switch "E" circuit

P2126 Throttle/pedal position sensor/switch "E" circuit range/performance

P2127 Throttle/pedal position sensor/switch "E" circuit low input

P2128 Throttle/pedal position sensor/switch "E" circuit high input

P2129 Throttle/pedal position sensor/switch "E" circuit intermittent

P2130 Throttle/pedal position sensor/switch "F" circuit

P2131 Throttle/pedal position sensor/switch "F" circuit range performance

P2132 Throttle/pedal position sensor/switch "F" circuit low input

P2133 Throttle/pedal position sensor/switch "F" circuit high input

P2134 Throttle/pedal position sensor/switch "F" circuit intermittent

P2135 Throttle/pedal position sensor/switch "A"/ "B" voltage correlation

P2136 Throttle/pedal position sensor/switch "A"/ "C" voltage correlation

P2137 Throttle/pedal position sensor/switch "B" / "C" voltage correlation

P2138 Throttle/pedal position sensor/switch "D" / "E" voltage correlation

P2139 Throttle/pedal position sensor/switch "D" /"F" voltage correlation

P2140 Throttle/pedal position sensor/switch "E" / "F" voltage correlation

P2141 Exhaust gas recirculation (EGR) throttle control valve - circuit low

P2142 Exhaust gas recirculation (EGR) throttle control valve - circuit high

P2143 Exhaust gas recirculation (EGR) vent control - open circuit

P2144 Exhaust gas recirculation (EGR) vent control - circuit low

P2145 Exhaust gas recirculation (EGR) vent control - circuit high

P2146 Injector - group A, supply voltage - open circuit

P2147 Injector - group A, supply voltage - circuit low

P2148 Injector - group A, supply voltage - circuit high

P2149 Injector - group B, supply voltage - open circuit

P2150 Injector - group B, supply voltage - circuit low

P2151 Injector - group B, supply voltage - circuit high

P2152 Injector - group C, supply voltage - open circuit

P2153 Injector - group C, supply voltage - circuit low

P2154 Injector - group C, supply voltage - circuit high

P2155 Injector - group D, supply voltage - open circuit

P2156 Injector - group D, supply voltage - circuit low

P2157 Injector - group D, supply voltage - circuit high

P2158 Vehicle speed sensor (VSS) B - circuit malfunction

P2159 Vehicle speed sensor (VSS) B - range/ performance

P2160 Vehicle speed sensor (VSS) B - circuit low

P2161 Vehicle speed sensor (VSS) B - circuit intermittent/erratic

P2162 Vehicle speed sensor (VSS) A/B - correlation

P2163 Throttle/pedal position sensor A - maximum stop performance

P2164 Throttle/pedal position sensor B - maximum stop performance

P2165 Throttle/pedal position sensor C - maximum stop performance

P2166 Throttle/pedal position sensor D - maximum stop performance

P2167 Throttle/pedal position sensor E - maximum stop performance

P2168 Throttle/pedal position sensor F - maximum stop performance

P2169 Exhaust gas pressure regulator vent solenoid - circuit open

P2170 Exhaust gas pressure regulator vent solenoid - circuit low

P2171 Exhaust gas pressure regulator vent solenoid - circuit high

P2172 Throttle actuator control (TAC) system - sudden high airflow detected

P2173 Throttle actuator control (TAC) system - high airflow detected

P2174 Throttle actuator control (TAC) system - sudden low airflow detected

P2175 Throttle actuator control (TAC) system - low airflow detected

P2176   Throttle actuator control (TAC) system - idle position not learned

P2177   System too lean off idle, bank 1

P2178   System too rich off idle, bank 1

P2179   System too lean off idle, bank 2

P2180   System too rich off idle, bank 2

P2181   Cooling system performance

P2182   Engine coolant temperature (ECT) sensor 2 - circuit malfunction

P2183   Engine coolant temperature (ECT) sensor 2 - range/performance

P2184   Engine coolant temperature (ECT) sensor 2 - circuit low

P2185   Engine coolant temperature (ECT) sensor 2 - circuit high

P2186   Engine coolant temperature (ECT) sensor 2 - circuit intermittent/erratic

P2187   System too lean at idle, bank 1

P2188   System too rich at idle, bank 1

P2189   System too lean at idle, bank 2

P2190   System too rich at idle, bank 2

P2191   System too lean at higher load, bank 1

P2192   System too rich at higher load, bank I

P2193   System too lean at higher load, bank 2

P2194   System too rich at higher load, bank 2

P2195   O2 sensor signal stuck lean bank 1, sensor 1

P2196   O2 sensor signal stuck rich bank 1, sensor 1

P2197   O2 sensor signal stuck lean bank 2, sensor 1

P2198   O2 sensor signal stuck rich bank 2, sensor 1

P2199   Intake air temperature (IAT) sensor 1/2 - correlation

P2200   Nitrogen oxides (NOx) sensor, bank 1 - circuit malfunction

P2201   Nitrogen oxides (NOx) sensor, bank 1 - range/performance

P2202   Nitrogen oxides (NOx) sensor, bank 1 - low input

P2203   Nitrogen oxides (NOx) sensor, bank 1 - intermittent input

P2205   Nitrogen oxides (NOx) sensor, bank 1, heater control - open circuit

P2206   Nitrogen oxides (NOx) sensor, bank 1, heater control - circuit low

P2207   Nitrogen oxides (NOx) sensor, bank 1, heater control - circuit high

P2208   Nitrogen oxides (NOx) sensor, bank 1, heater sense circuit - malfunction

P2209   Nitrogen oxides (NOx) sensor, bank 1, heater sense circuit - range/performance

P2210   Nitrogen oxides (NOx) sensor, bank 1, heater sense circuit - low input

P2211   Nitrogen oxides (NOx) sensor, bank 1, heater sense circuit - high input

P2212   Nitrogen oxides (NOx) sensor, bank 1, heater sense circuit - circuit intermittent

P2213   Nitrogen oxides (NOx) sensor, bank 2 - circuit malfunction

P2214   Nitrogen oxides (NOx) sensor, bank 2 - range/performance

P2215   Nitrogen oxides (NOx) sensor, bank 2 - low input

P2216   Nitrogen oxides (NOx) sensor, bank 2 - high input

P2217   Nitrogen oxides (NOx) sensor, bank 2 - intermittent input

P2218   Nitrogen oxides (NOx) sensor, bank 2, heater control - open circuit

P2219   Nitrogen oxides (NOx) sensor, bank 2, heater control - circuit low

P2220   Nitrogen oxides (NOx) sensor, bank 2, heater control - circuit high

P2221   Nitrogen oxides (NOx) sensor, bank 2, heater sense circuit - circuit malfunction

P2222   Nitrogen oxides (NOx) sensor, bank 2, heater sense circuit - range/performance

P2223   Nitrogen oxides (NOx) sensor, bank 2, heater sense circuit - circuit low

P2224 Nitrogen oxides (NOx) sensor, bank 2, heater sense circuit - circuit high

P2225 Nitrogen oxides (NOx) sensor, bank 2, heater sense circuit - circuit intermittent

P2226 Barometric pressure (BARO) sensor - circuit malfunction

P2227 Barometric pressure (BARO) sensor - range/ performance sensor - circuit low

P2229 Barometric pressure (BARO) sensor - circuit high

P2230 Barometric pressure (BARO) sensor - circuit intermittent

P2231 Heated oxygen sensor (HO2S) 1, bank 1 - signal circuit shorted to heater circuit

P2232 Heated oxygen sensor (HO2S) 2, bank 1 - signal circuit shorted to heater circuit

P2233 Heated oxygen sensor (HO2S) 3, bank 1 - signal circuit shorted to heater circuit

P2234 Heated oxygen sensor (HO2S) 1, bank 2 - signal circuit shorted to heater circuit

P2235 Heated oxygen sensor (HO2S) 2, bank 2 - signal circuit shorted to heater circuit

P2236 Heated oxygen sensor (HO2S) 3, bank 2 - signal circuit shorted to heater circuit

P2238 O2 sensor positive current control circuit low bank 1, sensor 1

P2239 O2 sensor positive current control circuit high bank 1, sensor 1

P2240 O2 sensor positive current control circuit/ open bank 2, sensor 1

P2241 O2 sensor positive current control circuit low bank 2, sensor 1

P2242 O2 sensor positive current control circuit high bank 2, sensor 1

P2243 O2 sensor reference voltage circuit/open bank 1, sensor 1

P2244 O2 sensor reference voltage performance bank 1, sensor 1

P2245 O2 sensor reference voltage circuit low bank 1, sensor 1

P2246 O2 sensor reference voltage circuit high bank 1, sensor 1

P2247 O2 sensor reference voltage circuit/open bank 2, sensor 1

P2248 O2 sensor reference voltage performance bank 2, sensor 1

P2249 O2 sensor reference voltage circuit low bank 2, sensor 1

P2250 O2 sensor reference voltage circuit high bank 2, sensor 1

P2251 O2 sensor negative current control circuit/ open bank 1, sensor 1

P2252 O2 sensor negative current control circuit low bank 1, sensor 1

P2253 O2 sensor negative current control circuit high bank 1, sensor 1

P2254 O2 sensor negative current control circuit/ open bank 2, sensor 1

P2255 O2 sensor negative current control circuit low bank 2, sensor 1

P2256 O2 sensor negative current control circuit high bank 2, sensor 1

P2257 Secondary air injection (AIR) system, control A - circuit low

P2258 Secondary air injection (AIR) system, control A - circuit high

P2259 Secondary air injection (AIR) system, control B - circuit low

P2260 Secondary air injection (AIR) system, control B - circuit high

P2261 Turbocharger (TC) bypass valve/ supercharger (SC) bypass valve

P2262 Turbocharger (TC) boost pressure not detected

P2263 Turbocharger (TC) boost pressure/ supercharger (SC) boost pressure - performance problem

P2264 Fuel/water separator sensor - circuit malfunction

P2265 Fuel/water separator sensor - range/ performance

P2266 Fuel/water separator sensor - circuit low

P2267 Fuel/water separator sensor - circuit high

P2268 Fuel/water separator sensor - circuit intermittent

P2 - codes (continued)

P2269 Water in fuel

P2270 O2 sensor signal stuck lean bank 1, sensor 2

P2271 O2 sensor signal stuck rich bank 1, sensor 2

P2272 O2 sensor signal stuck lean bank 2, sensor 2

P2273 O2 sensor signal stuck rich bank 2, sensor 2

P2274 O2 sensor signal stuck lean bank 1, sensor 3

P2275 O2 sensor signal stuck rich bank 1, sensor 3

P2276 O2 sensor signal stuck lean bank 2, sensor 3

P2277 O2 sensor signal stuck rich bank 2, sensor 3

P2278 O2 sensor signals swapped bank 1, sensor 3/bank 2, sensor 3

P2279 Intake air leak

P2280 Air leak/blockage between air filter and mass air flow (MAF) sensor

P2281 Air leak between MAF sensor and throttle body

P2282 Air leak between throttle body and intake valves

P2283 Injector control pressure sensor - circuit malfunction

P2284 Injector control pressure sensor - range/performance

P2285 Injector control pressure sensor - circuit low

P2286 Injector control pressure sensor - circuit high

P2287 Injector control pressure sensor - circuit intermittent

P2288 Injector control pressure - pressure too high

P2289 Injector control pressure, engine off - pressure too high

P2290 Injector control pressure - pressure too low

P2291 Injector control pressure, engine cranking - pressure too low

P2292 Injector control pressure - erratic

P2293 Fuel pressure regulator 2 - performance problem

P2294 Fuel pressure regulator 2 - circuit malfunction

P2295 Fuel pressure regulator 2 - circuit low

P2296 Fuel pressure regulator 2 - circuit high

P2297 O2 sensor out of range during deceleration bank 1, sensor 1

P2298 O2 sensor out of range during deceleration bank 2, sensor 1

P2299 Brake pedal position (BPP) switch/accelerator pedal position (APP) sensor - signals incompatible

P2300 Ignition coil A, primary circuit - circuit low

P2301 Ignition coil A, primary circuit - circuit high

P2302 Ignition coil A, secondary circuit - malfunction

P2303 Ignition coil B, primary circuit - circuit low

P2304 Ignition coil B, primary circuit - circuit high

P2305 Ignition coil B, secondary circuit - malfunction

P2306 Ignition coil C, primary circuit - circuit low

P2307 Ignition coil C, primary circuit - circuit high

P2308 Ignition coil C, secondary circuit - malfunction

P2309 Ignition coil D, primary circuit - circuit low

P2310 Ignition coil D, primary circuit - circuit high

P2311 Ignition coil D, secondary circuit - malfunction

P2312 Ignition coil E, primary circuit - circuit low

P2313 Ignition coil E, primary circuit - circuit high

P2314 Ignition coil E, secondary circuit - malfunction

P2315 Ignition coil F, primary circuit - circuit low

P2316 Ignition coil F, primary circuit - circuit high

P2317 Ignition coil F, secondary circuit - malfunction

P2318 Ignition coil G, primary circuit - circuit low

P2319 Ignition coil G, primary circuit - circuit high

P2320 Ignition coil G, secondary circuit - malfunction

P2321 Ignition coil H, primary circuit - circuit low

P2322 Ignition coil H, primary circuit - circuit high

P2323 Ignition coil H, secondary circuit - malfunction

P2324 Ignition coil 1, primary circuit - circuit low

P2325	Ignition coil 1, primary circuit - circuit high
P2326	Ignition coil 1, secondary circuit - malfunction
P2327	Ignition coil J, primary circuit - circuit low
P2328	Ignition coil J, primary circuit - circuit high
P2329	Ignition coil J, secondary circuit - malfunction
P2330	Ignition coil K, primary circuit - circuit low
P2331	Ignition coil K, primary circuit - circuit high
P2332	Ignition coil K, secondary circuit - malfunction
P2333	Ignition coil L, primary circuit - circuit low
P2334	Ignition coil L, primary circuit - circuit high
P2335	Ignition coil L, secondary circuit - malfunction
P2336	Cylinder 1 - above knock threshold
P2337	Cylinder 2 - above knock threshold
P2338	Cylinder 3 - above knock threshold
P2339	Cylinder 4 - above knock threshold
P2340	Cylinder 5 - above knock threshold
P2341	Cylinder 6 - above knock threshold
P2342	Cylinder 7 - above knock threshold
P2343	Cylinder 8 - above knock threshold
P2344	Cylinder 9 - above knock threshold
P2345	Cylinder 10 - above knock threshold
P2346	Cylinder 11 - above knock threshold
P2347	Cylinder 12 - above knock threshold
P2400	Evaporative emission (EVAP) leak detection pump, control - open circuit
P2401	Evaporative emission (EVAP) leak detection pump, control - circuit low
P2402	Evaporative emission (EVAP) leak detection pump, control - circuit high
P2403	Evaporative emission (EVAP) leak detection pump, sense circuit - open circuit
P2404	Evaporative emission (EVAP) leak detection pump, sense circuit - range/performance
P2405	Evaporative emission (EVAP) leak detection pump, sense circuit - circuit low
P2406	Evaporative emission (EVAP) leak detection pump, sense circuit - circuit high
P2407	Evaporative emission (EVAP) leak detection pump, sense circuit - circuit intermittent/ erratic
P2408	Fuel filler cap warning sensor/switch - circuit malfunction
P2409	Fuel filler cap warning sensor/switch - range/ performance
P2410	Fuel filler cap warning sensor/switch - circuit low
P2411	Fuel filler cap warning sensor/switch - circuit high
P2412	Fuel filler cap warning sensor/switch - circuit intermittent/erratic
P2413	Exhaust gas recirculation (EGR) system - performance problem
P2414	O2 sensor exhaust sample error bank 1, sensor 1
P2415	O2 sensor exhaust sample error bank 2, sensor 1
P2416	O2 sensor signals swapped bank 1, sensor 2/bank 1, sensor 3
P2417	O2 sensor signals swapped bank 2, sensor 2/bank 2, sensor 3
P2418	Evaporative emission (EVAP) switching valve open circuit
P2419	Evaporative emission (EVAP) switching valve circuit low
P2420	Evaporative emission (EVAP) switching valve circuit high
P2421	Evaporative emission (EVAP) vent valve - valve stuck open
P2422	Evaporative emission (EVAP) vent valve - valve stuck closed
P2423	Hydrocarbon (HC) catalytic converter, bank 1 efficiency below threshold
P2424	Hydrocarbon (HC) catalytic converter, bank 2 efficiency below threshold
P2425	Exhaust gas recirculation (EGR) cooling valve open circuit
P2426	Exhaust gas recirculation (EGR) cooling valve circuit low
P2427	Exhaust gas recirculation (EGR) cooling valve circuit high

P2 - codes (continued)

P2428 Exhaust gas temperature (EGT), bank 1 - temperature too high

P2429 Exhaust gas temperature (EGT), bank 2 - temperature too high

P2430 Secondary air injection (AIR) system, air flow /pressure sensor, bank 1 - circuit malfunction

P2431 Secondary air injection (AIR) system, air flow/pressure sensor, bank 1 - range/ performance

P2432 Secondary air injection (AIR) system, air flow/pressure sensor, bank 1 - circuit low

P2433 Secondary air injection (AIR) system, air flow/pressure sensor, bank 1 - circuit high

P2434 Secondary air injection (AIR) system, air flow / pressure sensor, bank 1 - circuit intermittent/erratic

P2435 Secondary air injection (AIR) system, air flow/pressure sensor, bank 2 - circuit malfunction

P2436 Secondary air injection (AIR) system, air flow/pressure sensor, bank 2 - range/ performance

P2437 Secondary air injection (AIR) system, air flow/pressure sensor, bank 2 - circuit low

P2438 Secondary air injection (AIR) system, air flow/pressure sensor, bank 2 - circuit high

P2439 Secondary air injection (AIR) system, air flow / pressure sensor, bank 2 - circuit intermittent/erratic

P2440 Secondary air injection (AIR) switching valve, bank 1 - valve stuck open

P2441 Secondary air injection (AIR) switching valve, bank 1 - valve stuck closed

P2442 Secondary air injection (AIR) switching valve, bank 2 - valve stuck open

P2443 Secondary air injection (AIR) switching valve, bank 2 - valve stuck closed

P2444 Secondary air injection (AIR) pump, bank 1 - pump stuck on

P2445 Secondary air injection (AIR) pump, bank 1 - pump stuck off

P2446 Secondary air injection (AIR) pump, bank 2 - pump stuck on

P2447 Secondary air injection (AIR) pump, bank 2 - pump stuck off

P2500 Alternator warning lamp, L-terminal - circuit low

P2501 Alternator warning lamp, L-terminal - circuit high

P2502 Charging system voltage

P2503 Charging system - voltage low

P2504 Charging system - voltage high

P2505 Engine control module (ECM) - supply voltage

P2506 Engine control module (ECM) - supply voltage, range/performance

P2507 Engine control module (ECIVI) - supply voltage low

P2508 Engine control module (ECM) - supply voltage high

P2509 Engine control module (ECM) - supply voltage, intermittent

P2510 Engine control (EC) relay, sense circuit - range/performance

P2511 Engine control (EC) relay, sense circuit - circuit intermittent

P2512 Event data recorder request - open circuit

P2513 Event data recorder request - circuit low

P2514 Event data recorder request - circuit high

P2515 A/C refrigerant pressure sensor B - circuit malfunction

P2516 A/C refrigerant pressure sensor B - range/ performance

P2517 A/C refrigerant pressure sensor B - circuit low

P2518 A/C refrigerant pressure sensor B - circuit high

P2519 A/C request A - circuit malfunction

P2520 A/C request A - circuit low

P2521   A/C request A - circuit high

P2522   A/C request B - circuit malfunction

P2523   A/C request B - circuit low

P2524   A/C request B - circuit high

P2525   Vacuum reservoir pressure sensor - circuit malfunction

P2526   Vacuum reservoir pressure sensor - range/performance

P2527   Vacuum reservoir pressure sensor - circuit low

P2528   Vacuum reservoir pressure sensor - circuit high

P2529   Vacuum reservoir pressure sensor - circuit intermittent

P2530   Ignition switch, ON position - circuit malfunction

P2531   Ignition switch, ON position - circuit low

P2532   Ignition switch, ON position - circuit high

P2533   Ignition switch, ON/start position - circuit malfunction

P2534   Ignition switch, ON/start position - circuit low

P2535   Ignition switch, ON/start position - circuit high

P2536   Ignition switch, accessory position - circuit malfunction

P2537   Ignition switch, accessory position - circuit low

P2538   Ignition switch, accessory position - circuit high

P2539   Fuel low pressure sensor - circuit malfunction

P2540   Fuel low pressure sensor - range/performance

P2541   Fuel low pressure sensor - circuit low

P2542   Fuel low pressure sensor - circuit high

P2543   Fuel low pressure sensor - circuit intermittent

P2544   Torque management request, input signal A - malfunction

P2545   Torque management request, input signal A - range/performance

P2546   Torque management request, input signal A - signal low

P2547   Torque management request, input signal A - signal high

P2548   Torque management request, input signal B - malfunction

P2549   Torque management request, input signal B - range/performance

P2550   Torque management request, input signal B - signal low

P2551   Torque management request, input signal B - signal high

P2552   Throttle/fuel inhibit - circuit malfunction

P2553   Throttle/fuel inhibit - range/performance

P2554   Throttle/fuel inhibit - circuit low

P2555   Throttle/fuel inhibit - circuit high

P2556   Engine coolant "low" sensor/switch - circuit malfunction

P2557   Engine coolant "low" sensor/switch - range/performance

P2558   Engine coolant "low" sensor/switch - circuit low

P2559   Engine coolant "low" sensor/switch - circuit high

P2560   Engine coolant level low

P2561   A/C control module - MIL activation requested

P2562   Turbocharger (TC) boost control position sensor - circuit malfunction

P2563   Turbocharger (TC) boost control position sensor - range/performance

P2564   Turbocharger (TC) boost control position sensor - circuit low

P2565   Turbocharger (TC) boost control position sensor - circuit high

P2566   Turbocharger (TC) boost control position sensor - circuit intermittent

P2567   Direct ozone reduction catalytic converter temperature sensor - circuit malfunction

P2568   Direct ozone reduction catalytic converter temperature sensor - range/performance

P2569   Direct ozone reduction catalytic converter temperature sensor - circuit low

P2570 Direct ozone reduction catalytic converter temperature sensor - circuit high

P2571 Direct ozone reduction catalytic converter temperature sensor - circuit intermittent/erratic

P2572 Direct ozone reduction catalytic converter deterioration sensor

P2573 Direct ozone reduction catalytic converter deterioration sensor - range/performance

P2574 Direct ozone reduction catalytic converter deterioration sensor - circuit low

P2575 Direct ozone reduction catalytic converter deterioration sensor - circuit high

P2576 Direct ozone reduction catalytic converter deterioration sensor - circuit intermittent/erratic

P2577 Direct ozone reduction catalytic converter - efficiency below threshold

P2600 Engine coolant pump motor - open circuit

P2601 Engine coolant pump motor - range/performance

P2602 Engine coolant pump motor - circuit low

P2603 Engine coolant pump motor - circuit high

P2604 Intake air heater A - range/performance

P2605 Intake air heater A - open circuit

P2606 Intake air heater B - range/performance

P2607 Intake air heater B - circuit low

P2608 Intake air heater B - circuit high

P2609 Intake air heater system - performance problem

P2610 Engine control module (ECM) - internal engine timer performance

P2611 A/C refrigerant distribution valve - open circuit

P2612 A/C refrigerant distribution valve - circuit low

P2613 A/C refrigerant distribution valve - circuit high

P2614 Camshaft position (CMP), output signal - open circuit

P2615 Camshaft position (CMP), output signal - circuit low

P2616 Camshaft position (CMP), output signal - circuit high

P2617 Crankshaft position (CKP), output signal - open circuit

P2618 Crankshaft position (CKP), output signal - circuit low

P2619 Crankshaft position (CKP), output signal - circuit high

P2620 Throttle position (TP), output signal - open circuit

P2621 Throttle position (TP), output signal - circuit low

P2622 Throttle position (TP), output signal-- circuit high

P2623 Injector control pressure regulator - open circuit

P2624 Injector control pressure regulator - circuit low

P2625 Injector control pressure regulator - circuit high

P2626 O2 sensor pumping current trim circuit/open bank 1, sensor 1

P2627 O2 sensor pumping current trim circuit low bank 1, sensor 1

P2628 O2 sensor pumping current trim circuit high bank 1 sensor 1

P2629 O2 sensor pumping current trim circuit/open bank 2 sensor 1

P2630 O2 sensor pumping current trim circuit low bank 2 sensor 1

P2631 O2 sensor pumping current trim circuit high bank 2 sensor 1

P2632 Fuel pump (FP) B, control - open circuit

P2633 Fuel pump (FP) B, control - circuit low

P2634 Fuel pump (FP) B, control - circuit high

P2635 Fuel pump (FP) A - low flow/performance problem

P2636   Fuel pump (FP) B - low flow/performance problem

P2637   Torque management, feedback signal A - malfunction

P2638   Torque management, feedback signal A - range/performance

P2639   Torque management, feedback signal A - signal low

P2640   Torque management, feedback signal A - signal high

P2641   Torque management, feedback signal B - malfunction

P2642   Torque management, feedback signal B - range/performance

P2643   Torque management, feedback signal B - signal low

P2644   Torque management, feedback signal B - signal high

P2645   Rocker arm actuator A, bank 1 - open circuit

P2646   Rocker arm actuator A, bank 1 - performance problem or actuator stuck off

P2647   Rocker arm actuator A, bank 1 - actuator stuck on

P2648   Rocker arm actuator A, bank 1 - circuit low

P2649   Rocker arm actuator A, bank 1 - circuit high

P2650   Rocker arm actuator B, bank 1 - open circuit

P2651   Rocker arm actuator B, bank 1 - performance problem or actuator stuck off

P2652   Rocker arm actuator B, bank 1 - actuator stuck on

P2653   Rocker arm actuator B, bank 1 - circuit low

P2654   Rocker arm actuator B, bank 1 - circuit high

P2655   Rocker arm actuator A, bank 2 - open circuit

P2656   Rocker arm actuator A, bank 2 - performance problem or actuator stuck off

P2657   Rocker arm actuator A, bank 2 - actuator stuck on

P2658   Rocker arm actuator A, bank 2 - circuit low

P2659   Rocker arm actuator A, bank 2 - circuit high

P2660   Rocker arm actuator B, bank 2 - open circuit

P2661   Rocker arm actuator B, bank 2 - performance problem or actuator stuck off

P2662   Rocker arm actuator B, bank 2 - actuator stuck on

P2663   Rocker arm actuator B, bank 2 - circuit low

P2664   Rocker arm actuator B, bank 2 - circuit high

P2665   Fuel shut-off solenoid B - open circuit

P2666   Fuel shut-off solenoid B - circuit low

P2667   Fuel shut-off solenoid B - circuit high

P2668   Fuel mode indicator lamp - circuit malfunction

P2669   Actuator supply voltage B - open circuit

P2670   Actuator supply voltage B - circuit low

P2671   Actuator supply voltage B - circuit high

P2700   Transmission friction element A, apply time - range/performance

P2701   Transmission friction element B, apply time - range/performance

P2702   Transmission friction element C, apply time - range/performance

P2703   Transmission friction element D, apply time - range/performance

P2704   Transmission friction element E, apply time - range/performance

P2705   Shift solenoid (SS) F - circuit malfunction

P2707   Shift solenoid (SS) F - performance problem or solenoid stuck off

P2708   Shift solenoid (SS) F - solenoid stuck on

P2709   Shift solenoid (SS) F - electrical

P2710   Shift solenoid (SS) F - intermittent

P2711   Unexpected mechanical gear disengagement

P2712   Hydraulic power unit leakage

P2713   Transmission fluid pressure (TFP) solenoid D - circuit malfunction

P2714   Transmission fluid pressure (TFP) solenoid D - performance problem or solenoid stuck off

P2715   Transmission fluid pressure (TFP) solenoid D - solenoid stuck on

P2716   Transmission fluid pressure (TFP) solenoid D - electrical

P2717 Transmission fluid pressure (TFP) solenoid D - circuit intermittent

P2718 Transmission fluid pressure (TFP) solenoid D - open circuit

P2719 Transmission fluid pressure (TFP) solenoid D - range/performance

P2720 Transmission fluid pressure (TFP) solenoid D - circuit low

P2721 Transmission fluid pressure (TFP) solenoid D - circuit high

P2722 Transmission fluid pressure (TFP) solenoid E - circuit malfunction

P2723 Transmission fluid pressure (TFP) solenoid E - performance problem or solenoid stuck off

P2724 Transmission fluid pressure (TFP) solenoid E - solenoid stuck on

P2725 Transmission fluid pressure (TFP) solenoid E - electrical

P2726 Transmission fluid pressure (TFP) solenoid E - circuit intermittent

P2727 Transmission fluid pressure (TFP) solenoid E - open circuit

P2728 Transmission fluid pressure (TFP) solenoid E -range/performance

P2729 Transmission fluid pressure (TFP) solenoid E - circuit low

P2730 Transmission fluid pressure (TFP) solenoid E - circuit high

P2731 Transmission fluid pressure (TFP) solenoid F - circuit malfunction

P2732 Transmission fluid pressure (TFP) solenoid F - performance problem or solenoid stuck off

P2733 Transmission fluid pressure (TFP) solenoid F - solenoid stuck on

P2734 Transmission fluid pressure (TFP) solenoid F - electrical

P2735 Transmission fluid pressure (TFP) solenoid F - circuit intermittent

P2736 Transmission fluid pressure (TFP) solenoid F - open circuit

P2737 Transmission fluid pressure (TFP) solenoid F - range/performance

P2738 Transmission fluid pressure (TFP) solenoid F - circuit low

P2739 Transmission fluid pressure (TFP) solenoid F - circuit high

P2740 Transmission fluid temperature (TFT) sensor B - circuit malfunction

P2741 Transmission fluid temperature (TFT) sensor B - circuit range/performance

P2742 Transmission fluid temperature (TFT) sensor B - circuit low

P2743 Transmission fluid temperature (TFT) sensor B - circuit high

P2744 Transmission fluid temperature (TFT) sensor B - circuit intermittent

P2745 Transmission intermediate shaft speed sensor B - circuit malfunction

P2746 Transmission intermediate shaft speed sensor B - range/performance

P2747 Transmission intermediate shaft speed sensor B - no signal

P2748 Transmission intermediate shaft speed sensor B - circuit intermittent

P2749 Transmission intermediate shaft speed sensor C - circuit malfunction

P2750 Transmission intermediate shaft speed sensor C - range/performance

P2751 Transmission intermediate shaft speed sensor C - no signal

P2752 Transmission intermediate shaft speed sensor C - circuit intermittent

P2753 Transmission fluid cooler - open circuit

P2754 Transmission fluid cooler - circuit low

P2755 Transmission fluid cooler - circuit high

P2756 Torque converter clutch (TCC) pressure control solenoid - circuit malfunction

P2757 Torque converter clutch (TCC) pressure control solenoid - performance problem or solenoid stuck off

P2758   Torque converter clutch (TCC) pressure control solenoid - solenoid stuck on

P2759   Torque converter clutch (TCC) pressure control solenoid - electrical fault

P2760   Torque converter clutch (TCC) pressure control solenoid - circuit intermittent

P2761   Torque converter clutch (TCC) pressure control solenoid - open circuit

P2762   Torque converter clutch (TCC) pressure control solenoid - range/performance

P2763   Torque converter clutch (TCC) pressure control solenoid - circuit high

P2764   Torque converter clutch (TCC) pressure control solenoid - circuit low

P2765   Transmission input/turbine shaft speed (TSS) sensor B - circuit malfunction

P2766   Transmission input/turbine shaft speed (TSS) sensor B - range/performance

P2767   Transmission input/turbine shaft speed (TSS) sensor B - no signal

P2768   Transmission input/turbine shaft speed (TSS) sensor B - circuit intermittent

P2769   Torque converter clutch (TCC) - circuit low

P2770   Torque converter clutch (TCC) - circuit high

P2771   Four wheel drive, low gear ratio switch - circuit malfunction

P2772   Four wheel drive, low gear ratio switch - range/performance

P2773   Four wheel drive, low gear ratio switch - circuit low

P2774   Four wheel drive, low gear ratio switch - circuit high

P2775   Transmission gear selection switch, upshift - range/performance

P2776   Transmission gear selection switch, upshift - circuit low

P2777   Transmission gear selection switch, upshift - circuit high

P2778   Transmission gear selection switch, upshift - circuit intermittent/erratic

P2779   Transmission gear selection switch, downshift range/performance

P2780   Transmission gear selection switch, downshift - circuit low

P2781   Transmission gear selection switch, downshift - circuit high

P2782   Transmission gear selection switch, downshift - circuit intermittent/erratic

P2783   Torque converter - temperature too high

P2784   Transmission input/turbine shaft speed (TSS) sensor A/B - correlation

P2785   Clutch actuator - temperature too high

P2786   Gear shift actuator - temperature too high

P2787   Clutch - temperature too high

P2788   Auto shift manual (ASM) transmission, adaptive learning - at limit

P2789   Clutch, adaptive learning - at limit

P2790   Gate select direction - circuit malfunction

P2791   Gate select direction - circuit low

P2792   Gate select direction - circuit high

P2793   Gear shift direction - circuit malfunction

P2794   Gear shift direction - circuit low

P2795   Gear shift direction - circuit high

P3 - codes

Note: The following list of OBD-II trouble codes is a generic list applicable to all models equipped with an OBD-II system, although not all codes apply to all models.

P3400 Cylinder deactivation system bank 1

P3401 Cylinder 1 deactivation/intake valve control circuit/open

P3402 Cylinder 1 deactivation/intake valve control performance

P3403 Cylinder 1 deactivation/intake valve control circuit low

P3404 Cylinder 1 deactivation/intake valve control circuit high

P3405 Cylinder 1 exhaust valve control circuit/open

P3406 Cylinder 1 exhaust valve control performance

P3407 Cylinder 1 exhaust valve control circuit low

P3408 Cylinder 1 exhaust valve control circuit high

P3409 Cylinder 2 deactivation/intake valve control circuit/open

P3410 Cylinder 2 deactivation/intake valve control performance

P3411 Cylinder 2 deactivation/intake valve control circuit low

P3412 Cylinder 2 deactivation/intake valve control circuit high

P3413 Cylinder 2 exhaust valve control circuit/open

P3414 Cylinder 2 exhaust valve control performance

P3415 Cylinder 2 exhaust valve control circuit low

P3416 Cylinder 2 exhaust valve control circuit high

P3417 Cylinder 3 deactivation/intake valve control circuit/open

P3418 Cylinder 3 deactivation/intake valve control performance

P3419 Cylinder 3 deactivation/intake valve control circuit low

P3420 Cylinder 3 deactivation/intake valve control circuit high

P3421 Cylinder 3 exhaust valve control circuit/open

P3422 Cylinder 3 exhaust valve control performance

P3423 Cylinder 3 exhaust valve control circuit low

P3424 Cylinder 3 exhaust valve control circuit high

P3425 Cylinder 4 deactivation/intake valve control circuit/open

P3426 Cylinder 4 deactivation/intake valve control performance

P3427 Cylinder 4 deactivation/intake valve control circuit low

P3428 Cylinder 4 deactivation/intake valve control circuit high

P3429 Cylinder 4 exhaust valve control circuit/open

P3430 Cylinder 4 exhaust valve control performance

P3431 Cylinder 4 exhaust valve control circuit low

P3432 Cylinder 4 exhaust valve control circuit high

P3433 Cylinder 5 deactivation/intake valve control circuit/open

P3434 Cylinder 5 deactivation/intake valve control performance

P3435 Cylinder 5 deactivation/intake valve control circuit low

P3436 Cylinder 5 deactivation/intake valve control circuit high

P3437 Cylinder 5 exhaust valve control circuit/open

P3438 Cylinder 5 exhaust valve control performance

P3439 Cylinder 5 exhaust valve control circuit low

P3440 Cylinder 5 exhaust valve control circuit high

P3441 Cylinder 6 deactivation/intake valve control circuit/open

P3442 Cylinder 6 deactivation/intake valve control performance

P3443 Cylinder 6 deactivation/intake valve control circuit low

P3444 Cylinder 6 deactivation/intake valve control circuit high

P3445 Cylinder 6 exhaust valve control circuit/open

P3446 Cylinder 6 exhaust valve control performance

P3447 Cylinder 6 exhaust valve control circuit low

P3448 Cylinder 6 exhaust valve control circuit high

P3449 Cylinder 7 deactivation/intake valve control circuit/open

P3450 Cylinder 7 deactivation/intake valve control performance

P3451 Cylinder 7 deactivation/intake valve control circuit low

P3452 Cylinder 7 deactivation/intake valve control circuit high

P3453 Cylinder 7 exhaust valve control circuit/open

P3454 Cylinder 7 exhaust valve control performance

P3455 Cylinder 7 exhaust valve control circuit low

P3456 Cylinder 7 exhaust valve control circuit high

P3457 Cylinder 8 deactivation/intake valve control circuit/open

P3458 Cylinder 8 deactivation/intake valve control performance

P3459 Cylinder 8 deactivation/intake valve control circuit low

P3460 Cylinder 8 deactivation/intake valve control circuit high

P3461 Cylinder 8 exhaust valve control circuit/open

P3462 Cylinder 8 exhaust valve control performance

P3463 Cylinder 8 exhaust valve control circuit low

P3464 Cylinder 8 exhaust valve control circuit high

P3465 Cylinder 9 deactivation/intake valve control circuit - open

P3466 Cylinder 9 deactivation/intake valve control performance

P3467 Cylinder 9 deactivation/intake valve control circuit low

P3468 Cylinder 9 deactivation/intake valve control circuit high

P3469 Cylinder 9 exhaust valve control circuit/open

P3470 Cylinder 9 exhaust valve control performance

P3471 Cylinder 9 exhaust valve control circuit low

P3472 Cylinder 9 exhaust valve control circuit high

P3473 Cylinder 10 deactivation/intake valve control circuit/open

P3474 Cylinder 10 deactivation/intake valve control performance

P3475 Cylinder 10 deactivation/intake valve control circuit low

P3476 Cylinder 10 deactivation/intake valve control circuit high

P3477 Cylinder 10 exhaust valve control circuit/open

P3478 Cylinder 10 exhaust valve control performance

P3479 Cylinder 10 exhaust valve control circuit low

P3480 Cylinder 10 exhaust valve control circuit high

P3481 Cylinder 11 deactivation/intake valve control circuit/open

P3482 Cylinder 11 deactivation/intake valve control performance

P3483 Cylinder 11 deactivation/intake valve control circuit low

P3484 Cylinder 11 deactivation/intake valve control circuit high

P3485 Cylinder 11 exhaust valve control circuit/open

P3486 Cylinder 11 exhaust valve control performance

P3487 Cylinder 11 exhaust valve control circuit low

P3488 Cylinder 11 exhaust valve control circuit high

P3489 Cylinder 12 deactivation/intake valve control circuit/open

P3490 Cylinder 12 deactivation/intake valve control performance

P3491 Cylinder 12 deactivation/intake valve control circuit low

P3492 Cylinder 12 deactivation/intake valve control circuit high

P3493 Cylinder 12 exhaust valve control circuit/open

P3494 Cylinder 12 exhaust valve control performance

P3495 Cylinder 12 exhaust valve control circuit low

P3496 Cylinder 12 exhaust valve control circuit high

P3497 Cylinder deactivation system bank 2

OBD-II Manufacturer-Specific DTCs
General Motors

Note: *The following list of OBD-II trouble codes is a manufacturer-specific list applicable to all GM models equipped with an OBD-II system, although not all codes apply to all models.*

P1031   HO2S heater current monitor control (sensor 1, banks 1 & 2)

P1032   HO2S heater warm-up control circuit (sensor 1, banks 1 & 2)

P1106   Manifold absolute pressure (MAP) sensor circuit intermittent high voltage

P1107   Manifold absolute pressure (MAP) sensor circuit intermittent low voltage

P1108   BARO to MAP sensor input comparison too high

P1111   Intake air temperature (IAT) sensor circuit intermittent high voltage

P1112   Intake air temperature (IAT) sensor circuit intermittent low voltage

P1113   Intake resonance switchover valve circuit conditions

P1114   Engine coolant temperature (ECT) sensor circuit intermittent low voltage

P1115   Engine coolant temperature (ECT) sensor circuit intermittent high voltage

P1120   Throttle position (TP) sensor 1 circuit - out of range

P1121   Throttle position (TP) sensor circuit intermittent high voltage

P1122   Throttle position (TP) sensor circuit intermittent low voltage

P1125   Accelerator pedal position (APP) system

P1132   HO2S circuit shorted to heater circuit conditions bank 1 , sensor 1

P1133 or P1153   HO2S insufficient switching

P1134 or P1154   HO2S transition time ratio

P1137   HO2S circuit low voltage during power enrichment sensor 2

P1138   HO2S circuit high voltage during decel fuel cutoff sensor 2

P1139   HO2S insufficient switching conditions bank 1, sensor 2

P1140   HO2S transition time ratio conditions bank 1, sensor 2

P1141   HO2S heater control circuit conditions bank 1, sensor 2

P1152   HO2S circuit shorted to heater circuit conditions bank 2, sensor 1

P1153   HO2S insufficient switching conditions bank 2, sensor 1

P1154   HO2S insufficient transition time ratio bank 2, sensor 1

P1158   HO2S shift rich conditions bank 2, sensor 2

P1161   HO2S heater control circuit conditions bank 2, sensor 2

P1171   Fuel system lean during acceleration

P1172   Sec fuel pump insufficient/no fuel flow

P1187   Engine oil temperature sensor low input conditions

P1188   Engine oil temperature sensor high input conditions

P1189   Engine oil pressure (EOP) switch circuit

P1191   Intake air (IA) duct air leak

P1200   Injector control circuit

P1201   Gas mass flow sensor performance conditions

P1202   Gas mass flow sensor low frequency conditions

P1203   Gas mass flow sensor low frequency conditions

P1214   Injection pump timing offset

P1215   PCM driver circuit

P1216   Fuel solenoid response time too short

P1217 Fuel solenoid response time too long

P1218 Injection pump calibration

P1220 Throttle position (TP) sensor 2 circuit

P1221 Throttle position (TP) sensor 1-2 correlation

P1222 Injector control circuit intermittent

P1223 Injector 1 output circuit

P1226 Injector 2 output circuit

P1229 Injector 3 output circuit

P1232 Injector 4 output circuit

P1235 Injector 5 output circuit

P1238 Injector 6 output circuit

P1241 Injector 7 output circuit

P1244 Injector 8 output circuit

P1245 Intake plenum switchover valve

P1250 Early fuel evaporation (EFE) heater circuit

P1257 Supercharger system overboost fault

P1258 Engine coolant over-temperature - protection mode active

P1260 Fuel pump speed relay control circuit

P1261 Injector positive voltage control circuit

P1262 Injector positive voltage control circuit group 2

P1270 Accelerator pedal position (APP) sensor analog to digital performance

P1271 Accelerator pedal position (APP) sensor 1-2 correlation

P1272 Accelerator pedal position (APP) sensor 2-3 correlation

P1273 Accelerator pedal position (APP) sensor 1-3 correlation

P1275 Accelerator pedal position (APP) sensor 1 circuit

P1276 Accelerator pedal position (APP) sensor 1 performance

P1277 Accelerator pedal position (APP) sensor 1 circuit low voltage

P1278 Accelerator pedal position (APP) sensor 1 circuit low voltage

P1280 Accelerator pedal position (APP) sensor 2 circuit

P1281 Accelerator pedal position (APP) sensor 2 performance

P1282 Accelerator pedal position (APP) sensor 2 circuit low voltage

P1283 Accelerator pedal position (APP) sensor 2 circuit High voltage

P1285 Accelerator pedal position (APP) sensor 3 circuit

P1286 Accelerator pedal position (APP) sensor 3 performance

P1287 Accelerator pedal position (APP) sensor 3 circuit low voltage

P1288 Accelerator pedal position (APP) sensor 3 circuit high voltage

P1293 Injector circuit low to high current transition time bank 1

P1294 Injector circuit low to high current transition time bank 2

P1295 Injector circuit low to low current transition time bank 1

P1296 Injector circuit low to low current transition time bank 2

P1300 Ignition coil 1 primary feedback circuit

P1305 Ignition coil 2 primary feedback circuit

P1310 Ignition coil 3 primary feedback circuit

P1315 Ignition coil 4 primary feedback circuit

P1320 ICM 4X reference circuit intermittent, no pulses

P1323 ICM 24X reference circuit low frequency

P1335 Crankshaft position sensor circuit

P1336 Crankshaft position (CKP) system variation not learned

P1345 Crankshaft position (CKP) camshaft position (CMP) correlation

P1346 Intake camshaft position system performance

P1349 Intake camshaft position system

P1350 Ignition control (IC) circuit malfunction

P1351 Ignition coil control circuit high voltage

P1352 Ignition bypass circuit high voltage

P1359 Ignition coil group 1 control circuit

P1360 Ignition coil group 2 control circuit

P1361 Ignition control (IC) circuit low voltage

P1362 Ignition bypass circuit low voltage

P1370 IC module 4X reference circuit to many pulses

P1371 DI ignition Low-resolution circuit

P1372 Crankshaft position (CKP) sensor A-B correlation

P1374 Crankshaft position (CKP) high to low resolution frequency correlation

P1380 Misfire detected - rough road data not available

P1381 Misfire detected - no communication with brake control module

P1401 Exhaust gas recirculation flow test

P1403 Exhaust gas recirculation (EGR) valve position circuit low voltage

P1404 Exhaust gas recirculation (EGR) valve closed position performance

P1405 Exhaust gas recirculation (EGR) valve position circuit high voltage

P1406 EGR pintle position error

P1410 Fuel tank pressure control circuit

P1415 or P1416 Secondary air injection (AIR) system

P1431 Fuel level sensor 2 performance

P1432 Fuel level sensor 2 circuit low voltage

P1433 Fuel level sensor 2 circuit high voltage

P1441 Evaporative emission (EVAP) system flow during non-purge

P1442 EVAP vacuum switch circuit

P1450 Barometric pressure sensor circuit

P1451 Barometric pressure sensor performance

P1450 Barometric pressure sensor circuit

P1451 Barometric pressure sensor performance

P1480 Cooling fan relay control circuit high input

P1481 Cooling fan speed sensor circuit

P1482 Cooling fan speed output circuit

P1483 Engine cooling system performance

P1484 Cooling fan system performance

P1500 Starter signal circuit

P1501 Theft deterrent system fault

P1502 Theft deterrent system signal not received

P1503 Theft deterrent system password incorrect

P1508 Idle speed low

P1509 Idle speed high

P1510 Throttle control system - in limitation

P1511 Throttle control system - limp home system performance

P1512 Throttle shaft position - out of range

P1514 Throttle body performance

P1515 Control module throttle actuator position performance

P1516 Throttle actuator control (TAC) module throttle actuator position performance

P1517 Throttle actuator control (TAC) module performance

P1518 Throttle actuator control (TAC) module serial data circuit

P1519 Throttle actuator command (TAC) module

P1520 Park neutral position switch circuit

P1523 Throttle return performance

P1524 Throttle position (TPS) sensor learned closed throttle degrees out-of-range

P1526 Throttle position (TPS) sensor learn not done after reprogramming

P1530 Throttle control system - amplifier adjustment

P1536 Engine coolant over-temperature - air conditioning (A/C) Disabled

P1539 Air conditioning (A/C) clutch feedback circuit high voltage

P1540 Air conditioning (A/C) refrigerant overpressure - air conditioning (A/C) disabled

P1545 Air conditioning (A/C) clutch relay control circuit

P1546 Air conditioning (A/C) clutch feedback circuit low voltage

P1550 Fuel injector control module system voltage

P1551 Throttle valve rest position not reached during learn

P1554 Cruise control feedback circuit

P1555 EVO Solenoid Control circuit

P1560 Transaxle not in drive - cruise control disabled

P1564 Vehicle acceleration too high - cruise control disabled

P1566 Engine RPM too high - cruise control disabled

P1567 Active banking control active - cruise control disabled

P1570 Traction control active - cruise control disabled

P1571 Transmission torque request circuit

P1574 Stop lamp switch circuit

P1575 Extended travel brake switch circuit

P1580 Cruise control move circuit low voltage

P1581 Cruise control move circuit high voltage

P1582 Cruise control direction circuit low voltage

P1583 Cruise control direction circuit high voltage

P1584 Cruise control disabled

P1585 Cruise control inhibit output circuit

P1599 Engine stall detected

P1601 PCM serial communications

P1602 PCM serial communications

P1617 Engine oil level switch circuit

P1619 Engine oil monitor reset

P1620 Low engine coolant

P1621 PCM long term memory performance

P1623 TFT sensor pull-up resistor

P1624 Customer snapshot requested - data available

P1625 PCM checksum - transaxle memory

P1626 Theft deterrent fuel enable signal lost

P1627 Control module analog to digital performance

P1628 ECT pull-up resistor

P1629 Theft deterrent start enable signal not received

P1630 Theft deterrent learn mode active

P1631 Theft deterrent start enable signal not correct

P1632 Theft deterrent fuel disable signal received

P1633 Ignition 0 switch circuit

P1634 Ignition 1 switch circuit

P1635 5 volt reference 1 circuit

P1637 Generator L-terminal circuit

P1638 Generator F-terminal circuit

P1639 5 volt reference 2 circuit

P1640 Control module output A circuit

P1641 Malfunction Indicator Lamp (MIL) control circuit

P1643 Wait to start lamp control circuit

P1644 Traction control delivered torque output circuit

P1650 Control module output B circuit

P1652 Powertrain induced chassis pitch output circuit

P1654 Service throttle soon lamp control circuit

P1656 Wastegate solenoid control circuit

P1658 Fuel injector control module driver performance

P1660 Control module output C circuit

P1665 Fuel level output circuit

P1670 Control module output D circuit

P1680 Ignition 1 voltage not present

General Motors (continued)

P1682 Electronic throttle control (ETC) - voltage incorrect

P1687 Fuel injector control module driver stuck on

P1688 Unmanaged engine torque signal delivered to TCM

P1689 Traction control delivered torque output circuit

P1691 Coolant gauge circuit

P1693 Tachometer circuit

P1695 Remote keyless entry circuit low voltage

P1696 Remote keyless entry circuit high voltage

P1709 Transmission pressure switch solenoid E circuit

P1710 Transmission pressure switch solenoid E circuit stuck open

P1711 Transmission pressure switch solenoid E circuit stuck closed

P1712 Transmission pressure switch solenoid E circuit high

P1713 Transmission reverse pressure switch circuit malfunction

P1714 Transmission reverse pressure switch circuit stuck open

P1720 Solenoid A controlled clutch stuck Off

P1721 Solenoid B controlled clutch stuck Off

P1723 Solenoid A controlled clutch stuck On

P1724 Solenoid B controlled clutch stuck On

P1726 Solenoid D engaged during upshift

P1727 Solenoid, E engaged during upshift

P1760 TCM supply voltage

P1779 Torque delivered signal

P1780 Transmission control module (TCM) requested MIL illumination

P1781 Transmission control module (TCM) MIL request circuit

P1791 Throttle/pedal position signal

P1792 Engine coolant signal

P1795 Throttle actuator control (TAC) system signal

P1810 TFP valve position switch circuit

P1811 Maximum adapt and long shift

P1814 Torque converter overstressed

P1815 Transmission fluid Pressure (TFP) valve position switch - start in wrong range

P1816 Transmission fluid pressure (TFP) valve position switch indicates Park/Neutral (P/N) with drive ratio

P1817 Transmission fluid pressure (TFP) valve position switch - reverse with drive ratio

P1818 Transmission fluid pressure (TFP) valve position switch indicates drive without drive ratio

P1819 Internal mode switch - no start/wrong range

P1820 Internal mode switch circuit A low

P1822 Internal mode switch circuit B high

P1823 Internal mode switch circuit P low

P1825 Internal mode switch - invalid range

P1826 Internal mode switch C circuit high voltage

P1842 1-2 Shift solenoid circuit low voltage

P1843 1-2 Shift solenoid circuit high voltage

P1845 2-3 Shift solenoid circuit low voltage

P1847 2-3 Shift solenoid circuit high voltage

P1860 TCC PWM solenoid circuit electrical

P1868 Transmission fluid life

P1870 Transmission component slipping

P1875 Four wheel drive (4WD) low switch circuit

P1887 TCC release switch circuit

Ford

Note: *The following list of OBD-II trouble codes is a manufacturer-specific list applicable to all Ford models equipped with an OBD-II system, although not all codes apply to all models.*

P1000 On board diagnostic (OBD) system readiness test not complete

P1001 KOER not able to complete, KOER aborted

P1100 Mass air flow (MAF) sensor intermittent

P1101 Mass air flow (MAF) sensor out of self-test range

P1109 Intake air temperature (IAT) sensor 2 intermittent

P1111 System pass 49 state except Econoline

P1112 Intake air temperature (IAT) sensor intermittent

P1114 Intake air temperature (IAT) sensor 2 circuit low input

P1115 Intake air temperature (IAT) sensor 2 circuit high input

P1116 Engine coolant temperature (ECT) sensor out of self-test range

P1117 Engine coolant temperature (ECT) sensor intermittent

P1120 Throttle position (TP) sensor out of range low (RATCH too low)

P1121 Throttle position (TP) sensor inconsistent with MAF sensor

P1124 Throttle position (TP) sensor out of self - test range

P1125 Throttle position (TP) sensor intermittent

P1127 Exhaust not warm enough, downstream heated oxygen sensors (HO2S) not tested

P1128 Upstream oxygen sensors swapped from bank to bank (HO2S - bank1, sensor 1/bank 2, sensor1)

P1129 Downstream oxygen sensors swapped from bank to bank (HO2S - bank 1, sensor 2/bank 2, sensor 2)

P1130 Lack of HO2S bank 1, sensor 1 switches, fuel trim at limit

P1131 Lack of HO2S bank 1, sensor 1 switches, sensor indicates lean

P1132 Lack of HO2S bank 1, sensor 1 switches, sensor indicates rich

P1137 Lack of HO2S bank 1, sensor 2 switches, sensor indicates lean

P1138 Lack of HO2S bank 1, sensor 2 switches, sensor indicates rich

P1150 Lack of HO2S bank 2, sensor 1 switches, fuel trim at limit

P1151 Lack of HO2S bank 2, sensor 1 switches, sensor indicates lean

P1152 Lack of HO2S bank 2, sensor 1 switches, sensor indicates rich

P1157 Lack of HO2S bank 2, sensor 2 switches, sensor indicates lean

P1158 Lack of HO2S bank 2, sensor 2 switches, sensor indicates rich

P1168 Fuel rail pressure (FRP) sensor in range but low

P1169 Fuel rail pressure (FRP) sensor in range but high

P1180 Fuel delivery system - low

P1181 Fuel delivery system - high

P1183 Engine oil temperature (EOT) sensor circuit

P1184 Engine oil temperature (EOT) sensor out of self-test range

P1195 Barometric (BARO) pressure sensor circuit malfunction (signal is from EGR boost sensor)

P1196 Starter switch circuit malfunction

P1209 Injection control pressure (ICP) peak fault

P1210 Injection control pressure (ICP) above expected level

P1211 Injection control pressure (ICP) not controllable-pressure above/below desired

P1212 Injection control pressure (ICP) voltage not at expected level

Ford (continued)

P1218 Cylinder identification (CID) stuck high

P1219 Cylinder identification (CID) stuck low

P1220 Series throttle control malfunction (traction control system)

P1224 Throttle position sensor "B" (TP-B) out of self-test range (traction control system)

P1229 Supercharger intercooler pump (ICP) pump not operating

P1230 Fuel pump low speed malfunction

P1231 Fuel pump secondary circuit low with high speed pump on

P1232 Low speed fuel pump primary circuit malfunction

P1233 Fuel system disabled or offline

P1234 Fuel system disabled or offline

P1235 Fuel pump control out of range

P1236 Fuel pump control out of range

P1237 Fuel pump secondary circuit malfunction

P1238 Fuel pump secondary circuit malfunction

P1244 Generator load input high

P1245 Generator load input low

P1246 Generator load input failed

P1250 Fuel pressure regulator control (FPRC) solenoid malfunction

P1260 Theft detected - Vehicle Immobilized

P1261 High to low side short - cylinder #1 (indicates low side circuit is shorted to B+ or to the high side between the IDM and the injector)

P1262 High to low side short - cylinder #2 (indicates low side circuit is shorted to B+ or to the high side between the IDM and the injector)

P1263 High to low side short - cylinder #3 (indicates low side circuit is shorted to B+ or to the high side between the IDM and the injector)

P1264 High to low side short - cylinder #4 (indicates low side circuit is shorted to B+ or to the high side between the IDM and the injector)

P1265 High to low side short - cylinder #5 (indicates low side circuit is shorted to B+ or to the high side between the IDM and the injector)

P1266 High to low side short - cylinder #6 (indicates low side circuit is shorted to B+ or to the high side between the IDM and the injector)

P1267 High to low side short - cylinder #7 (indicates low side circuit is shorted to B+ or to the high side between the IDM and the injector)

P1268 High to low side short - cylinder #8 (indicates low side circuit is shorted to B+ or to the high side between the IDM and the injector

P1270 Engine RPM/Vehicle speed limiter

P1271 High to low side open - cylinder #1 (indicates a high to low side open between the injector and the IDM)

P1272 High to low side open - cylinder #2 (indicates a high to low side open between the injector and the IDM)

P1273 High to low side open - cylinder #3 (indicates a high to low side open between the injector and the IDM)

P1274 High to low side open - cylinder #4 (indicates a high to low side open between the injector and the IDM)

P1275 High to low side open - cylinder #5 (indicates a high to low side open between the injector and the IDM)

P1276 High to low side open - cylinder #6 (indicates a high to low side open between the injector and the IDM)

P1277 High to low side open - cylinder #7 (indicates a high to low side open between the injector and the IDM)

P1278 High to low side open - cylinder #8 (indicates a high to low side open between the injector and the IDM)

P1280 Injection control pressure (ICP) circuit out of range low

P1281 Injection control pressure (ICP) circuit out of range high

P1282 Injection control pressure (ICP) excessive

P1283 Injection pressure regulator (IPR) circuit failure

P1284 Injection control pressure (ICP) failure-aborts KOER or CCT test

P1285 Cylinder head over temperature sensed

P1288 Cylinder head temperature (CHT) sensor circuit out of self-test range

P1289 Cylinder head temperature (CHT) sensor circuit high input

P1290 Cylinder head temperature (CHT) sensor circuit low input

P1291 IDM to injector high side circuit #1 (Right bank) short to GND or B+

P1292 IDM to injector high side circuit #2 (Right bank) short to GND or B+

P1293 IDM to injector high side circuit open bank #1 (right bank)

P1294 IDM to injector high side circuit open bank #2 (left bank)

P1295 Multiple IDM/injector circuit faults on bank #1 (right bank)

P1296 Multiple IDM/injector circuit faults on bank#2 (left bank)

P1297 High sides shorted together

P1298 IDM failure

P1299 Cylinder head over temperature protection active

P1309 Misfire monitor disabled

P1316 Injector circuit/IDM codes detected

P1320 Distributor signal interrupt

P1336 CKP and or CMP input signal to PCM concerns

P1345 No camshaft position sensor signal

P1351 Ignition diagnostic monitor (IDM) circuit input malfunction

P1351 Indicates ignition system malfunction

P1352 Indicates ignition system malfunction

P1353 Indicates ignition system malfunction

P1354 Indicates ignition system malfunction

P1355 Indicates ignition system malfunction

P1356 PIPs occurred while ignition diagnostic monitor (IDM) pulse width indicates engine not turning

P1357 Ignition diagnostic monitor (IDM) pulse width not defined

P1358 Ignition diagnostic monitor (IDM) signal out of self-test range

P1359 Spark output circuit malfunction

P1364 Spark output circuit malfunction

P1380 Variable cam timing solenoid a circuit malfunction (bank 1)

P1381 Variable cam timing over-advanced (bank 1)

P1383 Variable cam timing over-retarded (bank 1)

P1385 Variable cam timing solenoid a circuit malfunction (bank 2)

P1386 Variable cam timing over-advanced (bank 2)

P1388 Variable cam timing over-retarded (bank 2)

P1390 Octane adjust (OCT ADJ) out of self-test range

P1391 Glow plug circuit low input bank 1 (right)

P1392 Glow plug circuit high input bank 1 (right)

P1393 Glow plug circuit low input bank 2 (left)

P1394 Glow plug circuit high input bank 2 (left)

P1395 Glow plug monitor fault bank 1

P1396 Glow Plug monitor fault bank 2

P1397 System voltage out of self test range

P1400 DPF EGR sensor circuit low voltage detected

P1401 DPF EGR sensor circuit high voltage detected

P1402 EGR valve position sensor open or short

P1403 Differential pressure feedback EGR (DPFE) sensor hoses reversed

P1405 DPF EGR sensor Upstream hose off or plugged

P1406 DPF EGR sensor downstream hose off or plugged

P1407 Exhaust gas recirculation (EGR) no flow detected (valve stuck closed or inoperative)

P1408 EGR flow out of self-test range (Non MIL)

P1409 EGR vacuum regulator solenoid circuit malfunction

P1410 Check that fuel pressure regulator control solenoid and the EGR check solenoid connectors are not swapped

P1411 Secondary air injection (AIR) system downstream flow

P1413 Secondary air injection (AIR) system monitor circuit low

P1414 Secondary air injection (AIR) system monitor circuit high

P1432 Thermostat Heater control (THTRC) circuit failure

P1436 A/C Evaporator temperature (ACET) circuit low input

P1437 A/C Evaporator temperature (ACET) circuit high input

P1442 Evaporative emission control system small leak detected

P1443 Very small or No purge flow condition

P1444 Purge flow sensor (PFS) circuit low input

P1445 Purge flow sensor (PFS) circuit high input

P1449 Evaporative emission control system unable to hold vacuum

P1450 Unable to bleed Up fuel tank vacuum

P1451 EVAP control system canister vent solenoid circuit malfunction

P1452 Unable to bleed up fuel tank vacuum

P1455 Evaporative emission control system control leak detected (gross leak)

P1460 Wide open throttle A/C cutout primary circuit malfunction

P1461 Air conditioning pressure sensor (ACP) sensor high voltage detected

P1462 Air conditioning pressure sensor (ACP) sensor low voltage detected

P1463 Air conditioning pressure sensor (ACP) insufficient pressure change

P1464 A/C demand out of self-test range

P1469 Low A/C cycling period

P1473 Fan secondary high, with fan(s) off

P1474 Low fan control (LFC) primary circuit failure (applications with relay controlled electric cooling fan(s))

P1477 Medium fan control (MFC) primary circuit failure

P1479 High fan control (HFC) primary circuit failure

P1480 Fan secondary low, with low fan on

P1481 Fan secondary low, with high fan on

P1483 Power to fan circuit over current

P1484 Open power/ground to variable load control module (VLCM)

P1485 EGR control solenoid open or short

P1486 EGR Vent solenoid open or short

P1487 EGR boost check solenoid open or short

P1489 PCV heater control circuit

P1500 Vehicle speed sensor (VSS) intermittent

P1501 Vehicle speed sensor (VSS) out of self test range

P1502 Vehicle speed sensor (VSS) intermittent

P1504 Idle air control (IAC) circuit malfunction

P1505 Idle air control (IAC) system at adaptive clip

P1506 Idle air control (IAC) overspeed error

P1507 Idle air control (IAC) underspeed error

P1512 Intake manifold runner control (IMRC) malfunction (bank 1 stuck closed)

P1513 Intake manifold runner control (IMRC) malfunction (bank 2 stuck closed)

P1516 Intake manifold runner control (IMRC) input error (bank 1)

P1517 Intake manifold runner control (IMRC) input error (bank 2)

P1518 Intake manifold runner control (IMRC) malfunction (stuck open)

P1519 Intake manifold runner control (IMRC) malfunction (stuck closed)

P1520 Intake manifold runner control (IMRC) circuit malfunction

P1521 Variable resonance Induction system (VRIS) solenoid #1 open or short

P1522 Variable resonance induction system (VRIS) solenoid #2 open or short

P1523 High speed Inlet air (HSIA) solenoid open or short

P1530 Air condition (A/C) clutch circuit malfunction

P1531 Invalid test-accelerator pedal movement

P1536 Parking brake applied failure

P1537 Intake manifold runner control (IMRC) malfunction (bank 1 stuck open)

P1538 Intake manifold runner control (IMRC) malfunction (bank 2 stuck open)

P1539 Power to air condition (A/C) clutch circuit overcurrent

P1549 Intake manifold communication control circuit malfunction

P1550 Power steering pressure (PSP) sensor malfunction

P1565 Speed control command switch out of range high

P1566 Speed control command switch out of range low

P1567 Speed control output circuit continuity

P1568 Speed control unable to hold speed

P1572 Brake pedal switch circuit

P1582 Electronic throttle monitor data available

P1601 Serial communication error

P1605 Powertrain control module (PCM)-Keep alive Memory (KAM) test error

P1608 PCM Internal circuit malfunction

P1609 PCM Internal circuit malfunction (2.5L only)

P1625 B+ supply to variable load control module (VLCM) fan circuit malfunction

P1626 B+ supply to variable load control module (VLCM) air conditioning (A/C) circuit

P1633 Keep alive power voltage too low

P1635 Tire/axle ratio out of acceptable range

P1636 Inductive signature chip communication error

P1639 Vehicle ID block not programmed or is corrupt

P1640 Powertrain DTC's available in another module

P1641 Fuel primary circuit malfunction

P1650 Power steering pressure (PSP) switch malfunction

P1651 Power steering pressure (PSP) switch signal malfunction

P1660 Output circuit check signal high

P1661 Output circuit check signal low

P1662 Injection driver module Enable (IDM EN) circuit failure

P1663 Fuel delivery command signal (FDCS) circuit failure

P1667 Cylinder identification (CID) circuit failure

P1668 PCM-IDM diagnostic communication error

P1670 EF feedback signal not detected

P1674 Control module software corrupted

P1700 Transaxle mechanical failure

P1701 Reverse engagement error

P1701 Fuel trim malfunction (Villager)

P1702 TR sensor intermittent

P1703 Brake switch out of self-test range

P1704 TR sensor range fault

P1705 Transmission range sensor out of self-test range

P1706 High vehicle speed in Park

P1709 Park/Neutral position switch out of self-test range

P1729 4x4L switch circuit malfunction

P1740 TCC solenoid mechanical fault

P1741 TCC engagement error

P1742 TCC solenoid failed on

P1743 TCC solenoid failed on

Ford (continued)

P1744 TCC system mechanically stuck in off position

P1746 EPC solenoid Low

P1747 EPC solenoid

P1749 EPC solenoid failed low

P1751 Shift solenoid 1 performance

P1754 Coast clutch solenoid circuit

P1756 Shift solenoid 2 performance

P1760 Transmission system fault

P1761 Shift solenoid 3 performance

P1767 Shift solenoid performance

P1780 Transmission control switch out of self-test range

P1781 4x4L switch out of self-test range

P1783 Transmission over-temperature

P1784 Transmission system first or reverse gear fault

P1785 Transmission system first or second gear fault

P1786 Transmission system second or third gear fault

P1787 Transmission system third or fourth gear fault

P1788 3-2 Timing/coast clutch solenoid circuit open

P1789 3-2 Timing/coast clutch solenoid circuit shorted

P1900 Output shaft speed sensor circuit intermittent failure

P1901 Turbine shaft speed (TSS) sensor circuit Intermittent

Chrysler/Dodge

Note: *The following list of OBD-II trouble codes is a manufacturer-specific list applicable to all Chrysler/Dodge models equipped with an OBD-II system, although not all codes apply to all models.*

P1105 BARO Read only solenoid circuit

P1110 Decreased engine performance (high IAT temp.)

P1115 General temperature rationality

P1180 Decreased engine performance (high IAT temp.)

P1192 Inlet air temp sensor voltage low

P1193 Inlet air temp sensor voltage high

P1195 O2 sensor slow during catalyst monitor (bank 1, sensor 1)

P1196 O2 sensor slow during catalyst monitor (bank 2, sensor 1)

P1197 O2 sensor slow during catalyst monitor (bank 1, sensor 2)

P1198 Radiator temperature sensor voltage too high

P1199 Radiator temperature sensor voltage too low

P1281 Engine is cold too long

P1282 Fuel pump relay control circuit

P1283 Idle select signal invalid

P1284 Fuel injection pump battery voltage out-of-range

P1285 Fuel injection pump controller always on

P1286 Acceleration position sensor supply voltage low

P1288 Intake manifold short runner solenoid circuit

P1289 Manifold tuning valve solenoid circuit

P1290 CNG fuel system pressure too high (if equipped)

P1291 No temperature rise seen from the intake heaters

P1292 CNG pressure sensor voltage too high (if equipped)

P1293 CNG pressure sensor voltage too low (if equipped)

P1294 Target idle not reached

P1295 No 5 volts to the throttle position sensor

P1296 No 5 volts to the MAP sensor

P1297 No change in MAP from start to run

P1298 Lean operation at wide open throttle

P1299 Vacuum leak found (IAC fully seated)

P1300 Ignition timing adjustment circuit

P1388 Auto shut down (ASD) relay control circuit

P1389 No ASD relay output voltage at PCM

P1390 Timing belt skipped 1 tooth or more

P1391 Intermittent loss of CMP or CKP

P1398 Misfire adaptive numerator at limit

P1399 Wait to start lamp circuit

P1400 Manifold differential pressure sensor

P1403 Loss of 5 volt feed to the EGR position sensor

P1475 Auxiliary 5-volt supply voltage too high

P1476 Too little secondary air

P1477 Too much secondary air

P1478 Battery temperature sensor voltage out of limit

P1479 Transmission fan relay circuit

P1480 PCV solenoid circuit

P1481 EATX RPM pulse generator signal for misfire detection does not correlate with expected value

P1482 Catalyst temperature sensor circuit shorted low

P1483 Catalyst temperature sensor circuit shorted high

P1484 Catalytic converter overheat detected

P1485 Air injection solenoid circuit

P1486 EVAP system obstruction found

P1487 High speed radiator fan control relay circuit

P1488 Auxiliary 5 volt supply output too low

P1489 High speed fan control relay circuit

P1490 Low speed fan control relay circuit

P1491 Radiator fan control relay circuit

P1492 Ambient/battery temp sensor voltage too high

P1493 Ambient/ battery temp sensor voltage too low

P1494 Leak detection pump pressure switch or mechanical fault

P1495 Leak detection pump solenoid circuit

P1496 5 Volt supply output too low

P1498 High speed radiator fan ground control relay circuit

P1500 Alternator FR terminal circuit

P1501 Vehicle speed sensor 1/2 correlation - drive wheels

P1502 Vehicle speed sensor 1/2 correlation - non drive wheels

P1572 Brake pedal stuck on

P1573 Brake pedal stuck off

P1594 Charging system voltage too high

P1595 Speed control solenoid circuits

P1596 Speed control switch always high

P1597 Speed control switch always low

P1598 A/C pressure sensor voltage too high

P1599 A/C pressure sensor voltage too low

P1602 PCM not programmed

P1603 PCM Internal Dual-Port RAM communication failure

P1604 PCM Internal Dual-Port RAM read/write integrity failure

P1607 PCM internal shutdown timer rationality

P1680 Clutch released switch circuit

P1681 No instrument panel cluster CCD/J1850 messages received

P1682 Charging system voltage too low

Chrysler/Dodge (continued)

P1683   Speed control power relay; or speed control 12 volt driver circuit

P1684   The battery has been disconnected within the last 50 starts

P1685   Smart Key Immobilizer Module (SKIM) invalid key

P1686   No SKIM BUS messages received

P1687   No mechanical instrument cluster (MIC) BUS message

P1688   Internal fuel injection pump controller failure

P1689   No communication between ECM and I/P module

P1690   Fuel I/P CKP does not agree with CKP signal

P1691   Fuel injection pump controller calibration error

P1692   Diagnostic trouble code set in the ECM

P1693   Diagnostic trouble code set in the companion module

P1694   No CCD messages received from the ECM

P1695   PCM fault, no CCD messages from BCM

P1696   PCM EEPROM fault write denied

P1697   PCM fault, SRI mileage not stored

P1698   No CCD messages from the transmission or body control module (TCM or BCM)

P1719   Skip shift solenoid circuit

P1740   Rationality error detected in the torque converter clutch solenoid or overdrive solenoid systems

P1756   Governor pressure not equal to target @ 15-20 PSI (mid pressure malfunction)

P1757   Governor pressure not equal to target @ 15-20 PSI (zero pressure malfunction)

P1762   Governor pressure sensor offset voltage too low or high

P1763   Governor pressure sensor voltage too high

P1764   Governor pressure sensor voltage too low

P1765   Trans. 12 volt supply relay control circuit

P1899   P/N switch failure

P1899   P/N switch stuck in PARK or in gear

Toyota/Lexus

Note: *The following list of OBD-II trouble codes is a manufacturer-specific list applicable to all Toyota/Lexus models equipped with an OBD-II system, although not all codes apply to all models.*

P1010   Oil control valve/variable valve lift - LH bank - circuit malfunction

P1011   Oil control valve/variable valve lift - LH bank - open malfunction

P1012   Oil control valve/variable valve lift - LH bank - close malfunction

P1100   Barometric pressure sensor circuit

P1120   Accelerator pedal position sensor circuit malfunction

P1121   Accelerator pedal position sensor range/performance problem

P1125   Throttle control motor circuit malfunction

P1126   Magnetic clutch circuit malfunction

P1127   ETCS actuator power source circuit malfunction

P1128   Throttle control motor lock malfunction

P1129   Electric throttle control system malfunction

P1130   A/F sensor circuit range/performance malfunction (bank 1, sensor 1)

P1133   A/F sensor circuit response malfunction (bank 1, sensor 1)

P1135   A/F sensor heater circuit malfunction (bank 1, sensor 1)

P1150   A/F sensor circuit range/performance, malfunction (bank 2, sensor 1)

P1153   A/F sensor circuit response malfunction (bank 2, sensor 1)

P1155   A/F sensor heater circuit malfunction (bank 2, sensor 1)

P1200   Fuel pump relay/ECU circuit malfunction

P1300   Ignition circuit malfunction (No.1)

P1305   Ignition circuit malfunction (No.2)

P1310   Ignition circuit malfunction (No.3)

P1315   Ignition circuit malfunction (No.4)

P1320   Ignition circuit malfunction (No.5)

P1325   Ignition circuit malfunction (No.6)

P1330   Ignition circuit malfunction (No.7)

P1335   Crankshaft position sensor circuit malfunction (during engine running)

P1340   Ignition circuit malfunction (No.8)

P1341   Camshaft position (CMP) sensor 2, bank 1 - range/performance problem

P1345   Variable valve timing (VVT) sensor/camshaft position sensor circuit malfunction (bank 1)

P1346   VVT sensor/camshaft position sensor circuit range/performance problem (bank 1)

P1349   VVT system malfunction (bank 1)

P1350   VVT sensor/camshaft position sensor circuit malfunction (bank 2)

P1351   VVT sensor/camshaft position sensor circuit range/performance problem (bank 2)

P1354   VVT system malfunction (bank 2)

P1400   Sub-throttle position sensor circuit

P1401   Sub-throttle position sensor performance

P1405   Turbocharger (TC) pressure sensor - circuit malfunction

P1406   Turbocharger (TC) pressure sensor - range/performance problem

P1410   EGR valve position sensor circuit

P1411   EGR valve position sensor performance

P1500   Starter signal circuit

P1510   Intake air volume too low with supercharger on

P1511   Turbocharger (TC) pressure - too low

P1512   Turbocharger (TC) pressure - too high

P1520   Stop light switch circuit malfunction

P1532   Cruise control switch circuit

P1565   Cruise control switch circuit

P1566   Cruise control main switch circuit

P1570   Cruise control laser radar sensor - malfunction

P1572   Cruise control laser radar sensor - improper aiming of beam axis

P1575   Cruise control/skid control warning buzzer - malfunction

P1578   Brake system malfunction

P1600   PCM BATT malfunction

P1605   Knock control CPU fault

P1615   Data Bus, cruise control module - communication error

P1616   Data Bus, cruise control module - communication error

P1630   Traction control system - malfunction

P1633   PCM malfunction (ETCS circuit)

P1645   Body ECU fault

P1646   Transmission control module (TCM) - system malfunction

P1647   Transmission control module (TCM) - system malfunction

P1652   Turbocharger (TC) 2 air control solenoid - circuit malfunction

P1656   Oil control valve (OCV) circuit malfunction (bank 1)

P1658   Turbocharger (TC) wastegate regulating valve - circuit malfunction

P1661   Turbocharger (TC) 2 exhaust gas control valve - circuit malfunction

Toyota/Lexus (continued)

P1662 Exhaust bypass valve - circuit malfunction

P1663 Oil control valve (OCV) circuit malfunction (bank 2)

P1690 Oil control valve (OCV) circuit

P1692 Oil control valve (OCV) open fault

P1693 Variable valve timing - malfunction

P1694 Oil control valve (OCV) closed fault

P1700 Vehicle speed sensor 2 circuit

P1705 NC2 revolution sensor circuit malfunction

P1715 Rear wheel speed sensor(s) - malfunction

P1725 NT revolution sensor circuit malfunction

P1730 NC revolution sensor circuit malfunction

P1755 Torque converter clutch (TCC) solenoid - circuit malfunction

P1760 Linear solenoid for line pressure control circuit malfunction

P1765 Linear solenoid for accumulator pressure control circuit malfunction

P1770 Differential lock solenoid - circuit malfunction

P1780 Park/Neutral position switch malfunction

P1781 Shift lever switch - malfunction

P1782 Transfer box low ratio switch - circuit malfunction

P1783 Transfer box neutral switch - circuit malfunction

P1790 Shift/timing solenoid

P1810 CAN data bus malfunction

P1815 Shift control solenoid - malfunction

P1818 Shift control solenoid - circuit malfunction

Honda/Acura

Note: *The following list of OBD-II trouble codes is a manufacturer-specific list applicable to all Honda/Acura models equipped with an OBD-II system, although not all codes apply to all models.*

P1009 VTEC system malfunction

P1077 Intake manifold tuning (IMT) (intake manifold runner control (IMRC)) valve stuck short

P1078 Intake manifold tuning (IMT) (intake manifold runner control (IMRC)) valve stuck long

P1102 Mass air flow (MAF) sensor - signal higher than expected

P1103 Mass air flow (MAF) sensor - signal higher than expected

P1106 Barometric pressure (BARO) sensor range/performance problem

P1107 Barometric pressure (BARO) sensor circuit low voltage

P1108 Barometric pressure (BARO) sensor circuit high voltage

P1109 Barometric pressure (BARO) sensor circuit out of range high

P1111 Intake air temperature (IAT) sensor - circuit/intermittent voltage high

P1112 Intake air temperature (IAT) sensor - circuit/intermittent voltage low

P1114 Engine coolant temperature (ECT) sensor - circuit/intermittent voltage high

P1115 Engine coolant temperature (ECT) sensor - circuit/intermittent voltage low

P1116 Engine coolant temperature (ECT) sensor performance problem

P1120 Throttle motor position sensor 1 - circuit malfunction

P1121 Throttle position (TP) sensor signal low

P1122 Throttle position (TP) sensor signal high

P1125 Throttle position (TP) motor - fail safe mode

P1128 Manifold absolute pressure (MAP) sensor circuit lower than expected

P1129 Manifold absolute pressure (MAP) sensor circuit higher than expected

P1130 Demand for changing both secondary heated oxygen sensor (SHO2S (sensor 2)) and third heated oxygen sensor (THO2S (sensor 3))

P1133 Heated oxygen sensor (HO2S) - insufficient switching

P1134 Heated oxygen sensor (HO2S) - slow operation

P1149 Air fuel ratio (A/F) sensor (sensor 1) range/ performance problem

P1153 Heated oxygen sensor (HO2S) - insufficient switching

P1154 Heated oxygen sensor (HO2S) - LH front - slow operation

P1157 Air fuel ratio (A/F) sensor (sensor 1) line high voltage

P1158 Air fuel ratio (A/F) sensor (sensor 1) AFS- terminal low voltage

P1159 Air fuel ratio (A/F) sensor (sensor 1) AFS+ terminal low voltage

P1162 Air fuel ratio (A/F) sensor (sensor 1) circuit malfunction

P1163 Air fuel ratio (A/F) sensor (sensor 1) slow response

P1164 Air fuel ratio (A/F) sensor (sensor 1) range/ performance problem

P1165 Air fuel ratio (A/F) sensor (sensor 1) range/ performance problem

P1166 Air fuel ratio (A/F) sensor (sensor 1) heater circuit malfunction

P1167 Air fuel ratio (A/F) sensor (sensor 1) heater circuit malfunction

P1168 HO2S (bank 1, sensor 1) label circuit low input (LAF sensor)

P1169 HO2S (bank 1, sensor 1) label circuit high input (LAF sensor)

P1171 Fuel system - mixture lean under acceleration

P1172 Air fuel ratio (A/F) sensor (sensor 1) circuit out of range high

P1174 Front air fuel ratio (A/F) sensor (bank 2, sensor 1) circuit out of range high

P1182 Fuel temperature sensor - low input

P1183 Fuel temperature sensor - high input

P1187 Fuel temperature sensor - low input

P1188 Fuel temperature sensor - high input

P1192 Fuel tank pressure sensor - low input

P1193 Fuel tank pressure sensor - high input

P1201 Cylinder No. 1 - misfire

P1202 Cylinder No. 2 - misfire

P1203 Cylinder No. 3 - misfire

P1204 Cylinder No. 4 - misfire

P1205 Cylinder No. 5 - misfire

P1206 Cylinder No. 6 - misfire

P1220 Throttle motor position sensor 2 - circuit malfunction

P1221 Throttle motor position sensor 1/2 - signal variation

P1241 Throttle valve control motor 1 circuit

P1242 Throttle valve control motor 2 circuit

P1243 Insufficient throttle position detected

P1244 Insufficient closed throttle position detected

P1246 Accelerator position sensor 1 circuit

P1247 Accelerator position sensor 2 circuit

P1248 Accelerator pedal position sensor correlation fault

P1253 VTEC system malfunction

P1257 VTEC system malfunction

P1258 VTEC system malfunction

P1259 VTEC system malfunction

P1271 Accelerator pedal position (APP) sensor 1/2 - signal variation

P1272 Accelerator pedal position (APP) sensor 2/3 - signal variation

P1273 Accelerator pedal position (APP) sensor 1/3 - signal variation

P1275 Accelerator pedal position (APP) sensor 1 - circuit malfunction

P1279 VTEC solenoid or switch circuit

P1280 Accelerator pedal position (APP) sensor 2 - circuit malfunction

P1285 Accelerator pedal position (APP) sensor 3 - circuit malfunction

P1290 Throttle position (TP) motor - forced idle mode

P1295 Throttle position (TP) motor - power management mode

P1297 Electric load detector (ELD) circuit low voltage

P1298 Electric load detector (ELD) circuit high voltage

P1299 Throttle position (TP) motor - forced engine shut down mode

P1300 Random misfire detected

P1301 Cylinder 1, misfire detected

P1302 Cylinder 2, misfire detected

P1303 Cylinder 3, misfire detected

P1304 Cylinder 4, misfire detected

P1305 Cylinder 5, misfire detected

P1306 Cylinder 6, misfire detected

P1310 Ignition control module (ICM) - diagnosis

P1311 Ignition control module (ICM) - ignition coil secondary coil signal, circuit 1

P1312 Ignition control module (ICM) - ignition coil secondary coil signal, circuit 2

P1316 Spark plug detection module circuit (bank 2)

P1317 Spark plug detection module circuit (bank 1)

P1318 Spark plug detection module reset fault (bank 2)

P1319 Spark plug detection module reset fault (bank 1)

P1324 Knock sensor power source circuit low voltage

P1326 Ignition control module (ICM) - combustion quality input signal

P1336 Crankshaft speed fluctuation sensor circuit

P1337 Crankshaft speed fluctuation sensor circuit no signal

P1340 Ignition control module (ICM) - cylinder identification/synchronization

P1359 Crankshaft position top dead center sensor circuit

P1361 Camshaft position (CMP) sensor B intermittent signal interruption

P1362 Camshaft position (CMP) sensor B no signal

P1366 Camshaft position (CMP) sensor - top dead center sensor 2 - intermittent signal

P1367 Camshaft position (CMP) sensor - top dead center sensor 2 - no signal

P1381 Camshaft position (CMP) sensor circuit (intermittent signal)

P1382 Camshaft position (CMP) sensor circuit (no signal)

P1386 Camshaft position (CMP) sensor 'B' circuit (intermittent signal)

P1387 Camshaft position (CMP) sensor 'B' circuit (no signal)

P1390 G-sensor - intermittent voltage low

P1391 G-sensor - performance

P1392 G-sensor - voltage low

P1393 G-sensor - voltage high

P1394 G-sensor - intermittent voltage high

P1399 Random misfire

P1404 Exhaust gas recirculation (EGR) valve - valve closed

P1406 Exhaust gas recirculation (EGR) valve position sensor - circuit problem

P1410 Secondary air injection (AIR) pump - malfunction

P1415 AIR pump electrical current sensor - circuit low

P1416 AIR pump electrical current sensor - circuit high

P1410 Secondary air injection (AIR) system - malfunction

P1419 Secondary air injection (AIR) system - malfunction

P1420 NOx adsorptive catalyst system efficiency below threshold

P1441 Evaporative emission (EVAP) canister purge system - leak detected

P1442 Evaporative emission (EVAP) canister purge system - vacuum switch malfunction

P1450 Evaporative emissions (EVAP) two way valve, bypass valve - voltage low

P1451 Evaporative emissions (EVAP) two way valve, bypass valve - voltage high

P1454 Evaporative emission control system fuel tank pressure (FTP) sensor range/ performance problem

P1456 Evaporative emissions (EVAP) control system leakage (fuel tank system)

P1457 Evaporative emissions (EVAP) control system leakage (EVAP canister system)

P1459 EVAP purge flow switch circuit

P1460 Fuel gauge tank sensor - supply circuit

P1486 Thermostat range/performance problem

P1491 Exhaust gas recirculation (EGR) valve insufficient lift

P1498 Exhaust gas recirculation (EGR) valve position sensor circuit high voltage

P1505 Intake air system leak detected

P1508 Idle air control valve circuit

P1509 Idle air control valve circuit

P1514 Throttle position (TP) sensor/mass air flow (MAF) sensor - signal variation

P1515 Throttle command/actual throttle position - signal variation

P1516 Throttle position motor - position performance

P1519 Idle air control (IAC) valve circuit malfunction

P1523 Throttle position motor - closed position performance

P1549 Charging system high voltage

P1571 Brake pedal position (BPP) switch - no operation

P16BB Alternator B terminal circuit low voltage

P16BC Alternator FR terminal circuit/IGP circuit low voltage

P1607 Engine control module (ECM) internal circuit malfunction

P1608 PCM internal fault 'B'

P1618 Engine control module (ECM) - internal fault

P1625 Engine control module (ECM) -unexpected reset

P1630 Transmission control module (TCM) processor error

P1635 Sensor supply voltage - circuit 1 malfunction

P1639 Sensor supply voltage - circuit 2 malfunction

P1640 Engine control module (ECM) - internal fault

P1646 Sensor supply voltage - circuit C malfunction

P1650 Engine control module quad driver/output driver

P1655 TMA or TMB signal line circuit

P1656 Electronic stability program (ESP) control module - communication malfunction

P1660 At to ECM - data line failure - V6

P1671 TCM A/T FI data line (no signal)

P1672 TCM A/T FI data line circuit

P1676 TCM A/T FI data line circuit

P1677 TCM A/T FI data line circuit

P1678 TCM A/T FPTDR signal line circuit

P1681 AT to ECM - signal A - voltage low

P1682 AT to ECM - signal A - voltage high

P1683 Throttle valve default position spring performance problem

P1684 Throttle valve return spring performance problem

P1686 AT to ECM - signal B - voltage low

Honda/Acura (continued)

P1687	AT to ECM - signal B - voltage high		P1790	TCM A/T TP sensor circuit
P1690	TCSTB data line circuit		P1791	TCM A/T vehicle speed sensor circuit
P1696	TCFC line low input		P1792	TCM A/T ECT sensor circuit
P1697	TCFC line high input		P1793	Automatic transmission
P1705	TCM A/T gear position switch circuit shorted		P1794	Automatic transmission - BARO signal - V6
P1706	TCM A/T gear position switch circuit open		P1795	Automatic transmission
P1709	TCM A/T controller circuit		P1835	AT - kick-down switch
P1710	TCN A/T - 2004 MDX - 1st gear hold switch		P1850	AT - brake band solenoid malfunction
P1717	TCM A/T gear selection malfunction		P1860	AT - torque converter clutch (TCC) solenoid circuit
P1730	TCM A/T gear shift malfunction		P1870	CVT - poor acceleration
P1731	TCM A/T gear shift malfunction		P1873	CVT - poor acceleration
P1732	TCM A/T gear shift malfunction		P1876	CVT - poor acceleration
P1733	TCM A/T gear shift malfunction		P1877	CVT - poor acceleration
P1734	TCM A/T gear shift malfunction		P1878	CVT - poor acceleration
P1735	TCM A/T gear shift malfunction		P1879	CVT - poor acceleration
P1736	TCM A/T gear shift malfunction		P1880	CVT - poor acceleration
P1738	TCM A/T controller circuit		P1881	CVT - poor acceleration
P1739	TCM A/T controller circuit		P1882	Constantly variable transmission (CVT)
P1740	TCM A/T - 4th clutch pressure switch		P1885	CVT - poor acceleration
P1750	TCM A/T - hydraulic system mechanical malfunction		P1886	CVT - poor acceleration
P1751	TCM A/T - hydraulic system mechanical malfunction		P1888	CVT - poor acceleration
			P1889	CVT - poor acceleration
P1753	TCM A/T lockup solenoid valve "A" circuit		P1890	CVT - poor acceleration
P1758	TCM A/T lockup solenoid valve 'B' circuit		P1891	CVT - poor acceleration
P1760	TCM A/T system fault		P1892	CVT - poor acceleration
P1761	TCM A/T system fault		P1893	CVT - poor acceleration
P1768	TCM A/T controller circuit		P1894	CVT - poor acceleration
P1773	TCM A/T controller circuit		P1895	CVT - poor acceleration
P1778	Shift solenoid (SS) C		P1896	CVT - poor acceleration
P1786	TCM A/T controller circuit		P1897	CVT - poor acceleration
P1787	TCM A/T - lock-up clutch malfunction		P1898	CVT - poor acceleration
P1788	TCM A/T - poor gear shift		P1899	CVT - poor acceleration

9 Diagnostic routines

Contents

OK. The Malfunction Indicator Light (MIL) is glowing on your instrument panel. You may or may not notice any difference in the way your car drives, but you know that light is on for a reason. So you pay your local auto parts store a visit and pick up a code reader or scan tool. After hooking up the tool and following the instructions furnished with the tool, you find that your car does indeed have a diagnostic trouble code (DTC) stored in the PCM's memory. That was easy, but now what?!!

Well, now that you have a trouble code (or *codes*), you have a direction in which to start. The PCM has identified a problem in a certain *circuit or system* - not necessarily a particular component - so your diagnosis will concentrate on that system to which the trouble code pertains.

This is sometimes, however, easier said than done. Outside influences that are seemingly unrelated to the circuit containing the problem can trigger a DTC. Vehicle-specific flow charts in factory service manuals can run into the

hundreds of pages, and in many cases those diagnostic procedures are tailored to the use of the manufacturer's proprietary scan tool. And obviously, in a book of this size, it would be impossible to include vehicle-specific troubleshooting information for all makes and models, and for every DTC that could potentially be set.

But there is a bright side to this lit-up MIL on your dash. With the advent of OBD-II, many of the fault-finding exercises have become somewhat standardized. Most diagnosis can be carried out with a generic scan tool and a multimeter. Perhaps the most valuable feature of being able to extract DTCs is knowing what code has been set - and, with the help of this manual, what the definition of the code is. Even if you don't attempt to get to the root of the problem yourself, armed with this information you can take your vehicle to an automotive repair facility with the confidence that you won't be sold an unnecessary repair.

First things first

The OBD-II software residing in your vehicle's PCM is incredibly sophisticated, but it isn't magic. It was designed to monitor various engine operating parameters and alert the driver of any faults that would cause emissions to rise to an unacceptable level. It was *not* designed to carry out routine maintenance and other aspects of normal vehicle care. That's up to you. You're still going to have to change your oil regularly, check your underhood hoses and drivebelts, replace your air filter and spark plugs occasionally, etc. Basically, don't let your vehicle fall into a sad state of disrepair - you'll fend off things that could cause more serious, costly and difficult-to-diagnose problems.

When you're faced with a problem, you first need to establish the general operating condition of the engine. The engine management system can't compensate for a cracked spark plug, worn piston rings (with the resulting low compression), a jumped timing belt, insufficiently filled cooling system, missing thermostat and the like. Don't overlook the basics, either. If the engine won't start, first make sure there's fuel in the tank! If there's a rough idle condition, a

thorough check under the hood just might reveal a broken wire or disconnected vacuum line. Chapter 4 is full of good, basic troubleshooting information; a little time spent reviewing the material presented there could save you lots of time and frustration in the long run.

Next things next

Alright, we're going to assume that the engine is generally in good health, but your MIL is lit up. Now it's time to pull trouble codes, and for this you'll need a code reader or scan tool, either of which should be available at your local auto parts store (see illustration 9.1). For information on the location of the diagnostic connector and hooking-up a code reader or scan tool, see Chapter 7.

If you've gone this far, you probably now have a trouble code that you need to know what to do with. Chapter 8 contains a list of the standardized SAE generic codes, as well as some manufacturer-specific codes from some of the major auto makers.

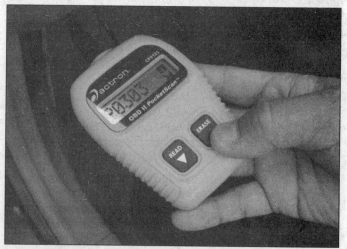

9.1 OK, now we know why the car was running rough - a misfire code (actually more than one!). This not only turned the MIL on, it made it flash, because a misfire can kill the catalytic converter in a short amount of time

9.2 At the very least you'll need a code reader if your MIL is on, but a scan tool is a far better choice if you plan on trying to fix the problem yourself

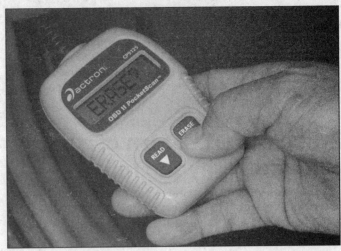

9.3 Once the repair has been completed, you can erase the code. If you're going to have the work done at an automotive repair shop, however, *don't* erase the code, because all of the data related to the code will also be erased!

As stated earlier, it would be impossible to cram complete vehicle-specific diagnostic flow charts for every trouble code into a book of this size, so trouble code diagnosis will be gathered into subsets, categorized by the basic *system* in which the problem lies, as indicated by the third character of the DTC. Also included are basic checks of the various input sensors and output actuators used by the OBD-II system. These simplified troubleshooting procedures, coupled with the definition of the actual trouble code (or codes) that you've obtained, will help you hunt down the cause of most failures.

Actual hands-on checking procedures will be based on the use of a scan tool (for looking at the PCM's data stream to check the parameters of various input sensors and out-put actuators) and/or a high-impedance digital multimeter, where feasible **(see illustration 9.2)**. Note that the following diagnostic procedures are geared toward P0 (generic powertrain) codes, but may be of some assistance when dealing with certain P1, P2 and P3 codes, too.

Make the repair

Once you've tracked down the source of the problem, you've pretty much made it to the summit. In most cases, the repair will be much easier than the diagnosis. If you have determined that the code was set by a faulty component, refer to Chapter 10, *Component replacement pro-*

If you have the capability, check for any Technical Service Bulletins (TSBs) that may have been issued that apply to your vehicle (see illustration). Do this before attempting to diagnose a problem. Perhaps a software update is available that may fix the problem that is causing a DTC to be set. (Actual software updates will have to be performed by a dealer service department or other qualified repair shop.)

An excellent resource for this information can be found at the National Automotive Service Task Force website (www.NASTF.org). This website is essentially a portal to all of the automotive manufacturers' service information and, while the information available there isn't free in most cases, it can be accessed on a temporary basis for a reasonable fee.

Before starting diagnosis, it's a good idea to see if any Technical Service Bulletins have been issued for your vehicle. Sometimes manufacturers discover an easy fix for a problem, or they may have found a software bug that can be repaired by reprogramming the PCM

cedures. There you'll find typical input sensor and output actuator removal and installation procedures. Just remember that the procedures there are *typical* representations of OBD-II components on various vehicles on the road today. If the information there is not helpful to your situation, refer to the *Haynes Automotive Repair Manual* for your particular vehicle.

Erase the DTC, turn off that MIL and verify the repair

Once you've completed the repair, use your code reader or scan tool to erase the trouble code and turn off the light **(see illustration 9.3)**. Generally this involves simply press-ing a button, but on some tools you'll have to locate this function by using the menu on the tool's display. If it isn't obvious, follow the instructions that came with your tool.

To verify the repair, start the vehicle, take it on a test run and perform a "drive cycle." While there is no "generic" drive cycle, the typical example described in Chapter 6 will most likely result in a test drive that will allow all of the OBD-II monitors to run, giving the PCM a chance to check your work. **Note:** *Some problems require more than one drive cycle to turn on the MIL.*

When you get back from your test drive, plug in your code reader or scan tool and make sure that the code (or codes) have not set again, no pending codes are present, and no new codes have been introduced. (Remember, not all codes turn on the Malfunction Indicator Light.)

1 Fuel, intake air or emissions control system faults (3rd character of DTC = 0, 1, 2)

1a Oxygen sensor or circuit

Oxygen sensor

Symptoms caused by problems with the oxygen sensor(s) or circuit(s) can include excessive emissions, sulfur-like smell from the exhaust, stalling, rough idle, possible inability to enter closed loop operation, overly rich or lean fuel mixture (perhaps with an accompanying misfire), poor gas mileage and sluggish throttle response/poor overall engine performance. **Note 1:** *The following diagnostic information applies to zirconia sensors only, which are the most common type. The other type, titania sensors, don't produce a voltage. They are fed a reference voltage (1-volt) from the PCM; the resistance of the sensor changes with the amount of oxygen in the exhaust, and the PCM monitors the resulting voltage change.* **Note 2:** *On a "V" engine, diagnosis can be narrowed down to one cylinder bank or the other, since the trouble code will indicate in which cylinder bank the problem lies. Bank 1 refers to the cylinder bank that contains cylinder no. 1, and Bank 2 is the other cylinder bank. Sensor 1 refers to the upstream (before the catalytic converter) oxygen sensor, while sensor 2 refers to the downstream (after the catalytic converter) sensor.*

Scan tool checks:

1   Connect your scan tool to the DLC and warm up the engine to normal operating temperature. Raise the engine speed to approximately 2000 rpm and check the performance of the oxygen sensor parameters on the tool **(see illustration 9.4)**:

* Upstream oxygen sensors should fluctuate rapidly (about one to five times a second or so), between approximately 0.1 volt and 0.9 volt (100 millivolts to 900 millivolts). If your scan tool is capable of measuring oxygen sensor cross-counts, check the cross-count value. Cross-counts are the rate at which the sensor's voltage crosses the 450 millivolt point per second. The cross-count value will vary, between perhaps one every two seconds to five per second, depending on engine speed, load, and the individual vehicle. Generally, the more the better (for an upstream sensor).

* Downstream oxygen sensors should fluctuate very slowly, and their range of fluctuation should be much less (from above 200 millivolts to below 800 millivolts) if the catalytic converter is doing its job. (If the catalytic converter is not doing an effective job, the sensor's reading will look very much like that of a healthy upstream oxygen sensor.)

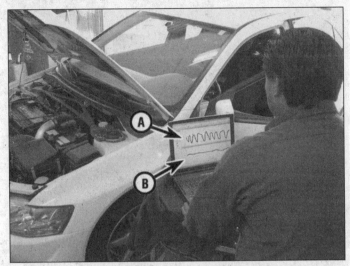

9.4 Shown here on a laptop equipped with scan tool software are the upstream (A) and downstream (B) oxygen sensor waveforms. The upstream sensor is fluctuating rapidly between approximately 100 millivolts to 900 millivolts, while the downstream sensor is fluctuating much more slowly, indicating the catalytic converter is doing its job

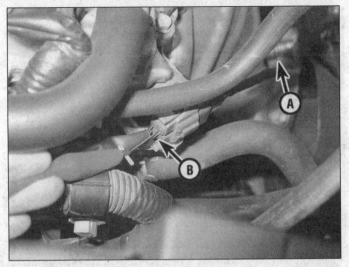

9.5 Oxygen sensor connectors aren't always easy to access. They're usually at the end of a wiring harness at least six inches away from the sensor.

A   Upstream oxygen sensor
B   T-pin backprobing the connector, looking for the signal wire

Multimeter checks:

2   An oxygen sensor can be checked with a high-imped-ance voltmeter connected to the sensor's output wire, by backprobing the proper terminal of the sensor's electrical connector **(see illustration 9.5)**. Voltage fluctuations should be noted as described under *"Scan tool checks,"* although voltage fluctuations are more difficult to see on the meter's display. Some high-end digital multimeters have a bar graph display which makes watching these fluctuations easier.

3   Heated oxygen sensors have either three or four wires; on three-wire sensors, one is for the sensor output (with ground being provided through the sensor body), and the other two are for the oxygen sensor heater power and ground. On four-wire sensors, the additional wire is a ground wire for the sensor (instead of it grounding through its body). To find the sensor's output wire, backprobe the ter-minals with your meter set on the 15 or 20-volt scale to find the terminal with battery voltage supplied to it (sensor heater feed). Now, with the engine warmed-up and running and the meter set on the millivolt scale, probe the other two or three terminals, locating the one that isn't "dead." This will be the sensor's output terminal and should allow you to monitor the output voltage of the sensor.

Other things to check:

4   If the upstream oxygen sensor is not fluctuating as it should, and is holding a fairly steady reading, chances are good that it is a "lazy" sensor; one that can't react properly because of contamination (engine coolant, fumes from sili-cone sealant used on certain engine gaskets, contaminated engine oil, lead, fouling due to excessively rich running con-ditions) or wear (caused by age, overheating or physical damage).

5   The sensor's ability to sense rich or lean conditions can

be measured by artificially inducing an overly rich or overly lean condition.

6   To see if the sensor can react to a very lean condition, create a vacuum leak (disconnect a hose from the intake manifold); the oxygen sensor output should drop down to 0.2 volt (200 millivolts) or below, almost instantly.

7   To create a rich condition, administer propane gas (bot-tled) into the air intake tract (open the propane valve only partially and do so a little at a time to prevent over-richening the mixture); the oxygen sensor output should go full-rich, or 0.9 volt (900 millivolts) **(see illustration 9.6)**. **Warning:** *Pro-pane gas is highly flammable. Be sure there are no leaks in your connections, and no flames, cigarettes, sparks or arc-ing wires in the vicinity, or an explosion could result).* **Note:** *Another way to richen the mixture is by disconnecting (and*

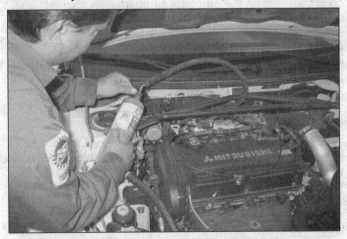

9.6 Here a rich condition is being created by administering propane gas into the intake tract. If the oxygen sensor is working properly, the sensor's output on the scan tool or voltmeter should go full-rich (approximately 900 millivolts)

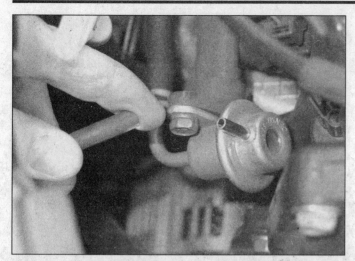

9.7 Another way to create a rich condition is to disconnect and plug the vacuum hose from the fuel pressure regulator

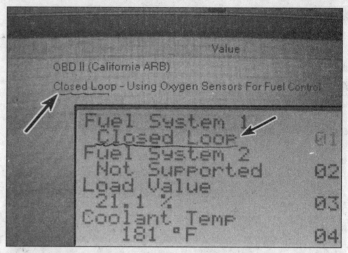

9.8 Whether you're using PC-based software or a scan tool (inset), closed-loop should be indicated within two to four minutes after the engine has been started cold

plugging) the vacuum hose from the fuel pressure regulator **(see illustration 9.7)** *(this won't work on returnless type fuel systems because there is no fuel pressure regulator on the fuel rail)*. If the sensor won't react to either of these conditions, it is most likely faulty.

8   If the sensor can "see" the lean and rich condition created in the last two Steps, it's probably OK.

9   Other factors that can affect oxygen sensor performance include intake air leaks (false air), vacuum leaks, exhaust leaks, misfire, incorrect fuel pressure, dirty fuel injectors, bad grounds (including a loose sensor or excessively rusty exhaust system), EGR system problems or MAP sensor/circuit problems. Make sure none of these conditions (or any trouble codes related to them) are present before replacing an oxygen sensor with a new one. Remember, lean running conditions will show up as low sensor voltage, and rich running conditions will show up as high sensor voltage ("low" and "high" being relative terms in the millivolt range).

10   Obviously, the sensor's wiring harness must be in good condition. Inspect the wiring for an open or short-circuit condition (short to ground *and* short to voltage).

Oxygen sensor heater

Problems with the oxygen sensor heater or circuit will result in an excessive amount of time before the engine goes into closed-loop operation.

Scan tool checks:

1   Begin this check with the engine cold. Connect the scan tool, start the engine and watch for the engine to go into closed loop, indicated by the upstream oxygen sensor voltage beginning to fluctuate. The scan tool should also display 'closed loop' **(see illustration 9.8)**. If the sensor's heater is working like it should, this should occur in about three minutes or so.

Multimeter checks:

2   Check for power to the sensor heater, and make sure the ground is good, as well (see *Multimeter checks* under

Oxygen sensor). If the sensor heater has power and ground, the oxygen sensor heater is most likely at fault.

3   If there is a power or ground problem, trace the circuit for an open or short-circuit condition (short to ground *and* short to voltage). Other possible causes include a faulty EFI or ASD relay (depending on manufacturer), or a faulty PCM. If any of these problems are suspected, it is recommended that the vehicle be diagnosed by an automotive service technician, since electrical parts are expensive and usually non-returnable.

1b Fuel trim problems (system too lean or too rich)

Symptoms caused by problems with the fuel trim function of the PCM can include diminished engine performance and reduced gas mileage. Short Term Fuel Trim (STFT) and Long Term Fuel Trim (LTFT) work together to control injector pulse width to keep the air fuel mixture as close to the stoichiometric ideal of 14.7:1 as possible. The PCM uses the oxygen sensor(s) to measure the amount of oxygen in the exhaust to control these values. **Note:** *On a "V" engine, diagnosis can be narrowed down to one cylinder bank or the other, since the trouble code will indicate in which cylinder bank the problem lies. Bank 1 refers to the cylinder bank that contains cylinder no. 1, and Bank 2 is the other cylinder bank.*

Scan tool checks:

1   Connect your scan tool to the DLC and warm up the engine to normal operating temperature, making sure the engine has gone into closed loop operation. Check the STFT and LTFT parameters on the scan tool display **(see illustration 9.9)**.

2   If the values are in the positive range, the PCM is trying to compensate for a lean condition by adding fuel (increas-

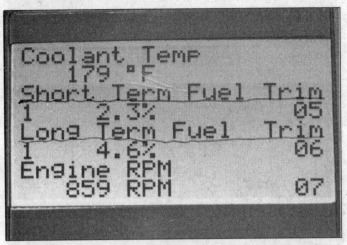

9.9 Here's the Short Term Fuel Trim (STFT) and Long Term Fuel Trim (LTFT) displayed on a scan tool. Both are on the positive side of 0-percent, but just barely, indicating that the PCM is only having to alter the injector pulse width a little so the engine isn't running *too* lean. This engine is running lean and clean!

ing injector pulse width, or on-time).

3   Conversely, if the values are in the negative range, the PCM is attempting to correct an overly rich running condition by decreasing injector pulse width (therefore reducing the amount of fuel injected).

4   Typically, STFT values shouldn't exceed an average of 20-percent in the positive range or 10-percent in the negative range, and LTFT values shouldn't exceed an average of 15-percent in the positive range or 25-percent in the negative range. **Note:** *If the LTFT is in the positive range (above 10-percent) and the STFT is in the negative range, chances are that the MAF/VAF sensor is faulty.*

Multimeter checks:

Although you can't monitor STFT or LTFT values with a multimeter, you can monitor oxygen sensor operation (as described in *Oxygen sensor or circuit problems*) to determine if the engine is running too rich or too lean, which will push STFT and LTFT to (or past) their normal operating ranges in either direction.

Other things to check:

1   If a rich condition exists (STFT in the negative range), start with the easiest thing to check first: the air filter element. If it's really dirty, replace it, erase the DTC, perform a few drive cycles and see if the DTC resets. Other possibilities include excessive fuel pressure, leaking fuel injector(s), clogged IAC valve (or clogged passage in the throttle body), malfunctioning TPS, MAF, MAP or ECT sensor, malfunctioning EGR system, a restricted exhaust system, or a malfunctioning canister purge system.

2   A contaminated or "lazy" oxygen sensor could also be the cause, but with your scan tool you can watch the O2 sensor's activity. If you induce a lean condition by discon-

necting a vacuum hose, you should see the O2 sensor output voltage drop, and the STFT value swing toward the positive range.

3   If a lean condition exists (STFT in the positive range), check for intake air leaks, vacuum leaks and exhaust leaks. Other possibilities include problems with the MAF or MAP sensors, insufficient fuel pressure, dirty or inoperative fuel injector(s), or a secondary air injection system operating when it shouldn't (during closed loop). Contaminated fuel, although unlikely, is also a possibility.

4   If both cylinder banks on a V engine are rich (resulting in a fuel trim code for each bank), the fuel pressure might be too high, the EVAP purge solenoid might be stuck open, the ECT sensor could be skewed toward a lower temperature, or the MAF signal voltage could be skewed toward a higher voltage.

5   Conversely, if both cylinder banks on a V engine are lean (resulting in a fuel trim code for each bank), the fuel pressure might be too low, there may be a vacuum leak, the ECT sensor could be skewed toward a higher temperature, or the MAF signal voltage could be skewed toward a lower voltage.

1c Intake Air Temperature (IAT) sensor or circuit

Symptoms caused by problems with the IAT sensor or circuit can include hard starting when cold, reduced gas mileage, pinging, and sluggish performance.

Scan tool checks:

1   With the engine cold, connect your scan tool to the DLC and turn the ignition on (but don't start the engine). Check the IAT sensor value and compare it to the engine coolant temperature (ECT) sensor value - they should be about the same, plus or minus a few degrees **(see illustrations 9.10a and 9.10b)**. **Note:** *Keep in mind the IAT sensor is more sus-*

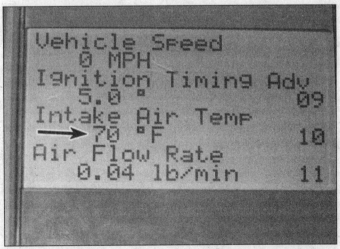

9.10a With the engine cold, the Intake Air Temperature (IAT) reading . . .

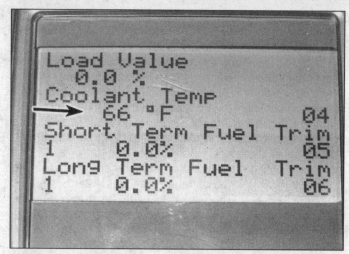

9.10b . . . and Engine Coolant Temperature (ECT) reading should be fairly close to each other

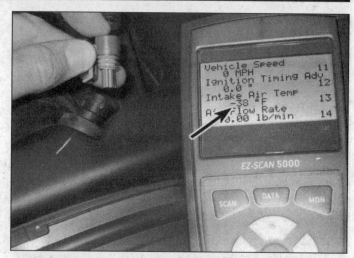

9.11a If the wiring harness and PCM are OK, the IAT value should indicate a very cold temperature when the sensor is unplugged . . .

ceptible to changes in ambient temperature than the ECT sensor.

2   If the IAT sensor value is way out of range, unplug the electrical connector from the sensor and check the sensor value on the scan tool; it should read very cold (around -40 degrees or so) **(see illustration 9.11a)**. Now connect the terminals of the electrical connector with a jumper wire and check the reading; it should now indicate a very high temperature **(see illustration 9.11b)**. **Note:** *We found that some vehicles wouldn't reflect this change until the ignition key was cycled off and back on again, or until the engine was started. On most vehicles, though, the change is immediate.*

3   If the scan tool reflects this, the IAT sensor is probably faulty, since the PCM is properly "seeing" the open and closed circuit conditions that you caused. If values don't change as described, check the wiring between the sensor and the PCM. If the wiring is OK, the PCM may be at

fault. At this point it is recommended that the vehicle be diagnosed by a dealer service department or other qualified repair shop, as the PCM is very expensive and is not returnable (and would most likely have to be programmed with a proprietary scan tool anyway).

Multimeter checks:

1   Disconnect the electrical connector from the IAT sensor, turn the ignition on (but don't start the engine), and check for a 5-volt reference voltage on one of the terminals of the electrical connector **(see illustration 9.12)**. If no voltage is present, check the wiring between the connector and the PCM.

2   Turn the ignition off and check for ground on the other terminal of the electrical connector by connecting the leads of the voltmeter across the terminals of the connector **(see**

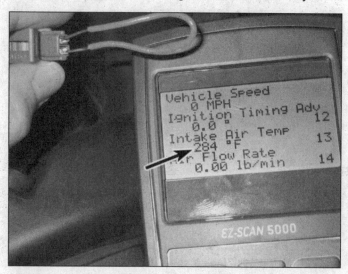

9.11b . . . and a very hot temperature when the terminals of the wiring connector are jumped

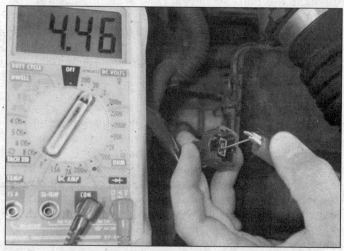

9.12 Checking for reference voltage at the IAT sensor electrical connector. **Caution:** *When probing the terminals of a connector, insert the pin to the **side** of the connector, not in the center of the terminal (which could spread the terminal apart and cause poor contact when reconnected)*

9.13 A good ground is indicated if the meter still registers a reference voltage when probing both terminals of the connector

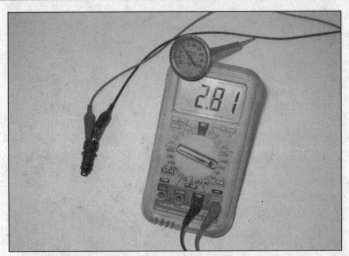

9.14 Check the resistance of the IAT sensor at various temperatures and see how it responds

illustration 9.13). If reference voltage was present in the last Step but not now, the ground circuit is open; check the wiring between the connector and the PCM.

3 If the wiring is OK but either reference voltage or ground is not present, the PCM is probably faulty. At this point it is recommended that the vehicle be diagnosed by a dealer service department or other qualified repair shop, as the PCM is very expensive and is not returnable (and would most likely have to be programmed with a proprietary scan tool anyway). If reference voltage and ground are OK, the IAT sensor is most likely faulty.

4 The performance of the IAT sensor can be checked by removing it from the vehicle and measuring its resistance at room temperature **(see illustration 9.14)**, then cooling it in a freezer and measuring its resistance cold, then heating it

up with a hair dryer or heat gun and measuring its resistance hot.

- At room temperature (approximately 70-degrees F) the resistance should be about 1500 ohms.
- When cold (32-degrees F), the resistance should be high (approximately 5000 to 6000 ohms).
- When hot (around 175-degrees F), the resistance should be low (approximately 260 ohms).

Keep in mind these resistance figures are approximate (you'd need to consult a factory service manual for the specific resistances for the sensor on your vehicle) - the important thing is that the resistance changes as the temperature of the sensor changes **(see illustration 9.15)**. If it doesn't, replace the sensor with a new one.

1d Mass Air Flow (MAF) sensor or circuit

Symptoms caused by problems with the MAF sensor or circuit can include hard starting (hot and cold), stalling, stumble on acceleration, reduced engine performance, reduced gas mileage, black smoke, rough idle, surging, and sometimes pinging. Fuel trim-related codes may also be present.

Preliminary checks:

1 Start by unplugging the electrical connector from the sensor (with the ignition key off), start the engine and see how it idles. If idle quality is better now than before, replace the sensor.

2 Next, check the air filter element - if it's extremely dirty replace it, erase the DTC, perform a few drive cycles and see if the DTC resets (and if the engine runs better).

3 Other outside factors that could result in an erroneous MAF sensor signal could be leaks in the ducting between the throttle body and the intake manifold, and vacuum leaks,

Temp (F)	Resistance (ohms)
32	4800 to 6800
50	4000
68	2200 to 2800
86	1300
104	1000 to 1200
122	1000
140	800
176	260 to 380
212	150

10206-9-9.18 HAYNES

9.15 Typical temperature-to-resistance chart applicable to IAT and ECT sensors. Note: *Resistance values are approximate*

9.16 The duct between the MAF sensor and the throttle body is notorious for cracking, which will result in unmeasured air entering the engine. Also make sure the clamps on either end are tight

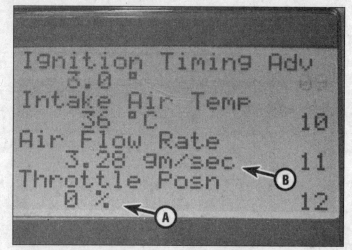

9.17a At idle, the throttle is closed (A) and the Mass Air Flow sensor is registering a little over 3 grams-per-second (B) on this turbocharged four-cylinder in a Lancer Evolution

so check all vacuum hoses and intake ducts carefully **(see illustration 9.16)**. Any air finding its way into the intake tract without passing through the MAF sensor will cause the PCM to send an insufficient pulse width to the fuel injectors. **Note:** *On models so equipped, don't forget to check the Positive Crankcase Ventilation (PCV) valve, hose and grommet.*

Scan tool checks:

1   Connect your scan tool to the DLC and warm up the engine to normal operating temperature, making sure the engine has gone into closed loop. Check the Short Term Fuel Trim (STFT) and Long Term Fuel Trim (LTFT) values. If the LTFT is in the positive range (above 10-percent) and the STFT is in the negative range, chances are that the MAF/VAF sensor is at fault.

2   With the engine running, observe the STFT and (if your scan tool is capable) injector pulse width parameters at idle, mid-throttle and while revving the engine. Injector pulse width and STFT should noticeably increase as engine speed increases. If they don't, the MAF sensor is probably faulty.

3   If the STFT and LTFT don't look suspicious, check the MAF sensor reading at idle - most scan tools will read this value in pounds-per-minute or grams-per-second (gm/sec, sometimes expressed as gps). The actual values depend on engine displacement, engine speed and load, but you can expect to see a reading of approximately 3 to 6 gm/sec at idle **(see illustration 9.17a)**. Now smoothly open the throttle and observe the reading. The transition of gm/sec should increase smoothly in proportion to throttle opening, from a low gm/sec reading at idle to a high gm/sec at wide open throttle **(see illustrations 9.17b and 9.17c)**. If this is not the case, or if the gm/sec value jumps abruptly, the sensor is probably faulty.

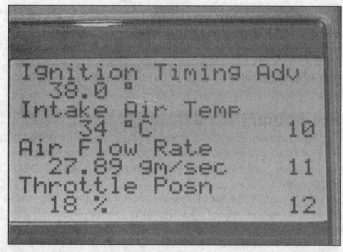

9.17b At part throttle (about 1/4 of the way open) the MAF reading has increased to 27.89 grams-per-second . . .

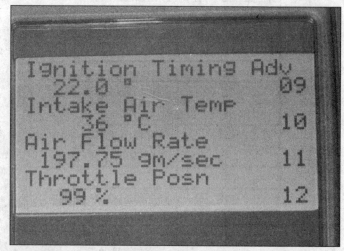

9.17c . . . and almost 198 gm/sec at Wide Open Throttle (WOT)! The transition from idle to WOT was smooth, indicating the MAF sensor is in good shape. Caution: *Don't hold the engine at a high rpm for longer than a moment or serious damage could occur*

9.18 Backprobing a MAF sensor, at idle, with T-pins on the signal and ground wires. Voltage should increase with engine speed

9.19 With the ignition key ON and the engine Off, the MAP reading should indicate the atmospheric (barometric) pressure where you are

Multimeter checks:

The typical MAF sensor has a 12-volt feed wire, a 5-volt reference wire from the PCM, a signal wire back to the PCM, and a ground wire (a wiring diagram for your specific vehicle should be used to identify the terminals of the sensor). Some MAF sensors send the PCM a signal voltage, while others send a frequency (measured in Hertz).

- **Signal voltage type sensors:** Using a high-impedance digital voltmeter and a T-pin, you can backprobe the signal wire and check the signal voltage to the PCM **(see illustration 9.18)**. A typical signal voltage at idle would be approximately 1.5 to 2.5 volts, and should increase as engine speed increases.
- **Frequency-based sensors:** Some multimeters are capable of measuring frequency; backprobe the signal wire as described previously and start the engine. A typical frequency reading should be about 2.5 kHz at idle, increasing in a linear fashion up to around 5 kHz at 3,500 rpm.
- **Either type:** The change in signal voltage or frequency from idle to wide open throttle should be smooth and linear. Any glitches or readings that don't increase in a linear fashion indicate a faulty sensor.

Other things to check:

1   With the engine idling, tap sharply on the MAF sensor with your fingers; if the engine stumbles, replace the sensor (not all sensors that are bad will react like this, however).
2   Vacuum leaks, MAP and TP sensor problems, and a restricted exhaust system are other factors that could result in a MAF sensor code being set.
3   Obviously, the wiring between the sensor and the PCM must be free of opens or shorts, and the connections must be secure and free of corrosion. If none of the checks reveal a sensor problem, and the wiring looks OK, the PCM could be at fault. At this point it is recommended that the vehicle be diagnosed by a dealer service department or other qualified repair shop, as the PCM is very expensive and is not returnable (and would most likely have to be programmed with a proprietary scan tool anyway).
4   Aftermarket air filters that require occasional oiling can also foul a MAF sensor.

1e Manifold Absolute Pressure (MAP) sensor or circuit

Symptoms caused by problems with the MAP sensor or circuit can include hard starting, stalling, rough idle, sluggish performance, black smoke, and sometimes oxygen sensor or fuel trim codes.

Scan tool checks:

1   Connect your scan tool to the DLC, check the MAP value on the tool's display and write it down **(see illustration 9.19)**. This value should reflect the atmospheric pressure where you are (some scan tools may actually display this value as a BARO reading, for barometric pressure). At sea level, atmospheric pressure is 29.92 in.Hg (inches of mercury). **Note:** *To compensate for higher elevations, subtract one inch of mercury from 29.92 for every 1,000 feet of elevation gain above approximately 2000 feet.* Also check the MAP value; with the engine at rest, it should be about the same as the BARO reading (within 10-percent).
2   Connect a vacuum gauge to manifold vacuum (not ported, or throttle body vacuum). Start the engine and allow it to warm up to normal operating temperature, then check the MAP sensor reading to see if it reacts properly to manifold vacuum **(see illustrations 9.20a and 9.20b)**. To convert

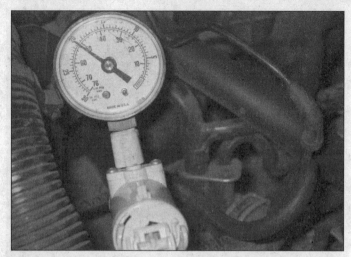

9.20a Here a vacuum gauge has been teed into the vacuum line to the fuel pressure regulator and the engine has been started. To determine if the MAP sensor is operating correctly, subtract this vacuum reading (20 in.Hg) from the barometric pressure reading (which was 30 in.Hg) . . .

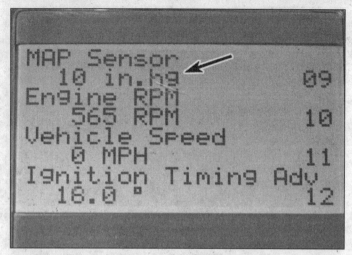

9.20b . . . and you get 10 in. Hg, which is exactly the MAP value that the scan tool is now showing at idle

the manifold vacuum reading to manifold absolute pressure, subtract the vacuum gauge reading from the barometric pressure reading taken in the last step.

3   Repeat Step 2 with the engine running at different speeds, using the vacuum gauge readings and calculating manifold absolute pressure at various rpms. If the sensor's operating parameters don't reflect the calculated manifold absolute pressures at various engine speeds, and there are no vacuum leaks, it is probably faulty.

4   This test can also be performed by connecting a hand-held vacuum pump to the port on the sensor and monitoring the sensor's activity at various applications of vacuum with the key on/engine off. **Caution:** *Don't pull a vacuum of more than 20 in.Hg, as the sensor could be damaged.*

Multimeter checks:

Analog-type MAP sensors

1   Most MAP sensors have three wires: a five-volt reference from the PCM, a ground, and a signal return back to the PCM. Using a high-impedance digital voltmeter you can backprobe these three wires at the sensor's electrical connector to see if the sensor is receiving voltage, putting out voltage and has a good ground. The signal return back to the PCM should vary with changes in manifold absolute pressure, typically from about 1 or 2 volts at idle (high vacuum) and close to five volts with the key on/engine off, and at wide open throttle (low vacuum).

2   This test can also be performed by connecting a hand-held vacuum pump to the port on the sensor and monitoring the sensor's activity at various applications of vacuum with the key on/engine off **(see illustration 9.21)**. **Caution:** *Don't pull a vacuum of more than 20 in.Hg, as the sensor could be damaged.*

3   If the MAP sensor doesn't react as described, and there is a five volt reference voltage and a good ground (and there are no vacuum leaks), the sensor is probably faulty.

Frequency-based MAP sensors

1   Frequency-based MAP sensors are used by some manufacturers, most notably Ford. If your multimeter is capable of measuring frequency, backprobe the signal return wire and start the engine. The frequency reading should vary, typically from about 95 Hz at idle (high vacuum) to approximately 150 Hz at wide open throttle (low vacuum).

2   This test can also be performed by connecting a hand-held vacuum pump to the port on the sensor and monitoring the sensor's activity at various applications of vacuum with the key on/engine off. **Caution:** *Don't pull a vacuum of more than 20 in.Hg, as the sensor could be damaged.*

Other things to check:

1   For the MAP sensor to report the proper values to the PCM, it's imperative that no vacuum leaks exist. Check the

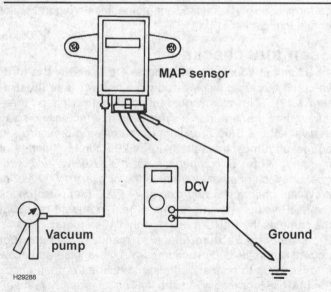

9.21 Checking a MAF sensor with a voltmeter and a hand-held vacuum pump

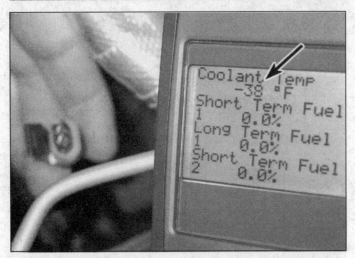

9.22a With the ECT sensor unplugged, the coolant temperature value on the scan tool should read very cold . . .

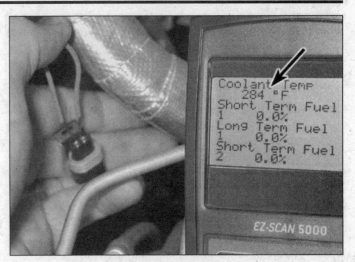

9.22b . . . and very hot with the terminals of the connector bridged

gasket or grommet on the sensor itself (manifold-mounted sensors), the hose from the intake manifold to the sensor (remotely mounted sensors), the throttle body gasket, intake manifold gasket, and all hoses connected to the intake manifold for leaks.

2   It's also important for the sensor to *receive* a vacuum signal. Make sure the sensor's port, or the hose leading to the sensor, isn't plugged. If you have a hose, make sure it's not soft, which will cause it to collapse under vacuum.

3   Check the wiring and all connectors from the sensor to the PCM. If no problems turn up during inspection or while performing the scan tool and/or multimeter checks, it's recommended that the vehicle be diagnosed by a dealer service department or other qualified repair shop.

1f Engine Coolant Temperature (ECT) sensor or circuit problems

Symptoms caused by problems with the ECT sensor can include black smoky exhaust, sluggish performance, poor gas mileage, engine overheating, and inoperative air conditioning.

Scan tool checks:

1   With the engine cold, connect your scan tool to the DLC and turn the ignition on (but don't start the engine). Check the ECT sensor value and compare it to the intake air temperature (IAT) sensor value - they should be about the same, plus or minus a few degrees **(see illustrations 9.10a and 9.10b)**.

2   If the ECT sensor value is way out of range, unplug the electrical connector from the sensor and check the sensor value on the scan tool; it should read very cold (around -40 degrees or so). Now connect the terminals of the electrical connector with a jumper wire and check the reading; it should now indicate a very high temperature **(see illustra-**

tions 9.22a and 9.22b).

3   If the scan tool reflects this, the ECT sensor is probably faulty, since the PCM is properly "seeing" the open and closed circuit conditions that you caused. If values don't change as described, check the wiring between the sensor and the PCM. If the wiring is OK, the PCM may be at fault. At this point it is recommended that the vehicle be diagnosed by a dealer service department or other qualified repair shop, as the PCM is very expensive and is not returnable (and would most likely have to be programmed with a proprietary scan tool anyway).

Multimeter checks:

1   Disconnect the electrical connector from the ECT sensor, turn the ignition on (but don't start the engine), and check for a 5-volt reference voltage on one of the terminals of the electrical connector **(see illustration 9.23)**. If no voltage is present, check the wiring between the connector and the PCM. If voltage is present, verify that there is a good

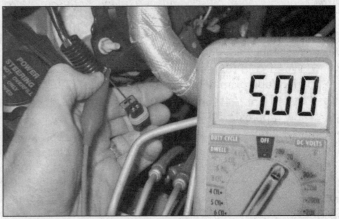

9.23 Checking for reference voltage at the ECT sensor electrical connector. Caution: *When probing the terminals of a connector, insert the pin to the **side** of the connector, not in the center of the terminal (which could spread the terminal apart and cause poor contact when reconnected)*

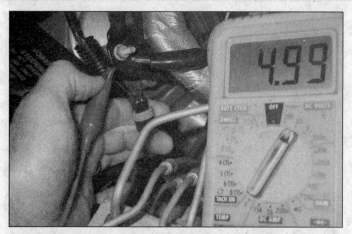

9.24 A good ground is indicated if the meter still registers a reference voltage when probing both terminals of the connector

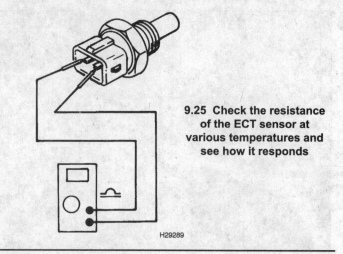

9.25 Check the resistance of the ECT sensor at various temperatures and see how it responds

ground by connecting the leads of the voltmeter to the terminals of the connector (see illustration 9.24). If there is no voltage present now, a bad ground is indicated.

2   If the wiring is OK but voltage is not present, the PCM is probably faulty. At this point it is recommended that the vehicle be diagnosed by a dealer service department or other qualified repair shop, as the PCM is very expensive and is not returnable (and would most likely have to be programmed with a proprietary scan tool anyway). If reference voltage and ground are OK, the ECT sensor is most likely faulty.

3   The performance of the ECT sensor can be checked by removing it from the vehicle and measuring its resistance at room temperature, then cooling it in a freezer and measuring its resistance cold, then heating it up with a heat gun (or placing the tip of the sensor in a pot of boiling water, but care must be taken not to scald yourself!) and measuring its resistance hot (see illustration 9.25). Warning: *The engine must be completely cool before removing the ECT sensor. Also, the ECT sensor is threaded into the water jacket, so the cooling system must be drained (at least partially) before removing the sensor.*

- At room temperature (approximately 70-degrees F) the resistance should be about 1500 ohms.
- When cold (32-degrees F), the resistance should be high (approximately 5000 to 6000 ohms).
- When hot (212-degrees F), the resistance should be low (approximately 150 ohms).

Keep in mind these resistance figures are approximate (you'd need to consult a factory service manual for the specific resistances for the sensor on your vehicle) - the important thing is that the resistance changes as the temperature of the sensor changes (see illustration 9.15). If it doesn't, replace the sensor with a new one.

Other things to check:

1   Since the ECT sensor is immersed in engine coolant, it is imperative that the coolant level is sufficient. If the coolant level is low, check the cooling system for leaks.

2   It is also important for the coolant to be able to circulate through the system properly. A partially blocked radiator or an eroded water pump impeller will affect coolant circulation and contribute to overheating, which will also result in ECT problems.

3   Obviously, the wiring between the sensor and the PCM must be free of opens or shorts, and the connections must be secure and free of corrosion. If none of the checks reveal a sensor problem, and the wiring looks OK, the PCM could be at fault. At this point it is recommended that the vehicle be diagnosed by a dealer service department or other qualified repair shop, as the PCM is very expensive and is not returnable (and would most likely have to be programmed with a proprietary scan tool anyway).

1g Throttle Position (TP) sensor/Accelerator Pedal Position (APP) sensor or circuit

Symptoms caused by problems with the TP/APP sensor can include slow or delayed throttle response, hesitation or flat spot on acceleration, idle speed too high or too low, and overall poor engine performance. On some vehicles with automatic transmissions the sensor also affects the operation of the torque converter clutch.

Scan tool checks:

1   Connect your scan tool to the DLC and check the TP reading with the key on and the engine off. Watch the value change as the throttle is moved slowly from idle to wide open (see illustration 9.26). Note: *On vehicles without an accelerator cable the engine must be running to perform this check.* The TP reading should change smoothly and linearly, with no jumps or glitches. If the change is not smooth, the sensor is probably bad. The change should also be smooth as the throttle is returned to its at-rest position.

2   If nothing happens during the check, proceed to the *Multimeter checks.*

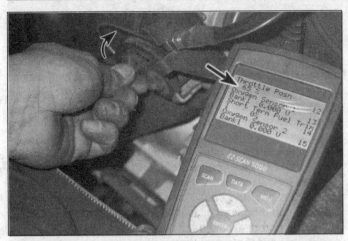

9.26 Watch the TP sensor value as the throttle is opened - the transition from idle to Wide Open Throttle (WOT) should be smooth

Multimeter checks:

1   Most TP sensors have three wires: a five-volt reference from the PCM, a ground, and a signal return back to the PCM. With the key on and the engine off, use a high-impedance digital voltmeter to backprobe these three wires at the sensor's electrical connector to see if the sensor is receiving voltage and has a good ground, and is putting out a signal return voltage.

2   With the key on and the engine off, there should be 4.5 to 5.0-volts across the reference voltage and ground wires (backprobe the 5-volt reference wire and the ground wire simultaneously) **(see illustration 9.27)**. If it's less than 4.5-volts, check the wiring between the sensor and the PCM. If the voltage is more than 5.0-volts, check the reference voltage wire for a short to power. **Note:** *Take into consideration the Note in Step 4.*

3   If the wiring and connections are OK, but the voltage on the reference wire is out of range, the PCM may be faulty. At this point it is recommended that the vehicle be diagnosed by a dealer service department or other qualified repair

shop, as the PCM is very expensive and is not returnable (and would most likely have to be programmed with a proprietary scan tool anyway).

4   The signal return back to the PCM should vary with changes in throttle position, typically from about 0.5-volt with the throttle at rest to approximately 4.0 to 5.0 volts with the throttle opened all the way **(see illustration 9.28)**. As with the scan tool check, the change should be smooth in both directions. **Note:** *On some vehicles the TP sensor works exactly opposite (putting out a higher voltage at idle and a lower voltage at wide open throttle), but the transition should still be smooth.*

5   If the reference voltage at the sensor is within range and the ground is good, but the signal return voltage is out of range or doesn't change smoothly, the sensor is probably bad.

1h Fuel temperature sensor (FTS) or circuit

1   The FTS measures the fuel temperature in the fuel rail.

2   The majority of FTSs used in motor vehicles are of the negative temperature coefficient (NTC) type. An NTC sensor is a thermistor in which the resistance decreases as the temperature rises.

3   The general method of testing, and the resistance and voltages, are similar to the engine coolant temperature (ECT) sensor previously described (see Section 1f).

1i Fuel injector or circuit

Problems with the fuel injector control circuit can mimic those of a bad throttle position sensor. Symptoms include stalling, flat spots or hesitation during acceleration, bad gas mileage and sluggish engine performance. A misfire DTC might also be set, so diagnose that code first to help isolate the cylinder in which the problem is occurring (if it is, in fact, happening on only one cylinder).

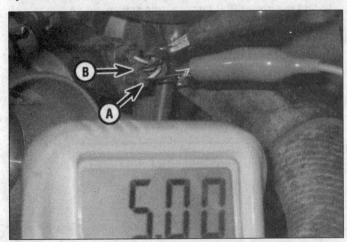

9.27 Backprobing the reference voltage (A) and ground (B) wires at the TP sensor on a 2003 Toyota Corolla

9.28 Checking the TP sensor signal voltage by backprobing the signal return wire. The voltage reading should change smoothly from idle to full-throttle

Checks:

1   Refer to Chapter 4, *Fuel injection system general checks* and perform the injector tests described there.

2   If the injector is operating, keep in mind that the problem could be intermittent or only occur during certain operating conditions, or the injector could be electrically OK but mechanically defective (restricted, clogged or leaking).

3   Carefully check all of the fuel injector electrical connectors for evidence of corrosion caused by "fretting," or slight movement between the terminals of the connector and the terminals of the injector. Any corrosion in these connectors can interfere with injector operation.

4   If the injector isn't receiving a signal from the PCM, there may be a problem in the wiring or in the PCM. If no problems can be found in the wiring or connections, it is recommended that the vehicle be diagnosed by a dealer service department or other qualified repair shop, as the PCM is very expensive and is not returnable (and would most likely have to be programmed with a proprietary scan tool anyway).

1j   Fuel pump or circuit

The Powertrain Control Module (PCM) may set a DTC if it detects a problem in the fuel pump circuit. Symptoms of a fuel pump circuit problem could range from a no-start condition to general reduced performance, stalling and hesitation on acceleration.

Checks:

1   If the vehicle won't start, check for the presence of voltage at the fuel pump electrical connector when the ignition key is turned on (power should be available for about two seconds as the PCM energizes the pump) or as the engine is cranked. If voltage is present, the fuel pump is most likely faulty. If the fuel pump has failed, be sure to check the fuel tank for evidence of contamination that could have destroyed the pump.

2   If no power is present, suspect the fuel pump relay. If you have access to a wiring diagram for your vehicle, remove the fuel pump relay and, using a jumper wire, bridge the terminals of the fuse/relay block that feed power to the fuel pump **(see illustration 9.29)**. If the pump now receives voltage when the ignition key is turned on, check for power

and ground to the relay control circuit using a high-impedance digital voltmeter. If power and ground are present when the engine is cranked, replace the relay. If no power is available, the PCM may be the problem. At this point it is recommended that the vehicle be diagnosed by a dealer service department or other qualified repair shop, as the PCM is very expensive and is not returnable (and would most likely have to be programmed with a proprietary scan tool anyway).

3   If the fuel pump is operational, check the fuel pressure with a fuel pressure gauge (refer to the *Haynes Automotive Repair Manual* for your vehicle). If the pressure is within the specified range, the cause of the DTC is probably intermittent and could be very difficult to re-create and diagnose.

4   Other potential causes of a DTC related to the fuel pump circuit would include problems with components that signal the PCM to operate the fuel pump, such as the crankshaft position sensor (CKP), oil pressure sensor (or low engine oil pressure). Additionally, some vehicles have a separate control module through which the fuel pump is activated.

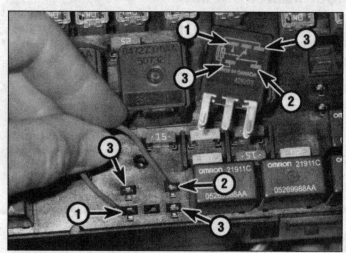

9.29 Bypassing the fuel pump relay with a jumper wire. Some relays have a schematic printed on the side to indicate the control and power circuits, but it's best to use a test light first to find the power (B+) terminal (the schematic on this relay turned out to be a mirror image)

1   B+   3   Control circuit
2   To fuel pump

2 Ignition system/misfire faults (3rd character of DTC = 3)

2a Misfire detected (random or cylinder-specific)

Symptoms caused by a misfire resulting in a DTC being set include rough idle and sluggish performance, poor gas mileage, and/or a restricted catalytic converter. **Note:** *Keep in mind that the diagnostic information presented here assumes that the engine is in good mechanical condition.*

Random cylinder misfire

Scan tool checks:

1   Connect your scan tool to the DLC and, if your scanner is capable, check the misfire history data. If one cylinder is showing more misfire counts than the others, concentrate on factors that would affect that particular cylinder, at least to begin with. (However, keep in mind that a specific cylinder misfire code would likely be set if the problem were limited to one particular cylinder.)

Other things to check:

2   If the vehicle is equipped with spark plug wires, make sure all of the wires are clean. Check also for evidence of arcing. As spark plug wires age, their ability to transmit high secondary voltage to the spark plugs can be reduced, and their insulating properties can be compromised as well. These problems often occur only when the engine is under load, so it's not always easy to determine if the wires are breaking down and causing a misfire. Sometimes arcing wires can be seen by running the engine in a darkened garage (do this at night, and with the garage door open so there is adequate ventilation). If the vehicle has accumulated many miles, it's not a bad idea to install a new set of spark plug wires, clear the DTC and see if the code resets.

3   If the engine is equipped with a distributor, check the distributor cap and rotor for evidence of arcing, too. If in doubt, replace them.

4   Check carefully for vacuum leaks.

5   Check the EGR valve, if equipped, making sure it closes all the way and doesn't leak. If an EGR leak is suspected, remove the EGR valve and clean it thoroughly to remove all carbon deposits so it can maintain a good seal when closed.

6   Check the fuel pressure with a fuel pressure gauge (refer to the *Haynes Automotive Repair Manual* for your vehicle). If the pressure is too low, that could be the cause of a random misfire.

7   Low fuel volume could cause a random misfire, too. A restricted fuel filter could cause low fuel volume, even while the fuel pressure reading is indicating proper fuel pressure.

8   Sometimes having the fuel injectors pressure-cleaned will cure a random- or multiple-cylinder misfire.

9   Check the crankshaft position sensor for debris/metallic contamination. Also check the reluctor wheel for debris and/or missing teeth. A CKP sensor with an intermittent electrical condition (open or short) could be the cause of a random misfire.

10   A malfunctioning chassis acceleration ("rough road") sensor could cause a random misfire DTC.

11   Although unlikely, contaminated fuel could result in a random cylinder misfire.

12   A faulty ignition module or PCM could be the cause. If none of the other checks turn up a problem, have the vehicle diagnosed by a dealer service department or other qualified repair shop.

Cylinder-specific misfire

1   When diagnosing a cylinder-specific (or multiple-cylinder) misfire, begin diagnosis with the ignition system.

2   If only one misfire DTC has been set, check the spark plug for the affected cylinder. Look for cracks in the insulator, carbon tracking and signs of physical damage. Replace the spark plug if any undesirable conditions are found, then clear the code and drive the vehicle to see if the code sets again.

3   If more than one DTC has set, and they are related to companion cylinders on a vehicle that uses coil packs, suspect a faulty coil pack. This can be confirmed by swapping the suspected bad coil pack with a coil pack that fires two other cylinders, then erasing the DTCs and driving the vehicle. If, after performing a test drive the problem shifts to the cylinders that received the suspect coil pack, you can conclude that the coil pack is the problem.

4   On vehicles that use one individual ignition coil-per-cylinder, swap the coil on the cylinder that the DTC pertains to with another cylinder, erase the DTC and drive the vehicle.

9.30 If you have a cylinder-specific misfire on an engine with coil-over-plug ignition, on cylinder number 1, for example, swap coil no. 1 with coil no. 2, then clear the DTC and drive the vehicle. If a misfire code now sets for cylinder number 2, you know the coil is bad

If the problem shifts to the cylinder that received the suspect coil, you can condemn that coil as being faulty **(see illustration 9.30)**. If the problem does not shift, the ignition coil might not be receiving a signal from the PCM; check the wiring and electrical connectors between the coil and the PCM.

5   An alternative to the method described in the previous Step would be to use a calibrated ignition tester to see if the coil is capable of firing the spark plug (see Chapter 4, **illustration 4.36).**

6   On distributor-equipped vehicles, the test described in the Step 4 can be applied to the spark plug wire for the cylinder that the DTC pertains to. If the problem clears up, it is recommended that all of the spark plug wires be replaced (see Step 2 under *Random cylinder misfire*).

7   If you have ruled out the ignition system as the source of the problem, refer to Chapter 4, *Fuel injection system general checks* and perform the injector tests described there. If the injector is receiving a signal from the PCM (as evidenced by the "noid light" test), you can swap the injector from the cylinder that the DTC pertains to with another injector (refer to the *Haynes Automotive Repair Manual* for your vehicle for the fuel rail and injector removal and installation procedure). If, after clearing the code and driving the vehicle the problem travels to the other cylinder, you can assume that the injector is faulty.

8   Sometimes having the fuel injectors pressure-cleaned will cure a misfire.

9   Although unlikely to cause a cylinder-specific misfire, see the items in Steps 4, 5, 9, and 12 under *Random cylinder misfire*.

2b Crankshaft Position (CKP) sensor or circuit

A problem with the CKP sensor or circuit can result in a no-start condition, stalling, poor performance, rough running engine, and misfiring. In some instances the engine will stall,

9.31a Typical inductive-type crankshaft position sensor

then may restart after sitting for awhile. **Note:** *If a CKP sensor-related DTC and a misfire-related DTC is set, troubleshoot the CKP-related code first, because chances are that it is causing the misfire.*

Preliminary checks:

1   If the vehicle won't start at all, check all the fuses first. Replace any blown fuses and trace the circuit to find the cause.

2   Make sure all the electrical connectors between the sensor and the PCM are secure.

3   Make sure the sensor is mounted securely.

4   Remove the sensor and check the tip for damage and/or the accumulation of debris, as this would interfere with the signal.

5   Some CKP sensors are adjustable - the air gap between the sensor tip and the trigger wheel must be set. If your sensor is adjustable, make sure the air gap is correct (refer to the *Haynes Automotive Repair Manual* for your vehicle).

6   On Hall-effect type sensors, make sure none of the trigger vanes are broken.

7   Check the routing of the CKP sensor's wiring harness. Make sure it doesn't travel too close to any spark plug wires or any aftermarket electrical equipment that may cause electromagnetic interference.

Multimeter checks:

Inductive-type sensor

1   Follow the wiring harness from the CKP sensor to its electrical connector, then unplug the connector **(see illustration 9.31a)**. Measure the CKP resistance **(see illustration 9.31b)**. Typical resistance for the CKP is in the range of 200 to 2000 ohms (the actual resistance for the sensor on your vehicle may be different). Most importantly, though, is that the sensor isn't open- or short-circuited. **Note:** *Even if the resistance is within the quoted specifications, this does not prove that the CKP can generate an acceptable signal.*

2   Check the CKP signal:

a) Detach the sensor's electrical connector (if not already done).

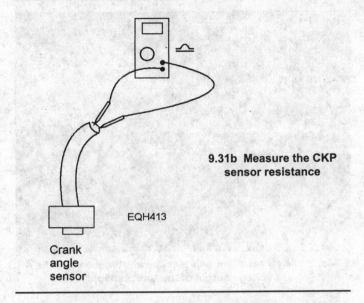

9.31b Measure the CKP sensor resistance

EQH413

Crank angle sensor

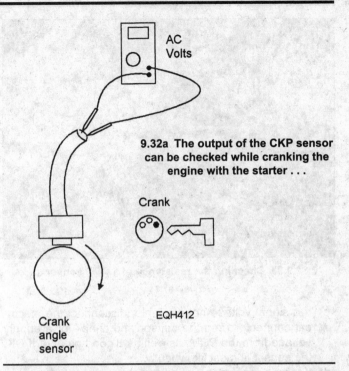

AC Volts

9.32a The output of the CKP sensor can be checked while cranking the engine with the starter . . .

Crank

EQH412

Crank angle sensor

b) Connect the multimeter, set on the AC voltage scale, between the two terminals of the sensor. If a third terminal or wire is present, it will be a shield terminal or wire.

c) Crank the engine (or turn it over manually with a large ratchet or breaker bar) and watch the meter; an AC voltage should be produced **(see illustrations 9.32a and 9.32b)**.

Note: *The AC voltmeter at least proves that a signal is being generated by the sensor. However, the AC voltage is an average voltage, and does not clearly indicate if there is damage to the CKP trigger wheel or that the sine wave is regular in formation.*

3   In some systems, the CKP may be shielded. To test the shielding, proceed as follows:

a) Locate the electrical connector and unplug it.

b) Attach an ohmmeter probe to one of the sensor terminals.

c) Attach the other ohmmeter probe to the shield wire terminal. A reading of infinity should be obtained.

9.32b . . . or while turning it over with a large breaker bar

d) Move the ohmmeter probe from the shield wire terminal and connect it to a good ground. A reading of infinity should also be obtained.

Note: *The shield wire on the CKP in some systems is connected to the CKP ground return wire. In such a case, continuity will be registered on the ohmmeter, and this is normal for that vehicle.*

4   If these checks don't reveal any problems with the CKP sensor or circuit, the ignition module (if equipped) or PCM could be at fault. At this point it is recommended that the vehicle be diagnosed by a dealer service department or other qualified repair shop, as the PCM is very expensive and is not returnable (and would most likely have to be programmed with a proprietary scan tool anyway).

Hall-effect type sensor

1   Roll back the rubber protection boot to the sensor's electrical connector.

2   Connect the voltmeter negative or dwell meter probe to an engine ground.

3   Identify the supply, signal and ground terminals.

4   Connect the voltmeter positive or dwell meter probe to the wire attached to the sensor's signal terminal.

5   Start the engine (if possible) and allow it to idle.

6   An average voltage of approximately 7 to 8 volts, or an approximate duty cycle of 35% should be obtained.

7   If a signal voltage or duty cycle signal is not available:

a) Turn the ignition key to the on position, then connect the voltmeter positive probe to the signal terminal at the sensor.

b) Turn the engine over slowly. As the trigger vane cutout space moves in and out of the air gap, the voltage should alternate between 10 to 12 volts and zero volts.

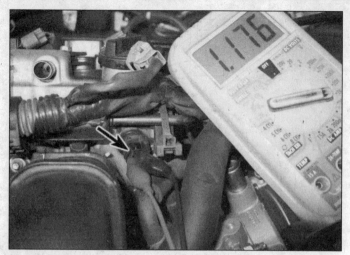

9.33 Checking the resistance of a CMP sensor

9.34a While an assistant operates the starter, measure the AC voltage output of the CMP sensor

c) If a signal voltage not available, disconnect the electrical connector from the sensor and check for a supply voltage from the PCM, as well as a good ground. If OK, the sensor is most likely faulty.

d) If there is no supply voltage or ground, check the wiring between the sensor and the PCM. If the wiring is OK, the PCM is suspect. At this point it is recommended that the vehicle be diagnosed by a dealer service department or other qualified repair shop, as the PCM is very expensive and is not returnable (and would most likely have to be programmed with a proprietary scan tool anyway).

2c Camshaft Position (CMP) sensor or circuit

The PCM uses the signal from the CMP sensor and the CKP sensor to determine Top Dead Center (TDC) compression for cylinder number 1. When a CMP-related code sets, the vehicle may start normally, might not start at all, or cranking times may be longer than normal before the engine does start.

Inductive-type sensor

1   The camshaft position sensor may be installed inside the distributor or mounted on the valve cover, in close proximity to the camshaft or camshaft sprocket.

2   Detach the sensor's electrical connector.

3   Measure the sensor's resistance (see illustration 9.33); a typical resistance value would be in the 200 to 900 ohm range (the actual specification for the sensor on your vehicle may be different). If it's open or shorted, replace it.

4   Connect an AC voltmeter between the two terminals at the sensor. Remove the fuel pump relay or EFI relay so the engine won't start.

5   Crank the engine. A small AC voltage output should be obtained (see illustrations 9.34a and 9.34b). If no voltage is generated, replace the sensor.

6   Reconnect the electrical connector and reinstall the EFI or fuel pump relay.

7   Backprobe the signal and ground terminals.

8   Start the engine and allow it to idle. An AC voltage of about 0.75 volts should be obtained.

a) If the voltage is no greater now than in Step 5, check the connectors and wiring between the sensor and the PCM for problems such as corrosion (in the connectors) and open or short-circuit conditions.

b) If the connectors and wiring are OK, the PCM might be the source of the problem. At this point it is recommended that the vehicle be diagnosed by a dealer service department or other qualified repair shop, as the PCM is very expensive and is not returnable (and would most likely have to be programmed with a proprietary scan tool anyway).

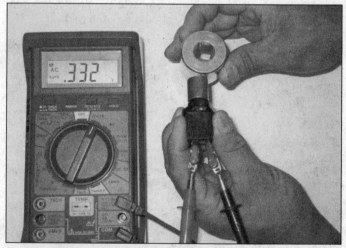

9.34b The CMP sensor can also be checked off the vehicle. Connect the leads of a voltmeter (set on the AC scale) to the sensor and pass a metal object back-and-forth in front of the sensor - a small AC voltage should be indicated on the meter

Hall-effect type sensor

1   The Hall-effect type sensor may be installed inside the distributor or mounted on the valve cover in close proximity to the camshaft. The following procedures describe how to test the distributor-located sensor. Testing the camshaft-located type will follow similar lines.

2   Connect the voltmeter negative or dwell meter probe to an engine ground.

3   Identify the supply, signal and ground terminals. The terminals may be marked as follows:

   0   Output
   +   Signal
   -    Ground

4   Connect the voltmeter positive or dwell meter probe to the wire attached to the sensor's signal terminal. **Note:** *The electrical connector must be connected.*

5   Allow the engine to idle. An average voltage of approximately 2.5 volts or an approximate duty cycle of 50% should be obtained.

6   If signal voltage or duty cycle signal not available:

 a) Stop the engine.
 b) If the sensor is located in the distributor, remove the distributor cap.
 c) Turn the ignition to the On position (with the sensor's electrical connector still connected).
 d) Connect the voltmeter positive probe to the signal terminal.
 e) Turn the engine over slowly. As the trigger vane cut-out space moves in and out of the air gap, the voltage should alternate between 5.0 volts and zero volts.

7   If no signal voltage is generated in the previous test:

 a) Disconnect the electrical connector from the sensor and check for a supply voltage from the PCM, as well as a good ground. If OK, the sensor is most likely faulty
 b) If there is no supply voltage or ground, check the wiring between the sensor and the PCM. If the wiring is OK, the PCM is suspect. At this point it is recommended that the vehicle be diagnosed by a dealer service department or other qualified repair shop, as the PCM is very expensive and is not returnable (and would most likely have to be programmed with a proprietary scan tool anyway).

Other things to check:

Other factors to consider would include worn-out timing chain or belt, a timing belt that has jumped a tooth, a faulty cam sprocket, a broken trigger vane (Hall-effect type sensors) or a defective ignition control module.

2d Ignition coil or circuit

Refer to *Cylinder-specific misfire* earlier in Section 2a.

2e Knock (KS) sensor or circuit

Symptoms accompanying knock sensor-related DTCs include spark knock (pinging), sluggish performance (especially under load) and sometimes a misfire-related trouble code.

Scan tool checks:

1   Connect your scan tool to the DLC, start the engine and allow it to reach normal operating temperature (and go into closed-loop).

2   If your scan tool is capable of displaying the knock sensor value, it should be 0-degrees at idle, but should increase when the engine is suddenly revved to about 3000 rpm.

Multimeter checks:

1   Unplug the electrical connector from the sensor. Using an ohmmeter, measure the resistance of the sensor. Sensor resistance values vary between vehicles, but the reading shouldn't be zero (shorted) or infinite (open).

2   Some knock sensors receive a reference voltage from the PCM. Disconnect the electrical connector from the sensor and turn the ignition key to the on position. Using a high-impedance digital voltmeter, measure the voltage across the terminals of the electrical connector. If no voltage is present, check the wiring harness and all electrical connections between the knock sensor and the PCM.

Other checks:

1   Knock sensor torque is critical, especially on knock sensors that are retained by a bolt passing through the center of the sensor. An overtightened knock sensor may not function properly. A typical knock sensor torque would be in the range of 15 to 20 ft-lbs for the bolted-type, or 20 to 25 ft-lbs for the threaded-type.

2   A faulty PCM could be the cause of a recurring knock sensor DTC. If this is suspected, it is recommended that the vehicle be diagnosed by a dealer service department or other qualified repair shop, as the PCM is very expensive and is not returnable (and would most likely have to be programmed with a proprietary scan tool anyway).

3 Emissions control system faults (3rd character of DTC = 4)

3a EGR system

A common symptom of a faulty EGR system is an engine that has a rough idle or stalls. Other symptoms can include a failed emissions test (excessive NOx), pinging (spark knock) during acceleration, reduced engine performance, surging during a cruise condition, and accompanying fuel trim and/or misfire codes. **Note:** *It's a good idea to check for any Technical Service Bulletins (TSBs) and the latest PCM software updates for your vehicle. It's not uncommon for manufacturers to modify the PCM's programming to account for bugs in the software or vehicle operating characteristics that are discovered after a certain model has been released and in circulation for awhile.*

Flow related codes (DTCs P0400 - P0402)

1   These codes indicate that the EGR valve is allowing too much or not enough exhaust gas to flow through the valve and into the intake manifold. These problems are usually caused by a bad hose (on vacuum-actuated valves), a dirty valve and/or restricted EGR passages. A worn EGR valve could also be the cause.

2   Refer to Chapter 4, Section 10, for basic EGR system checking procedures.

3   The best course of action to take (after inspecting all hoses for leaks) is to remove the EGR valve and clean the valve pintle and its seat. The EGR passage in the intake manifold may require cleaning, too. While the valve is off, check it for freedom of movement (on valves where this is possible).

4   The PCM infers EGR flow in different ways, depending on the system. It can use information from a differential pressure feedback sensor, an EGR temperature sensor, or it can monitor changes in manifold absolute pressure or changes in Short Term Fuel Trim (STFT) when the PCM runs the EGR monitor. If the PCM sees a change in valve position but no change in pressure, temperature or fuel trim (depending on system), it will set a DTC. These parameters can be viewed on most scan tools.

5   If cleaning the valve and ports and erasing the code doesn't solve the problem, and the hoses are OK, the valve itself, or solenoid may be faulty. Other possibilities include wiring problems or a faulty PCM.

Other EGR codes

1   Other EGR DTCs are related to solenoid or valve position sensor and circuit problems. Some of these problems can also be rectified by removing the valve and cleaning it.

2   Other problems related to these codes indicate wiring problems or problems with the PCM.

3b Secondary air system

The secondary air system is only supposed to operate when the engine is in open loop. A malfunction in this system can result in closed-loop operation taking too long to achieve (if it isn't pumping air as it should) or oxygen sensor-related codes, catalyst efficiency codes and fuel trim codes (if it stays on too long). Ultimately, if ignored and the system doesn't turn off, the catalytic converter could be destroyed by overheating.

Preliminary checks:

1   On systems that use a belt-driven pump, check the condition and tension of the drivebelt.

2   Check all hoses and valves related to the system for leaks **(see illustration 9.35)**.

3   Check the electrical connector at the pump (electric pump systems), pump clutch (belt-driven pump with clutch), and any other valves and/or switches for tightness and lack of corrosion.

4   With the engine cold, disconnect the hose from one of the check valves and confirm that air is being pumped out when the engine is running **(see illustrations 9.36a, 9.36b and 9.36c)**.

9.35 Locations of the secondary air system check valves vary, but most valves look like this. Check the valve(s) for deterioration (holes, cracks), and all hoses, clamps and pipes, too

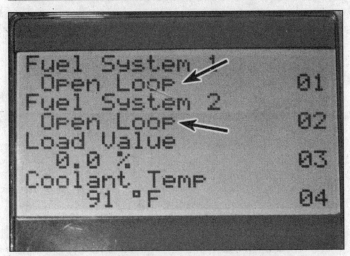

9.36a From a cold start-up, verify that the engine is in open loop . . .

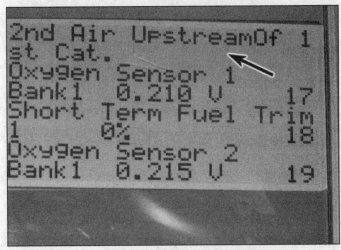

9.36b . . . and the secondary air system is activated . . .

Scan tool check:

1   With the engine cold, connect your scan tool to the DLC, start the engine and watch the secondary air pump parameter - it should read "ON" (or something similar) until the engine goes into closed loop, then it should read "OFF". If the tool doesn't reflect this, the PCM may be faulty. At this point it is recommended that the vehicle be diagnosed by a dealer service department or other qualified repair shop, as the PCM is very expensive and is not returnable (and would most likely have to be programmed with a proprietary scan tool anyway).

2   On systems with a belt-driven pump and a PCM actuated clutch the pump works in a similar fashion as an air conditioning compressor clutch. Make sure the clutch engages and the pump actually turns when it receives the ON command from the PCM.

Multimeter check:

1   With the engine cold (and in open loop), check for power

9.36c . . . then check for airflow from one of the secondary air system hoses

and ground at the pump or pump clutch electrical connector while the engine is idling. If one or the other is not present, check the wiring harness between the pump and PCM for an open or short-circuit condition.

2   If the pump isn't working due to a lack of power or ground, the PCM may be faulty. At this point it is recommended that the vehicle be diagnosed by a dealer service department or other qualified repair shop, as the PCM is very expensive and is not returnable (and would most likely have to be programmed with a proprietary scan tool anyway).

3c Catalyst efficiency

A catalyst efficiency-related DTC might not be accompanied by any driveability problems at all (just a lit-up MIL), or it might be accompanied by symptoms such as stalling, rough idle, a rotten egg smell and/or sluggish performance.

Preliminary checks:

1   With the engine completely cool (after sitting for several hours to allow the catalytic converter to cool off), raise the vehicle and support it securely on jackstands.

• Get under the vehicle and look for clues that the converter has been overheated, such as discoloring of the converter casing. If the converter looks as though it has been overheated and there is an accompanying DTC, it's a pretty good indication of a failed converter (but the diagnosis should be confirmed by monitoring the oxygen sensors). Also look for dents and evidence of leakage.

• Strike the converter with a rubber mallet or the heel of your hand. If the converter rattles (aside from any noise made by heat shields) the catalyst inside may have broken.

2   Make sure there are no other DTCs that could affect converter operation, such as codes related to oxygen sensor, misfire or secondary air injection system problems.

Scan tool checks:

1   Connect your scan tool to the DLC and warm up the engine to normal operating temperature. Raise the engine speed to approximately 2000 rpm and check the performance of the oxygen sensor parameters on the tool:

- Upstream oxygen sensors should fluctuate rapidly (about one to five times a second or so), between approximately 0.1 volt and 0.9 volt (100 millivolts to 900 millivolts). If your scan tool is capable of measuring oxygen sensor cross-counts, check that parameter also. Cross-counts are the rate at which the sensor's voltage crosses the 450 millivolt point per second.

- Downstream oxygen sensors *should* fluctuate very *slowly*, and their range of fluctuation should be much less (from above 200 millivolts to below 800 millivolts) if the catalytic converter is doing its job. A degraded, weak or non-functioning catalytic converter will have a lower downstream oxygen sensor amplitude than the upstream sensor, but will resemble the upstream sensor's voltage fluctuations (or cross-counts).

2   If the downstream oxygen sensor is performing similar to the upstream sensor, the catalytic converter isn't working properly and must be replaced. Before doing so, however, try to determine the cause of failure so the new converter doesn't get destroyed. Check the fuel trim parameters under *Fuel trim problems*. If out of range, check the items listed there, especially the fuel pressure (excessive fuel pressure can cause an overly-rich mixture).

Multimeter checks:

Refer to *Oxygen sensor or circuit problems* for multimeter-based oxygen sensor tests. compare the results with the information presented in Steps 1 and 2 under *Scan tool checks*.

3d EVAP system

Leak-related DTCs

The cause of these problems can be very difficult to hunt down, since a "large" leak is classified as a hole as small as 0.040-inch. That's about the diameter of the pin on a typical thumbtack! Some shops use a machine that pumps smoke into the system; the technician can then find the leak by looking for the plume of smoke emanating from the hole or bad connection. Without such a machine, a leak may still be discovered by careful inspection of all the hoses and connections in the system. Probably the most common cause of a leak-related code is a fuel filler cap that has been left off or not tightened all the way **(see illustration 9.37)**.

Circuit-related DTCs

Most often these DTC relate to open or shorted circuits or components in the EVAP system, such as the canister purge solenoid, vent control solenoid or pressure sensor **(see illustration 9.38)**. These components can be checked with an ohmmeter to detect an open or shorted condition, as well as the wiring between the component and the PCM.

9.37 A common cause of a leak-related EVAP system code is a gas cap that hasn't been fully tightened. Also, check the condition of the cap's O-ring

Performance-related DTCs

Performance related EVAP codes can also be triggered by an open- or short-circuit condition of one of the electrical components in the system, but can also be caused by flow-related malfunctions in the system. Check to make sure that none of the hoses and valves in the system are obstructed.

3f Fuel level sensor or circuit

If the fuel level sensor isn't working properly, the PCM might not be able to run the EVAP monitor, in which case a DTC will be set. The most common symptom associated with a fuel level sensor DTC is an inaccurate fuel gauge.

Scan tool check:

1   If your scan tool is capable of displaying fuel level sensor parameters, connect your scanner to the DLC, turn the ignition to the On position and check the fuel level sensor value - it should roughly be equal to the fuel level that the gauge on the instrument panel is showing.

9.38 EVAP system solenoids can be checked for an open- or short-circuit condition with an ohmmeter

2   This check can be performed right after refueling, then later after the vehicle has been driven a substantial distance to see if the fuel level sensor is registering a lesser quantity of fuel in the tank when it's low.

3   If the fuel level value on the scan tool conflicts with the gauge on the dash, the sensor is probably bad. To confirm this, the sensor should be checked with a multimeter.

Multimeter check:

1   Relieve the fuel system pressure, then remove the fuel pump/fuel level sending unit from the fuel tank (refer to the *Haynes Automotive Repair Manual* for your vehicle. **Warning:** *Gasoline is extremely flammable, so take extra precautions when you work on any part of the fuel system. Don't smoke or allow open flames or bare light bulbs near the work area, and don't work in a garage where a gas-type appliance (such as a water heater or a clothes dryer) is present. Since gasoline is carcinogenic, wear fuel-resistant gloves when there's a possibility of being exposed to fuel, and, if you spill any fuel on your skin, rinse it off immediately with soap and water. Mop up any spills immediately and do not store fuel-soaked rags where they could ignite. The fuel system is under constant pressure, so, if any fuel lines are to be disconnected, the fuel pressure in the system must be relieved first. When you perform any kind of work on the fuel system, wear safety glasses and have a Class B type fire extinguisher on hand.*

2   Connect the probes of an ohmmeter to the fuel level sensor terminals. Usually this can be determined by following the sensor leads to the electrical connector. If not, you'll have to consult a wiring diagram for your vehicle.

3   Position the float in the down (empty) position and note the reading on the meter.

4   Move the float up to the full position while watching the meter.

5   If the resistance does not change smoothly as the float travels from empty to full, replace the sensor.

6   If the sensor seems to be working properly but the code sets again after erasing it, the problem may be intermittent. It could be a bad sensor, a problem in the wiring to the sensor or a faulty PCM. At this point it is recommended that the vehicle be diagnosed by a dealer service department or other qualified repair shop, as the PCM is very expensive and is not returnable (and would most likely have to be programmed with a proprietary scan tool anyway).

3g Purge flow sensor or circuit

Refer to the information given in the *EVAP system* section.

3h Exhaust pressure sensor/ control valve or circuit

Refer to the information given in the *EGR system* section.

3i Cooling fan control circuit

Symptoms accompanying cooling fan control circuit-related DTCs include overheating and/or a non-operational air conditioning system.

Preliminary check:

As with any electrical component check, it's a good idea to first check all fuses related to the circuit. If a blown fuse is found, replace it and see if it blows again. If it does, trace the circuit to find the source of the short.

Scan tool check:

1   Connect your scan tool to the DLC and warm up the engine to normal operating temperature. Keep an eye on the coolant temperature (ECT) parameter to make sure the fan comes on when it's supposed to. Most fans will come on at some temperature between 200 and 228-degrees F.

2   Turn the air conditioning on and make sure the condenser cooling fan (or auxiliary fan) comes on.

3   If the main fan doesn't come on when it's supposed to, or the auxiliary fan doesn't come on when the air conditioning is turned on, disconnect the electrical connector from the inoperative fan and, using jumper wires, connect power and ground to the terminals of the fan connector. The fan should operate - if it doesn't, replace the fan motor.

4   If the fan does work, the problem might be intermittent. Clear the DTC and see if it resets.

Other possibilities:

Other possible causes of an inoperative fan include an open or shorted circuit between the PCM and the fan, a faulty fan relay, a faulty cooling fan control module (if equipped), or a faulty PCM. If no problems are found after checking the wiring and relay, the vehicle should be checked by a dealer service department or other qualified repair shop.

4 Vehicle speed, idle speed control or auxiliary input faults (3rd character of DTC = 5)

4a Vehicle Speed Sensor (VSS)

A VSS-related DTC can result in an inoperative (or inaccurate) speedometer, erratic or incorrect transmission shift points and torque converter clutch operation, and other driveability problems.

Scan tool check:

Connect your scan tool to the DLC and drive the vehicle or raise the drive wheels off the ground and support the vehicle securely on jackstands; the VSS parameter should match the speed shown on the speedometer **(see illustration 9.39)**. **Warning:** *If the drive wheels are raised off the ground, don't exceed approximately 10 miles per hour.* If no speed is indicated, or the speed on the scan tool doesn't match the speed on the speedometer, check the VSS.

Multimeter check:

Hall-effect type switch

1   The VSS may be located on the transmission, on the speedometer drive behind the instrument panel, or on the rear axle.
2   Connect the voltmeter negative or dwell meter probe to an engine ground.
3   Identify the supply, signal and ground terminals.

9.39 Checking the vehicle speed reading on the scan tool against the speedometer

4   Connect a voltmeter positive or dwell meter probe to the wire attached to the VSS signal terminal.
5   The drive wheels must rotate for a signal to be generated. This may be accomplished by using one of the two following methods:
a) Push the vehicle forward.
b) Raise the vehicle and support it securely on jackstands so the drive wheels can freely turn.
6   Rotate the wheels by hand so that a duty cycle or voltage can be obtained.
7   If there is no signal or an erratic duty cycle or voltage:
a) Check the voltage at the signal terminal with the VSS electrical connector disconnected, and the ignition on. A voltage between 8.5 and 10.0 volts should be obtained.
b) Check the voltage supply at the VSS supply terminal. A voltage slightly less than battery voltage should be obtained.
c) Check the VSS ground connection.
8   If the supply and ground voltages are satisfactory, the VSS is suspect, or the VSS is not being rotated by the speedometer drive (i.e. broken cable or transmission fault).
9   If there is no signal voltage, check the diode in the wire between the PCM and VSS (if present). Also check the continuity of the signal wiring.
10 Check all voltage supplies and ground connections to the PCM. If the voltage supplies and ground connections are satisfactory, the PCM is suspect. At this point it is recommended that the vehicle be diagnosed by a dealer service department or other qualified repair shop, as the PCM is very expensive and is not returnable (and would most likely have to be programmed with a proprietary scan tool anyway).

Reed switch type

11 The signal output with the drive wheels rotating is essentially that of a square waveform. Switching is from zero to five volts, or from zero to battery voltage. A duty cycle of 40 to 60-percent may also be obtained.

Inductive type

12 The signal output with the drive wheels rotating is essentially that of an AC waveform. The signal output will vary according to speed of rotation, in a similar fashion to the Crankshaft Position (CKP) sensor described earlier in this Chapter.

4b Idle control system

Common symptoms of an idle control system-related DTC would be an out-of-range idle speed (too low or high), surging at idle, or a stalling condition.

Preliminary checks:

1   On some vehicles, an idle relearn procedure must be performed if the battery has been replaced or disconnected. Refer to your *Haynes Automotive Repair Manual* or other service information to see if this is the case with your vehicle.
2   Check to make sure that no air leaks or vacuum leaks exist (see Chapter 4 for general engine troubleshooting procedures.
3   Make sure the throttle cable isn't too tight, preventing the throttle plate from closing all the way.
4   Remove the air intake duct and make sure the throttle plate isn't excessively dirty, which could prevent it from closing completely.

Scan tool check:

1   Connect your scan tool to the DLC, start the engine and allow it to idle. Take note of the idle rpm and the IAC parameter value (it may be expressed as a percentage, or in "counts," from 0 to 255 (completely extended to completely retracted).
2   Turn on as many electrical loads as you can think of (such as the headlights, rear window defroster, air conditioning and blower fan), and turn the steering wheel to its stop in one direction. If the idle speed control system is working properly, the engine shouldn't bog down; the idle speed should stay the same.
3   If the engine speed drops, but the IAC parameter changes, the fault is probably a bad IAC valve, or a plugged passage in the valve or throttle body. Remove the IAC valve and inspect. A wiring problem or corroded electrical connector could also be the cause.
4   If the engine speed drops and the IAC parameter doesn't change, one of the load-sensing devices could be defective. These could include the air conditioning pressure switch, the power steering pressure (PSP) switch, or the electrical load input to the PCM. The PCM could also be faulty, in which case the vehicle should be diagnosed by a dealer service department or other qualified repair shop, as the PCM is very expensive and is not returnable (and would most likely have to be programmed with a proprietary scan tool anyway).
5   If the engine speed stays the same, the problem could be intermittent. Erase the DTC and drive the vehicle to see if the code resets.

Multimeter checks:

Two-wire IAC valves

1   A voltmeter and/or dwell meter are suitable instruments for testing the two-wire IAC valves in most systems. **Note:** *A dwell meter will not give good results when connected*

to Ford systems - a voltmeter or oscilloscope is a better choice.
2   Connect the negative probe to an engine ground.
3   Connect the voltmeter positive or dwell meter probe to the wire attached to the IAC signal terminal.
4   Start the engine and allow it to idle.
5   With the engine hot, a varying voltage between 7.0 to 9.0 volts, a duty cycle of 40 to 44%, and a frequency of 110 are likely to be obtained.
6   When the engine is cold or placed under load, the voltage will decrease and the duty cycle will increase. Frequency is likely to remain stable for most idle control valves (the frequency will usually alter in Ford valves). **Note:** *The reading on a digital voltmeter will indicate the average voltage.*
7   Load the engine by switching on the headlights, rear window defroster, air conditioning and blower fan. The average voltage will decrease and the duty cycle will increase. The frequency of pulse should remain constant.
8   If an air leak or another fault is present resulting in more air bypassing the throttle, the IAC duty cycle will be lower than normal as the PCM pulses the valve less open.
9   When more load is placed upon the engine, the PCM pulses the valve more open (larger duty cycle) to increase the idle speed.
10   In addition, if the engine is mechanically unsound or the throttle valve is dirty, the PCM may pulse the valve more open to increase the idle speed. This may result in an uneven idle and a larger than normal duty cycle.
11   If the IAC valve signal is not available:

a) Check the IAC valve resistance. Typically, a resistance of 8 to 16 ohms should be obtained.
b) With the ignition on, check for battery voltage at the supply terminal. If there is no voltage, trace the wiring back to the main relay or ignition switch as appropriate.
c) Disconnect the electrical connector from the IAC valve. With the ignition on, use a jumper lead to very briefly touch the actuator pin in the valves electrical connector to ground. If the valve does not actuate, check for continuity of wiring between the electrical connector and the PCM. If the valve actuates, check the PCM main voltage supplies and grounds. If testing reveals no fault, the PCM is suspect. At this point it is recommended that the vehicle be diagnosed by a dealer service department or other qualified repair shop, as the PCM is very expensive and is not returnable (and would most likely have to be programmed with a proprietary scan tool anyway).

Bosch three-wire IAC valves

1   A voltmeter and a dwell meter are suitable instruments for testing the Bosch three-wire IAC valve.
2   Connect the voltmeter negative or dwell meter probe to an engine ground.
3   Connect the voltmeter positive or dwell meter probe to the wire attached to one of the two IAC signal terminals.
4   Start the engine and allow it to idle.
5   When the engine is hot, a varying voltage or a duty

cycle of either approximately 31% or 69% will be obtained. The duty cycle obtained will depend upon which terminal the instrument is connected.

6 When the engine is cold or placed under load, the voltage will decrease and the duty cycle will increase. **Note:** *The reading on a digital voltmeter will indicate the average voltage.*

7 Load the engine by switching on the headlights, rear window defroster, air conditioning and blower fan. The average voltage will decrease and the duty cycle will increase.

8 If an air leak or another fault is present resulting in more air bypassing the throttle, the valve's duty cycle will be lower than normal as the PCM pulses the valve less open.

9 When more load is placed upon the engine, the PCM pulses the valve more open (larger duty cycle) to increase the idle speed.

10 In addition, if the engine is mechanically unsound or the throttle valve is dirty, the PCM may pulse the valve more open to increase the idle speed. This may result in an uneven idle and a larger than normal duty cycle.

11 Switch the voltmeter positive or dwell meter probe to the wire attached to the other one of the two signal terminals.

12 With the engine hot, a varying voltage or a duty cycle of either approximately 31% or 69% will be obtained. The duty cycle obtained will depend upon which terminal the instrument is connected.

13 If the IAC valve signal is not available:

a) Check the IAC valve resistance (see below).

b) With the ignition on, check for battery voltage at the supply terminal.

c) If there is no voltage, trace the wiring back to the main relay or ignition switch as appropriate.

d) Disconnect the IAC valve electrical connector. Switch on the ignition and use a jumper lead to very briefly touch one of the two actuator pins in the ISCV multi-plug to ground. If the valve actuates, check the PCM main voltage supplies and grounds. If the ISCV does not actuate, check for continuity of wiring between the valve's electrical connector and the PCM. If testing reveals no fault, the PCM is suspect. At this point it is recommended that the vehicle be diagnosed by a dealer service department or other qualified repair shop, as the PCM is very expensive and is not returnable (and would most likely have to be programmed with a proprietary scan tool anyway).

e) Switch the jumper lead to very briefly touch the other ISCV actuator pin in the ISCV multi-plug to ground. Evaluate the results as in paragraphs as described in paragraph d) above.

14 Check the resistance of the IAC valve **(see illustration 9.40)**:

a) Disconnect the IAC valve electrical connector.

b) Connect an ohmmeter between the center terminal and one of the outer terminals. A resistance value should be obtained; this value will vary between manufacturers, but the thing to remember is that it shouldn't be an open or short-circuit condition.

9.40 Checking the resistance of a three-terminal IAC valve. The resistance between the center terminal and each of the outer terminals should be fairly close to each other

c) Reconnect the ohmmeter between the center terminal and the other outer terminal. A resistance similar to the one in the last check should be obtained.

Stepper motors

1 The typical stepper motor employs two motor windings. The PCM positions the stepper motor by energizing the windings in one direction and then the reverse. A voltmeter could be used to test for a stepper motor signal. However, although a signal can usually be obtained on all of the motor terminals, the signal is fleeting and will only be generated as the motor winding is actuated.

2 Check the resistance of both sets of windings and compare them to each other. Values are usually under 100 ohms.

VW/Audi idle control motors

The type of control motor fitted to many current VW/Audi vehicles incorporates a reversible stepper motor winding, a Hall sensor that signals the stepper motor position, a TPS, and an idle switch. An 8-terminal electrical connector connects the motor to the wiring harness. The component parts that make up the control motor can be tested by referring to the test procedures described under the headings for individual components.

4c Closed throttle position switch or circuit

See the *Throttle Position (TP) sensor/Accelerator Pedal Position (APP) sensor or circuit problems* (Section 1g) earlier in this Chapter.

4d Starter/immobilizer circuit

DTCs related to starter/immobilizer systems usually indicate a problem with the ignition key/programming, the remote entry module or the PCM. Due to the wide variety of sys-

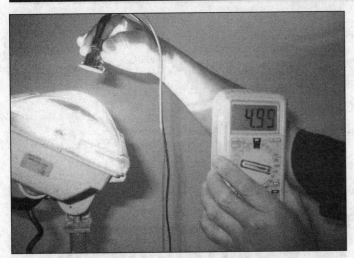

9.41 Checking the resistance of a battery temperature sensor. As it heats up, the resistance should decrease

tems from various manufacturers using this technology, any problems causing one of these DTCs to set should be performed by a dealer service department or other qualified repair shop.

4e Battery temperature sensor or circuit

Multimeter check:

Most battery temperature sensors are negative temperature coefficient (NTC) type thermistors. While sensor values may vary between manufacturers, the resistance can be checked with an ohmmeter. When cold, the resistance reading should be high. When warmed (you can hold it in front of a light bulb), the resistance should drop **(see illustration 9.41)**. If the resistance doesn't change, a faulty sensor is indicated.

Other checks:

If the sensor checks out OK, check the electrical connector for corrosion, and the wiring between the sensor and the PCM for an open or short-circuit condition. The PCM could also be the cause. If the sensor, connectors and wiring appear to be OK, it is recommended that the vehicle be diagnosed by a dealer service department or other qualified repair shop, as the PCM is very expensive and is not returnable (and would most likely have to be programmed with a proprietary scan tool anyway).

4f Power steering pressure (PSP) switch or circuit

1   The PSP operates when the steering is turned. The information from the switch is used to increase the engine idle speed, to compensate for the extra load placed on the engine by the power steering pump.

Multimeter check:

2   Supply to the PSP is usually made from a switched battery supply or from the PCM.
3   Battery voltage will be available at both the supply and ground side of the switch when the wheels are in the straight-ahead position.
4   Zero voltage will be obtained at the ground side of the switch when the wheels are turned. Note: In some systems, zero voltage will be obtained with the wheels straight-ahead, and battery voltage when the wheels are turned. **Note:** *In some systems, zero voltage will be obtained with the wheels straight-ahead, and battery voltage when the wheels are turned.*

Other checks:

5   If the switch doesn't operate as described, check the electrical connection for corrosion and the wiring harness for an open or short-circuit condition. The PCM could also be the cause. If the switch, connectors and wiring appear to be OK, it is recommended that the vehicle be diagnosed by a dealer service department or other qualified repair shop, as the PCM is very expensive and is not returnable (and would most likely have to be programmed with a proprietary scan tool anyway).

4g System voltage-related DTCs

System voltage problems, whether high, low or unstable, generally point to the battery or alternator as the source of the fault. Refer to Chapter 4 for battery and charging system checking procedures. Other things to check would be the wiring between the alternator and the battery, and between the fuse block and the PCM. The PCM could also be the cause of the problem but an affirmative diagnosis should be made by a dealer service department or other qualified repair shop before replacing the PCM, as the PCM is very expensive and is not returnable (and would most likely have to be programmed with a proprietary scan tool anyway).

5 Computer or auxiliary output faults (3rd character of DTC = 6)/Transmission control system faults (3rd character of DTC = 7, 8 and 9)

5a Powertrain Control Module (PCM)-related DTCs

Trouble codes caused by PCM faults should be diagnosed by a dealer service department or other qualified repair shop, as the PCM is very expensive and is not returnable (and would most likely have to be programmed with a proprietary scan tool anyway).

However, before taking the vehicle in for diagnosis, check all fuses, replacing any that are blown, and try to find the short-circuit condition. Then, clear the DTC and see if the problem happens again.

5b Transmission Control Module (TCM)-related DTCs

Just like PCM-related DTCs, TCM-related trouble codes should also be diagnosed by a dealer service department or other qualified repair shop. (The advice pertaining to fuses and clearing the DTC applies here, too.)

5c Starter relay circuit-related DTCs

These DTCs are generally set when the PCM detects a starter signal when the vehicle is in operation. The trouble areas could be the relay itself, but more commonly the Park/Neutral Position (PNP) switch or the ignition switch. The PCM could also be the problem, but if this is suspected, the vehicle should be diagnosed by a dealer service department or other qualified repair shop.

5d Fuel pump control circuit-related DTCs

Refer to *Fuel pump or circuit problems* under *Fuel, intake air or emissions control system faults* earlier in this Chapter.

5e Throttle actuator control circuit-related DTCs

These codes apply only to vehicles without an accelerator cable. If a throttle actuator control DTC is set, the PCM will usually default to a "limp-home" mode, enabling the vehicle to be driven at a very slow speed (basically just to get it off the road). If no other TP sensor or throttle actuator codes are set along with a P0638 or P0639, the problem is most likely a mechanical one within the throttle body assembly, such as a binding throttle plate or weakened return springs. However, there's always the possibility of a problem with the wiring harness or the PCM, so a definitive diagnosis should be made by a dealer service department or other qualified repair shop.

5f Intake manifold tuning valve-related DTCs

These DTCs apply to systems that use an intake manifold tuning valve (IMTV), as well as intake manifold runner control (IMRC) systems. Some of these systems are vacuum-actuated, others are electrically actuated.

Things to check:

On vacuum-actuated systems, check all vacuum hoses and servo motors for leaks. On systems that use a cable to actuate the valve, check the cable for freedom of movement. Check the valve for freedom of movement, too. On all systems, check all electrical connectors, making sure they are tight and that the terminals aren't corroded. Check the fuses, too. If no obvious problems are found, clear the DTC and drive the vehicle. If it sets again, have the vehicle diagnosed by a dealer service department or other qualified repair shop.

5g Input shaft/turbine speed sensor or circuit/Output shaft speed sensor or circuit

Most input and output shaft speed sensors are inductive-type permanent magnet generators that produce an AC voltage, which the PCM or TCM converts to a digital signal. They can be checked in a similar fashion to that of an inductive-type crankshaft position sensor, explained earlier in this Chapter. The input shaft (or turbine) speed sensor can be checked with the vehicle parked and the engine running, while the output shaft speed sensor must be checked with the drive wheels turning (the drive wheels can be raised and the vehicle supported securely on jackstands). **Warning:** *If the drive wheels are raised off the ground, don't exceed approximately 10 miles per hour.*

Other problems that could result in a DTC related to one of these sensors include corroded or loose electrical con-

nectors, faulty wiring, or a faulty PCM or TCM. If no obvious problems are found, have the vehicle diagnosed by a dealer service department or other qualified repair shop.

5h Shift solenoid/circuit

Problems with a shift solenoid or circuit can range from a faulty solenoid (leaking, stuck on or stuck off), the shift valve in the valve body that the solenoid controls (stuck on or off), the wiring between the solenoid and the PCM or TCM, or the wiring between the underhood fuse block and the transmission. A faulty PCM or TCM could also be the cause. If no obvious problems can be found (chafed wires, loose connections), have the vehicle diagnosed by a dealer service department or transmission specialist.

5i Other transmission control system-related DTCs

Aside from checking fuses, wiring harness and electrical connectors, and erasing the DTC to see if it sets again, other transmission-related DTCs should be diagnosed by a dealer service department or other qualified automotive repair shop. Most of the diagnostic procedures that must be followed to troubleshoot these problems are vehicle-specific and will require the use of a factory service manual, special tools and, in many cases, transmission removal and/or partial or complete disassembly.

Notes

10 Component replacement procedures

Contents

This chapter provides replacement procedures for the components that are monitored and controlled by the OBD-II system. Since there are many different design fuel systems and engine management components used on today's vehicles, these procedures are generic in nature and represent typical procedures that will apply to most vehicles. If necessary, more specific procedures can be found in the *Haynes Automotive Repair Manual* for your vehicle. For a description of how a component works, or what it's function is, you can refer to Chapter 5.

1 Catalytic converter

Warning: *Make sure that the exhaust system is completely cooled down before proceeding. If the vehicle has just been driven, the catalytic converter can be hot enough to cause serious burns.*

Note 1: *Because of a Federally-mandated extended warranty which covers emission-related components such as the catalytic converter, check with a dealer service department before replacing the converter at your own expense.*

Note 2: *The photos accompanying this procedure are of a vehicle with a single catalyst, two short pipes welded to either end of the catalyst, a two-hole mounting flange at the front end of the forward pipe and a straight pipe behind the catalyst that uses a clamp to secure it to the pipe going to*

the muffler. If your vehicle doesn't use a slip joint behind the catalyst, but is welded to the rear exhaust pipe instead, you will have to either cut it off yourself or have it cut off at an automotive repair shop.

1 Raise the vehicle and support it securely on jackstands.

2 Spray a liberal amount of penetrant onto the threads of the exhaust pipe-to-exhaust manifold bolts and the clamp bolt behind the catalytic converter **(see illustrations 10.1 and 10.2)** and wait awhile for the penetrant to loosen things up.

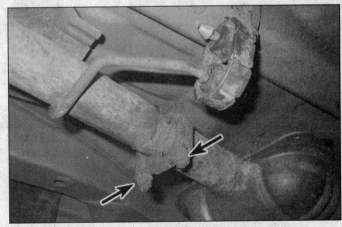

10.1 Back off the nuts to loosen this type of clamp. If it's hard to loosen, spray some penetrant onto the threads

10.2 On this model, the catalyst's exhaust pipe is connected to the exhaust manifold by two bolts and nuts

10.3 This PCM connector is attached by this bolt

3   While you're waiting for the penetrant to do its work, disconnect the electrical connectors for the upstream and downstream oxygen sensor and remove both oxygen sensors.

4   Unscrew the upper exhaust pipe-to-exhaust manifold flange bolts. If they're still difficult to loosen, spray the threads with some more penetrant, wait awhile and try again.

5   To loosen a clamp that secures the slip joint between the exhaust pipe behind the catalytic converter and the pipe ahead of the muffler, back off the nut. If it's still difficult to loosen, spray the threads with some more penetrant, wait awhile and try again.

6   Remove the catalytic converter assembly. Remove and discard the old flange gasket.

7   Installation is the reverse of removal. Be sure to use a new flange gasket at the exhaust manifold mounting flange. Use new bolts at the front flange. Although the slip joint clamp doesn't get as overheated as the exhaust manifold flange bolts, it's still a good idea to use a new clamp. Coat the threads of the fasteners with anti-seize compound to facilitate future removal. Tighten the fasteners securely.

2   Powertrain Control Module (PCM)

Caution: *Avoid static electricity damage to the Powertrain Control Module (PCM) by grounding yourself to the body of the vehicle before touching the PCM and using a special anti-static pad on which to store the PCM once it's removed.*

Note 1: *Anytime the PCM is replaced with a new unit, it must be reprogrammed with a scan tool by a dealership service department or other qualified repair shop.*

Note 2: *Anytime the battery is disconnected, stored operating parameters may be lost from the PCM, causing the engine to run rough for a period of time while the PCM relearns the information.*

1   The PCM may be located in different locations depending on the manufacturer. The most common locations are behind the right or left side kick panels under the dash, or under the driver's or passenger's seat. On some vehicles it is located in the engine compartment, near the firewall.

2   Disconnect the cable from the negative terminal of the battery.

10.4 After removing the bolt, pull the connector straight out

10.5 Other connectors can be disconnected by depressing plastic tabs on the connectors, then unplugging them

10.6 Most PCMs are attached by a few fasteners . . .

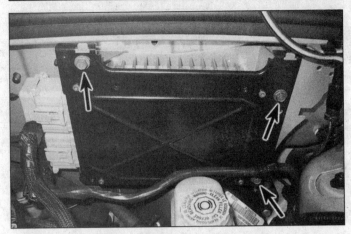

10.7 . . . or a mounting bracket

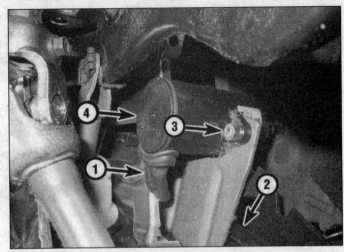

10.8 Typically the Accelerator Pedal Position (APP) sensors is located on a mounting bracket near the top of the accelerator pedal arm. To remove it:

3   Carefully disconnect the PCM electrical connector(s) **(see illustrations 10.3, 10.4 and 10.5).**
4   Unscrew the PCM mounting bolts and remove the PCM **(see illustrations 10.6 and 10.7).**
5   Installation is the reverse of removal.

1   Trace the electrical lead up to the connector and dis-
connect it (connector not visible in this photo)
2   Follow the upper end of the accelerator pedal arm all
the way to the top, where it's connected to the APP
sensor linkage arm by a link rod. Remove the retainer
and disconnect the link rod's Heim joint from the APP
sensor linkage arm by prying it loose with a screw-
driver
3   Remove the two APP sensor mounting bolts (other
bolt, on front side of sensor, not visible in this photo)
4   Remove the APP sensor from its mounting bracket

3   Accelerator Pedal Position (APP) sensor

1   Disconnect the cable from the negative terminal of the battery.
2   Using a flashlight, locate the APP sensor on its mounting bracket at the top of the accelerator pedal arm. Unplug the electrical connector, detach the linkage, unscrew the fasteners and detach the sensor **(see illustration 10.8).**
3   Installation is the reverse of removal.

it's found at the top of the brake pedal arm **(see illustration 10.9).**
2   Disconnect the electrical connector from the switch **(see illustration 10.10).**
3   Loosen the locknut, then unscrew and remove the switch, or simply rotate the switch in its bracket to unlock it (depending on type) **(see illustrations 10.11, 10.12 and 10.13).**
4   Installation is the reverse of removal.

4   Brake Pedal Position (BPP) switch

1   Use a flashlight and locate the BPP switch; usually

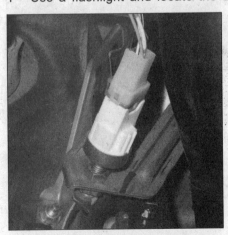

10.9 Typically, the BPP switch is attached to a bracket near the top of the brake pedal

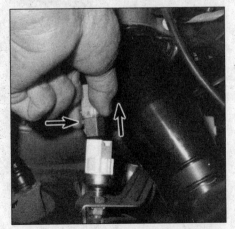

10.10 Disconnect the BPP switch electrical connector

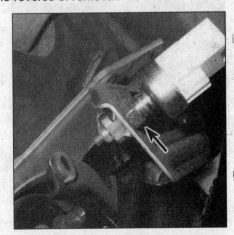

10.11 This BPP switch has a locknut that secures the switch . . .

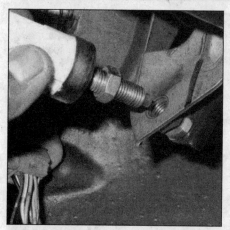

10.12 . . . after removing the locknut, the switch can be unscrewed and removed from the mounting bracket

10.13 Others have locking tabs that secure the switch. Typically these types of switches require the switch to be rotated to unlock the switch from the mounting bracket

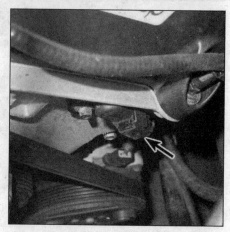

10.14 Typically the CMP sensor can be found at the front . . .

10.15 . . . or the side of the cylinder head

5 Camshaft Position (CMP) sensor

1   Disconnect the cable from the negative terminal of the battery.

2   Disconnect the electrical connector from the CMP sensor (see illustrations 10.14 and 10.15).

3   Remove the sensor mounting bolt and remove the CMP sensor (see illustrations 10.16 and 10.17).

4   Inspect the CMP sensor O-ring for cracks, tears and other deterioration. If it's damaged, replace it (see illustration 10.18).

5   When installing the CMP sensor, apply a small dab of clean engine oil to the sensor O-ring, then use a slight rocking motion to work the O-ring into the sensor mounting bore. Do NOT use a twisting motion or you will damage the O-ring.

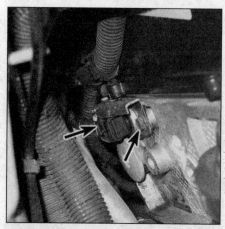

10.16 Remove the connector and the sensor mounting bolt . . .

10.17 . . . and remove it from the cylinder head

10.18 Inspect the CMP sensor O-ring; if it's cracked, torn or deteriorated, replace it; be sure to coat the new O-ring with clean engine oil before installing it on the CMP sensor

10.19 The CKP sensor typically can be found on the timing chain cover at the front of the engine, near the crankshaft pulley . . .

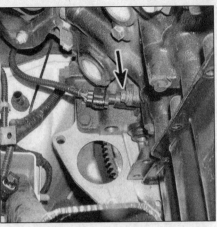

10.20 . . . or on the side of the engine block

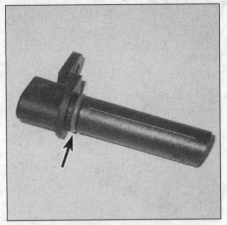

10.21 Inspect the CKP sensor O-ring; if it's cracked, torn or deteriorated, replace it; be sure to coat the new O-ring with clean engine oil before installing it on the CKP sensor

6   Make sure that the CMP sensor mounting flange is fully seated flat against the mounting surface around the sensor mounting hole.
7   Installation is otherwise the reverse of removal. Be sure to tighten the CMP sensor mounting bolt securely.

6   Crankshaft Position (CKP) sensor

1   Disconnect the cable from the negative terminal of the battery.
2   Locate the CKP sensor and disconnect the electrical connector **(see illustrations 10.19 and 10.20)**.
3   Remove the CKP sensor mounting bolt and remove the CKP sensor.
4   Inspect the CKP sensor O-ring for cracks, tears and other deterioration. If it's damaged, replace it **(see illustration 10.21)**.

5   Make sure that the CKP sensor mounting flange is fully seated flat against the mounting surface around the sensor mounting hole.
6   Installation is otherwise the reverse of removal. Be sure to tighten the CKP sensor mounting bolt.

7   Engine Coolant Temperature (ECT) sensor

Warning: *Wait until the engine is completely cool before beginning this procedure.*
1   Partially drain the cooling system.
2   Disconnect the cable from the negative battery terminal.
2   Locate the ECT sensor and disconnect the electrical connector **(see illustrations 10.22 and 10.23)**.
4   Using a deep socket, carefully unscrew the ECT sensor from the intake manifold.

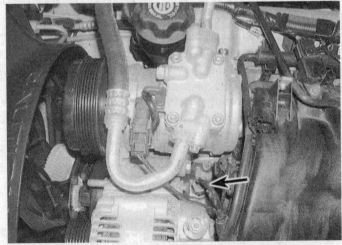

10.22 Most ECT sensors are located on the intake manifold . . .

10.23 . . . or the thermostat housing

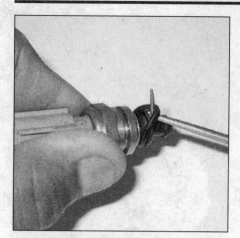

10.24 Inspect the ECT sensor O-ring; if it's cracked, torn or deteriorated, replace it . . .

10.25 . . . if the sensor is not equipped with an O-ring, wrap the threads of the ECT sensor with Teflon sealing tape

10.26 The fuel tank pressure sensor is typically located somewhere on top of the fuel tank . . .

5   On ECT sensors equipped with an O-ring, inspect the sensor O-ring for cracks, tears and other deterioration. If it's damaged, replace it. If the sensor is not equipped with an O-ring, wrap the threads of the ECT sensor with Teflon sealing tape before installing the sensor **(see illustrations 10.24 and 10.25)**.

6   Installation is otherwise the reverse of removal.

7   Refill the cooling system.

8   Fuel Tank Pressure (FTP) sensor

Warning: *Gasoline is extremely flammable, so take extra precautions when you work on any part of the fuel system. Don't smoke or allow open flames or bare light bulbs near the work area, and don't work in a garage where a natural gas-type appliance (such as a water heater or a clothes dryer) with a pilot light is present. Since gasoline is carcinogenic, wear latex gloves when there's a possibility of being exposed to fuel, and, if you spill any fuel on your skin, rinse it off immediately with soap and water. Mop up any spills immediately and do not store fuel-soaked rags where they could ignite. The fuel system is under constant pressure, so, if any fuel lines are to be disconnected, the fuel pressure in the system must be relieved first. When you perform any kind of work on the fuel system, wear safety glasses and have a Class B type fire extinguisher on hand.*

1   Relieve the fuel system pressure.

2   Access the FTP sensor, then disconnect the electrical connector for the FTP sensor **(see illustrations 10.26 and 10.27)**.

3   Remove the FTP sensor.

4   Be sure to install a new gasket or O-ring.

5   Installation is the reverse of removal.

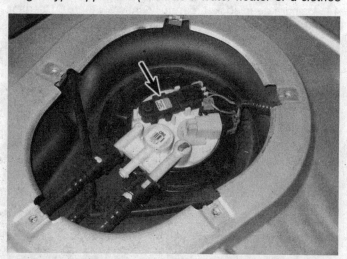

10.27 . . . or on the fuel pump/fuel gauge sending unit mounting flange

9   Input Shaft Speed (ISS) sensor/Output Shaft Speed (OSS) sensors

1   Disconnect the cable from the negative terminal of the battery.

2   Disconnect the electrical connector from the ISS or OSS sensor **(see illustration 10.28)**.

3   Place a drain pan under the sensor you're going to remove. Remove the sensor mounting bolt and pull out the sensor.

4   Be sure to install a new gasket or O-ring.

5   Installation is the reverse of removal. When you're done, be sure to check the transmission fluid level and add fluid as necessary.

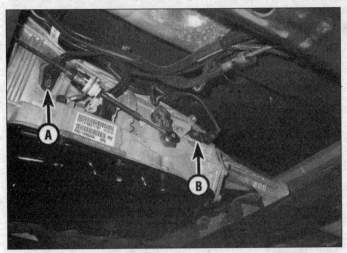

10.28 Typical ISS sensor (A) and OSS sensor (B)

10.29 On some vehicles, the IAT sensor is located on the air filter housing . . .

10 Intake Air Temperature (IAT) sensor

1   Locate the IAT sensor, then disconnect the electrical connector from the sensor (see illustrations 10.29, 10.30, 10.31 and 10.32).
2   Remove the IAT sensor.
3   Installation is the reverse of removal.
4   If equipped, be sure to install a new gasket or O-ring (see illustration 10.33).

10.30 . . . or it's located on the air intake duct . . .

10.31 . . . On others, it's located on the intake manifold plenum . . .

10.32 . . . or it's an integral component of the Mass Air Flow (MAF) sensor (to replace this type of IAT sensor, you'll have to replace the MAF sensor)

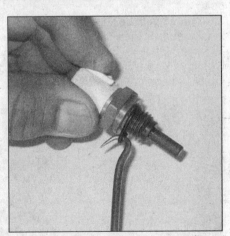

10.33 If equipped, be sure to remove and discard the old IAT sensor O-ring or gasket - use a new O-ring or gasket when installing the IAT sensor (regardless of whether you're installing the old IAT sensor or a new unit)

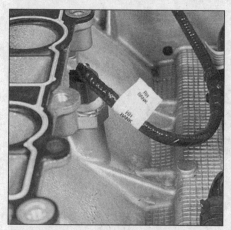

10.34 Knock sensors can be difficult to locate because they're often buried under intake or exhaust manifolds and miscellaneous engine plumbing and wiring

10.35 On some engines the knock sensors are threaded into the side of the engine block (with the type of sensor shown, trace the electrical lead from the knock sensor up to the sensor electrical connector and disconnect it)

10.36 If equipped, be sure to remove and discard the old knock sensor O-ring - use a new O-ring when installing the knock sensor (regardless of whether you're installing the old knock sensor or a new unit)

11 Knock sensor

Warning: *The knock sensor(s) on some vehicles may be threaded into a water jacket. If you're not completely sure if the sensor on your engine is or isn't, wait until the engine is completely cool and drain the cooling system before removing the sensor.*

1   Access the knock sensor, then disconnect the electrical connector from the sensor **(see illustrations 10.34 and 10.35).**

2   Remove the knock sensor. Most knock sensors are threaded into the engine block or fastened with a mounting bolt.

3   If equipped, be sure to install a new O-ring before installing the sensor **(see illustration 10.36).**

4   Installation is the reverse of removal. Tighten bolted-type knock sensors to 15 to 20 ft-lbs. Tighten threaded-type knock sensors to 20 to 25 ft-lbs.

12 Manifold Absolute Pressure (MAP) sensor

1   Access the MAP sensor, then disconnect the electrical connector for the MAP sensor **(see illustrations 10.37 and 10.38).** If equipped, detach the vacuum hose from the sensor.

2   Remove the MAP sensor from the throttle body or intake manifold plenum. Usually, the MAP sensor is mounted by fasteners, but sometimes it can be found threaded into an intake manifold plenum.

3   If equipped, be sure to install a new O-ring **(see illustration 10.39).**

4   Installation is the reverse of removal.

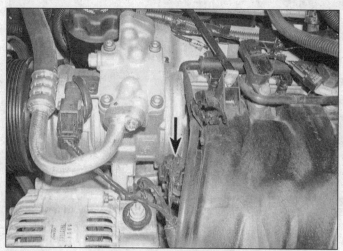

10.37 On some vehicles, the MAP sensor is located on the intake manifold plenum . . .

10.38 . . . while on others, it's located on the throttle body (shown here) or on a bracket on the firewall (and connected to the manifold by a vacuum hose)

10.39 If equipped, be sure to remove and discard the old MAP sensor O-ring - use a new O-ring when installing the MAP sensor (regardless of whether you're installing the old MAP sensor or a new unit)

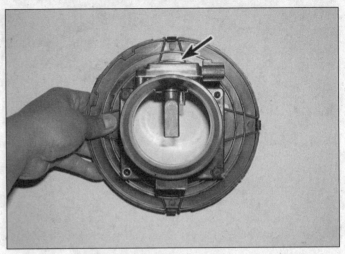

10.40 The MAF sensor is a black plastic or cast aluminum housing located in the intake tract somewhere between the air filter housing and the throttle body.

13 Mass Air Flow (MAF) sensor

1   Access the MAF sensor, then disconnect the electrical connector from the sensor (see illustration 10.40).
2   Generally, a MAF sensor can be removed by removing a couple of screws that secure it to air filter housing.
3   Installation is the reverse of removal.

14 Oxygen sensors

Note: *Because it is installed in the exhaust manifold or pipe, which contracts when cool, the oxygen sensor may be very difficult to loosen when the engine is cold. Rather than risk damage to the sensor (if you are planning to reuse it*

in another manifold or pipe), start and run the engine for a minute or two, then shut it off. Be careful not to burn yourself during the following procedure.

1   Access the oxygen sensor harness and then unplug the electrical connector. If necessary, raise the vehicle and support it securely on jackstands. **Note:** *The electrical connector is usually located at least six inches from the sensor.*
2   Unscrew the sensor from the exhaust manifold or exhaust pipe (see illustration 10.41 and 10.42). **Note:** *The best tool for removing an oxygen sensor is a special slotted socket, especially if you're planning to reuse a sensor. If you don't have this tool and you plan to reuse the sensor, be extremely careful when unscrewing the sensor.*
3   Apply anti-seize compound to the threads of the sensor to facilitate future removal. The threads of new sensors should already be coated with this compound, but if you're planning to reuse an old sensor, re-coat the threads. Install the sensor and tighten it securely.

10.41 Each pre-catalyst oxygen sensor (A) is installed in the exhaust manifold or in the exhaust pipe right below the exhaust manifold, and each post-catalyst oxygen sensor is installed somewhere after the upstream catalyst (B)

10.42 Use a slotted socket to remove the oxygen sensor

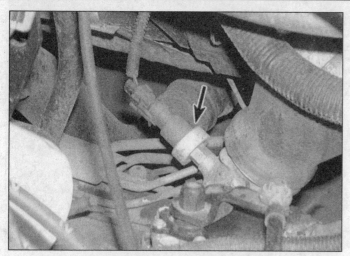

10.43 Typical steering gear-mounted Power Steering Pressure (PSP) switch . . .

10.44 . . . and a typical PSP switch mounted on the power steering pump

4   Reconnect the electrical connector of the pigtail lead to the main wiring harness.
5   Lower the vehicle (if it was raised), test drive the vehicle and verify that no trouble codes have been set.

15 Power Steering Pressure (PSP) switch

1   Access the PSP sensor, then disconnect the electrical connector for the PSP sensor (see illustrations 10.43 and 10.44).
2   Position a suitable drain pan below the switch to catch any fluid draining from the steering gear or power steering pump.
3   Using a wrench, unscrew the switch from the steering gear or power steering pump.

4   Before installing the PSP switch, wrap the threads with Teflon tape to prevent leaks.
5   Installation is the reverse of removal.
6   Add power steering fluid as required.

16 Throttle Position (TP) sensor

1   Access the TP sensor, then disconnect the electrical connector (see illustration 10.45).
2   Remove the TP sensor mounting fasteners and then remove the TP sensor.
3   Remove and discard the old TP sensor O-ring, if equipped (see illustration 10.46).
4   Installation is the reverse of removal. Note: Some TP sensors require adjustment (those with slotted mounting holes). See the Haynes Repair Manual for your vehicle.

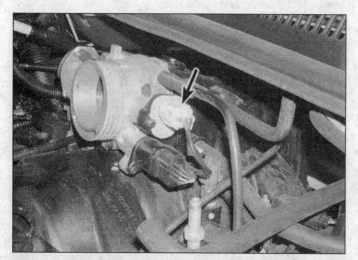

10.45 Typical Throttle Position (TP) sensor

10.46 If the TP sensor is equipped with an O-ring, remove and discard it. To prevent air leaks, use a new O-ring even if you're installing the old TP sensor

10.47 The TR sensor is located at the manual lever on automatic transaxles . . .

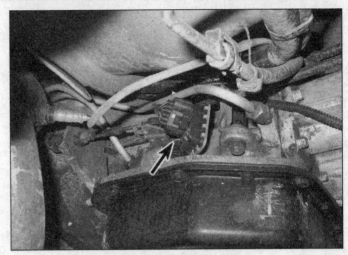

10.48 . . . and transmissions

17 Transmission Range (TR) sensor

Note : *Sometimes a special tool is required for this procedure - without it, chances are you won't be able to adjust the sensor properly, and a trouble code will then be set (along with driveability problems). If your sensor is adjustable (has slotted mounting bolt holes) refer to the Haynes Automotive Repair Manual for your vehicle.*

1   Set the parking brake, then place the shift lever in Neutral.
2   Locate the TR sensor, then disconnect the electrical connector(s) **(see illustrations 10.47 and 10.48).**
3   Unscrew the fasteners and remove the sensor.
4   Installation is the reverse of the removal procedure.

18 Air Injection system components

AIR vacuum check valve

1   Locate the AIR vacuum check valve in the vacuum line **(see illustration 10.49).**
2   To remove the AIR vacuum check valve, simply disconnect the vacuum lines from both ends of the valve.
3   Installation is the reverse of removal. When installing the AIR vacuum check valve, check to see if it's labeled "VAC" or "V." If it is, make sure that side is facing toward the vacuum source, i.e. toward the throttle body.

AIR pump solenoid

4   Locate the AIR pump solenoid **(see illustration 10.50).**
5   Disconnect the electrical connector from the AIR pump solenoid.
6   Disconnect the vacuum hoses from the AIR pump solenoid.
7   Remove the AIR pump solenoid retaining fastener.
8   Installation is the reverse of removal.

10.49 The typical location for the AIR vacuum check valve is in the vacuum line between the throttle body and the AIR pump solenoid; to remove the vacuum check valve, simply disconnect the vacuum lines from both ends of the valve

10.50 Typical AIR pump solenoid

10.51 Typical AIR shutoff valve

10.52 Typical AIR check valve

AIR shut-off valve

9   Locate the AIR shutoff valve (see illustration 10.51).
10   Disconnect the AIR pump solenoid vacuum line from the AIR shutoff valve.
11   Disconnect the AIR pump hose from the shutoff valve.
12   Disconnect the hose that connects the shutoff valve to the AIR check valve.
13   Installation is the reverse of removal.

AIR check valve

14   Locate the AIR check valve (see illustration 10.52).
15   Disconnect the hose from the check valve.
16   Using a back-up wrench on the AIR pipe hex nut (to prevent the pipe from twisting), unscrew the AIR check valve from the AIR pipe.
17   When installing the check valve, it's a good idea to apply anti-seize compound to the threads of the check valve and the AIR pipe to facilitate future removal.
18   Installation is otherwise the reverse of removal.

AIR pipe

19   Locate the AIR pipe between the AIR check valve and the exhaust manifold (see illustration 10.53).
20   Remove the AIR shutoff valve and the AIR check valve.
21   Remove the AIR pipe mounting bolts that attach the pipe to the exhaust manifold and remove the AIR pipe.
22   Remove and discard the old gasket from the AIR pipe mounting flange.
23   Installation is the reverse of removal. Be sure to use a new gasket.

AIR pump

Electric AIR injection pump

24   Locate the AIR pump (see illustration 10.54).
25   Remove the AIR pump mounting bolts.
26   Pull down the AIR pump and disconnect the electrical connector and the inlet and outlet hoses.
27   Installation is the reverse of removal.

10.53 The AIR pipe is located between the exhaust manifold and the AIR check valve

10.54 Typical electric AIR injection pump

10.55 Typical location of a belt-driven AIR injection pump

10.56 EVAP canister purge control solenoid valves are commonly found at the firewall . . .

10.57 . . . or on the fenderwells in the engine compartment

Belt-driven AIR injection pump

28 Locate the AIR pump (see illustration 10.55).
29 Disconnect the hoses or tubes from the AIR injection pump.
30 Relieve the tension on the drivebelt and remove the drivebelt.
31 Locate the mounting bolts for the AIR injection pump and remove the bolts, then remove the pump.
32 Installation is the reverse of removal.

19 EVAP canister purge control solenoid valve

1 Locate the EVAP canister purge control solenoid valve (see illustrations 10.56 and 10.57).
2 Disconnect the electrical connector from the purge control solenoid valve.
3 Clearly label and detach the vacuum lines.
4 Remove the mounting fastener, if equipped, then remove the purge control solenoid valve.
5 Installation is the reverse of removal.

20 EVAP canister vent shut valve

1 Locate the EVAP canister vent shut valve (see illustrations 10.58 and 10.59).
2 Disconnect the vent shut valve electrical connector.
3 Disconnect the vapor hose from the vent shut valve.
4 Remove fasteners securing the vent shut valve to the EVAP canister or mounting bracket, then remove the valve.
5 If equipped, replace the O-ring on the vent shut valve (see illustration 10.60).
6 Installation is the reverse of removal.

10.58 The EVAP canister vent shut valve is located underneath the vehicle, usually near . . .

10.59 . . . or on the EVAP canister

10.60 If the EVAP canister vent shut valve is equipped with an O-ring, remove and discard it; to prevent air leaks, use a new O-ring even if you're installing the old valve

10.61 The EGR valve is usually located on the intake manifold . . .

10.62 . . . but it can be mounted on a coolant casting . . .

21 Exhaust Gas Recirculation (EGR) valve

1 Locate the EGR valve (**see illustrations 10.61, 10.62 and 10.63**).
2 Disconnect the electrical connector and vacuum line, if equipped, from the EGR valve.
3 Disconnect the EGR pipes, if equipped, from the EGR valve.
4 Remove the EGR valve mounting fasteners.
5 Remove the EGR valve and the old gasket (**see illustration 10.64**).
6 Installation is the reverse of removal. Be sure to use a new EGR valve gasket, and tighten the EGR valve mounting fasteners securely.

10.63 . . . or directly on the cylinder head

22 Fuel injectors

Warning: *Gasoline is extremely flammable, so take extra precautions when you work on any part of the fuel system. Don't smoke or allow open flames or bare light bulbs near the work area, and don't work in a garage where a gas-type appliance (such as a water heater or a clothes dryer) is present. Since gasoline is carcinogenic, wear fuel-resistant gloves when there's a possibility of being exposed to fuel, and, if you spill any fuel on your skin, rinse it off immediately with soap and water. Mop up any spills immediately and do not store fuel-soaked rags where they could ignite. The fuel system is under constant pressure, so, if any fuel lines are to be disconnected, the fuel pressure in the system must be relieved first. When you perform any kind of work on the fuel system, wear safety glasses and have a Class B type fire extinguisher on hand.*

1 Relieve the fuel system pressure by removing the fuel pump fuse or unplugging the electrical connector from the fuel pump, then starting the engine and allowing it to die.

10.64 Be sure to remove and discard the old EGR valve gasket. If the gasket sticks to the mating surfaces (as it did here) be sure to remove all traces of old gasket material with a gasket scraper, and be extremely careful not to scratch or gouge the surfaces

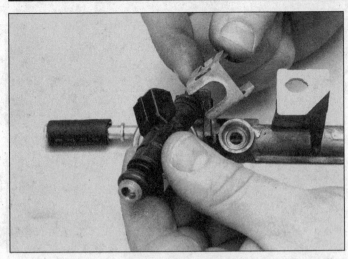

10.65 Generally, to disengage an injector from the fuel rail, remove the clamp and pull the injector straight out of the fuel rail (wiggle and pull at the same time if the O-ring is stuck to the injector bore) . . .

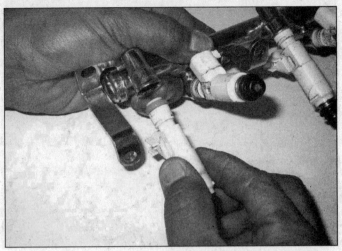

10.66 . . . or on other types, simply wiggle it side to side a little to loosen the O-ring and then pull it straight out as shown

Note: *Refer to the Haynes Automotive Repair Manual for your particular vehicle if you're not sure how to do this.* Also equalize tank pressure by removing the fuel filler cap.

2   Disconnect the cable from the negative battery terminal.

3   Disconnect the fuel supply line from the fuel rail.

4   Disconnect the electrical connectors from the fuel injectors.

5   Remove the fuel rail mounting bolts.

6   Remove the fuel rail and injectors as a single assembly. Be prepared for some fuel spillage.

7   Remove the fuel injectors from the fuel rail **(see illustrations 10.65 and 10.66).**

8   Remove the old O-rings from each injector **(see illustration 10.67)** and discard them. Always install new O-rings on the injectors before reassembling the injectors and the fuel rail.

9   Installation is otherwise the reverse of removal. To ensure that the new injector O-rings are not damaged when

the injectors are installed into the fuel rail and into the intake manifold, lubricate them with clean engine oil.

10   Start the engine and verify that there are no fuel leaks.

23 Idle Air Control (IAC) valve

1   Locate the IAC valve **(see illustration 10.68).**

2   Disconnect the IAC valve electrical connector.

3   Remove the IAC valve mounting fasteners and detach the IAC valve from the throttle body.

4   If equipped, replace the O-ring on the IAC valve **(see illustration 10.69).**

5   Installation is the reverse of removal. **Note:** *On some IAC valves, the pintle must be retracted before the valve is installed. If the pintle bottoms out in the throttle body before the flange of the valve seats, wiggle the pintle back-and-forth while pushing it inwards to retract it.*

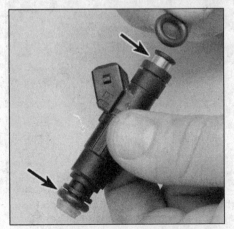

10.67 Always remove and discard the old injector O-rings and install new O-rings on each injector

10.68 The IAC valve is usually located on the throttle body

10.69 If equipped, remove and discard the old O-ring from the IAC valve, then install a new one

10.70 Disconnect the electrical connector from the coil pack

10.71 Generally, ignition coils are secured by one . . .

24 Ignition coils

1 Disconnect the cable from the negative battery terminal.

2 Disconnect the electrical connector from the ignition coil **(see illustration 10.70).**

3 Remove the coil mounting fastener(s) **(see illustrations 10.71 and 10.72).**

4 Remove the ignition coil **(see illustration 10.73).**

5 Clean the coil(s) with a dampened cloth and dry them thoroughly.

6 Inspect each coil for cracks, damage and carbon tracking. If damage exists, replace the coil.

7 Coat the inside of the spark plug boot with silicone dielectric compound **(see illustration 10.74).**

8 Installation is otherwise the reverse of removal.

10.72 . . . or two mounting fasteners

10.73 To remove the ignition coil, pull it straight out

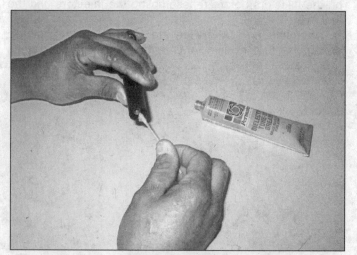

10.74 Before pushing the spark plug boot back onto the spark plug, coat the inside of the boot with silicone dielectric compound

11 OBD-II and performance programming

Why is a performance Chapter part of a book on OBD-II diagnostics? Other Chapters in this book explain how the on-board diagnostics system works on computer-controlled powertrains. However, in addition to the great benefits of fuel economy, reliability, cleaner air and self-diagnostic capabilities that such vehicles give us today, the programming of that computer also provides us with a simple means of gaining more performance from our vehicle, without ever getting our hands dirty!

The PCM is the "brain" of the electronically controlled engine management and emissions system, and is specifically calibrated to optimize the performance, emissions, fuel economy and driveability of one specific vehicle/engine/transaxle/accessories package in one make/model/year of vehicle. This programming is 90% generic in nature and common to all vehicles, but the other 10% is very specific to that make and model. Parameters such as ignition timing and fuel calibration play a big role in how the vehicle drives, and factory programming is designed to keep the emissions low enough to meet Federal standards, yet keep the fuel curve rich enough to provide a "safety factor" for all kinds of driving and all climactic zones of the country.

This programming is of necessity a compromise, and the vehicle manufacturers' goal is usually not maximum performance. The goals of enthusiasts are more in the high-performance sphere and their programming needs are slightly different. The average vehicle owner will never see 5000 rpm in the vehicle's lifetime, but the average enthusiast wants to see the upper power band now and again and also experience more power down low as well.

Performance chips

For improved performance, many enthusiasts upgrade their engine management systems with aftermarket programming. The advantages are increased fuel flow, an improved ignition advance curve and higher revving capability. While replacing or "tuning" computer components can provide substantial performance gains by themselves, they can be very helpful, if not crucial, when combined with mechanical engine upgrades. Power adders such as superchargers and turbochargers may have special needs in terms of fuel and spark mapping, and these can be satisfied with aftermarket chips or other programming.

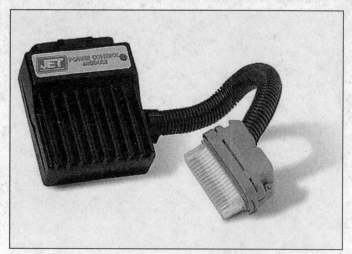

11.1 For a minimal outlay of cash and trouble, a simple upgrade for your PCM can improve engine response with increased timing. This is a typical plug-in Power Programmer from Jet Performance. For some models, computer upgrade work can be done by mail and Jet will ship your PCM back to you in 24 hours, all with special packaging they will supply

11.2 Before you order a custom chip for your vehicle, you must copy all the information from the label on your PCM (including the bar code), so the techs know exactly what factory program and spark/fuel parameters they're working with

Where the factory PCM programming needs some "help" for performance use is in the ignition timing and fuel curves. Virtually all new vehicles are designed to run on the lowest grade of unleaded pump gas, with an 87-octane rating. To get more performance, the ignition curve can be given more advanced timing and the fuel curve adjusted for more fuel at higher rpm, but the octane rating of the gas now may become a problem. When timing is advanced, the engine may have more tendency to exhibit detonation or ping, signs of improper burning in the combustion chamber and potentially dangerous to the lifespan of the engine. Thus, if you want more timing in your computer for more power, you'll probably have to up the grade of gasoline you buy. In fact, the more serious engine modifications you make, the more you will probably have to "reprogram" your PCM. Over the process of modifying your vehicle's engine, your programming needs may change. As you make more and different changes, different tweaks need to be applied to the "brain." Hopefully, you have located a trustworthy "tuning" shop near you. They'll be able to help you with computer upgrades.

In many new cars, the programming that affects the areas we want to modify is part of a "chip" on the motherboard of the PCM. The chip is a very small piece of silicon semiconductor material carrying many integrated circuits. These are usually called PROM chips, for Programmable Read Only Memory. In some cases, the chip is a "plug-in" which can be easily removed from the PCM and replaced with a custom chip; other chips are factory-soldered to the board. Cars with plug-in chips aren't difficult to modify, but some vehicles do not have replaceable chips.

It isn't recommended to remove a soldered chip from the motherboard at home. Your factory PCM is very expensive to replace and just a tiny mistake with the solder or the heat source could ruin it. Aftermarket companies offer repro-

gramming services for these kinds of PCMs, and some tuning shops also have equipment to do this. In some cases you remove your PCM and send it to the company by overnight mail, they modify it and overnight-mail it back to you.

The performance chip generally will not void your warranty, but you might want to remove it if you bring your vehicle in to a dealer for diagnostic work, in case the dealership downloads an updated factory program as part of your service. If there is a warranty problem with your vehicle, and the dealer determines that an aftermarket part such as a programmer was installed and was responsible for the problem, the dealer will most likely *not* cover the problem under warranty. Read the fine print in your warranty for the exact wording.

Based on the information you have given them about your vehicle, driving needs, and modifications you have made to the engine, they will custom-program the timing, fuel and even the transmission shifting information on vehicles with PCM-controlled electronic automatic transaxles. On vehicles so equipped, they can even change the factory-set rev limiter or top-speed limiter. On most applications, your vehicle will require a better grade of gas than before, so factor the increased fuel cost in your budget.

Towing is another consideration when "chipping" a vehicle like a light truck. The octane requirement goes up seriously with increased load. Lighter vehicles require less octane with all other factors being equal. If you even occasionally tow heavy loads (boat, car trailer, etc.), make sure this is taken into consideration before investing in a new program or chip. You should also tell the chip company if you have changed to a non-stock gear ratio or installed much-taller tires and wheels. The new program can help gain back any performance you may have lost with large-diameter wheels or gears and even correct your speedometer readings.

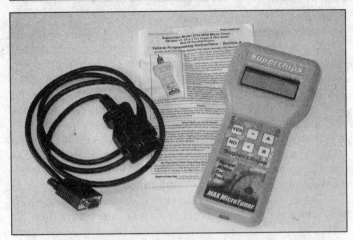

11.3 The Superchips MAX MicroTuner is capable of saving a version of your stock PCM's data, then downloading one of three performance-level programs into your vehicle's management system: a conservative 87-octane-rated program; a performance/towing program, 91-octane required; and a performance only, 91-octane program not suited for towing - instructions and a computer cable are included and you can switch programs or go back to stock with the tool anytime

11.4 With most hand-held programmers, simply hook the cable to the programmer at one end and the other to the diagnostic port of your vehicle, and the instructions walk you through the simple steps to entering the programming that best suits your needs

Depending on the year and model of the truck, a plug-in chip may be available from the aftermarket for your vehicle. In these cases, you don't have to send your PCM to the company, just give them the complete serial number and codes on the decal of your PCM and they'll supply the correct plug-in for you.

Hand-held programmers

The advent of the standardization that came with OBD-II, including the codes and diagnostic connector, has given rise to the popularity of hand-held programmers that you can use at home to do what the chip companies have been doing. The nature of computer tweakers is such that they constantly seek new challenges, and some of these data-stream wizards went from PC's to vehicle computers. The PCMs in our vehicles today are fast and adaptable - it's been said that they're more powerful than NASA navigational computers!

The hand-held units pack a lot of computing information in a package that looks like a controller for a video game. They come with a cable to connect directly to your diagnostic test port, just like a scan tool. You follow the manufacturer's instructions and push buttons on the programmer to alter programming in your vehicle's PCM, all with the engine off. Included are the installation instructions, the computer cable, and instruction book for using the tuner later as a diagnostic code-reader.

Some models of programmers have a feature where the unit copies and stores the stock programming of your specific vehicle (you punch your VIN number into the programmer). Often you have a choice of several performance programs you can install back into your PCM in place of the original. The program choices usually vary in intensity and

the octane rating that the program requires. A program for using 87-octane gas will be on the milder side, a step up could offer more performance with 89-octane, and the strongest program could offer 15 to 30 horsepower with the use of 91 or 93-octane, depending on the vehicle.

An advantage of the programmers versus chips is that you can switch programs or go back to stock anytime. If you carry the tool in your glove box, you can change the tune even when you're out on the road (not while driving, though). If you're set for 91-octane and you're stuck in the boonies where there's a single pump with 87, you can go back to a milder or stock program in minutes, thus avoiding detonation and possible engine damage. Likewise, when travelling empty you can have one program and switch to a less-aggressive one when you hook up to your RV trailer or tow a boat or car.

As with having your PCM "chipped," hand-held programmers offer the option of adjusting your vehicle's program to correct the speedometer for different gearing or tire sizes. Transmission shift points, speed limiters and rev limiters can also be adjusted with hand-held programmers. By keeping the programmer, you can change any of these parameters back and forth as needed, and use it as a code reader anytime. Models are available for most domestic cars and trucks, usually with brand-specific models, such as one for a Chevy, one for Dodge and one for Ford vehicles.

Performance programming for diesels

The hottest area of PCM reprogramming in the last five years has been the availability of performance tuning for diesel engines, primarily in light and medium-duty trucks. Once thought of as stinky, noisy workhorses suitable only for towing duty, today's diesel trucks are enjoying popularity for many uses, and performance programming has come along to make any job easier for them, even if it's just to accelerate

11.5 Diesel trucks also respond well to aftermarket programmers - this is a PowerPDA from Banks Engineering that interfaces wirelessly with their Six-Gun diesel programmer - you can select power on the fly, time runs, log data, and it displays EGT, boost pressure and several other parameters important to a performance diesel truck

hard up an on-ramp to the freeway.

Back when diesels all had mechanical fuel injection, there was little that could be done to tweak the performance without upgrading the turbocharger or other hard parts, but today's breed of diesel engines in light and medium-duty trucks all have electronic injectors, which makes them eminently suitable for reprogramming. Diesel engines differ in several major ways from gasoline engines, chiefly in that there is no ignition system, and the fuel is injected directly into the cylinders where it is auto-ignited by the heat and force of extreme compression.

The diesel engine takes in the air that it needs without a lot of controls on the intake side; it is the injection of *fuel* that makes all the difference. The computers governing modern diesel engines control the fuel delivery very closely, in effect being the "distributor" as well as the "carburetor". Besides the amount of fuel an injector is told to deliver, the fuel pressure and the precise *time* the injector squirts for each cylinder is important. Injecting the fuel a little sooner can allow more cylinder pressure to build. Programmers for diesel engines have become very popular, often allowing you to choose "on the fly" from several different performance programs.

There is a caveat to this kind of "instant" horsepower, however. Programmers promise horsepower gains from 50 to 100 to even 300 for some expensive models. Since these gains are made by introducing more fuel and more fuel sooner, the bang inside each cylinder gets bigger. It can get explosive enough to literally stretch the head bolts and lift the cylinder heads on some engines! Blown head gaskets are not uncommon when diesels are fueled to the limit and driven for hard acceleration. Do your research, talk to other diesel owners before you purchase a programmer, and stay conservative on the level of horsepower increase, especially if you're towing heavy loads. If you go for the higher levels of power, you should definitely install an EGT (exhaust gas temperature) gauge to monitor your engine, since these high levels of power can raise EGT dangerously.

Experts recommend that anytime you install programming in your diesel vehicle you should have the engine fully warmed up first, otherwise the glow plug system can put a drain on your battery during the KOEO (Key On, Engine Off) period when you're programming.

How to: Predator Tuning Tool

Technology in vehicle computing moves almost as fast as in desktop computing, and a new hand-held programmer from Diablosport called the *Predator* has several interesting features. The shape and the translucent case may look like a computer-game controller, but inside is some clever technology.

In addition to the "standard" tweaks that Diablosport has developed for most vehicles, the Predator tool also has advanced diagnostic capabilities. The performance "tune-ups" are easy to install and offer between 15 and 30 horsepower improvement, depending on the specific vehicle. Even cars and trucks that are already "performance models" can gain extra power, although Diablosport stresses that all the user-selectable tuning points are still within a "safe" range for the engine.

Where the *Predator* differs from most hand-helds is that you once you buy it you don't have to stop there. Diablosport has a dealer network around the country, and most dealers have a chassis dyno and performance tuners on staff who are constantly tweaking, testing and recording data. When

Warning: *Virtually all "tuning" chips and/or hand-held programmers are technically illegal for street/highway use. Most such products have a small warning on their box to let you know these tools are designed "for off-road use only". Unlike other traditional engine modifications such as special induction parts, exhaust headers and hotter camshafts, performance computer tuning is virtually undetectable. Thus chips and programmers are used often on street vehicles. If your state has an annual I/M (inspection & maintenance) program, you are advised to revert back to the stock programming your specific vehicle came with from the factory before you go in for a test. Most aftermarket programming tools have the capability of "saving" the stock program in memory so that it can be reinstalled at any time.*

11.6 A supercharged Ford F-150 Lightning pickup is a strong performer to begin with, but with a Predator programmer and some expert tuning by John Morris of Altered Speed (French Camp, CA), it turned into a road-rocket!

11.7 A preliminary run on the Mustang chassis dyno will establish a performance baseline and, with the use of exhaust analysis, determine the factory fuel curve. The only connection required underhood for the dyno work is the clip-on lead for the ignition coil pack to read engine rpm

these dealers discover new model-specific improvements, they send them to Diablosport, who in turn tests them and makes the best ones available to all their dealers. If you have a *Predator*, you can go to one of their dealers and have new tweaks installed in your vehicle. They can fine-tune the parameters for your specific needs, and back the results up with runs on their dyno.

11.8 With a driver in the truck to operate the throttle, John controls the dyno's load at the rear wheels to determine the vehicle's horsepower and torque in stock form. Even vehicles of the same exact model will have different figures due to variables in each powertrain

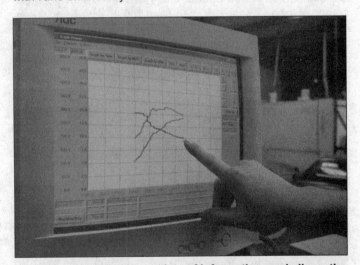

11.10 The computer stores lots of information, and allows the tuner to look at it in various ways. There are the three basic curves being considered here: the uppermost curve is the torque at various rpms; the lower curve is the horsepower at the rear wheels; and John is pointing to the Air/Fuel Ratio line. In this case the fuel curve starts getting too rich at 3400 rpm and falls off further after that, meaning the truck is too rich, either for clean air or good performance. The ideal A/F ratio is around 14.7:1 under light load, but for performance vehicles under a load like the dyno, it should be between 13.0:1 and 14.0:1. Supercharged vehicles like this Lightning pickup need more fuel under load to avoid detonation, in the range of 11.6:1 under load

11.9 The run takes only a short time, and with the truck shut down, John analyzes all the data on the dyno's computer

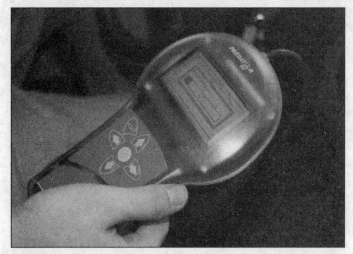

11.11 The Diablosport Predator programmer is hooked to the diagnostic port in the pickup's instrument panel and with the Key on but the engine Off, the instructions talk you through the steps to install the performance programming. In the first step, the Predator reads the VIN, anti-theft code and stock program of the vehicle, so it always has that as a reference

11.12 With the Diablosport instructions, anyone can install their choice of the Predator's performance "tunes," reading the screen and pushing the scroll arrows to navigate. A number of aftermarket supercharger packages come with a Predator loaded with a custom tune for that vehicle and supercharger

A dyno setup should have the capability to read the Air/Fuel ratio while idling or making runs under load. When under load at higher rpms, your OBD-II system is in the open-loop mode so the oxygen sensors aren't telling the PCM anything and codes aren't necessarily set during these conditions. At Altered Speed, they have an expensive wide-band oxygen sensor that can read much wider variations than a stock O2 sensor. High-performance vehicles usually run richer under load than the range handled by a stock sensor. They usually unplug the after-catalyst sensor and plug their sensor in while dyno-tuning, since the factory after-cat sensor is used primarily to test the effectiveness of the con-verter, not to influence the everyday tuning of the engine. After a dyno session, the stock after-cat sensor can go back in place.

Another cool feature of this programmer is that you can interface your *Predator* with your desktop or laptop computer. Besides the usual tunable elements, the *Predator* can log dynamic data at 90 samples per second for a half-hour, then export this into your home computer for storage and analysis. In most cases, the tool can not only read and clear the universal OBD-II P-codes, but also the manufacturer-specific codes usually available only through an expensive scan tool.

11.13 Another dyno run is made with the standard predator program, and the truck picked up 3 horsepower, but the torque went up 13 ft-lbs and reached its peak at 3600 rpm, rather than the 4350 rpm when stock. Low-end torque is what you feel when driving, but John determined there was still more to be gained with custom tuning

11.14 Predator owners can plug their programmer into their PC supplied software, and store/analyze live data recorded on the Predator. Authorized dealers like Altered Speed can plug into their computer software and make custom tweaks for specific applications and/or download special tuning from Diablosport and transfer it into the hand-held Predator

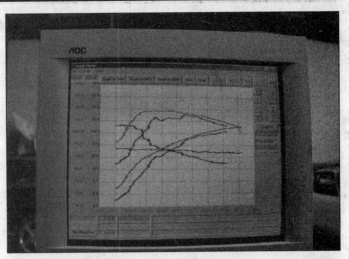

11.16 After the custom tweaking, horsepower was up to 305 at 5350 rpm, torque went to 347.6 @3600 rpm, and the A/F ratio (middle two lines) was more of an even line rather than a downward (too rich) curve. This screen compares the run with the basic Predator tune to the later runs with the custom tuning. Note how the power and torque lines are not only higher, but also smoother. The consistent A/F ratio under load may even help fuel economy and spark plug life

11.15 Dealers and customers can talk directly to Diablosport factory customer service techs for help when using a Predator or upgrading to a custom tune

We followed a 1999 Ford Lightning F-150 pickup as it received the performance *Predator* treatment at Altered Speed in French Camp, California, a Diablosport dealer. Already a factory-performance vehicle, the truck gained some 21 new horsepower at the rear wheels, an equal amount of new low-end torque for a whole new feel to street driving, and an improvement in quarter-mile times from 14.26 to 13.81. That's pretty impressive for not picking up a wrench through the entire process!

Glossary

A

Absolute Pressure - Pressure measured from the point of total vacuum. For instance, absolute atmospheric pressure at sea level is 14.7 psi (1 bar, 100 kPa or 29.92 in. hg) at a temperature of 80 degrees Fahrenheit (26.7 degrees Centigrade.)

Acceleration - The moment the throttle is open with the engine running and the vacuum in the intake manifold drops.

Actuator - One name for any computer-controlled output device, such as a fuel injector, an EGR solenoid valve, an EVAP solenoid purge valve, etc. The term also refers to a specific component, the pressure actuator, used on Bosch KE-Jetronic and KE-Motronic continuous injection systems. See pressure actuator.

Adaptive control - The ability of a control unit to adapt its closed-loop operation to changing operating conditions - such as engine wear, fuel quality or altitude - to maintain proper air-fuel mixture control, ignition timing or idle rpm. Also referred to as self-learning.

Adaptive memory - A feature of computer memory that allows the microprocessor to adjust its memory for computing open-loop operation, based on changes in engine operation.

Adjustable timing light - A timing light that delays flashes as an adjusting knob is turned. The delay is displayed as degrees on a meter, usually incorporated in the timing light.

After Top Dead Center (ATDC) - The position of a piston after it has passed top dead center. Usually expressed in degrees.

Air Charge Temperature sensor (ACT) - A thermistor used to measure intake air temperature or air-fuel mixture temperature.

Air-Flow Controlled (AFC) - A Bosch term for early L-Jetronic fuel injection systems, used to distinguish L-Jet from the earlier D-Jetronic, which was a pressure-controlled system. AFC also refers to many other fuel injection systems that measure the amount of air flowing past a sensor to determine engine fuel requirements

Air-fuel ratio - The amount of air compared to the amount of fuel in the air-fuel mixture, almost always expressed in terms of mass. See also Stoichiometric Ratio.

Airflow meter - In Bosch systems, any device that measures the amount of air being used by the engine. The control unit uses this information to determine the load on the engine. The two most common examples of airflow meters are the airflow sensor used in the Bosch L-Jetronic and the air mass sensor used in the Bosch LH-Jetronic systems. See airflow sensor and air mass sensor.

Airflow sensor - A sensor used to measure the volume of air entering the engine on many fuel injection systems. Continuous injection systems use an airflow sensor plate to measure airflow volume; electronic systems use a vane or flap-type airflow sensor.

Air gap - The space between the spark plug electrodes, motor and generator armatures, field shoes, etc.

Air injection - A way of reducing exhaust emissions by injecting air into each of the exhaust ports of an engine. The air mixes with the hot exhaust gasses and oxidizes the HC and CO to form H_2O and CO_2.

Air mass sensor - An airflow meter that uses the changing resistance of a heated wire in the intake airstream to measure the mass of the air being drawn into the engine. Also referred to as a hot-wire sensor.

AIR monitor - The AIR monitor runs passive and, if necessary, active tests of the Secondary Air Injection system. The passive test monitors oxygen sensor voltage from start-up to closed-loop operation to determine whether the oxygen sensor is switching back and forth the way that it's supposed to in closed loop. If so, the AIR monitor passes and doesn't bother with the active test, which is only run *after the engine management system has already entered closed-loop operation*. In the active test, the AIR monitor uses the oxygen sensor to tell it whether the oxygen content in the exhaust changes as the AIR system is turned on and off by the PCM. The AIR monitor looks for a change in oxygen sensor voltage and in STFT as air is pumped into the exhaust stream. When extra air is introduced into the exhaust gases during closed loop, the oxygen sensor voltage should go low and the STFT should indicate that it has richened the air/fuel mixture by increasing injector pulse-width. If the PCM doesn't see these results, the AIR monitor fails.

Air vane - The pivoting flap inside an L-Jetronic or Motronic airflow sensor that swings open in relation to the amount of air flowing through the airflow sensor.

Alternating current - A flow of electricity through a conductor, first in one direction, then in the opposite direction.

Ambient temperature - The temperature of the surrounding air.

Ammeter - An electric meter used to measure current.

Amperage - The total amount of current (amperage) flowing in a circuit.

Ampere (Amp) - The unit of measure for the flow of current in a circuit. The amount of current produced by one volt acting against one ohm of resistance.

Amplifier - An electronic device (usually an electron tube or transistor) used in a circuit to strengthen or increase an input signal.

Amplitude - The maximum rise (or fall) of a voltage signal from 0 volts.

Analog - A voltage signal or processing action that is continuously variable relative to the operation being measured or controlled.

Analog Volt-Ohmmeter (VOM) - A multi-function meter which measures voltage and resistance. Measurements are made with a D'arsenval meter movement (needle) instead of a digital display.

Anti-knock value - The characteristic of gasoline that helps prevent detonation or knocking

Antioxidant inhibitor - A gasoline additive used to prevent oxidation and the formation of gum.

Armature - The spring-loaded part in an injector that's magnetically attracted by the solenoid coil when it is energized. Also another name for the solenoid itself.

Atmospheric pressure - Normal pressure in the surrounding atmosphere, generated by the weight of the air pressing down from above. At sea level, atmospheric pressure is about 14.7 psi, above vacuum or zero absolute, pressure (1 bar, 100 kPa or 29.92 in. hg) at a temperature of 80 degrees Fahrenheit (26.7 degrees Centigrade). See barometric pressure.

Atomization - breaking down into small particles or a fine mist.

Auxiliary air valve - A special valve which bypasses the closed throttle valve. The auxiliary air valve admits extra air into the intake manifold during cold engine starting for a higher idle speed during warm-up.

Available voltage - The measured voltage at the source or other point in a circuit with respect to ground.

B

Backfire - The accidental combustion of gasses in an engine's intake or exhaust manifold.

Backpressure - The resistance, caused by turbulence and friction, that is created as a gas or liquid is forced through a passage.

Baffle - A plate or obstruction that restricts the flow of air or liquids. The baffle in a fuel tank keeps the fuel from sloshing as the car moves.

Ballast resistor - A resistor connected in series between the ignition switch and the ignition coil to reduce voltage and current to the coil when the engine is running.

Bank 1 - The bank of cylinders containing cylinder #1.

Bank 2 - The bank of cylinders opposite cylinder #1 (V6, V8, V10, etc.).

Bar - The metric unit of measurement used in the measurement of both air and fuel. One bar is about 14.7 psi (1 bar, 100 kPa or 29.92 in. hg, at a temperature of 80 degrees Fahrenheit [26.7 degrees Centigrade]) at sea level.

Barometric Pressure - Another term for atmospheric pressure, expressed in inches of Mercury (in-Hg). Barometric pressure is determined by how high atmospheric pressure (relative to zero absolute pressure) forces mercury up a glass tube. 14.7 psi = 1 bar, 100 kPa or 29.92 in. hg, at a temperature of 80 degrees Fahrenheit [26.7 degrees Centigrade]) at sea level.

Base idle - The idle rpm when the throttle lever rests on the throttle stop and the Idle Speed Control motor or solenoid is fully retracted and disconnected.

Battery - A group of two or more cells connected together for the production of an electric current. It converts chemical energy into electrical energy.

Battery-hot - Refers to a circuit that is fed directly from the starter relay terminal. Voltage is available whenever the battery is charged.

Battery voltage - Voltage measured between the two terminals of a battery.

Bimetal - A spring or strip made of two different metals with different thermal expansion rates. A rising temperature causes a bimetal element to bend or twist one way when it's cold and the other way when it's warm.

Binary - A mathematical system consisting of only two digits (0 and 1) which allows a digital computer to read and process input voltage signals.

Block learn - Long-term recorded memory of air fuel ratios stored in the computer (if electrical power is lost, by disconnecting the battery for example, the memory in the block learn will be lost)

Blown - A melted fuse filament caused by electrical overload.

Boost - A condition of over-pressure (above atmospheric) in the intake manifold; caused by intake air being forced in by a turbocharger or supercharger.

Bottom Dead Center - (BDC) - The exact bottom of a piston stroke.

Bypass - A passage inside a throttle body casting that allows air to go around a closed throttle valve.

C

Calibration - The act of determining or rectifying the graduations used on a testing instrument.

Calibration Package - More commonly known as CALPAK is installed in the computer in case of PROM or ECM failure, to give a preset air/fuel ratio and timing so that the vehicle can be driven to a repair facility.

Camshaft overlap - The period of camshaft rotation in degrees during which both the intake and the exhaust valve are open.

CAN - Communication between system computers.

Canister - A container in an evaporative emission control system that contains charcoal to trap vapors from the fuel system.

Capacitance - The ability of a condenser (capacitor) to receive and hold an electrical charge.

Capacitor - An electrical device made up of two conductors made of metal foil, separated by a very thin insulating material and rolled up and housed (usually) in a metal container. A capacitor has the ability to store an electrical charge.

Capacity - The quantity of electricity that can be delivered under specified conditions, as from a battery at a given rate of discharge in amp hours.

Carbon dioxide (CO_2) - One of the many by-products of combustion. CO_2 is one of the harmless gases produced by normal combustion or by converting HC and CO inside the catalytic converter. However, it should be noted that many scientists throughout the world regard CO_2 as a *greenhouse gas*, i.e. a gas that retains heat. These same scientists warn that the excessive level of CO_2 in the earth's atmosphere is responsible for global warming trends.

Carbon monoxide (CO) - CO is the colorless, odorless and highly toxic byproduct of a rich fuel mixture. Most CO is converted into carbon dioxide (CO_2) and oxygen in the oxidation catalyst.

Catalyst - In chemistry, a catalyst is a substance, usually present in minute amounts relative to the *reactants* (the stuff that it catalyzes) that modifies and increases the rate of a chemical reaction without itself being consumed in the process. In automotive terminology, the term is also often used to mean "catalytic converter."

Catalyst monitor - The catalyst monitor compares the voltage signals from the upstream and downstream oxygen sensors to measure the amount of oxygen being stored by the catalytic converter. As the catalyst deteriorates or becomes contaminated, its ability to store oxygen decreases. As the storage capacity of the catalyst decreases, more oxygen exits the outlet end of the catalyst, producing a switching rate at the downstream oxygen sensor similar to the switching rate of the upstream sensor. When the switching rate of the downstream sensor matches the switching rate of the upstream sensor, the catalyst monitor fails.

Catalytic converter - A reaction chamber containing a *monolithic substrate* through which exhaust gases pass on their way to the tailpipe. There are really two catalysts inside the converter: the reduction catalyst and the oxidation catalyst. The *reduction catalyst* reduces NOx to nitrogen and oxygen. The *oxidation* catalyst oxidizes (adds oxygen to) HC and CO, which converts them into carbon dioxide (CO_2) and water (H_2O).

Cavitation - The rapid formation and collapse of gas or vapor-filled cavities in a liquid, in regions of very low pressure (behind the vanes of a fuel pump rotor, for example). The point at which a pump begins to lose efficiency.

Centigrade - Unit of measuring temperature where water boils at 100 degrees and freezes at 0 degrees at sea level altitude (boiling points will decrease as altitude increases).

Charge - Any condition where electricity is available. To restore the active materials in a battery cell by electrically reversing the chemical action.

Check Engine Light (CEL) - A dash panel light used to alert the driver of a problem in one or more of the systems monitored by the Powertrain Control Module.

Check Valve - A one way valve which allows a vacuum or gas to flow in one direction only. Preventing backflow.

Circuit - A circle or unbroken path through which electric current can flow.

Circuit breaker - A device other than a fuse which interrupts a circuit under infrequent abnormal conditions.

Clearance volume - The volume of a combustion chamber when the piston is at top dead center.

Closed circuit - A circuit which is uninterrupted from the current source and back to the current source.

Closed loop - The mode of operation that a system with an oxygen sensor goes into once the engine is sufficiently warmed up. When the system is in closed-loop operation, an oxygen sensor monitors the oxygen content of the exhaust gas and sends a varying voltage signal to the control unit, which alters the air/fuel mixture ratio accordingly.

Cold-start injector - A solenoid-type injector, installed in the intake plenum, that injects extra fuel during cold-engine starts. Also referred to as a cold start valve.

Cold-start valve - See cold-start injector.

Combustion - Controlled, rapid burning of the air-fuel mixture in the engine cylinders.

Combustion chamber - Space left between the cylinder head and the top of the piston at TDC; where combustion of the air-fuel mixture takes place.

Comprehensive Component Monitor (CCM) - The CCM continuously monitors all sensors and circuits not already being monitored by some other monitor. This list includes, but is not limited to, the CMP sensor, the CKP sensor, the ECT sensor, the knock sensor, the MAP sensor, the MAF sensor, the TP sensor, etc.

Compression ratio - The ratio of maximum engine cylinder volume (when the piston is at the bottom of its stroke) to minimum engine cylinder volume (with the piston at TDC). Thus, the theoretical amount that the air-fuel mixture is compressed in the cylinder.

Computed timing - The total spark advance in degrees before top dead center. Calculated by the computer based on inputs from a number of sensors.

Condenser - A device for holding or storing an electric charge. See capacitor.

Conductor - A material that allows easy flow of electricity.

Conflict - Sometimes the Diagnostic Executive can't run two monitors at the same time because doing so will alter the outcome of one or both of the test results. If the Diagnostic Executive sees a *conflict* between running two monitors at one time, it holds up one monitor until the other monitor has been run to completion.

Continuity - Little or no resistance in an electrical circuit to the flow of current. A solid electrical connection between two points in a circuit. The opposite of an open circuit.

Continuous Injection System (CIS) - A Bosch-developed fuel injection system that injects fuel continuously. Unlike an electronic injection system, which uses a computer to control the pulse-width of electronic solenoid injectors, CIS uses hydraulic controls to alter the amount of fuel injected. There are four basic types of CIS: K-Jetronic, K-Jetronic with Lambda (oxygen sensor), KE-Jetronic and KE-Motronic.

Controller - One of several names for a solid state micro-computer which monitors engine conditions and controls certain engine functions, i.e. air/fuel ratio, injection and ignition timing, etc. Specific names such as ECM, ECU, Power Module, Logic Module, SBEC and SMEC are generically referred to as controllers in many different instances to refer to all of these computers.

Control module - A transistorized device that processes electrical inputs and produces output signals to control various engine functions. One of several names for a solid-state micro-computer.

Control plunger - In Bosch CIS, the component inside the fuel distributor that rises and falls with the airflow sensor plate lever, which controls fuel flow to the injectors.

Control pressure - In Bosch CIS, the pressurized fuel used as a hydraulic control fluid to apply a counterforce to the control plunger in Bosch CIS. Control pressure alters the air-fuel ratio through the operation of the control-pressure regulator.

Control pressure regulator - In Bosch CIS, the control-pressure regulator is a thermal-hydraulic device that alters the control pressure by returning the excess fuel from the control pressure circuit to the fuel tank. The control pressure regulator controls the counterforce pressure on top of the control plunger. Also referred to as the warm-up regulator.

Control unit - An electronic computer that processes electrical inputs and produces electrical outputs to control a series of actuators which alter engine operating conditions. Also referred to as an electronic control assembly (ECA), electronic control module (ECM), electronic control unit (ECU), logic module, or simply, the computer.

Conventional Theory of Current Flow - The current flow theory which says electricity flows from positive to negative. Also called positive current flow theory.

Converter circuits - Area of the computer where the input data in a form of analog signals coming from sensors are converted into digital signals.

Core - The center conductor part or a wire of the iron magnetic material or a solenoid magnet.

Counterforce - The force of the fuel-pressure applied to the top of the control plunger to balance the force of the airflow pushing against the sensor plate. See control pressure.

Cross-circuit short - A current flow path between hot wires in two different circuits.

Cross-counts - The number of times that an oxygen sensor crosses the center voltage level between rich and lean.

Current - Amount or intensity of flow of electricity. Measure in amperes.

Current flow - The current flow theory which says electricity flows from positive to negative. Also called positive current flow theory.

Current-limiting resistor - A resistor inserted in a circuit to limit the current.

Cycle - A complete alternation in an alternating current.

D

Dampener - A device, sometimes called an accumulator, installed inline between the fuel pump and the fuel filter on many fuel injection systems, which dampens the pulsations of the fuel pump. The accumulator also maintains residual pressure in the fuel delivery system, even after the engine has been turned off, to prevent vapor lock.

Dead short - A zero-resistance short circuit.

Deceleration - The moment the throttle is released with the engine running and the vacuum in the intake manifold increases.

De-energized - Having the electric current or energy source turned off.

Density - The ratio of the mass of something (air, in this book) to the volume it occupies. Air has less density when it's warm or when the vehicle is operating at higher altitude. It has more density when it's cool, and at lower altitude.

Detonation - See knock.

Diagnostic Executive - The Ford and General Motors term for the software that decides whether enabling criteria are present and manages the sequence for running different monitors. The Diagnostic Executive also makes sure that the monitors are run at the right time, and in the correct sequence, so that there are no conflicts between monitors and between the monitors and vehicle performance. Other manufacturers use other terms. For example, Chrysler uses the term Task Manager, etc. In this manual, we use the term Diagnostic Executive.

Diagnostic mode - This operation mode is used by the Engine Control Computer (ECU) and provides historical data to the technician that indicates any malfunctions or discrepancies that have been stored in memory.

Diaphragm - A component which moves a control lever accordingly when supplied with a vacuum signal.

Dielectric - The insulating material used between the plates of a capacitor (condenser).

Dieseling - A condition in a gasoline engine in which extreme heat in the combustion chamber continues to ignite fuel after the ignition has been turned off.

Differential pressure - In Bosch KE-Jetronic systems, the difference between actuator fuel pressure in the lower chambers of the differential-pressure valves and the system pressure entering the pressure actuator. See pressure-drop.

Differential-pressure regulator - See pressure actuator.

Differential-pressure valves - Inside the Bosch CIS fuel distributor, these valves (there's one for each cylinder) maintain a constant pressure drop at each of the control-plunger slits, regardless of changes in the quantity of fuel flow.

Digifant - Volkswagen collaborated with Bosch to develop this electronic injection system. Digifant is similar to a Motronic system, except that its timing control map is less complicated than the Motronic map. And it doesn't have a knock sensor.

Digifant II - A refined version of Volkswagen's Digifant. This system has some control improvements and uses a knock sensor for improved timing control.

Digital - A two-level voltage signal or processing function that is either on/off or high/low.

Digital control - Circuits which handle information by switching the current on and off.

Digital Fuel Injection (DFI) - A General Motors system, similar to earlier electronic fuel injection systems, but with digital microprocessors. Analog inputs from various engine sensors are converted to digital signals before processing. The system is self-monitoring and self-diagnosing. It also has the capabilities of compensating for failed components and remembering intermittent failures.

Digital volt-ohm meter - A highly accurate multimeter. To indicate meter readings, it uses integrated circuits and a digital display instead of conventional needle movement.

Diode - A form of semiconductor that allows electricity to flow only in one direction.

Displacement - A measurement of the volume of air displaced by a piston as it moves from bottom to top of its stroke. Engine displacement is the piston displacement multiplied by the number of pistons in an engine.

Distributor pipe - Another name for the fuel rail.

D-Jetronic - D-Jetronic is the term used by Bosch to describe a fuel injection system controlled by manifold pressure. The D is short for druck, the German word for "pressure." Manifold pressure is measured to indicate engine load (how much air the engine is using). This pressure is an input signal to the control unit (ECU) for calculation of the correct amount of fuel delivery.

Draw - The amount of electricity current any load or circuit uses.

Driveability - The operating characteristics of a vehicle.

Drive cycle - The OBD-II drive cycle is similar to the Federal Test Procedure (FTP). Typically, a drive cycle consists of a cold start, warm-up, idle, first acceleration, first steady-state cruising, first deceleration, second acceleration, second steady-state cruising and, finally, second deceleration.

Duty cycle - Many solenoid-operated metering devices cycle on and off. The duty cycle is a measurement of the amount of time a device is energized, or turned on, expressed as a percentage of the complete on-off cycle of that device. In other words, the duty cycle is the ratio of the pulse width to the complete cycle width.

Dwell - The amount of time that primary voltage is applied to the ignition coil to energize it. Dwell is also a measurement of the duration of time a component is on, relative to the time it's off. Dwell measurements are expressed in degrees (degrees of crankshaft rotation, for example). See duty cycle.

Dynamometer - A device used to measure mechanical power, such as the power of an engine.

E

Eccentric - Off center. A shaft lobe which has a center different from that of the shaft.

Electro-hydraulic pressure actuator - See pressure actuator.

Electromagnetic - Refers to a device which incorporates both electronic and magnetic principles together in its operation.

Electromechanical - Refers to a device which incorporates both electronic and mechanical principles together in its operation.

Electron Theory of Current Flow - The current flow theory which says electricity flows from negative to positive.

Electronic - Pertaining to the control of systems or devices by the use of small electrical signals and various semiconductors, devices and circuits.

Electronic Control Unit (ECU) - One (of many) names for the system computer. Often referred to as simply the "control unit."

Electronic Lean Burn (ELB) - This was the first electronic system introduced by Chrysler Motors to fire an extremely lean air/fuel ratio. This system only controlled ignition timing.

Emissions - Unburned parts of the air-fuel mixture released in the exhaust. Refers mostly to carbon monoxide (CO), hydrocarbons (HC), and nitrous oxide (NOx)

Enabling criteria - A specified set of operating conditions that must be present before an OBD-II PCM will run a diagnostic monitor.

Energized - Having the electric current or source turned on.

Engine mapping - Vehicle operation simulation procedure used to tailor the onboard computer program to a specific engine/powertrain combination. This program is stored in a PROM or calibration assembly.

Ethanol - Ethyl alcohol distilled from grain or sugar cane.

EVAP monitor - The EVAP monitor tests the EVAP system for leaks. Depending on the manufacturer, EVAP monitors employ one of three basic strategies to test the EVAP system. Some EVAP monitors use vacuum switching valves to isolate each part of the EVAP system plumbing, then use vacuum sensors to verify that each part of the system can hold a vacuum. Other monitors use a small electric pump to pressurize the system and a pressure sensor to determine whether the system leaks. Other monitors use an intrusive strategy: The EVAP monitor turns on the EVAP canister purge solenoid and watches how it affects STFT and idle air control.

Evaporative Emission Control (EEC) - A way of controlling HC emissions by collecting fuel vapors from the fuel tank and carburetor fuel bowl vents and directing them through an engine's intake.

F

Fahrenheit - Unit of measuring temperature where water boils at 212 degrees and freezes at 32 degrees at sea level altitude (boiling points decrease as altitude increases).

Fast-burn combustion chamber - A compact combustion chamber with a centrally located spark plug. The chamber is designed to shorten the combustion period by reducing the distance of flame front travel.

Fault codes - A series of numbers representing the results of On-Board Diagnostic or Vehicle Diagnostics. The computer communicates this service information via the Diagnostic Connector as a series of timed pulses read either on a SCAN Tool or as flashes of the "Power Loss/Check Engine" light.

Federal Test Procedure (FTP) - The mandated certification test that a new vehicle must pass before it wins EPA approval. Basically, there are four parts to the test. First, the vehicle is driven and its fuel economy is measured. Next, the vapor recovery system is tested while the vehicle is being refueled. Then the vehicle is placed on a dynamometer and its emissions are measured as it's driven under various driving conditions. Finally, the vehicle is placed in a sealed room, where the fuel vapor recovery system is tested for leaks.

Feed circuit - The power supply or hot wire.

Feedback carburetor - A form of carburetor that has a mixture control solenoid and is controlled by a computer

Firing order - The order in which combustion occurs in the cylinders of an engine.

Flat spot - The brief hesitation or stumble of an engine caused by a momentary overly lean air-fuel mixture due to the sudden opening of the throttle.

Flooding - An excess of fuel in the cylinder, from an over-rich mixture, that prevents combustion.

Flux lines - The lines of magnetic force. Also called Maxwells.

Freeze frame data - When one of the PCM's monitors detects a fault in some monitored emissions component or system, it sets a Diagnostic Trouble Code (DTC). And it also saves in memory a "freeze frame" or snapshot of the important engine operating conditions (sensor circuit voltage, for example) at the moment the DTC was set. This freeze frame data is extremely helpful when diagnosing what might be wrong with an emissions system, component or circuit because it can help you pinpoint which component, sensor, circuit, etc. jumped out of range, shorted, grounded, went open, etc. at the moment that the DTC was set.

Frequency - The number of cycles (complete alterations) of an alternating current per second.

Frequency valve - In Bosch CIS, a device that regulates pressure in the lower chamber of the differential-pressure valve, in response to a signal from the lambda (oxygen) sensor. Also referred to as a Lambda valve (Bosch's term) or a timing valve.

Fuel distributor - On Bosch CIS, the device that supplies the injectors with pressurized fuel in proportion to air volume, measured by the airflow sensor plate. The fuel distributor houses the control plunger and the differential-pressure valves. All fuel metering takes place inside the fuel distributor.

Fuel filter - Filters fuel before delivery to protect injection system components (on the frame of the vehicle) and the fuel pump (inside the gas tank).

Fuel injector - In all systems (except CIS, CIS/Lambda and CIS-E systems), a spring-loaded, solenoid (electromagnetic) valve which delivers fuel into the intake manifold, in response to electrical signals from the control module. In CIS, CIS/Lambda and CIS-E systems, a spring-loaded, pressure sensitive valve which opens at a preset value.

Fuel metering - Control of the amount of fuel that is mixed with engine intake air to form a combustible mixture.

Fuel pump - Delivers fuel from the tank to the injection system and provides system pressure. On fuel-injected vehicles, the pump is always electric.

Fuel rail - The hollow pipe, tube or manifold that delivers fuel at system pressure to the injectors. The fuel rail also serves as the mounting point for the upper ends of the injectors, and for the damper (if equipped) and the pressure regulator.

Fuel rich/lean - A qualitative evaluation of air/fuel ratio based on an air/fuel value known as stoichiometry or 14.7:1. This is determined by a voltage signal from the oxygen sensor. An excess of oxygen (lean) is a voltage of less than .4 volts. A rich condition is indicated by a voltage of greater than .6 volts.

Fuel system monitor - The PCM monitors Short-Term Fuel Trim (STFT) and Long-Term Fuel Trim (LTFT) to calculate the total fuel correction needed to maintain closed loop operation. The PCM uses the fuel system monitor to watch STFT and LTFT. The fuel system monitor runs only when the engine is warmed up, the system is in closed loop, the signals from all sensors (MAP, ECT, IAT, TPS, VSS, BARO, RPM, etc.) are present, and long-term and short-term fuel trim data is available and within design parameters. The fuel system monitor is another continuous monitor, like the misfire monitor and the Comprehensive Component Monitor (CCM).

Full-load - The load condition of the engine when the throttle is wide open. Full-load can occur at any rpm.

Full-load enrichment - The extra fuel injected during acceleration to enrich the mixture when the throttle is wide open. On some systems, the computer goes open-loop during full-load enrichment.

Functionality test - One of the tests that the Comprehensive Component Monitor (CCM) runs continuously. The functionality test simply monitors certain sensor circuits for electrical continuity and out-of-range readings. A functionality test is similar to the type of scrutiny imposed on the sensor circuits by an OBD-I computer.

Fuse - A device containing a soft piece of metal which melts and breaks the circuit when it is overloaded.

Fusible link - A device that protects a circuit from damage if a short to ground occurs or if the polarity of the battery or charger is reversed.

G

Galvanic battery - The principle of operation of an oxygen sensor; a galvanic battery generates a direct current voltage as a result of a chemical reaction.

Gasohol - A blend of ethanol and unleaded gasoline, usually at a one to nine ratio.

Generate - To produce electricity by electromagnetic induction.

G-lader - A type of supercharger pump which compresses air by squeezing it through an internal spiral, then forcing it through ports in the engine.

Goose - A brief opening and closing of the throttle (Dynamic Response Test)

Ground - In automobile terms is refer to the negative side of the electrical system, examples are battery negative post and/or cable chassis and engine block.

Gulp valve - A valve used in an air injection system to prevent backfire. During deceleration it redirects air from the air pump to the intake manifold where the air leans out the rich air-fuel mixture.

H

Hall Effect pick-up assembly - This device performs the same job as a pick up coil and reluctor. The Hall Effect pick-up is usually mounted in the distributor and is stationary. Some are used for sensing crankshaft or camshaft position, such as General Motors Computer-Controlled Coil Ignition (C3i) system. The shutter blades (reluctor component) are mounted to the rotor and turn with the rotor. The blades (one for each cylinder) pass through the pick-up switch. As this happens the magnetic field is strengthened, sending a signal to the electronic control unit.

Headers - Exhaust manifolds on high-performance engines that reduce back-pressure by using larger passages with gentle curves.

Hertz (Hz) - A measure of frequency, measured in cycles per second.

Hg (Mercury) - A calibration material used as a standard for vacuum measurement.

High impedance DVOM - This voltmeter has high opposition to the flow of electrical current. It is good for reading circuits with low current flow as found in electronic systems. It allows a test to be made without affecting the circuit.

High-speed surge - A sudden increase in engine speed caused by high manifold vacuum pulling in an excess air-fuel mixture.

High-Swirl Combustion (HSC) chamber - A combustion chamber in which the intake valve is shrouded or masked to direct the incoming air-fuel charge and create turbulence that will circulate the mixture more evenly and rapidly.

Hot start - Starting the engine when it's at or near its normal operating temperature.

Horsepower - The rate of doing work. A common measure of engine output.

Hot-wire sensor - See air mass sensor.

Hydrocarbon (HC) - A chemical compound made up of hydrogen and carbon. Gasoline, itself, is a hydrocarbon compound. HC is a toxic byproduct of incomplete combustion, which can be caused by misfires, preignition, detonation, etc. Hydrocarbons can also escape in the form of vapors from a leaking fuel system component or from the Evaporative Emissions Control (EVAP) system. Most HC is converted into harmless H_2O and CO_2 by the oxidation catalyst.

I

Ideal air-fuel ratio - See stoichiometric ratio.

Idle limiter - A device to control minimum and maximum idle fuel richness. The idler limiter is intended to prevent unauthorized persons from making overly rich idle adjustments.

Idle-speed stabilizer - An electronically-controlled air bypass around the throttle. Also referred to as an idle speed actuator or a constant idle system.

Ignition coil - A device which transfers electrical energy from one circuit to another. Two wound coils of wire with different diameters, usually around an iron core. One coil wire uses more turns than the other coil of wire. This produces an output voltage greater than the input voltage.

Ignition interval (firing interval) - The number of degrees of crankshaft rotation between ignition sparks.

Ignitor - The term used by foreign automobile manufactures for an ignition module.

Impedance - The total opposition a circuit offers to the flow of current. It includes resistance and reactance and is measured in ohms (i.e. 10 megohms).

Impeller - A rotor or rotor blade (vane) used to force a gas or liquid in a certain direction under pressure.

Induction - the production of an electrical voltage in a conductor or coil by moving the conductor or coil through a magnetic field, or by moving the magnetic field past the conductor or coil.

Inductive Discharge Ignition - A method of igniting the air-fuel mixture in an engine cylinder. It is based on the induction of a high voltage in the secondary winding of a coil.

Inert gas - A gas that will not undergo chemical reaction.

Infinity reading - A reading of an ohmmeter that indicates an open circuit or an infinite resistance.

Information - Electrical signals received by the computer, sent by the sensors

In-Hg - Inches of mercury. Used to express the measurement of pressure or vacuum. See barometric pressure.

Injection pressure - In Bosch CIS, the pressure of the fuel in the lines between the differential-pressure valves and the injectors. Also referred to as injector fuel.

Injection valve - See injector.

Injector - This device opens to spray fuel into the throttle bore (throttle body injection) or into the intake port (electronic port injection systems and continuous injection systems). Electronic injectors are opened by an electric solenoid and closed by a spring; continuous injectors are opened by fuel pressure and closed by a spring. Injectors are also referred to as injection valves.

Injector fuel - See injection pressure.

Input conditioning - The process of amplifying or converting a voltage signal into a form usable by the computer's central processing unit.

Input sensors - A device which monitors an engine operating condition and sends a voltage signal to the control unit. This variable voltage signal varies in accordance with the changes in the condition being monitored. There can be anywhere from half a dozen to two dozen sensors on an engine, depending on the sophistication of the system.

Insulator - Any material which is a poor conductor of electricity or heat.

Integral coil - This is an ignition coil that is build compact enough to be placed inside the distributor cap as opposed to being a separate component from the distributor.

Integrator - The ability of the computer to make short-term corrections in fuel metering.

Intercooler - An air-to-air or air-to-liquid heat exchanger used to lower the temperature of the air-fuel mixture by removing heat from the intake air charge.

Intermittent - Occurs now and then (not continuously). In electrical circuits, it refers to an occasional open, short, or ground.

Ionize - To break up molecules into two or more oppositely charged ions. The air gap between the spark plug electrode is ionized when the air-fuel mixture is charged from a nonconductor to a conductor.

J

Jumper wire - Used to bypass sections of a circuit. The simplest type is a length of electrical wire with an alligator clip at each end.

K

K-Jetronic - K-Jetronic is the term used by Bosch to describe the original continuous injection system. The K is short for kontinuerlich, the German word for "continuous." Airflow is measured by a circular plate inside the airflow sensor part of the mixture control unit. Fuel delivery was purely mechanical, in relation to airflow, until 1980, i.e. there were no electronics used in the K-Jet system. VW, Audi and Mercedes refer to K-Jet as CIS.

K-Jetronic with Lambda - This second-generation K-Jet system, which began in 1980, uses a feedback loop consisting of an oxygen sensor and a control unit to provide some electronic control of the air-fuel mixture. This system is also referred to as "CIS with Lambda." "Lambda" is the Bosch term for an oxygen sensor.

KE-Jetronic - This third-generation K-Jet system combines mechanical control with electronic regulation of the mixture. Many of the sensors it uses are the same as those used in L-Jetronic systems. VW, Audi and Mercedes refer to it as CIS-E.

KE-Motronic - This Bosch system is similar to KE-Jetronic, except that it has ignition-timing control and all the other features as any other Motronic system. See Motronic.

Keep Alive Memory - More frequently known as KAM, records the trouble codes of a malfunction, also records what is going on in the engine managing system every second. Power failure such as disconnecting the battery will erase its memory.

Kilohertz (kHz) - 1000 Hertz (Hz), the unit of frequency. See Hertz.

Kilopascal (kPa) - 1,000 Pascal, a unit of pressure. 100 kPa = Atmospheric Pressure at sea level.

Knock - A sudden increase in cylinder pressure caused by preignition of some of the air-fuel mixture as the flame front moves out from the spark plug ignition point. Pressure waves in the combustion chamber crash into the piston or cylinder walls. The result is a sound known as knock or pinging. Knock can be caused by using fuel with an octane rating that's too low, overheating, by excessively advanced ignition timing, or by a compression ratio that's been raised by hot carbon deposits on the piston or cylinder head.

Knock sensor - A vibration sensor mounted on the cylinder block that generates a voltage when the knock (detonation) occurs. The voltage signals the control unit, which alters the ignition timing by retarding it (and on turbocharged vehicles, limits boost) to stop the knock.

L

L-Jetronic - L-Jetronic is the term used by Bosch to describe a fuel injection system controlled by the air flowing through a sensor with a movable vane, or flap, which indicates engine load. The L is short for luft, the German word for "air." Later versions of L-Jet are equipped with a Lambda (oxygen) sensor for better mixture control. Bosch originally used the term Air-Flow Controlled (AFC) Injection to denote L-Jet systems in order to differentiate them from pressure-controlled D-Jetronic systems.

LH-Jetronic - Bosch LH-Jetronic systems measure air mass (weight of air) with a hot-wire sensor instead of measuring airflow with a vane, or flap, type air volume sensor used on L-Jet systems. The H is short for heiss, the German word for "hot."

LH-Motronic - This Bosch system is the same as any other Motronic system, except that it uses a hot-wire air-mass sensor (L is short for luft, the German word for "air" and H is short for heiss, which means "hot," hence hot wire). LH-Motronic systems also have idle stabilization.

Lambda (l) - Expresses the air/fuel ratio in terms of the stoichiometric ratio compared to the oxygen content of the exhaust. At the stoichiometric ratio, when all of the fuel is burned with all of the air in the combustion chamber, the oxygen content of the exhaust is said to be at lambda = 1. If there's excess oxygen in the exhaust (a lean mixture), then lambda is greater than 1 (l > 1); if there's an excess of fuel in the exhaust (a shortage of air - a rich mixture), then lambda is less than 1 (l < 1).

Lambda control - Bosch's term for a closed-loop system that adjusts the air-fuel ratio to lambda = 1, based on sensing the amount of excess oxygen in the exhaust.

Lambda control valve - See frequency valve.

Lambda sensor - Bosch's term for the oxygen sensor. See oxygen sensor.

Lean mixture - A fuel mixture that has more air than required (or not enough fuel) for a stoichiometric ratio.

Lean surge - A change in rpm caused by an extremely lean fuel mixture.

Light Emitting Diode (LED) - A gallium-arsenide diode that emits energy as light. Often used in automotive indicators.

"Limp-in", "limp-home" or limp-mode - used by many manufacturers to explain the driveability characteristics of a failed computer system. Many computer systems store information that can be used to get the vehicle to a repair facility. In this mode of operation, driveability is greatly reduced.

Linear - Any mathematically expressed relationship whose graphical representation is a straight line in the Cartesian coordinate system.

Liquid/vapor separator valve - A valve in some EEC fuel systems that separates liquid fuel from fuel vapors.

Load - The amount of work the engine must do. When the vehicle accelerates quickly from a standstill, or from a low speed, the engine is placed under a heavy load.

Lobes - The rounded protrusions on a camshaft that force, and govern, the opening of the intake and exhaust valves.

Logic module - See control module.

Logic probe - A simple hand-held device used to confirm the operational characteristics of a logic (On/Off) circuit.

Long-Term Fuel Trim (LTFT) - When the PCM runs the fuel system monitor during closed-loop operation, LTFT is one of the two factors used by the PCM to calculate the total fuel correction needed to maintain closed-loop (Short-Term Fuel Trim, or STFT is the other factor). When STFT is no longer used to keep the fuel system in closed-loop with minor corrections to the injector pulse-width, LTFT moves the baseline value stored in PCM memory closer to the corrections that are actually needed. These changes in long-term fuel corrections can only be stored in PCM memory when the system is already in closed-loop, and they remain in memory even after the engine is turned off.

Lucas Bosch - This system, used in Jaguars and Triumphs, is a Bosch L-Jetronic system licensed for production by Lucas.

M

Magnetic field - The area in which magnetic lines of forces exist.

Magnetic pick-up coil - Coil used in the electronic distributor ignition system to determine exactly when to switch off the coil secondary.

Magnetic pulse generator - A signal-generating switch that creates a voltage pulse as magnetic flux changes around a pickup coil.

Magnetic reluctance - That quality in a substance or material which tends to impede the flow of a magnetic field.

Magnetic saturation - The condition when a magnetic field reaches full strength and maximum flux density.

Malfunction Indicator Light (MIL) - An emissions warning light on the instrument cluster that tells the driver or mechanic that the PCM has stored a Diagnostic Trouble Code (DTC). Formerly referred to as the "Check Engine" light, the "Service Engine Soon" light and various other names, the term "Malfunction Indicator Light" (or its acronym, MIL) was adopted by manufacturers as the standard term for this light in 1996, the year that OBD-II began. Many people still continue to refer to the MIL by one of its old names, but the SAE J1930 list of standardized terminology makes clear that the term everyone should be using is MIL.

Manifold Absolute Pressure (MAP) - Manifold pressure measured on the absolute pressure scale, an indication of engine load.

Manifold Pressure Controlled (MPC) - A fuel injection system which determines engine load based on intake manifold pressure.

Manifold Tune Valve Solenoid - When engaged, alters the internal shape and air flow of the manifold in order to increase low end engine torque.

Manifold vacuum - Low pressure in an engine's intake manifold, located below the carburetor or TBI throttle plate.

Map - A pictorial representation of a series of data points stored in the memory of the control unit of systems with complete engine management. The control unit refers to the map to control variables such as fuel injection pulse width and ignition timing, an indication of engine load.

Mass - The amount of matter contained in an object or a volume. Also a measure of that object's resistance to acceleration. In the field of earth gravity, mass is roughly equivalent to the weight of the object or volume. In fuel injection terms, a measured air volume is corrected for temperature and density to determine its mass.

Matured fault - Once a *maturing* fault has exceeded the specified threshold for its reoccurrence - it could be a certain number of times or a certain duration of time during which it occurs - it *matures* into a full-blown fault, at which point the PCM stores a DTC and turns on the MIL.

Maturing fault - Also referred to as a *pending* fault. When the PCM detects a fault in a sensor or circuit the first time, it will store the fault in its memory, but it might or might not display the MIL, depending on how the software in the PCM was written. Each manufacturer has its own criteria for determining whether a fault is an isolated anomaly, an intermittent problem or a serious ongoing problem. A maturing fault is a "problem-in-the-making." It's not a full-blown problem yet, but it looks like it's headed that way, so the PCM stores the fault and keeps an eye on things for awhile. If the same fault occurs again or a third or fourth time the PCM, at some point, depending on the software, stores the DTC and displays the MIL. Once the maturing fault or code reaches this point, it's known as a *matured* fault or code.

Metering slits - In Bosch CIS, the narrow slits in the control-plunger barrel of the fuel distributor. Fuel flows through the slits in accordance with the lift of the control plunger and the pressure drop at the slits.

Methanol - Methyl alcohol distilled from wood or made from natural gas.

Micron - A unit of length equal to one millionth of a meter, one one-thousandth of a millimeter.

Milliampere (mA) - One one-thousandth of one ampere. The current flow to the pressure actuator in KE systems is measured in milliamps.

Misfire - Failure of the air-fuel mixture to ignite during the power stroke.

Misfire monitor - The misfire monitor is one of the more critical, if not *the* most critical, of all the monitors, because it watches for misfires, which are the number one catalyst killers. How does the misfire monitor work? Basically, it monitors the speed of the crankshaft. Every time a cylinder fires, the crank speeds up; every time a cylinder misfires, the crank slows down. The Crankshaft Position (CKP) sensor sends a signal to the PCM based on crank speed. If the signal is consistent in amplitude and frequency, everything is simpatico. But when the PCM detects a drop in crank speed after a certain cylinder fires (or after several cylinders fire), it stores a DTC. If the variation in crank speed is below a specified threshold, the PCM might not display the MIL until the second time that this event occurs. If the variation in crank speed is above that threshold (i.e. a gross misfire) the MIL begins flashing immediately to alert the driver to get the vehicle to a dealer for immediate attention.

Mixture control unit - In Bosch CIS, the collective term for the airflow sensor plate and the fuel distributor, which are integrated into a single component.

Mixture control (M/C) solenoid - Device, installed in computer controlled carburetors, which regulates the air/fuel ratio.

Mode - A particular state of operation.

Module - A self-contained, sealed unit that houses the solid-state circuits which control certain electrical or mechanical functions.

Monitor - A type of test conducted by an OBD-II PCM on certain subsystems and components to verify that they're working correctly. Typically, there are monitors for misfires, the fuel system, the oxygen sensors, the catalytic converter(s), the EVAP system, the EGR system and (if still equipped) the AIR system. There's also a Comprehensive Component Monitor (CCM), which detects failed sensor input and output circuits not already monitored by one of the other monitors. The CCM, fuel and misfire monitors run continuously, while the other monitors run only when all the enabling criteria are present.

Monolithic substrate - The substrate is the ceramic grid, inside a three-way catalytic converter, which is coated with the catalyzing material that reduces three toxic pollutants - HC, CO and NOx - into harmless substances. There are actually two catalysts inside a three-way converter. The reduction catalyst, which is located in the front part of the converter housing, separates NOx into nitrogen and oxygen molecules. The substrate inside this part of the converter is coated with platinum and rhodium. The oxidation catalyst, which is located in the rear part of the converter housing, oxidizes (adds oxygen to) HC and CO to convert them into CO_2 and H_2O. The substrate inside this part of the converter is coated with platinum and palladium.

Motronic - This term is used by Bosch to denote its engine management systems. The original Motronic system combined L-Jetronic with electronic ignition timing control in one control unit. Most Motronic-equipped engines also have electronic idle stabilization. Around 1986, Motronic systems got: Knock regulation by ignition timing of individual cylinders; adaptive circuitry, which adapts fuel delivery and ignition timing to actual conditions; diagnostic circuitry which enables the control unit to recognize system faults and store fault information in its memory. Motronic has also been integrated with KE-Jetronic systems, and is referred to as KE-Motronic.

Multigrade - An oil that has been tested at more than one temperature, and so has more than one SAE viscosity number.

Multi-Point Fuel Injection (MPFI) - A fuel injection system that uses one injector per cylinder, mounted on the engine to spray fuel near the intake valve area or the combustion chamber. Also referred to as Multi-Port Injection.

Mutual induction - The transfer of energy between two unconnected conductors, caused by the expanding or contracting magnetic flux lines of the current carrying conductor.

N

Negative ground electrical system - An automotive electrical system in which the battery negative terminal is connected to ground.

Negative polarity - Also called ground polarity. A correct polarity of the ignition coil connections. Coil voltage is delivered to the spark plugs so that the center electrode of the spark is negatively charged and the grounded electrode is positively charged.

Negative Temperature Coefficient (NTC) - A term used to describe a thermistor (temperature sensor) in which the resistance decreases as the temperature increases. The thermistors used on fuel injection systems are nearly all NTCs.

Noble metals - Metals that resist oxidation, such as platinum and palladium.

Normally aspirated - An engine that uses normal engine vacuum to draw in its air-fuel mixture. Not supercharged or turbocharged.

O

Octane rating - The measurement of the anti-knock value of a gasoline.

Ohm - An electrical unit used for measuring resistance, one ohm is the amount of resistance required for one volt to produce one ampere of electrical current.

Oil galleries - Passages in the block and head that carry oil under pressure to various parts of the engine.

On-Board Diagnostics (OBD) - This term refers to the ability of the computer system to analyze and verify the operational ability of itself.

Open circuit - A circuit which does not provide a complete path for the flow of current.

Open loop - An operational mode during which "default" (preprogrammed) values in the control unit memory are used to determine the air/fuel ratio, injection timing, etc., instead of "real" sensor inputs. The system goes into open loop during cold-engine operation, or when a particular sensor malfunctions and does not respond to feedback signals from the EGO sensor.

Orifice - The calibrated fuel delivery hole at the nozzle end of the fuel injector.

Oscillating - Moving back and forth with a steady rhythm.

Oxidation - The combination of an element with oxygen in a chemical process that often produces extreme heat as a byproduct.

Oxidation catalyst - The oxidation catalyst is the second of the two catalysts located inside a three-way catalytic converter. The oxidation catalyst, which is coated with platinum and palladium, oxidizes (adds oxygen to) HC and CO, which converts them into carbon dioxide (CO_2) and water (H_2O).

Oxide of Nitrogen (NOx) - Chemical compounds of nitrogen given off by an internal combustion engine. They combine with hydrocarbons to produce smog. NOx formation is affected by combustion chamber temperatures.

Oxygen sensor - A sensor, mounted in the exhaust manifold or exhaust pipe, that reacts to changes in the oxygen content of the exhaust gases. The voltage generated by the oxygen sensor is monitored by the control unit.

Oxygen sensor monitor - During closed-loop operation, the oxygen sensor monitor determines whether the upstream oxygen sensor is in good shape. First, it looks at how fast the oxygen sensor heater brings the oxygen sensor up to its normal operating temperature. Then it watches the voltage output level of the oxygen sensor, which must be high enough when the system is rich and low enough when the system is lean. Third, it watches how fast the oxygen sensor responds. Fourth, it watches oxygen sensor voltage levels that remain too high or too low, indicating a short or high resistance, respectively. If the oxygen sensor or circuit fails any of these tests, the oxygen sensor monitor fails.

Ozone - Ozone (O_3) is an allotrope (a structurally differentiated form) of oxygen that's derived or formed naturally from diatomic (made up of two atoms) oxygen by electric discharge or by exposure to ultraviolet radiation. Ozone is found in two places. Stratospheric ozone is the "good" ozone that forms a belt around the earth about 20 miles up. Because of its unique ability to filter out ultraviolet radiation from the sun, stratospheric ozone is the type of ozone that you heard or read about in the Nineties because it was being depleted by the chlorofluorocarbons (CFCs) in R-12 air conditioning refrigerant. Ground level ozone is the same stuff but it's the "bad" ozone because it's unhealthy for human beings. When ground level ozone and *volatile organic compounds* (VOCs), the vapors from different types of solvents, are mixed together with sunlight, you get *photochemical smog*.

P

Parallel circuit - A circuit with more than one path for the current to follow.

Particulates - Liquid or solid particles such as lead and carbon that are given off by an internal combustion engine as pollution.

Part-load - The throttle opening between idle and fully-open.

Part load enrichment - Extra fuel injected during throttle opening to enrich the mixture during transition. Usually occurs during closed-loop operation.

PCM timer - When you start the engine, the PCM timer starts its countdown. When the timer indicates to the PCM that the specified amount of time has elapsed since start-up, the PCM knows that the upstream oxygen sensor is ready to put out an accurate voltage signal in response to changes in the amount of oxygen in the exhaust stream. At this point the PCM puts the fuel system in closed-loop operation and starts monitoring the oxygen sensor. The PCM also puts a stopwatch on other critical sensors, such as the Engine Coolant Temperature (ECT) sensor, which must satisfy enabling criteria within a specified time.

Pending - If a defective or non-operational information sensor is a mandatory component of running a monitor, the Diagnostic Executive doesn't run the test *pending* repair or replacement of the sensor and/or its circuit.

Percolation - The bubbling and expansion of a liquid. Similar to boiling.

Photochemical smog - A combination of pollutants which, when acted upon by sunlight, forms chemical compounds that are harmful to human, animal, and plant life. When ground level ozone, nitrogen dioxide (NO_2) and volatile organic compounds (VOCs), which are the vapors from various solvents, are mixed together with sunlight, you get photochemical smog.

Pick-up coil - The pick-up coil is a coil of fine wire mounted to a permanent magnet. The pick-up coil develops a field that is sensitive to ferrous metal (like a reluctor). As the reluctor passes the pick-up coil, a small alternating current is produced. This alternating current is sent to the electronic control unit. The pick-up coil is sometimes called a stator or sensor.

Piezoelectric - Voltage caused by physical pressure applied to the faces of certain crystals.

Piezoresistive - A sensor whose resistance varies in relation to pressure or force applied to it. A piezoresistive sensor receives a constant reference voltage and returns a variable signal in relation to its varying resistance.

Pintle - In an injector, the tip of the needle that opens to allow pressurized fuel through the spray orifice. The shape of the pintle and the orifice determines the spray pattern of the atomized fuel.

Plenum - A chamber that stabilizes the air-fuel mixture and allows it to rise to a pressure slightly above atmospheric pressure.

Plunger - See control plunger.

Poppet valve - A valve that plugs and unplugs its opening by axial motion.

Ported vacuum - The low-pressure area (vacuum) just above the throttle in a carburetor.

Port injection - A fuel injection system in which the fuel is sprayed by individual injectors into each intake port, upstream of the intake valve.

Positive Crankcase Ventilation (PCV) - A way of controlling engine emissions by directing crankcase vapors (blow-by) back through an engine's intake system.

Positive ground electrical system - An automotive electrical system in which the battery positive terminal is connected to ground.

Positive polarity - Also called reverse polarity. An incorrect polarity of the ignition coil connections. Coil voltage is delivered to the spark plugs so that the center electrode of the spark plugs is positively charged and the grounded electrode is negatively charged.

Positive Temperature Coefficient (PTC) - A term used to describe a thermistor (temperature sensor) in which the resistance increases as the temperature increases. The thermistors used on most fuel injection systems are negative temperature coefficient (NTC) but a few Chryslers and some mid-80s Cadillacs used PTCs.

Potentiometer - A variable resistor element that acts as a voltage divider to produce a continuously variable output signal proportional to a mechanical position.

Power loss lamp - This was the term given to the instrument panel-mounted lamp on early Chrysler vehicles. It functions in the same manner as the Check Engine Light.

Power module - On Chryslers, the power module works in conjunction with the logic module. The power module is the primary power supply for the EFI system.

Pre-ignition - An engine condition in which the air-fuel mixture ignites prematurely due to excessive combustion chamber temperature.

Pressure actuator - On Bosch KE-Jetronic and KE-Motronic systems, an electronically-controlled hydraulic valve, affixed to the mixture-control unit, that regulates fuel flow through the lower chambers of the differential-pressure valves. The pressure actuator controls all adjustments to basic fuel metering and air-fuel ratio to compensate for changing operating conditions. Also referred to as a differential-pressure regulator and as an electro-hydraulic pressure actuator.

Pressure differential - A difference in pressure between two points.

Pressure drop - The difference in pressure where fuel metering occurs. In electronic injection systems, this is the difference between fuel system pressure and intake manifold pressure. In Bosch CIS, it's the difference between system pressure inside the control plunger and the pressure outside the slits, in the upper-chamber of the differential-pressure valves.

Pressure regulator - A spring-loaded diaphragm-type pressure-relief valve which controls the pressure of fuel delivered to the fuel injector(s) by returning excess fuel to the tank.

Pressure relief - What you must do to all fuel-injection systems before cracking a fuel line and opening up the system.

Pressure relief valve - Another name for the fuel-injection system test port.

Pressure tap - Another name for the fuel-injection system test port.

Primary circuit - The low voltage circuit in the ignition system. Sometimes 6 volts, but usually 12 volts.

Primary pressure - Another name for system pressure in a continuous injection system.

Processing - The computer receives information in the form of voltage and channels it through a logic electronic circuit according with the programmed instructions.

Programmable Read Only Memory - More commonly known as the PROM, carries all the particular information of the vehicle such as number of cylinders, weight, if it is automatic or standard, if it has fuel injection or carburetion, year built etc., and can't be changed from one vehicle to another, due to its peculiarities.

Pulse - An abrupt change in voltage whether positive or negative.

Pulse air system - Part of the emission control system that utilizes a reed-type check valve which allows air to be drawn into the exhaust system as a result of exhaust pulses.

Pulsed injection - A system that delivers fuel in intermittent pulses by the opening and closing of solenoid-controlled injectors. Also referred to as electronic fuel injection (EFI).

Pulse generator - Term used by foreign automobile manufactures for the pick-up coil. It generates signals or pulses, which are fed to the ignitor (ignition control unit). Sometime called signal generator.

Pulse period - The available time, depending on the speed of crankshaft rotation, for opening of pulsed solenoid injectors.

Pulse time - The amount of time that solenoid injectors are open to inject fuel. Also known as pulse width, especially when displayed on an oscilloscope as a voltage pattern.

Pulse width - The amount of time that a fuel injector is energized, measured in milliseconds. The duration of the pulse width is determined by the amount of fuel the engine needs at any time. The longer the pulse width, the richer the air-fuel mixture; the shorter the pulse width, the leaner the air/fuel mixture. During a cold start and subsequent warm-up period, the pulse width is fixed, i.e. it opens each time for the same time interval in accordance with a default setting in the PCM's map. When the PCM goes into closed-loop operation, the PCM begins to alter pulse width in response to the voltage signal(s) from the upstream oxygen sensor(s). Also referred to as pulse time.

Purge valve - A vacuum-operated valve used to draw fuel vapors from a vapor canister.

Push valve - In a continuous injection system, the push valve controls the return of fuel from the control-pressure regulator to the system-pressure regulator. When the engine is shut off, the push valve closes the control pressure circuit.

R

Random-Access Memory (RAM) - Temporary short-term or long term computer memory that can be read and changed, but is lost whenever power is shut off to the computer.

Ratio - The proportion of one value divided by another.

Rationality test - One of the tests that the Comprehensive Component Monitor (CCM) runs continuously. The CCM scrutinizes every circuit that it monitors to ensure *that it makes sense*. In other words, if one sensor circuit contradicts another circuit, it's flagged by the CCM as irrational and it fails the rationality test. But it doesn't necessarily turn on the MIL the first time that the CCM identifies a rationality failure. For example, if one sensor input contradicts another sensor input, even though both sensor circuits are within their specified operating ranges, the CCM software might wait for the anomaly to occur a *second* time before displaying the MIL. Why? Because sometimes an aberration like this that's detected by the CCM goes away the next trip, never to return again. Turning on the MIL too soon will only send the owner to the service department needlessly.

Reach - The length of the spark plug shell from the seat to the bottom of the shell.

Readiness flags - If a vehicle is started and run and if it satisfies all the enabling criteria needed to run all the monitors, and if it passes every test, the Diagnostic Executive puts a check mark next to the all of the monitors to indicate that they have passed. These check marks are commonly referred to as readiness flags.

Read Only Memory (ROM) - The permanent part of a computer's memory storage function. ROM can be read but not changed, and is retained when power is shut off to the computer.

Reciprocating engine - Also called piston engine. An engine in which the pistons move up and down or back and forth, as a result of combustion in the top of the piston cylinder.

Recombinant - A non-gassing battery design in which the oxygen released by the electrolyte recombines with the negative plates.

Rectified - Electrical current changed from alternating (A.C.) to direct (D.C.).

Reduction - A chemical process in which oxygen is taken away from a compound.

Reduction catalyst - The reduction catalyst is the first of the two catalysts located inside a three-way catalytic converter. The reduction catalyst, which is coated with platinum and rhodium, reduces NOx to nitrogen and oxygen.

Reed valve - A one-way check valve. A reed, or flap, opens to admit a fluid or gas under pressure from one direction, while closing to deny movement from the opposite direction.

Reference voltage - A constant voltage signal (below battery voltage) applied to a sensor by the computer. The sensor alters the voltage according to engine operating conditions and return it as a variable input signal to the computer which adjusts the system operation accordingly.

Relative pressure - In electronic injection systems, the difference in pressure between fuel pressure in the injector(s) and pressure in the intake manifold.

Relay - A switching device operated by a low current circuit which controls the opening and closing of another circuit of higher current capacity.

Relief valve - A pressure limiting valve located in the exhaust chamber of the thermactor air pump. It functions to relieve part of the exhaust air flow if the pressure exceeds a calibrated value.

Reluctance - The resistance that a magnetic circuit offers to lines of force in a magnetic field.

Reluctor - This is a piece of ferrous metal that resembles a wheel with spokes or teeth. It is sometimes called an armature, timing core or trigger wheel. Whatever it is called, the function is the same. As it rotates, the spokes or teeth pass a pick-up coil which generates a small alternating current.

Reserve capacity rating - A battery rating based on the number of minutes a battery at 80 degrees F can supply 25 amperes, with no battery cell falling bellow 1.75 volts.

Residual pressure - Fuel pressure maintained within the system after engine shutdown.

Resistance - Opposition to electrical current flow.

Resistor - Any electrical circuit element that provides resistance in a circuit.

Resistor type spark plugs - A plug that has a resistor in the center electrode to reduce the inductive portion of the spark discharge.

Response time - This term refers to the length of time that it takes an oxygen sensor to switch from rich to lean or lean to rich. Once the system is in closed loop, the oxygen sensor is monitored by the oxygen sensor monitor, which watches over, among other things, a fast response time from the oxygen sensor. The response time must be fast enough to provide the PCM with timely data so that it can alter the pulse-width of the fuel injectors quickly enough to keep the air/fuel mixture ratio at the ideal ratio of 14.7:1.

Rest pressure - Fuel pressure maintained within the fuel system after the engine has been shut down.

Rich mixture - Not enough air or too much fuel is drawn into the engine to maintain a stoichiometric ratio. There's still fuel left after the combustion process.

Road draft tube - The earliest type of crankcase ventilation; it vented blow-by gases to the atmosphere.

Runners - The passages in the intake manifold that connects the manifold's plenum chamber to the engine's inlet ports.

S

SAE viscosity grade - A system of numbers signifying an oil's viscosity at a specific temperature; assigned by the Society of Automotive Engineers.

Scavenging - A slight suction caused by a vacuum drop through a well designed exhaust header system. Scavenging helps pull exhaust gases out of an engine cylinder.

Secondary circuit - The high voltage circuit of the ignition system. Usually measured in thousands of volts (10,000 to as high as 80,000 volts).

Semiconductor - A semiconductor is simply a material that conducts electricity only when the conditions are right. Two basic types of semiconductors are used in the automobiles, they are the diodes and transistors types.

Sensor - A device which monitors an engine operating condition and sends a voltage signal to the control unit. This variable voltage signal varies in accordance with the changes in the condition being monitored. There can be anywhere from half a dozen to two dozen sensors on an engine, depending on the sophistication of the system.

Sensor plate - In Bosch CIS, the flat, round plate, bolted to a lever arm, which rises and falls with the flow of air through the airflow sensor, raising and lowering the control plunger in the fuel distributor.

Sensor test mode - This mode of diagnosis is used to read the output signal of a specific sensor when the engine is not running. Specific codes are used to select a specific sensor on the SCAN Tool. The output of this mode is actual output of the selected sensor (temperature, voltage, speed, etc.).

Sequential Electronic Fuel Injection (SEFI), or Sequential Fuel Injection (SFI) - A fuel injection system which uses a micro-computer to determine and control the amount of fuel required by, and injected into, a particular engine in the same sequence as engine firing sequence.

Series circuit - A circuit with only one path for the current to flow.

Series-parallel circuit - A circuit in which some loads are wired in series and some loads are wired in parallel.

Short circuit - An undesirable connection between a circuit and any other point.

Short-Term Fuel Trim (STFT) - When the PCM runs the fuel system monitor, STFT is one of the two factors used by the PCM to calculate the total fuel correction needed to maintain closed loop operation (Long-Term Fuel Trim, or LTFT, is the other factor). Based on information from certain sensors (MAP, ECT, IAT, TPS, VSS, BARO, RPM, etc.) STFT adjusts injector pulse-width to keep the system in closed loop. The system starts at a baseline value, then goes richer or leaner from there. If everything is running smoothly, these corrections are small. But STFT can only go so far. If the system gets too lean or too rich, the STFT corrections alone won't keep the system in closed loop. At that point, the LTFT comes into play (see *Long-Term Fuel Trim*). Short-term fuel corrections are erased from the PCM memory each time that the engine is turned off.

Signal - Another name for vacuum transmitted from one location, or component, to another.

Single grade - An oil that has been tested at only one temperature, and so has only one SAE viscosity number.

Sintered - Welded together without using heat to form a porous material, such as the metal disc used in some vacuum delay valves.

Siphoning - The flowing of liquid as a result of pressure differential, without the aid of a mechanical pump.

Slit - See metering slits.

"Soft" fault code - A circuit or component failure that does not reappear after you clear the codes and retest the system.

Solenoid - An electromagnetic actuator consisting of an electrical coil with a hollow center and an iron piece, the armature, that moves into the coil when it is energized. Solenoids are used to open fuel injectors and many other output actuators on fuel-injected vehicles.

Solenoid valve - A valve operated by a solenoid.

Solid-state - A method of controlling electrical current flow, in which the parts are primarily made of semiconductor materials.

Spark advance - Causing spark to occur earlier.

Spark retard - Causing less spark advance to be added, resulting in a spark which is introduced later.

Spark timing - A way of controlling exhaust emissions by controlling ignition timing. Vacuum advance is delayed or shut off at low and medium speeds, reducing NOx and HC emissions.

Spark voltage - The inductive portion of a spark that maintains the spark in the air gap between a spark plug's electrodes. Usually about one-quarter of the firing voltage level.

Specific gravity - The ratio of a weight of any volume of a substance to the weight of an equal volume of water. When battery electrolyte (acid) is tested, the result is the specific gravity of the electrolyte.

Starting bypass - A parallel circuit branch that bypasses the ballast resistor during engine cranking.

Starting safety switch - A neutral start switch. It keeps the starting system from operating when a car's transmission is in gear.

Stator - This is another name for a pick-up coil. The stator is sometimes called a pick-up coil, a sensor or a Hall Effect pick-up. See Pick-up coil.

Stepper motor - Digital devices actuators (motors) that work with DC current, that move in a fixed amount of increments from the off position.

Stoichiometric ratio - The ideal air/fuel mixture ratio (14.7:1) at which the best compromise between engine performance (richer mixture) and economy and low exhaust emissions (leaner mixture) is obtained. All of the air and all of the fuel is burned inside the combustion chamber.

Storage - The programmed instructions are stored in computer electronic memory.

Stratified charge engine - An engine that uses 2-stage combustion: first is the combustion of rich air-fuel mixture in a pre-combustion chamber, then combustion of a leaner air-fuel mixture occurs in the main combustion chamber.

Stroke - One complete top-to-bottom or bottom-to-top movement of an engine piston.

Sub oxygen sensor - The second oxygen sensor (after the catalytic converter), which monitors catalytic converter efficiency.

Substrate - The layer, or honey-comb, of aluminum oxide upon which the catalyst (platinum or palladium) in a catalytic converter is deposited.

Sulfation - The crystallization of lead sulfate on the plates of a constantly discharged battery.

Sulfur oxides - Chemical compounds given off by processing and burning gasoline and other fossil fuels. As they decompose, they combine with water to form sulfuric acid.

Supercharging - Use of an air pump to deliver an air-fuel mixture to the engine cylinders at a pressure greater than atmospheric pressure.

Suspend - If the Diagnostic Executive knows that it needs a correctly functioning information sensor to run a monitor, but a monitor is already running for the needed sensor, the Diagnostic Executive will *suspend* the second monitor until the monitor for the needed sensor is completed.

Switches - Are one of the simplest functions of sensors, they simply signal a condition of on/off.

Synthetic motor oil - Lubricants formed by artificially combining molecules of petroleum and other materials.

System pressure - The fuel pressure in the fuel lines and at the pressure regulator, created by the fuel pump.

System pressure regulator - In a continuous injection system, holds system fuel pressure constant.

T

Task Manager - Chrysler's term for the software that decides whether enabling criteria are present and that manages the sequence for running different monitors. See *Diagnostic Executive* (which is the term that we use in this manual).

Television-Radio-Suppression (TVRS) Cables - High-resistance, carbon-conductor ignition cables that suppress Radio Frequency Interference (RFI).

Temperature inversion - A weather pattern in which a layer or "lid" of warm air keeps the cooler air beneath it from rising.

Temperature sensor - A special type of solid-state resistor, known as a thermistor. Used to sense coolant and, on some systems, air temperature also. See thermistor.

Test port - The Schrader valve fitting located on the fuel rail of a port injection system. Used for relieving fuel pressure and for hooking up a fuel-pressure gauge.

Tetraethyl lead - A gasoline additive used to help prevent detonation.

Thermactor - A system for injection of air into the exhaust system to aid in the control of hydrocarbons and carbon monoxide in the exhaust.

Thermal cracking - A common oil refining process which uses heat to break down (crack) the larger components of the crude oil. The gasoline which is produced usually has a higher sulfur content than gasoline produced by catalytic cracking.

Thermistor - A special kind of resistor whose resistance decreases as its temperature increases. Thermistors are used for air and coolant temperature sensors. Also referred to as a Negative Temperature Coefficient (NTC) resistor. See temperature sensor.

Thermostatic - Referring to a device that automatically responds to temperature changes in order to activate a switch.

Throttle body - The carburetor-like aluminum casting that houses the throttle valve, the idle air bypass (if equipped), the throttle position sensor (TPS), the idle air control (IAC) motor, the throttle linkage and, on TBI systems, one or two injectors.

Throttle Body Injection (TBI) - Any of several injection systems which have the fuel injector(s) mounted in a centrally located throttle body, as opposed to positioning the injectors close to the intake ports.

Throttle valve - The movable plate, inside the throttle body, which is controlled by the accelerator pedal. The throttle valve controls the amount of air that can enter the engine.

Thyristor - A silicon-controlled rectifier (SCR) that normally blocks all current flow. A slight voltage applied to one layer of its semiconductor structure will allow current flow in one direction while blocking current flow in the other direction.

Time-in-run - The amount of time that the engine has been running.

Timing - Relationship between spark plug firing and piston position usually expressed in crankshaft degrees before (BTDC) or after (ATDC) top dead center of the piston.

Timing valve - See frequency valve.

Top Dead Center (TDC) - The exact top of a piston's stroke. Also is used for specifications when tuning an engine.

Total ignition advance - The sum of centrifugal advance, vacuum advance, and initial timing; expressed in crankshaft degrees.

T-Pin - A common type of sewing pin which is very useful in probing an electrical connector in order to make a test lead connection.

Transducer - A transducer converts or transduces a form of energy to another. All of the sensors or actuators are transducers.

Transistor - A three-terminal semiconductor used for current switching, detection, and amplification. Low current flows between another pair of terminals, with one common terminal.

Trigger wheel - This is another name for a reluctor or armature. It is a metallic timing device used in a system with a sensor. See reluctor.

Trip - Basically, the term "trip" refers to an engine start-up, followed by an appropriate length of time during which it runs, then a subsequent shutdown, which allows an OBD-II PCM to operate one or more of its monitors. But not all trips are the same to the PCM, which requires different enabling criteria to run different monitors. Some trips allow certain monitors to run, but not others. So an OBD-II trip is a start-up/run/shutdown cycle that meets the enabling criteria for a monitor to run.

Tuned Port Injection (TPI) - A General Motors fuel injection system that uses tuned air intake runners for improved airflow.

Turbo lag - The time interval required for a turbocharger to overcome inertia and spin up to speed.

Turbocharger - A supercharging device that uses exhaust gases to turn a turbine that forces extra air-fuel mixture into the cylinders.

V

Vacuum - Anything less than atmospheric pressure.

Vacuum advance - The use of engine vacuum to advance ignition spark timing by moving the distributor breaker plate.

Vacuum lock - A stoppage of fuel flow caused by insufficient air intake to the fuel tank.

Vacuum regulator - Provides constant vacuum output when the vehicle is at idle. Switches to engine vacuum at off idle.

Vaporization - Changing a liquid into a gas (vapor).

Vapor lock - A condition which occurs when the fuel becomes so hot that it vaporizes, slowing or stopping fuel flow in the fuel lines.

Variable dwell - The ignition dwell period varies in distributor degrees at different engine speeds, but remains relatively constant in duration or actual time.

Variable reluctance sensor - A non-contact transducer that converts mechanical motion into electrical control signals.

Varnish - An undesirable deposit, usually on engine pistons, formed by oxidation of fuel and of motor oil.

Venturi - A restriction in an airflow, such as in a carburetor or TBI, that speeds the airflow and creates a vacuum.

Venturi vacuum - Low pressure in the venturi of a carburetor, caused by the fast air flowing through the venturi.

Viscosity - The tendency of a liquid, such as oil, to resist flowing.

Volatility - The ease with which a liquid changes from a liquid to a gas vapor.

Volt - A unit of electrical pressure (electromotive force), which causes current to flow in a circuit. One volt causes one ampere of current to flow one ohm of resistance.

Voltage - The force (electromotive force) that moves electrons through a conductor. It can be visualized as the difference in electrical pressure. One volt moves one ampere of current through one ohm of resistance.

Voltage decay - The rapid oscillation and dissipation of secondary voltage after the spark in a spark plug air gap has stopped.

Voltage drop - The net difference in electrical pressure when measured across a resistance. Voltage drop is always measured in parallel.

Voltage reserve - The amount of coil voltage available in excess of the voltage required to fire the spark plug.

Volumetric Efficiency (VE) - Describes the efficiency of taking air into the cylinder. Taking 5.0L of air into a 5.0L engine is described as 100% volumetric efficiency. Must engines running at wide open throttle range from 70-80%. With a turbo/supercharger, compressing the intake air can raise it to over 100%.

W

Warm-up - In OBD-II, a warm-up consists of starting and running the engine until the engine coolant temperature reaches 160 degrees Fahrenheit AND the PCM sees an increase of at least 40 degrees Fahrenheit in coolant temperature. In other words, if you started an engine that was already 130 degrees and drove the vehicle until the engine coolant temperature was 160 degrees, that would not constitute a bona fide warm-up in OBD-II, because even though the engine reached the 160 degree threshold, it didn't increase at least 40 degrees. But if you started an engine that was 120 degrees and drove it until the coolant temperature reached 160 degrees, that would be a warm-up.

Warm-up counter - In an OBD-II PCM, the warm-up counter starts ticking when the Diagnostic Executive asks the PCM to turn off the MIL. The PCM turns off the MIL, but it doesn't erase the DTC that caused the MIL to come on. Instead, it uses the warm-up counter to count off 40 or 80 or some other number (depending on the manufacturer) of warm-ups (see *warm-up* above). If the fault that caused the PCM to store the DTC doesn't reoccur for the next 40 or 80 or whatever number of trips, the PCM then erases the DTC.

Warm-up regulator - On Bosch CIS, the original name for the control-pressure regulator.

Wastegate control - A solenoid or diaphragm used to control boost output on turbocharged models. The computer varies the duty cycle of the solenoid to match maximum boost to changing engine operating conditions.

Water injector - A method of lowering the air-fuel mixture temperature by injecting a fine spray of water which evaporates as it cools the intake charge.

Water jackets - Passages in the head and block that allow coolant to circulate throughout the engine.

Watt - The unit of measure that indicates electrical power applied in a direct current circuit. Watts are calculated by multiplying the current in amperes by the voltage.

Z

Zero absolute pressure - A total vacuum. Zero on the absolute pressure scale.

Acronyms

A

AAC - Auxiliary Air Control Valve
AAT - Ambient Air Temperature
AC - Alternating current
A/C - Air Conditioning
ACC - Air Conditioning Clutch
ACCS - Air Conditioning Cycling Switch
ACL - Air Cleaner
ACT- Air Charge Temperature
A/D - Analog-to-digital
A/F - Air Fuel Ratio
AFC - Air Flow Control
AIR - Air Injection Reactor
AIR - Secondary Air Injection
AISC - Air Induction System Control
AISM - Automatic Idle Speed Motor
ALDL - Assembly Line Data Link (GM)
ALU - Arithmetic Logic Unit
AP - Accelerator Pedal
APP - Accelerator Pedal Position
APS - Atmospheric Pressure Sensor
AS - Air Switch Solenoid
ASD - Automatic Shutdown
ASM - Auto Shift Manual
A/T - Automatic Transaxle
A/T - Automatic Transmission
ATDC - After Top Dead Center
ATS - Air Temperature sensor
AWD - All-Wheel Drive

B

B+ - Battery Positive Voltage.
BARO - Barometric Pressure
BATT (+) - Battery positive post or its circuit.
BATT (-) - Battery negative post or its circuit.
BC - Blower Control
BCS - Boost Control Solenoid
BLR - Blower
BOO - Brake On/Off
BPP - Brake Pedal Position

Acronyms

BPS - Brake Pedal Switch
BTDC - Before Top Dead Center
BTS - Battery Temperature Sensor
BUS N - Bus Negative
BUS P - Bus Positive

C

CAC - Charge Air Cooler
CAN - Controller Area Network
CANP - Canister Purge
CARB - California Air Resources Board
CARB LEV - Low Emission Vehicle
CARB ULEV - Ultra Low Emission Vehicle
CARB ZEV - Zero Emission Vehicle
CC - Climate Control
CCA - Cluster Control Assembly
CCD - Computer Controlled Dwell
CCM - Comprehensive Component Monitor
CCRM - Constant Control Relay Module
CCS - Coast Clutch Solenoid
CES - Clutch Engage Switch
CFI - Continuos Fuel Injection
CFV - Critical Flow Venturi
CHT - Cylinder Head Temperature
CI - Cylinder Injection
CID - Cylinder identification
CIS - Continuous Injection System
CKP - Crankshaft Position
CL - Closed Loop
CMFI - Central Multiport Fuel Injection
CMP - Camshaft Position
CO - Carbon Monoxide
CO$_2$ - Carbon Dioxide
COP - Coil On Plug Electronic Ignition
CPP - Clutch Pedal Position
CPU - Central Processing Unit
CTO - Clean Tachometer Output
CTOX - Continuous Trap Oxidizer
CTP - Closed Throttle Position
CTS - Coolant Temperature sensor
CVS - Constant Volume Sampler

D

D/A - Digital-to-analog
DATA + - Data Positive
DATA - - Data Negative
DCL - Data Communication Link
DFCO - Decel Fuel Cutoff Mode
DFI - Direct Fuel Injection
DI - Distributor Ignition
DIS - Direct Ignition System
DIS - Distributorless Ignition System.
DLC - Data Link Connector
DM - Drive Motor

DMCM - Drive Motor Control Module
DMCT - Drive Motor Coolant Temperature
DMPI - Drive Motor Power Inverter
DOL - Data Output Line
DTC - Diagnostic Trouble Code
DTM - Diagnostic Test Mode

E

EBCM - Electronic Brake Control Module
EC - Engine Control
ECGI - Electronically Controlled Gasoline Injection
ECL - Engine Coolant Level
ECM - Engine Control Module
ECT - Engine Coolant Temperature
ECU - Engine Control Unit
EEC - Electronic Engine Control
EEPROM - Electronically Erasable Programmable Read Only Memory
EFE - Early Fuel Evaporation
EFI - Electronic Fuel Injection
EFT - Engine Fuel Temperature
EGR - Exhaust Gas Recirculation
EGRGT - Exhaust Gas Recirculation Temperature
EGR Monitor - OBD-II EGR Test
EGRT - EGR Temperature
EGT - Exhaust Gas Temperature
EI - Electronic Ignition
ELD - Electrical Load Detector
ELD - Electronic Load Detector
EM - Engine Modification
EMR - Electronic Module Retard
EOP - Engine Oil Pressure
EOT - Engine Oil Temperature
EP - Exhaust Pressure
EPA - Environmental Protection Agency
EPR - Exhaust Pressure Regulator
EPROM - Erasable Programmable Read Only
ESC - Electronic Spark Control
EST - Electronic Spark Timing
E/T - Exhaust Temperature
ETB - Electronic Throttle Body
EVAP - Evaporative Emission Control
EVAP CV - Evaporative Canister Vent
EVR - EGR Vacuum Regulator
EXC - Exhaust Control

F

FC - Fan Control
FEEPROM - Flash Electronically Erasable Programmable Read Only Memory
FF - Flexible Fuel
FIC - Fuel Injector Control
FLI - Fuel Level Indicator
FMEM - Failure Mode Effect Mgmt.
FP - Fuel Pump

FPM - Fuel Pump Monitor
FPROM - Flash Erasable PROM
FRP - Fuel Rail Pressure
FRT - Fuel Rail Temperature
FRZF - Freeze Frame
FT - Fuel Trim
FTO - Filtered Tachometer Output
FTP - Federal Test Procedure
FTP - Fuel Tank Pressure
FTT - Fuel Tank Temperature
FWD - Front Wheel Drive

G

GCM - Governor Control Module
GEN - Generator
GND - Ground
GPM - Grams Per Mile
GVW - Gross Vehicle Weight
GVWR - Gross Vehicle Weight Rating (curb weight plus payload)

H

HC - Hydrocarbon
HDR-CKP - High Data Rate CKP Sensor
HEI - High Energy Ignition
HFP - High Fuel Pump (Relay) Control
HHDDE - Heavy Heavy Duty Diesel Engine
HHDE - Heavy Heavy Duty Engine
HO$_2$S - Heated Oxygen Sensor
HOC - Electrically Heated Oxidation Catalyst
HP - Horsepower
HPC - High Pressure Cutoff
HSC - High Swirl Combustion
HTWC - Heated 3-way Catalyst

I

IAC - Idle Air Control
IAT - Intake Air Temperature
IC - Ignition Control
ICM - Ignition Control Module
ICP - Injection Control Pressure
IDM - Ignition Diagnostic Monitor
IFI - Indirect Fuel Injection
IFS - Inertia Fuel Shutoff
IGN GND - Ignition Ground
ILEV - Inherently Low Emission Vehicle
I/M - Inspection and Maintenance
IMRC - Intake Manifold Runner Control
IMT - Intake Manifold Tuning
I/O - Input/Output
ISC - Idle Speed Control
ISS - Input Shaft Speed
ITS - Idle Tracking Switch

K

KAPWR - Direct Battery Power
KOEC - Key On, Engine Cranking
KOEO - Key On, Engine Off
KOER - Key On, Engine Running
KS - Knock Sensor

L

LDDT - Light Duty Diesel Truck categories
LDT - Light Duty Truck (gasoline) categories based on weight
LDV - Light Duty Vehicle, generally passenger cars and light trucks under 6000 pounds GVWR.
LEV - Low Emission Vehicle
LEV II - California regulations beginning in the 2004 model year.
LHDE - Light Heavy Duty Engine (several weight categories).
LOAD - Calculated Load Value
LOOP - Engine Operating Loop Status
LTFT - Long Term Fuel Trim
LVW - Loaded Vehicle Weight, curb weight plus 300 pounds

M

MAF - Mass Air Flow
MAP - Manifold Absolute Pressure
MAPT - Manifold Absolute Pressure and Temperature
MAT - Manifold Air Temperature
MC - Mixture Control
MDP - Manifold Differential Pressure
MDT - Medium Duty Truck categories based on weight
MDV - Medium Duty Vehicle
MFI - Multiport Fuel Injection
MHDE - Medium Heavy Duty Engine
MIL - Malfunction Indicator Light
MST - Manifold Surface Temperature
M/T - Manual Transaxle
M/T - Manual Transmission
MVZ - Manifold Vacuum Zone
MY - Model Year

N

NCP - Non-Compliance Penalty
NOx - Oxides of Nitrogen
NTC - Negative Temperature Coefficient
NVRAM - Non-Volatile Random Access Memory

O

O$_2$ - Oxygen
O$_2$S - Oxygen sensor
OBD - On-Board Diagnostics
OBD II - On-Board Diagnostics, Generation Two
OC - Oxidation Catalytic Converter
ODM - Output Device Monitor

OL - Open Loop
ORVR - On-Board Refueling Vapor Recovery
OSC - Oxygen Sensor Storage
OSS - Output Shaft Speed

P

PAIR - Pulsed Secondary Air Injection
PC - Passenger Car
PC - Pressure Control
PCM - Powertrain Control Module
PCV - Positive Crankcase Ventilation
PID - Parameter ID
PNP - Park/Neutral Position
PR - Pressure Relief
PRNDL - Park-Reverse-Neutral-Drive-Low
PROM - Programmable Read-Only Memory
PSP - Power Steering Pressure
PTC - Pending Trouble Code
PTO - Power Take-Off
PTOX - Periodic Trap Oxidizer
PWM - Pulse Width Modulation
PZEV - Partially Zero Emission Vehicle

R

RAM - Random Access Memory
RFI - Radio Frequency Interference
RM - Relay Module
ROM - Read Only Memory
RPM - Revolutions per Minute
RWD - Rear Wheel Drive

S

SAE - Society of Automotive Engineers
SBEC - Single Board Engine Controller
SC - Supercharger
SCB - Supercharger Bypass
SDM - Sensing Diagnostic Module
SFI - Sequential Fuel Injection
SI - Sequential Injection
SMEC - Single Module Engine Controller
SPARK ADV - Spark Advance
SPL - Smoke Puff Limiter
SRI - Service Reminder Indicator
SRT - System Readiness Test
SS - Shift Solenoid
ST - Scan Tool
STFT - Short Term Fuel Trim
SULEV - Super Ultra Low Emission Vehicle

T

TAC - Throttle Actuator Control
TB - Throttle Body
TBI - Throttle Body Injection
TC - Turbo Charger

TCC - Torque Converter Clutch
TCCP - Torque Converter Clutch Pressure
TCM - Transmission Control Module
TFP - Transmission Fluid Pressure
TFT - Transmission Fluid Temperature
Tier 1 - California regulations beginning in 1993 model year and Federal regulations beginning in 1994 model year.
Tier 2 - Federal regulations beginning in the 2004 model year.
TNA - Speed Signal
TOT - Transmission Oil Temperature
TP - Throttle Position
TPI - Tuned Port Injection
TPS - Throttle Position Sensor
TR - Transmission Range
TSS - Turbine Shaft Speed
TVV - Thermal Vacuum Valve
TWC - Three Way Catalyst
TWC+OC - Three Way + Oxidation Catalyst

U

ULEV - Ultra Low Emission Vehicle

V

VAC - Vacuum
VAF - Volume Air Flow
VCM - Vehicle Control Module
VCRM - Variable Control Relay Module
VECI - Vehicle Emission Control Information
VIN - Vehicle Identification Number
VR - Voltage Regulator
VSS - Vehicle Speed Sensor

W

WOT - Wide Open Throttle
WU-OC - Warm Up Oxidation Catalytic Converter
WU-TWC - Warm Up Three Way Catalytic Converter

Z

ZEV - Zero Emission Vehicle

Index

Haynes Automotive Manuals

NOTE: If you do not see a listing for your vehicle, consult your local Haynes dealer for the latest product information.

HAYNES XTREME CUSTOMIZING
11101 Sport Compact Customizing
11102 Sport Compact Performance
11110 In-car Entertainment
11150 Sport Utility Vehicle Customizing
11213 Acura
11255 GM Full-size Pick-ups
11314 Ford Focus
11315 Full-size Ford Pick-ups
11373 Honda Civic

ACURA
12020 Integra '86 thru '89 & Legend '86 thru '90
12021 Integra '90 thru '93 & Legend '91 thru '95

AMC
Jeep CJ - see JEEP (50020)
14020 Concord/Hornet/Gremlin/Spirit '70 thru '83
14025 (Renault) Alliance & Encore '83 thru '87

AUDI
15020 4000 all models '80 thru '87
15025 5000 all models '77 thru '83
15026 5000 all models '84 thru '88

AUSTIN
Healey Sprite - see MG Midget (66015)

BMW
18020 3/5 Series '82 thru '92
18021 3 Series including Z3 models '92 thru '98
18022 3-Series, E46 chassis '99 thru '05, Z4 models '03 thru '05
18025 320i all 4 cyl models '75 thru '83
18050 1500 thru 2002 except Turbo '59 thru '77

BUICK
19010 Buick Century '97 thru '05
Century (front-wheel drive) - see GM (38005)
19020 Buick, Oldsmobile & Pontiac Full-size (Front wheel drive) '85 thru '05
19025 Buick Oldsmobile & Pontiac Full-size (Rear wheel drive) '70 thru '90
19030 Mid-size Regal & Century '74 thru '87
Regal - see GENERAL MOTORS (38010)
Skyhawk - see GM (38030)
Skylark - see GM (38020, 38025)
Somerset - see GENERAL MOTORS (38025)

CADILLAC
21030 Cadillac Rear Wheel Drive '70 thru '93
Cimarron, Eldorado & Seville - see GM (38015, 38030, 38031)

CHEVROLET
10305 Chevrolet Engine Overhaul Manual
24010 Astro & GMC Safari Mini-vans '85 thru '05
24015 Camaro V8 all models '70 thru '81
24016 Camaro all models '82 thru '92, Cavalier - see GM (38015), Celebrity - see GM (38005)
24017 Camaro & Firebird '93 thru '02
24020 Chevelle, Malibu, El Camino '69 thru '87
24024 Chevette & Pontiac T1000 '76 thru '87 Citation - see GENERAL MOTORS (38020)
24027 Colorado & GMC Canyon '04 thru '06
24032 Corsica/Beretta all models '87 thru '96
24040 Corvette all V8 models '68 thru '82
24041 Corvette all models '84 thru '96
24045 Full-size Sedans Caprice, Impala, Biscayne, Bel Air & Wagons '69 thru '90
24046 Impala SS & Caprice and Buick Roadmaster '91 thru '96
Lumina '90 thru '94 - see GM (38010)
24048 Lumina & Monte Carlo '95 thru '05 Lumina APV - see GM (38035)
24050 Luv Pick-up all 2WD & 4WD '72 thru '82
Malibu - see GM (38026)
24055 Monte Carlo all models '70 thru '88
Monte Carlo '95 thru '01 - see LUMINA
24059 Nova all V8 models '69 thru '79
24060 Nova/Geo Prizm '85 thru '92
24064 Pick-ups '67 thru '87 - Chevrolet & GMC, all V8 & in-line 6 cyl, 2WD & 4WD '67 thru '87; Suburbans, Blazers & Jimmys '67 thru '91
24065 Pick-ups '88 thru '98 - Chevrolet & GMC, all full-size models '88 thru '98; C/K Classic '99 & '00; Blazer & Jimmy '92 thru '94; Suburban '92 thru '99; Tahoe & Yukon '95 thru '99
24066 Pick-ups '99 thru '06 - Chevrolet Silverado & GMC Sierra '99 thru '06; Suburban/Tahoe/ Yukon/Yukon XL/Avalanche '00 thru '06
24070 S-10 & GMC S-15 Pick-ups '82 thru '93
24071 S-10, Sonoma & Jimmy '94 thru '04
24072 Chevrolet TrailBlazer & TrailBlazer EXT, GMC Envoy & Envoy XL, Oldsmobile Bravada '02 thru '06
24075 Sprint '85 thru '88, Geo Metro '89 thru '01
24080 Vans - Chevrolet & GMC '68 thru '96
24081 Chevrolet Express & GMC Savana Full-size Vans '96 thru '05

CHRYSLER
10310 Chrysler Engine Overhaul Manual
25015 Chrysler Cirrus, Dodge Stratus, Plymouth Breeze, '95 thru '00
25020 Full-size Front-Wheel Drive '88 thru '93
K-Cars - see DODGE Aries (30008)
Laser - see DODGE Daytona (30030)
25025 Chrysler LHS, Concorde & New Yorker, Dodge Intrepid, Eagle Vision, '93 thru '97
25026 Chrysler LHS, Concorde, 300M, Dodge Intrepid '98 thru '03
25027 Chrysler 300, Dodge Charger & Magnum '05 thru '07
25030 Chrysler/Plym. Mid-size '82 thru '95
Rear-wheel Drive - see DODGE (30050)
25035 PT Cruiser all models '01 thru '03
25040 Chrysler Sebring/Dodge Avenger '95 thru '05, Dodge Stratus '01 thru '05

DATSUN
28005 200SX all models '80 thru '83
28007 B-210 all models '73 thru '78
28009 210 all models '78 thru '82
28012 240Z, 260Z & 280Z Coupe '70 thru '78
28014 280ZX Coupe & 2+2 '79 thru '83
300ZX - see NISSAN (72010)
28018 510 & PL521 Pick-up '68 thru '73
28020 510 all models '78 thru '81
28022 620 Series Pick-up all models '73 thru '79
720 Series Pick-up - NISSAN (72030)
28025 810/Maxima all gas models, '77 thru '84

DODGE
400 & 600 - see CHRYSLER (25030)
30008 Aries & Plymouth Reliant '81 thru '89
30010 Caravan & Ply. Voyager '84 thru '95
30011 Caravan & Ply. Voyager '96 thru '02
30012 Challenger/Plymouth Saporro '78 thru '83
Challenger '67-'76 - see DART (30025)
30013 Caravan, Chrysler Voyager, Town & Country '03 thru '06
30016 Colt/Plymouth Champ '78 thru '87
30020 Dakota Pick-ups all models '87 thru '96
30021 Durango '98 & '99, Dakota '97 thru '99
30022 Dodge Durango models '00 thru '03
Dodge Dakota Pick-ups '00 thru '04
30023 Dodge Durango '04 thru '06, Dakota '05 and '06
30025 Dart, Challenger/Plymouth Barracuda & Valiant 6 cyl models '67 thru '76
30030 Daytona & Chrysler Laser '84 thru '89
Intrepid - see Chrysler (25025, 25026)
30034 Dodge & Plymouth Neon '95 thru '99
30035 Omni & Plymouth Horizon '78 thru '90
30036 Dodge and Plymouth Neon '00 thru '05
30040 Pick-ups all full-size models '74 thru '93
30041 Pick-ups all full-size models '94 thru '01
30042 Dodge Full-size Pick-ups '02 thru '05
30045 Ram 50/D50 Pick-ups & Raider and Plymouth Arrow Pick-ups '79 thru '93
30050 Dodge/Ply./Chrysler RWD '71 thru '89
30055 Shadow/Plymouth Sundance '87 thru '94
30060 Spirit & Plymouth Acclaim '89 thru '95
30065 Vans - Dodge & Plymouth '71 thru '03

EAGLE
Talon - see MITSUBISHI (68030, 68031)
Vision - see CHRYSLER (25025)

FIAT
34010 124 Sport Coupe & Spider '68 thru '78
34025 X1/9 all models '74 thru '80

FORD
10355 Ford Automatic Transmission Overhaul
10320 Ford Engine Overhaul Manual
36004 Aerostar Mini-vans '86 thru '97
Aspire - see FORD Festiva (36030)
36006 Contour/Mercury Mystique '95 thru '00
36008 Courier Pick-up all models '72 thru '82
36012 Crown Victoria & Mercury Grand Marquis '88 thru '06
36016 Escort/Mercury Lynx '81 thru '90
36020 Escort/Mercury Tracer '91 thru '00
Expedition - see FORD Pick-up (36059)
36022 Ford Escape & Mazda Tribute '01 thru '03
36024 Explorer & Mazda Navajo '91 thru '01
36025 Ford Explorer & Mercury Mountaineer '02 thru '06
36028 Fairmont & Mercury Zephyr '78 thru '83
36030 Festiva & Aspire '88 thru '97
36032 Fiesta all models '77 thru '80
36034 Focus all models '00 thru '05
36036 Ford & Mercury Full-size '75 thru '87
36044 Ford & Mercury Mid-size '75 thru '86
36048 Mustang V8 all models '64-1/2 thru '73
36049 Mustang II 4 cyl, V6 & V8 '74 thru '78
36050 Mustang & Mercury Capri '79 thru '86
36051 Mustang all models '94 thru '04
36052 Mustang '05 thru '07
36054 Pick-ups and Bronco '73 thru '79
36058 Pick-ups and Bronco '80 thru '96
36059 F-150 & Expedition '97 thru '03, F-250 '97 thru '99 & Lincoln Navigator '98 thru '02
36060 Super Duty Pick-up, Excursion '99 thru '06
36061 F-150 full-size '04 thru '06
36062 Pinto & Mercury Bobcat '75 thru '80
36066 Probe all models '89 thru '92
36070 Ranger/Bronco II all models '83 thru '92
36071 Ford Ranger '93 thru '05 &
Mazda Pick-ups '94 thru '05
36074 Taurus & Mercury Sable '86 thru '95
36075 Taurus & Mercury Sable '96 thru '01
36078 Tempo & Mercury Topaz '84 thru '94
36082 Thunderbird/Mercury Cougar '83 thru '88
36086 Thunderbird/Mercury Cougar '89 thru '97
36090 Vans all V8 Econoline models '69 thru '91
36094 Vans full size '92 thru '05
36097 Windstar Mini-van '95 thru '03

GENERAL MOTORS
10360 GM Automatic Transmission Overhaul
38005 Buick Century, Chevrolet Celebrity, Olds Cutlass Ciera & Pontiac 6000 '82 thru '96
38010 Buick Regal, Chevrolet Lumina, Oldsmobile Cutlass Supreme & Pontiac Grand Prix front wheel drive '88 thru '05
38015 Buick Skyhawk, Cadillac Cimarron, Chevrolet Cavalier, Oldsmobile Firenza Pontiac J-2000 & Sunbird '82 thru '94
38016 Chevrolet Cavalier/Pontiac Sunfire '95 thru '04
38017 Chevrolet Cobalt & Pontiac G5 '05 thru '07
38020 Buick Skylark, Chevrolet Citation, Olds Omega, Pontiac Phoenix '80 thru '85
38025 Buick Skylark & Somerset, Olds Achieva, Calais & Pontiac Grand Am '85 thru '98
38026 Chevrolet Malibu, Olds Alero & Cutlass, Pontiac Grand Am '97 thru '03
38027 Chevrolet Malibu '04 thru '07
38030 Cadillac Eldorado & Oldsmobile Toronado '71 thru '85, Seville '80 thru '85, Buick Riviera '79 thru '85
38031 Cadillac Eldorado & Seville '86 thru '91, DeVille & Buick Riviera '86 thru '93, Fleetwood & Olds Toronado '86 thru '92
38032 DeVille '94 thru '05, Seville '92 thru '04
38035 Chevrolet Lumina APV, Oldsmobile Silhouette & Pontiac Trans Sport '90 thru '96
38036 Chevrolet Venture, Olds Silhouette, Pontiac Trans Sport & Montana '97 thru '05
General Motors Full-size Rear-wheel Drive - see BUICK (19025)

GEO
Metro - see CHEVROLET Sprint (24075)
Prizm - see CHEVROLET (24060) or TOYOTA (92036)
40030 Storm all models '90 thru '93
Tracker - see SUZUKI Samurai (90010)

GMC
Vans & Pick-ups - see CHEVROLET

HONDA
42010 Accord CVCC all models '76 thru '83
42011 Accord all models '84 thru '89
42012 Accord all models '90 thru '93
42013 Accord all models '94 thru '97
42014 Accord all models '98 thru '02
42015 Honda Accord models '03 thru '05
42020 Civic 1200 all models '73 thru '79
42021 Civic 1300 & 1500 CVCC '80 thru '83
42022 Civic 1500 CVCC all models '75 thru '79
42023 Civic all models '84 thru '91
42024 Civic & del Sol '92 thru '95
42025 Civic '96 thru '00, CR-V '97 thru '01, Acura Integra '94 thru '00
Passport - see ISUZU Rodeo (47017)
42026 Civic '01 thru '04, CR-V '02 thru '04
42035 Honda Odyssey models '99 thru '04
42037 Honda Pilot '03 thru '07, Acura MDX '01 thru '07
42040 Prelude CVCC all models '79 thru '89

HYUNDAI
43010 Elantra all models '96 thru '01
43015 Excel & Accent all models '86 thru '98

ISUZU
Hombre - see CHEVROLET S-10 (24071)
47017 Rodeo '91 thru '02, Amigo '89 thru '02, Honda Passport '95 thru '02
47020 Trooper '84 thru '91, Pick-up '81 thru '93

JAGUAR
49010 XJ6 all 6 cyl models '68 thru '86
49011 XJ6 all models '88 thru '94
49015 XJ12 & XJS all 12 cyl models '72 thru '85

JEEP
50010 Cherokee, Comanche & Wagoneer Limited all models '84 thru '01
50020 CJ all models '49 thru '86
50025 Grand Cherokee all models '93 thru '04
50029 Grand Wagoneer & Pick-up '72 thru '91
50030 Wrangler all models '87 thru '03
50035 Liberty '02 thru '04

KIA
54070 Sephia '94 thru '01, Spectra '00 thru '04

LEXUS
ES 300 - see TOYOTA Camry (92007)

LINCOLN
Navigator - see FORD Pick-up (36059)
59010 Rear Wheel Drive all models '70 thru '05

MAZDA
61010 GLC (rear wheel drive) '77 thru '83
61011 GLC (front wheel drive) '81 thru '85
61015 323 & Protegé '90 thru '00
61016 MX-5 Miata '90 thru '97
61020 MPV all models '89 thru '94
Navajo - see FORD Explorer (36024)
61030 Pick-ups '72 thru '93
Pick-ups '94 on - see Ford (36071)
61035 RX-7 all models '79 thru '85
61036 RX-7 all models '86 thru '91
61040 626 (rear wheel drive) '79 thru '82
61041 626 & MX-6 (front wheel drive) '83 thru '92
61042 626 '93 thru '01, & MX-6/Ford Probe '93 thru '01

MERCEDES-BENZ
63012 123 Series Diesel '76 thru '85
63015 190 Series 4-cyl gas models, '84 thru '88
63020 230, 250 & 280 6 cyl sohc '68 thru '72
63025 280 123 Series gas models '77 thru '81
63030 350 & 450 all models '71 thru '80

MERCURY
64200 Villager & Nissan Quest '93 thru '01
All other titles, see FORD listing.

MG
66010 MGB Roadster & GT Coupe '62 thru '80
66015 MG Midget & Austin Healey Sprite Roadster '58 thru '80

MITSUBISHI
68020 Cordia, Tredia, Galant, Precis & Mirage '83 thru '93
68030 Eclipse, Eagle Talon & Plymouth Laser '90 thru '94
68031 Eclipse '95 thru '01, Eagle Talon '95 thru '98
68035 Mitsubishi Galant '94 thru '03
68040 Pick-up '83 thru '96, Montero '83 thru '93

NISSAN
72010 300ZX all models incl. Turbo '84 thru '89
72015 Altima all models '93 thru '04
72020 Maxima all models '85 thru '92
72021 Maxima all models '93 thru '01
72030 Pick-ups '80 thru '97, Pathfinder '87 thru '95
72031 Frontier Pick-up '98 thru '04, Xterra '00 thru '04, Pathfinder '96 thru '04
72040 Pulsar all models '83 thru '86
72050 Sentra all models '82 thru '94
72051 Sentra & 200SX '95 thru '04
72060 Stanza all models '82 thru '90

OLDSMOBILE
73015 Cutlass '74 thru '88
For other OLDSMOBILE titles, see BUICK, CHEVROLET or GM listings.

PLYMOUTH
For PLYMOUTH titles, see DODGE.

PONTIAC
79008 Fiero all models '84 thru '88
79018 Firebird V8 except Turbo '70 thru '81
79019 Firebird all models '82 thru '92
79040 Mid-size Rear-wheel Drive '70 thru '87
For other PONTIAC titles, see BUICK, CHEVROLET or GM listings.

PORSCHE
80020 911 Coupe & Targa models '65 thru '89
80025 914 all 4 cyl models '69 thru '76
80030 924 all models incl. Turbo '76 thru '82
80035 944 all models incl. Turbo '83 thru '89

RENAULT
Alliance, Encore - see AMC (14020)

SAAB
84010 900 including Turbo '79 thru '88

SATURN
87010 Saturn all models '91 thru '02
87011 Saturn Ion '03 thru '07
87020 Saturn all L-series models '00 thru '04

SUBARU
89002 1100, 1300, 1400 & 1600 '71 thru '79
89003 1600 & 1800 2WD & 4WD '80 thru '94
89100 Legacy models '90 thru '99
89101 Legacy & Forester '00 thru '06

SUZUKI
90010 Samurai/Sidekick/Geo Tracker '86 thru '01

TOYOTA
92005 Camry all models '83 thru '91
92006 Camry all models '92 thru '96
92007 Camry/Avalon/Solara/Lexus ES 300 '97 thru '01
92008 Toyota Camry, Avalon and Solara & Lexus ES 300/330 all models '02 thru '05
92015 Celica Rear Wheel Drive '71 thru '85
92020 Celica Front Wheel Drive '86 thru '99
92025 Celica Supra all models '79 thru '92
92030 Corolla all models '75 thru '79
92032 Corolla rear wheel drive models '80 thru '87
92035 Corolla front wheel drive models '84 thru '92
92036 Corolla & Geo Prizm '93 thru '02
92037 Corolla models '03 thru '05
92040 Corolla Tercel all models '80 thru '82
92045 Corona all models '74 thru '82
92050 Cressida all models '78 thru '82
92055 Land Cruiser FJ40/43/45/55 '68 thru '82
92056 Land Cruiser FJ60/62/80/FZJ80 '80 thru '96
92065 MR2 all models '85 thru '87
92070 Pick-up all models '69 thru '78
92075 Pick-up all models '79 thru '95
92076 Tacoma '95 thru '04, 4Runner '96 thru '02, T100 '93 thru '98
92078 Tundra '00 thru '05, Sequoia '01 thru '05
92080 Previa all models '91 thru '95
92081 Prius '01 thru '08
92082 RAV4 all models '96 thru '05
92085 Tercel all models '87 thru '94
92090 Sienna all models '98 thru '02
92095 Highlander & Lexus RX-330 '99 thru '06

TRIUMPH
94007 Spitfire all models '62 thru '81
94010 TR7 all models '75 thru '81

VW
96008 Beetle & Karmann Ghia '54 thru '79
96009 New Beetle '98 thru '05
96016 Rabbit, Jetta, Scirocco, & Pick-up gas models '75 thru '92 & Convertible '80 thru '92
96017 Golf, GTI & Jetta '93 thru '98, Cabrio '95 thru '98
96018 Golf, GTI, Jetta & Cabrio '99 thru '02
96020 Rabbit, Jetta, Pick-up diesel '77 thru '84
96023 Passat '98 thru '01, Audi A4 '96 thru '01
96030 Transporter 1600 all models '68 thru '79
96035 Transporter 1700, 1800, 2000 '72 thru '79
96040 Type 3 1500 & 1600 '63 thru '73
96045 Vanagon air-cooled models '80 thru '83

VOLVO
97010 120, 130 Series & 1800 Sports '61 thru '73
97015 140 Series all models '66 thru '74
97020 240 Series all models '76 thru '93
97040 740 & 760 Series all models '82 thru '88

TECHBOOK MANUALS
10205 Automotive Computer Codes
10206 OBD-II & Electronic Engine Management Systems
10210 Automotive Emissions Control Manual
10215 Fuel Injection Manual, 1978 thru 1985
10220 Fuel Injection Manual, 1986 thru 1999
10225 Holley Carburetor Manual
10230 Rochester Carburetor Manual
10240 Weber/Zenith/Stromberg/SU Carburetor
10305 Chevrolet Engine Overhaul Manual
10310 Chrysler Engine Overhaul Manual
10320 Ford Engine Overhaul Manual
10330 GM and Ford Diesel Engine Repair
10333 Building Engine Power Manual
10340 Small Engine Repair Manual
10345 Suspension, Steering & Driveline
10355 Ford Automatic Transmission Overhaul
10360 GM Automatic Transmission Overhaul
10405 Automotive Body Repair & Painting
10410 Automotive Brake Manual
10415 Automotive Detailing Manual
10420 Automotive Electrical Manual
10425 Automotive Heating & Air Conditioning
10430 Automotive Reference Dictionary
10435 Automotive Tools Manual
10440 Used Car Buying Guide
10445 Welding Manual
10450 ATV Basics
10452 Scooters, Automatic Transmission 50cc to 250cc

SPANISH MANUALS
98903 Reparación de Carrocería & Pintura
98904 Carburadores para los modelos Holley & Rochester
98905 Códigos Automotrices de la Computadora
98910 Frenos Automotriz
98913 Electricidad Automotriz
98915 Inyección de Combustible 1986 al 1999
99040 Chevrolet & GMC Camionetas '67 al '87
99041 Chevrolet & GMC Camionetas '88 al '98
99042 Chevrolet Camionetas Cerradas '68 al '95
99055 Dodge Caravan/Ply. Voyager '84 al '95
99075 Ford Camionetas y Bronco '80 al '94
99077 Ford Camionetas Cerradas '69 al '91
99083 Ford Modelos de Tamaño Mediano '75 al '86
99088 Ford Taurus & Mercury Sable '86 al '95
99091 GM Modelos de Tamaño Grande '70 al '90
99095 GM Modelos de Tamaño Mediano '70 al '88
99100 Jeep Cherokee, Wagoneer & Comanche '84 al '00
99110 Nissan Camionetas '80 al '96, Pathfinder '87 al '95
99118 Nissan Sentra '82 al '94
99125 Toyota Camionetas y 4-Runner '79 al '95

Over 100 Haynes motorcycle manuals also available

10-07

Haynes North America, Inc., 861 Lawrence Drive, Newbury Park, CA 91320 • (805) 498-6703